TRUE PATRIOT DAY

ZY AARON

Martin and Bowman
1-855-921-1348

PART ONE

July 1

CHAPTER 1

"ALL RISE FOR THE Governor of the great State of California, the Honorable George Hunter!" the announcer bellowed, elongating each syllable with practiced precision.

Whispered conversations ceased on cue, and the entire press corps stood.

Governor Hunter strode to the podium and straightened his blue and gold tie, pushing the knot hard against his Adam's apple. He cleared his throat, scanned the room with focused eyes, like a cornered small animal seeking escape from a predator. "Please join me in a moment of silence in memory of a special man, an eminent attorney, and a great friend." He lifted his eyes toward the ceiling. "Jim Simmons, we'll be in your debt forever. We'll miss you."

Governor Hunter gripped his hands behind his back to conceal the slight shaking.

"Please sit. Without further ado, let's get down to business. I called this press conference to announce my choice for Attorney General. I know everyone expected me to appoint Ms. Mahoney to succeed Jim Simmons. However, after careful consideration, I went in a different direction. Please join me in congratulating Mr. Richard Clancy, California's new AG. Mr. Clancy, if you please."

Clancy took his time rising to his reed-thin six-foot-four-inch height, ignoring all eyes fixated on him. He buttoned his suit jacket, smoothed down his expensively cut salt-and-pepper hair, his tie, and his matching pocket square, although everything had been in pristine order.

Hunter continued. "With the untimely death of our dear colleague Jim Simmons, the people of the great State of California need a new leader to steer the Department of Justice through these tumultuous times. I nominate Richard Clancy for the position of Attorney General." He shook Clancy's hand, grinning for the cameras showing no teeth. "Congratulations, Mr. Clancy. I'm sure you will carry on Jim's exceptional work."

"Thank you, Governor, for the faith you placed in me. I will do my absolute best to honor that trust, and Jim's memory, while I faithfully serve the people of our great state."

The camera flashes produced intertwined shadows on the white wall behind them. They performed an obligatory handshake and beamed for the media. The Governor released Clancy's hand with haste, as if separating himself from a ghastly apparition.

"I will allow Mr. Clancy a few moments to introduce himself." Hunter grinned at the audience, focusing on the closest lenses. "Don't eat him alive yet. California and I need an Attorney General more than ever."

As the polite laughter died down, Hunter approached Clancy and, standing on his toes, hissed in his ear. "So long as you don't forget. *You* work for *me*."

CHAPTER 2

LISA JENSEN SAT MOTIONLESS on the comfy sofa as far as possible from Phil's desk. Phil replaced the receiver with unhurried, studied moves. He rubbed his strong, square chin, gazing out the large corner window. Lisa knew Phil preferred grandiose statements rather than present simple, concise facts. She often teased him about 'over-lawyering' everything.

They were alone in his ostentatious corner office. Phil's decorator had positioned the expensive leather and mahogany furniture with deliberate precision, to apprise visitors of the significant power living in that office. Phil's desk rested on a foot-tall pedestal, centered on the short wall. Behind it stood a wall-to-wall, floor-to-ceiling bookshelf bursting with law books. Phil, attired in a navy-blue pinstriped suit, stiffly starched white shirt, and blood-red polka-dotted silk tie, relaxed on his throne. A pretentious nameplate, centered at the edge of his desk, identified him as *Phillip L. Tomlinson, Orange County District Attorney*.

"Coroner just made the official call. He concurred with the police and classified Richter's death as self-inflicted," he stated in a rehearsed matter-of-fact tone. Crossing heavy arms on his portly chest, he continued, "Terrific news. There's nothing left for us to worry about." Seeing her grimace, he added, "Lisa, for what it's worth, I'm truly sorry for your loss."

After a dozen years, Lisa accepted Tomlinson as the self-serving, arrogant *politico* he was. She had enabled him, out of loyalty, respect, even out of irrational love. She resolved to end tolerating and ignoring his shenanigans. She lifted the envelope from her lap and held it between fingernails as if it were a dead critter. Lisa pulled at a single detached strand of strawberry-blond hair, which she wore swept upward into a spiraled bun, exposing her exquisite long neck. She squinted at his rotund face, searching, hoping for compassion.

Nothing there.

"You don't look well, Phil. The extra weight can't be good for you." Her tone was soft, caring, though she now wondered if he deserved it. "Take better care of yourself. Please."

"Yet, my dear, you get more eye-catching every day." Phil ogled her with ravenous, lustful eyes and hooted. "How do you do that? Hell, I think you are more gorgeous now than when I first saw you." He winked. "I had a crush on you from day one. George hit a home run recruiting you right out of law school."

"I don't have the stress of admin duties," Lisa replied. She ached for this day to be over. She resolved to plan the rest of her life, far away from Phil and his endless machinations.

"Would you like to be the OC DA?" He flashed a politician's overconfident smile.

Lisa shook off the slime flooding her skin. "I'm not ready for the political side of the job. You're too young to retire, aren't you?" Lisa closed her eyes and visualized herself taking a shower in a cleansing and rejuvenating brilliant white light.

"You're ready. I'll recommend you for it. Sooner than you think." He removed the soda cup lid and glinted at Lisa over its top. He gulped down the brown liquid, and an avalanche of ice cubes caused it to dribble out of the corner of his mouth onto his otherwise perfect shirt.

"Where would you go? I thought this was your dream job. You said this is where you make the greatest difference." She pondered the scene had the aura of an unpleasant *déjà vu*.

"Wherever I go, there is always room for you, like the old days. The unstoppable duo, Phillip L. Tomlinson and the heart stopping Lisa Jensen. We were always fabulous *together*," he added. Starting at her ankles, his gaze raked her legs, pausing in the middle and then on her bust before it settled on her face. "How about Sacramento for now?"

"We were not undefeated," Lisa retorted.

"Yes, we were!" Phil exclaimed. "How many significant murder cases did we work together and won? Twenty-five, thirty?"

"Sixteen," she hissed, revealing no teeth. "We lost the very first case I second-chaired for you." She clutched the wrinkled envelope as if it were a lifeline. She traced the heart-shaped piece of jewelry inside, separating it from the keys that shared the small package.

"It was a hung jury." Phil made a dismissive gesture. "Technically, we didn't lose."

"Now, we know we *should have lost*." Lisa marched to the door. She knew Phil was searching for another angle to exploit. She flashed an image of Phil as the epitome of a crooked public official caught stealing a baby's lollipop, licking it with contempt for all to see.

"Don't go yet!" he shouted, tracking her like a wolf stalking its prey. As he leaned over the desk, his tie fell like a giant tongue over his expanding belly. "You can never talk about this, about any of it. Think about the ramifications and unintended consequences."

She felt even more uncomfortable and fought the urge to sprint out of his office. Lisa wondered how many times Phil had lied to her and other ADAs. Day after day, year after year, she defended him, protected him. All of it in vain, undeserved.

"We dodged a big bullet, Lisa," he pleaded. "Her family needs to find that thing. No unanswered questions. Case closed. Let the sleeping dogs lie, will you? For old times' sake."

Lisa stopped at the door and studied the intricate pattern of wood fibers folding onto themselves under the expensive varnish. *Just like life.* "I know, damn it. No need to keep reminding me," she fought back agony and heavy tears. "Even if it goes against everything you and George taught me. What a waste. What a shame!"

"I want to make sure you understand what's at stake," Phil crossed his arms again. "No good can ever come out of this for anyone. Yourself included."

"I held full-time jobs, while I put myself through college and then Law School. I slept four hours a night for months on end. I made dean's list every semester, dedicated my entire life in service of those who needed a voice. I thought I learned from you all there is to know about truth, integrity, and the relentless pursuit of justice. Now, this. How can I look at myself in the mirror after this?"

"Lisa, our entire careers, everything we worked so hard for, and maybe our lives depend on this moment, right now. Don't throw it all away for both of us. We'll figure out another way to straighten it out, but I need you to do this for me. For us."

"I'll take care of it," Lisa replied, opening the door. She could not help herself and mocked his tone over her shoulder. "For old times' sake." She slammed the door, causing Phil's secretary to jump in her seat.

"Damn you, Phil," Lisa muttered. Clasping the wrinkled envelope, she felt tears brimming, and she clenched her jaw and fists. She endeavored to hold them back. She had committed long ago she would rather suffer eternal damnation than allow her colleagues to see her in such an emotional state. She had toiled and fought hard to create and maintain her reputation. She was the *tougher-than-diamonds prosecutor* fighting for justice, giving all victims a loud voice.

Fur-lined cape, please.

CHAPTER 3

THE WAREHOUSE WAS A giant rectangular cavernous space with a two-story office structure at its southern end, and small windows near the roof line on the long sides. A cloak of dust and diesel exhaust trailed the convoy of trucks and Humvees into the building.

The giant door rolled down with a long screeching sound as the trepidation of powerful motors rattled the windows. Excited men slapped high fives, disembarking the vehicles. Slamming door sounds replaced the noise of engines shutting off one by one.

Amid the chaos, yet somehow out of the way, Alvin Purcell remain standing tall, with that precise posture military officers adopted over a lifetime of service. Hands locked behind his back, Purcell took in the commotion, his alert eyes tracking the movement of the troops. He flicked a speck of dirt off his immaculate black trousers, caressing their precise pleats, and tugged at the spotless crimson shirt, making sure its sleeves had kept the sharp crease. Brushing a hand through his cropped gray hair, he stepped forward.

Purcell inventoried everything, as the troops scurried by with their consignments. "Leave the biohazard suits, medical supplies, weapons, and ammo in the trucks. Reload all other vehicles by areas of deployment. Make it snappy. Double-check and secure each load."

Two men, clad in black SWAT coveralls, approached. They steered a large trolley stacked with three metallic containers coated with faded military green paint.

"Sir, the special cases." The shorter man advanced towards Purcell.

"After everyone leaves, load them in the Humvees and lock them in." Purcell pointed to nearby vehicles. "Report back here at oh seven hundred tomorrow."

Purcell took a breath and leaned over to check the dual locks on the first rectangular box. His fingers crept with veneration over the Cyrillic lettering. Those were the tools of much-needed change. These devices would usher in a new age for his country. An era of essential law and order for the country. The clear direction that America had been missing for so long.

The two men retreated with the cart. Purcell stole a glance at the rest of the troops milling around. He reviewed every intricate detail of the operation in his head. "Goddamn bureaucrats almost fucked everything up. They couldn't wait until next week," he whispered, although nobody was within earshot.

The troops secured vehicles and cargo and then assembled in a loose formation in front of Purcell. All men and women wore bulletproof vests with various local, state, and federal law enforcement marks. Some of them wore military-style fatigues suggestive of special operations teams. Conversations ceased, and the buzz of excitement subsided. The setting sun cast orange stripes through exhaust fumes that swirled in lazy whirlpools around their ankles.

"I am impressed," Purcell said. "Notify everybody of our new location. The timeline remains unaltered. Thanks to your swift response, our operation is back on track. A magnificent new country awaits us. You proved, again, you're the right team for this job."

"America for Americans," a Highway Patrolman double slammed his right fist over his heart. All troops mimicked the gesture. The crowd stomped their feet and exchanged high fives again. The air shook with excitement and loud conversations. Purcell's hand came up. He waited with impatience for them to settle down before he resumed his speech.

"Soon enough. You are the undeniable new heroes of a proud nation."

"America for Americans!" The group's retort rocked the warehouse.

"Enjoy your evening." Purcell continued, unfazed. "Team leaders, we meet here at oh seven hundred tomorrow. We hand out last assignments at oh nine hundred. Dismissed."

Purcell stood still until the last man left through the side door, and then he headed to the ad hoc security and communications office, at the bottom of the staircase leading to the second floor. He waved a white key card at the sensor and placed his palm on the adjacent screen. The lock beeped and clicked, and he pushed the door open. He scanned the room and inspected with care the wiring, struggling to hide that he lacked the technological knowledge to comprehend the complexity and accuracy of the setup.

"Are we fully operational yet?" Purcell fought to mask his irritation. He could not assess the progress of the job and hated needing to ask the technicians.

"We'll be operational within the hour," Cross shook dust from his crumpled police coveralls. He gestured to his men to speed up activity. Facing Purcell again, he added, "We'll have limited capabilities until the rest of the equipment gets here, gets installed and tested. Too bad we had to leave all that gear behind—"

"Good job, Cross," Purcell cut him off, his mind already on the next task. "When your men finish setting up whatever we brought with us, go home. Simpson will be here with the rest of your gadgets and finish setting up tonight. Only you need to be here for the 7:00 A.M. briefing. Have your crew report here at oh nine hundred, along with everyone else." Without waiting for confirmation, Purcell turned on his heel and marched up the stairs.

On the second-floor bridge, he ran into Martin Bonds and Chris Wallace. Both men sported mirrored wraparound sunglasses. Arms akimbo and nose held high, Purcell addressed them. "Lose the damn shades. You look like cheap imitations of the Terminator. Find a new hero to worship."

The men complied with urgency and stepped aside with reverence. Walking between them, Purcell continued. "You have the first watch when Cross and his techs finish. The boss will be here in a few hours.

Simpson's crew will relieve you. Both of you report here at oh nine hundred tomorrow."

Purcell paced around, inspecting the giant multipurpose room occupying the entire second floor. Satisfied, he trotted back to the security office and knocked on the door, tapping his boot on the bare concrete floor as he waited. The door opened.

"Know who's on the other side before you open the door," he barked at Cross. "I'm going to check on things at Site B. I'll try to get back before the boss arrives. Carry on."

Purcell walked away with purpose. "In three days, this will all be over. I can finally see justice done. Stuff like that will never happen to anyone else. That's a dream worth chasing to the very end, no matter the cost," he whispered to himself, and strode out of the warehouse.

CHAPTER 4

"DADDY, WHERE ARE YOU?** Help us, Daddy. Please!" The infant girl's insistent voice echoed like crystal bells inside canyon walls. She sought aid with sky-blue eyes sparkling under giant tears, two magnificent sapphires soaked in liquid diamonds.

John Paul Morgan, J.P. to his friends, struggled under the tremendous pressure crushing his chest. He felt confined, trapped, like a lizard pinned by a ruthless giant finger.

"Daddy, I'm hurting. Mommy's dying!" The little one pleaded with quivering hiccups. She reached out with her whole being, the way toddlers do, her head lolling from side to side. The pitch of her voice increased. "Daaaaddddyyyyyyy. Daaaaddddyyyyyyy."

J.P. wriggled to break free and reach for the tiny cherub. Each one of her words pierced his soul like a stiletto thrust. Anguish became more intolerable with every unanswered cry. His heart threatened to break through his rib cage, and his muscles burned from exertion.

J.P. wanted to assure the baby girl that he would help and make the tormentors go away. No sounds escaped his scorched lips. Powerlessness brought on rekindled mental torture that singed his soul. All he could do was lie there, silent and defeated, watching the heavenly child beg for help. Help that would never come. Her innocent face contorted with terror and sorrow no child should know, and J.P. suffered another sharp pain jolt like a stake through his heart.

A stunning young woman emerged from the blackness, floating next to the little girl, scooping her up and enveloping her in arms of pure love. J.P. recalled that gorgeous face well. It belonged to the love of his life, Alice. His wife. His murdered wife. The feelings of anguish and misery increased a hundredfold.

"I am sorry, babe. Please forgive me." He felt the excruciating impulse to shout his regret. The words never formed in his parched throat.

"Where were you, J.P.? How could this happen? Why?" Alice's features twisted in endless grief, her steel-blue eyes as restless and unforgiving as the stormy sea.

J.P.'s subconscious mind realized it was *The Nightmare.* A dreadful hallucination seared into his brain for over a decade. His body relaxed on cue. He had realized long ago, no matter what, he could never change history. Alice, who taught him so much about life and love, had been dead for over a decade, along with their unborn, unnamed daughter. Only the heartache and guilt survived, channeled into a relentless self-flagellation routine.

The faces and voices faded away like vapors on a hot day. He longed to hold on to the wispy image. It was all he had left of them—this haunting picture. *The Nightmare.* J.P. expected the arduous feelings of sorrow and remorse, even welcomed them.

J.P. sat up with a jolt. Sweat glistened on his arms in the fading sunlight. He felt droplets snake their way through his thick hair. His heart hammered inside of his chest, endeavoring to break through. Thump. Thump. Thump.

The Nightmare *is back,* reflected J.P. *Why now, after all these years? What did Einstein say?* "Coincidence is God's way of remaining anonymous." Strange feelings flowed over him. J.P. shivered, attempting to shake them off, and glanced at the dashboard clock. 7:28 P.M.

He recalled closing his eyes at 5:00 P.M., intent on resting his eyes for a minute. He struggled to recall the last time he had awakened this disoriented. Dim, glowing lights of the electronic gear elicited his attention yet provided no answers.

Great job, Mr. Super PI. Maybe it is Super... pie. The bad guys could have stolen the entire world while you were sleeping on the job.

He jerked the lever, restoring the cot to a chair to get a better view out the windows of the SUV. He rubbed his eyes, wiping the cobwebs, and made a lighthearted mental note to buy Ginkgo Biloba—in bulk.

J.P.'s SUV, a Ford Expedition EL, doubled as his mobile office. A swivel chair that turned into a cot replaced the second and third-row seats. All around were banks of electronic gear and built-in cabinets. There was even a well-stocked mini fridge.

He studied the small park—one square block of lush grass and bonded rubber stone surrounding children's play areas. An oasis with middle-class homes lined up on the outer sides of one-way streets. He let his gaze drift across to Anna's home. Bright yellow Police Line tape marked the pale blue front door, her *personal gate to heaven*, like giant slanted crosshairs.

The excruciating news received that afternoon flooded J.P.'s mind. The agonizing reason that brought him there. He focused his eyes on the street across the small park, half a block down from Anna's lawn. The two plainclothes cops he had spotted earlier were still there, in the ash gray Dodge Charger. They kept the engine running, and their motionless mirrored shades trained on Anna's front door.

A blue Honda Accord skidded to a stop on the park side, across from Anna's stylish front yard. The driver got out and darted towards Anna's home. J.P. sat up straight. From behind, the woman appeared familiar, yet he did not recognize her. She had strawberry-blond hair pulled up in an exquisite bun and shapely long legs balancing on expensive high-heeled red pumps. She walked with the confidence of someone used to steady herself all day long in those shoes. A tailored Navy business suit adorned her slender, curvy body. She reminded him of Heather Locklear of his high school years. J.P. reasoned she was a lawyer, one of Anna's friends he probably met in her office.

He concentrated on her back as she climbed the stairs. The woman retrieved keys from her purse, and J.P.'s vision field narrowed to the back of the woman and the door. Anna did not trust anyone to access her home in her absence. Only Anna's mom and J.P. enjoyed that privilege. Not even her house cleaner had keys.

The plainclothes officers reached the bottom of the steps as the mysterious woman unlocked the second lock. Unaware of their presence, she pushed the door open and stooped under the Police Line tape. The powerful arm of the shorter, older cop prevented the door from closing. The younger, leaner one shoved the woman inside.

CHAPTER 5

"**F**OLKS, I KNOW YOU** live only to ask questions, but I have important work to do." Clancy raised his hand like a traffic cop. "Filling Jim Simmons's shoes is no simple task. My office will provide a press release kit soon. I look forward to our next opportunity to talk."

The relentless chorus of reporters shouted questions over each other.

"'s enhanced amnesty program for undocumented aliens continue?"

"What is your position regarding illegal immigration?"

"What legislation will you implement regarding taxpayer-funded benefits for illegal immigrants and undocumented people?"

"Do you support taxpayer-paid abortions for illegals?"

"Will California continue to provide medical insurance for undocumented..."

Clancy signaled them to be quiet and waited with a frown until the room fell silent. Damned be the vultures. They had no respect for anyone's time and schedule. All they cared about was asking senseless questions, hoping to get their stupid ratings up. He would have to do something about it later. Now, he had more important issues that demanded his attention.

"Ladies and gentlemen, please understand this has been unexpected. I have not had time to sit down with the Governor and discuss these matters. George and I will call a press conference to share all the details. Give us a chance, please."

He marched out of the room, ignoring the press corps. His bodyguards fell in step, struggling to keep up. Without bothering to look at them, Clancy said, "Have the secretary pool distribute the press kits. Get the team ready. We leave in ten minutes."

Clancy sunk in the brand new leather chair and executed two full 360 degree turns. He considered redecorating the office in a more dynamic theme to suit his disposition, or at least furnish it more expensively to match his customs. Yet he knew it would be a waste of time. He would switch offices again before the decorators even started planning the changes.

"For my actual office, I'll spare no expense," he toasted himself with the remains of his energy drink, then retrieved a mobile phone, and spoke fast, "Everything went smooth as silk. Your tip was perfect. Hunter performed admirably at the press conference, and no one is the wiser. Now it's just a matter of time. Hunter seemed relieved when it was all over."

Clancy hung up and leaned back, interlocking his fingers behind his head.

"Life is grand," he pronounced aloud. He mock saluted the pictures of President Cornell and Governor Hunter, then smacked his lips like a child eyeing a bowl of ice cream. "You boys look mismatched up there. Let's see what we can do about that. Quickly."

CHAPTER 6

J.P. GRABBED A PROTEIN bar and a bottle of cold water, then settled to wait for the woman to come out. The woman had keys to Anna's home. That intrigued J.P. Mentally, he made a list of questions he intended to ask her, without the cops breathing down their necks. He lifted a pair of binoculars and focused them on the yellow tape. He waited, still as a statue, for the woman and the police officers to reveal their faces when they exited.

The pale blue door opened. The older cop stepped outside. He squinted long and hard in both directions and then treaded to the Honda. He backed it up in Anna's driveway and popped the trunk. Then he hurried back inside, inspecting the street in both directions again.

On instinct, J.P. started recording video with his windshield mounted HD camera. The older cop returned and gazed again along the street in both directions. Satisfied, he held the door open for his lanky partner.

J.P. instantly nicknamed them *Rail* and *Fireplug*. Rail carried a rolled-up rug on his right shoulder. J.P. scratched his scalp and considered whether the two cops were robbing the home before the family took inventory. Was the blonde woman helping them?

Rail crouched under the tape and headed down the stairs. A red shoe fell from inside the rug. Almost before it hit the ground, *Fireplug* scooped it up. *Fireplug* reached inside the rug and retrieved the second shoe. Rail dumped his cargo in the Honda's trunk and then removed a woman's purse, concealed under his right arm. He threw it in on top of the rug. *Fireplug* tossed in the high heels and slammed the lid closed.

18

The entire event got more bizarre by the minute. J.P. had had plenty of experience with law enforcement types, yet this was a first for him. He had no illusions about all cops being straight and honest. However, he knew most of them to be hardworking people, doing an essential, dangerous job. Too many things did not add up about these two officers.

Then there was Anna's alleged suicide, which J.P. did not buy for one minute.

J.P. focused on the blue Honda's trunk, praying the woman in it was still alive. He contemplated calling 911 but had no evidence they had taken the woman against her will, and cops always looked out for each other. J.P.'s reason for being there rattled around in his head. Paramount was finding the proof Anna had called him about. He would talk to the police after he located the evidence. Whatever information Anna had found most likely led to her murder. If only she had told him what it was, instead of resorting to her usual hugger-muggers. That was Anna. Always ready for a pun and a riddle, "to turn that frown upside down."

J.P. watched *Fireplug* climb in the gray sedan. Rail followed in the Honda, bumper to bumper. This was the ideal time to search Anna's home, yet his famous childlike curiosity would never allow J.P. to ignore this conundrum. He resolved to return and comb through Anna's house after he made sure the woman was safe. Whoever she was.

J.P. drove to the end of the park, turned, and stayed on a parallel street for two blocks. He shadowed the small procession, pleading with God their cargo was merely unconscious. Otherwise, he would have to live with the fact he did nothing. Who could have expected police officers to harm innocent people for no apparent reason?

A line from an old Mel Gibson movie clattered in his tired brain, *"Dirty cops. Do they come any other way?"* "Yes, Mel, they do. However, it seems you got it right about these two," J.P. murmured to himself, shaking his giant frame to silence the alarms going off in his mind. "I have a bad feeling. This is shaping to be a long night, Mel."

CHAPTER 7

J.P. PULLED OVER AND watched the two sedans drive in a warehouse. The colossal building's foursquare block lot stood isolated from other structures. A ten-foot brand-new, shiny chain-link fence topped with four rows of barbed wire angled outward, surrounded the entire yard. The narrow backyard separated the building from the railroad tracks.

A thick layer of dry leaves and brush had formed in front of the left roll-up door. The two cars had used the right-side entrance. The screeching sound of the closing gate resonated in the warm air. J.P.'s mind switched gears. He needed to know what was inside that place.

The occupants of that building valued their privacy. No signs identifying a business or address. The whole place screamed. "Go away." J.P.'s inquisitiveness commanded he looked inside. He needed to figure out why the cops, if they were police officers, kept Anna's place under surveillance. More to the point, why they abducted the blonde woman.

Another warehouse nearby caught J.P.'s attention. Despite the late hour, it bustled with activity. People, trucks, cars, and forklifts scurried about the busy lot like well-defined ant trails. It was a great place to leave his vehicle undetected while he conducted reconnaissance.

J.P. grabbed various items from the SUV's built-in cabinets, stuffed them in the pockets of his "uniform," as Max called his usual attire— soft-soled black Skechers, black jeans, and a short-sleeved black shirt worn over a black T-shirt. At Max's suggestion, he once tried an all-charcoal, then a navy ensemble. It did not feel the same. The gray and blue did not mesh well with his jet-black hair and coal-black eyes. He felt more visible in them. Being a shadow among shadows was a matter of life and death in his profession, just as it had been most of his life.

J.P. selected a fresh shirt and made sure the button camera had a full charge and linked to the equipment in the truck. He set up his gear to record video feeds from all cameras and upload copies to his cloud storage. Then he donned a disposable black mask, a usual sight in the aftermath of COVID-19. He considered taking a gun and decided against it. The men he was stalking might be real cops, and he did not want to explain the gun, even though he had valid permits. Cops always had guns to spare. Need be, he could "borrow" one from them.

J.P. chose a path and analyzed it through a miniature night-vision scope. He spotted security cameras atop the target warehouse, protecting the adjacent areas in a crisscross pattern. He recognized the model. The cameras had motion and infrared sensors. The system monitored and recorded everything. Motion, or excessive heat, triggered floodlights and the alarms.

Penetrating this setup would not be a simple task. Its design and installation covered a 180-degree field, and its infrared motion detectors were impossible to beat. On the upside, the edge of the rooftop mounting limited the direct line of sight of the cameras to the path next to the walls. If, by some miracle, he could make it there unnoticed, he might have a chance. He prayed the night watchmen bored as easy as any other security guard in the world.

He advanced through the parking lot behind the neighboring building toward the train tracks. Sneaking along the railroad fence, he reached a spot that offered an unrestricted view of the rear area of the warehouse. Outside the backyard, halfway between the railroad and the street, stood a tall old tree. Floodlights atop of the target building created long shadows across the fence separating the two warehouses, the only partial blind spot for the motion sensors.

He shoved his giant hands into black nitrile gloves and became a ghost. Even now, COVID caused people to wear gloves with normal attire. He considered the infiltration task a breeze. He had broken into and out of far better fortified places, though not on this continent.

"I hear the train a-comin'. It's rollin' round the bend," he hummed Johnny Cash's tune as he slowed his breathing and patted his pockets, re-taking inventory of all tools.

Powerful ground trepidations announced the locomotive before J.P. saw its headlamp. After the floodlights turned on, he sauntered across the narrow lane, using the shadow of the tree to conceal his movements from the surveillance system. J.P. climbed on the tree's lower branch. In one fluid move, he skipped the barbed wire as the last of the five train cars passed by. Three giant leaps later, he flattened his back against the warehouse wall. *Thanks, Johnny.*

He chose one of the two back access doors as the potential entry point. J.P. moseyed sideways, his back glued to the wall and his head down. A bullet-shaped trash bin concealed a square box half buried in the stucco next to the door. He slid the cover and shook his head in disbelief. A biometric palm pad with a key card reader backup. Even if he bypassed the card reader with the tools in his pockets, he needed a palm print authorized to open the door.

The place piqued his interest even more. His mind buzzed with dread. Too much security for a run-of-the-mill warehouse. Everything looked brand-new, dust free, as if installed earlier that day. He considered walking to the front to ring the bell. That way, at least, he had a chance of gaining access. He also had an equal chance of catching a bullet on sight.

He proceeded along the wall to the second back door, located a third of the way from the opposite corner. There was no access pad, but that door had been closed for years. He walked to the metallic ladder at the far corner and climbed with surprising agility for someone his size. He spotted two roof access hatches, both alarmed and locked from inside. He scanned the entire flattop and noticed an abandoned bucket with rolls of rope and network cable.

J.P. tied cables to the cameras covering the backyard. He secured the rope to a metallic reinforcement beam running along the edge of the roof. He tested the rope's strength and then yanked on the wires, causing all cameras to the turn towards the dark sky.

Who said watching MacGyver was a waste of time? He had lots of good ideas.

CHAPTER 8

"NOT NO, BUT HELL NO!"** yelled Bonds. He smacked the monitors with the paperback he had been reading. "We barely got here, and the problems started."

"What's up?" Wallace asked, keeping his eyes glued to the magazine in his hands. Intoxicating pictures of attractive, scantily clad young women posing with expensive cars had his undivided attention. He struggled with the decision regarding his next car. A Maserati, a Bentley, or maybe an Aston Martin. Convertible, no doubt. Adorned with gorgeous babes.

"Goddamn techies," Martin spat his words. "The blasted thing is already on the fritz."

"It's just a temporary problem. Maybe the train loosened a wire. Just wait. It will come back." Wallace looked up from the magazine. "Simpson's guys will take care of it."

"We must keep this place secret," Bonds snapped. "Do you watch movies? That's how every break in starts. The security monitors go dark or flicker or some other damn thing."

"Paranoid much? Who in their right mind would barge in here?" Wallace asked.

"For the stuff we have out there?" Martin pointed to the door leading to the warehouse. "You bet your ass lots of people would kill us for it. If they knew."

"Exactly. We've been here six hours. It takes time to plan a successful infiltration into a place like this."

"All the same, go check it out," Bonds replied in anger. Seeing no reaction, he pushed Wallace's legs off the desk. "Now, Chris, I don't want any problems."

Wallace sauntered out of the office, uttering in a sarcastic tone, "Lock the door behind me. We don't want any problems."

CHAPTER 9

WALLACE KICKED THE DOOR open and stepped out in a shooter's stance, his Beretta and flashlight held tight. He lurched forward, did a slow full sweep, and then relaxed. He turned off the flashlight and stuck it in his belt, next to a much larger one.

Above the door, J.P. hung face down, with his feet planted against the wall. His face broadened into his signature *cat-that-ate-the-canary* smile, and he released the rope. He plummeted on top of Wallace, knocking his gun into the knee-high weeds.

As Wallace rose to his feet, J.P. assessed him to be five inches shorter but bulkier. Wallace scanned the lawn for his gun. He settled for the big flashlight, holding it like a bat.

J.P. invited his opponent to make the first move. Wallace raised the flashlight and propelled himself headfirst. J.P. stepped out of the way and delivered a blow as Wallace sailed by. The hit connected with Wallace's shoulder and sent him scrambling crablike on the grass.

"Got anything interesting in there?" asked J.P.

"Who the fuck are you?" blurted Wallace, collecting himself.

J.P. figured Wallace realized he faced an agile rival and considered a different strategy.

"A concerned citizen." J.P. locked his gaze on Wallace. "I witnessed crimes perpetrated by undercover police officers."

"What!?" Wallace asked, anxious and puzzled.

"I saw two cops kidnap a woman and steal a rug from my friend's house," J.P. explained in a mocking tone.

"What are you talking about?" Wallace half-lowered his guard.

J.P. feigned right and delivered a left hook to Wallace's exposed jaw. Wallace landed flat on his back. "I wondered about the rug," J.P. said. "Maybe Anna left it to me in her will. *Rail* and *Fireplug* looked like cops but behaved like criminals."

"*Rail? Fireplug?* What the hell?" Wallace stood and stumbled backward. "Oh, you're one of those sarcastic pricks who think everything they have to say is funny." Wallace attacked with the flashlight, connecting to J.P.'s left shoulder blade.

J.P. flicked off an imaginary speck from his shirt. "Uncertainty is my ally." J.P. cocked his head right, avoiding Wallace's direct jab. He locked Wallace's arm between his shoulder and left forearm, then he stepped under. J.P. twisted and flipped Wallace, slamming him on the ground. "Stay down. All I want from you is information."

"I'm a cop, asshole. There will be hell to pay for this." Wallace got up panting like an exhausted dog leaning with sweaty palms on his knees. "You'll be in prison forever."

"Catch me first, Grandpa."

"What did you say, motherfucker?" Wallace hurled himself at J.P. His flashlight sailed past J.P.'s temple. Wallace located his pistol and nose-dived for it.

A cheetah stalking a gazelle would have envied J.P.'s leap that pinned Wallace face down on the ground. Wallace pushed against the ground to shake J.P. off.

"Enough is enough," declared J.P. "This a vest, Grandpa? Or a girdle?" J.P. teased Wallace, his confidence as strong as his swing.

"You are dead. You hear me? You are a fucking ghost already. What do you care about that bitch? She's been nothing but trouble. If you want her, you can have her."

"She is a human being," J.P. juggled the flashlight. "Kidnapping is wrong. Maybe they taught that *after* you graduated cop school."

"Screw you." Wallace panted. He struggled with sweat dripping off his forehead.

"Give up, or do I have to knock you out?" J.P. half-yawned.

Wallace reached for his backup weapon holstered inside his left ankle. J.P. threw the flashlight, smashing Wallace's fingers against the butt of the revolver. He decided he had enough and directed a haymaker to the side of Wallace's head. "That will give one hell of a headache, but you will be out of my way."

J.P. gathered Wallace's guns, frisked him, and retrieved two extra clips from Wallace's belt. He dragged Wallace to the security palm pad. Wallace was wearing comfortable civilian clothes, not some second-rate uniform of a security company. When his shirt gave way, a bulletproof vest marked *POLICE* became visible.

"Hmm. Gramps was telling the truth," J.P. muttered.

A can of pepper spray, a stun gun, handcuffs, and two more spare magazines completed Wallace's arsenal. J.P. found a badge, a white security key card, keys, loose change, and other insignificant items. He shoved the useless stuff back in Wallace's pockets, keeping only the guns, badge, ammo clips, and security key card.

J.P. waved the card in front of the reader and scanned Wallace's palm on the biometric pad. He pulled the unconscious body inside and handcuffed him around the six-inch pipe next to the door. J.P. pocketed the spare magazines, then emptied Wallace's backup revolver and threw it atop a truck canopy.

One problem solved, one million to go. What did I get myself into, and for what?

CHAPTER 10

IN THE DIM LIGHT, J.P. studied Wallace's sidearm and magazines. He whistled quietly. Wallace used a Beretta 92 Combat Edition and hollow-point 9 mm rounds. Then J.P. inspected the Long Beach PD badge, reflecting that Wallace was outside of his jurisdiction, probably moonlighting as a security guard. For whom, though?

Though poor, the light allowed him to travel through the warehouse. The military-style trucks, Humvees, pallets, and piles of boxes obstructed his view of the entire ground floor. J.P. decided his priority was to locate the other guards and prevent them from raising an alarm.

Next on the list was to pinpoint the woman's whereabouts, find out who she was, and ask her about those damn keys. He planned to question the cops who kidnapped her, too. He could not figure out what all of it had to do with Anna Richter. There was no longer any doubt in his mind that Anna's death related to these folks and their secret warehouse.

A bluish glow flickered under the door by the staircase. The other doors on the ground floor were all dark. The only other light filtered under both doors on the second floor. J.P. squeezed his gigantic frame between two Humvees and approached the ground floor door.

Damn. The door had the same biometric lock and card reader. It would take too long to drag Wallace to the new lock. Another option would be to try the trick from Sneakers. It had worked for Redford. However, it was a noisy option that would alert unknown parties. He could also knock and see if the guards inside would open it. *No guts, no glory.*

He jiggled the key card and placed his gloved hand, obscuring the reader. The system produced a faint failure beep. J.P. smashed into the door as if he expected it to open. He waited for the biometric lock to reset itself and then repeated the steps. This time, he mumbled a curse under his breath and kicked the door.

"Chris, what's going on?" Bonds yelled from inside, irritated.

J.P. repeated the procedure and pushed the door, expecting it to remain closed.

"Stop, Chris. You'll break the door!" Bonds shouted as his chair scraped the floor.

J.P.'s smile widened. *Come to Papa Bear.*

The door cracked open. J.P. shouldered it, sending Bonds crashing backward. J.P. burst in with the Beretta leveled, scanning the room filled only with electronic gear. Bonds wriggled to regain balance. J.P. trained the gun on Bonds and motioned at him to lie down. J.P. spied yellow letters on Bonds's bulletproof vest: DEA. J.P. handcuffed Bonds to a shelf bolted to the wall. "Take a nap while I check out this place."

"If you live long enough, you'll wish you never did this." Bonds' face turned crimson.

"Let me worry about that," replied J.P. *Cops? Feds? If I lived long enough? Surreal.* "I have to help the poor woman you abducted. Deep down, I am a gentleman. Where is she?"

Bonds' eyes glanced toward the ceiling. "It doesn't matter. The boss doesn't tolerate mistakes. You just signed all our death warrants, yours included." Martin tested the cuffs.

J.P. pondered whether Bonds overstated the consequences. *Feds do not kill their own for such minor mistakes, do they? Oh, well. It is a paranoid world out there. I just live in it.*

He cold cocked Bonds and then seized his key card, wallet, and gun, a SIG Sauer P229 and four spare clips. "Sleep tight. Maybe we live."

J.P. released the SIG's clip, ejected the chambered round, and then threw everything under different vehicles outside. Martin's badge confirmed him as a DEA agent. New feelings of discomfort crept over J.P. as he scanned the room.

The security area housed a high-tech comms, tactical command, and electronic surveillance center—a modular one, designed to dismantle with ease and move with a moment's notice. Battlefield-style.

J.P. cut the networking wires coming out of the wall and then left the security room.

OK, lady. Who the hell are you, and what did I just do? Why am I here risking my neck, instead of having dinner and catching up on the much-needed sleep?

Climbing the stairs, J.P. scanned the cavernous structure for other guards. He walked to the first door in perfect silence. Someone had painted it shut long ago. He tiptoed to the second door and saw the biometric-lock-and-key card combo. Frustrated, he wondered what would justify this level of security for a crummy warehouse smack in the middle of South LA.

"She's not some whore from a jungle village. Are you insane? You know our DNA is on file," a strained male voice pleaded from the other side of the door, over light music.

"This bitch gets what she deserves." Decades of cigarettes and alcohol abuse marked the second male voice. "She went to Richter's house. She knows too much. There will be no time for forensic investigations. It would be a shame to let this good-looking piece of ass go to waste." The tone changed to bittersweet. "Isn't that right, baby?"

J.P. cringed, struggling to comprehend why peace officers threatened to rape a woman in custody. Then there was the fact she knew too much just because she went to Anna's house.

Scuffling sounds and a loud moan seeped through the door. The woman screamed, and J.P.'s heart skipped a beat. He needed a way in if he would help. Fast.

"Fuck!" the scruffy-voice owner shouted. "Scream all you want, bitch. No one can hear you. You'll beg to tell me what you know and die quickly. First, I'm gonna fuck your pretty brains out until you spill your guts. I bet you're one fun ride." He sniggered at his own joke.

"I'm not taking any risks that could jeopardize our mission," the younger voice replied. "If you're that horny, get yourself a hooker, or jerk off like always."

"Our mission is what I tell you it is, shithead. Get out of here before I shoot your limp dick off. If you're up for sloppy seconds, you can have it. Very sloppy seconds," he snickered.

"You're a sick dumbass. How did you ever make it on our team?"

"Your boss gets here in about an hour. Before that, I need to find out what this nosy bitch knows. I'm gonna soften her up then interrogate her properly. I'll use an oversized microphone, if you catch my drift. Get the fuck out of here. I don't enjoy being watched."

"Fucking moron." The younger voice trembled. "You'll pay for this."

Rail walked out, humiliated and furious. The tip of his nose lined up with the Beretta in J.P.'s hand. J.P. lifted his eyebrows and pointed with his chin toward the room. *Rail* froze, his eyes wide with astonishment. J.P. blocked the door with his foot, spun *Rail* around, and shoved him back into the room, holding him by the back of his shirt and the bulletproof vest.

J.P. scanned the room lit by fluorescent lights. At one end were a California wall map and a conference table with ten leather chairs. On the opposite side, laptops and papers covered several metal desks. Four dozen folding chairs stood arranged in neat rows. Between the doors were six metallic supply cabinets. Five pairs of metal bunk beds lined up on the opposite wall end to end. It was a modular, tactical briefing room found on battlefields, not in South LA.

The room felt warm. The air was dusty and smelled of sweat and gun oil.

The mysterious woman sat on the middle lower bed, her body against the wall. The upper bed shadow and her blue mask concealed her face. Flexi-cuffs bound her hands and ankles, and her suit jacket laid crumpled next to her. Her ripped white silk blouse revealed a white lace bra with a torn strap. She panted and wheezed, straining to resist the assault.

Fireplug stood in front of her, legs apart, working his fly with both hands, very much like an ancient captor about to exercise the power he had over the defenseless woman.

Using *Rail* as a shield, J.P. tiptoed into the room.

Fireplug noticed the woman's gaze drift past him. He turned in slow motion and stared down the barrel of J.P.'s Beretta. His left cheek sported a small welt and a fresh, bleeding cut.

You got a piece of him. Good for you, girl.

J.P. lifted *Rail*'s gun from its holster and released the magazine, letting them both drop to the floor. He kicked them under the conference table. A powerful blow to the back of his neck sent *Rail* to his knees. J.P. stepped on *Rail*'s left ankle, denying him access to his backup weapon. J.P. squeezed *Rail*'s carotid artery, limiting the flow of blood to the brain to render the man docile. "Try anything funny and I will tear your windpipe," J.P. stated in a calm voice.

Fireplug took in the scene. Recognition, followed by sheer surprise, registered on his pudgy face as if a flash-bang grenade went off. "What the fuck are *you* doing here?" he yelped.

"You bastard!" the woman shouted, wriggling toward the edge of the bed. "Of course, you're involved in this, Morgan. Is this your revenge?"

"Shut up, bitch," *Fireplug* yelled. "This doesn't concern you."

So much for wearing a mask. What? Do I have my name tattooed on my forehead?

"When I get out of here," the woman ignored him and continued her tirade, "I'll make sure this time you get the needle and the gas chamber after that. For good measure."

J.P.'s eyes bounced from *Fireplug* to the woman, doing his best to identify them.

The woman leaned forward and tried to stand. Her bound ankles and wrists lent the move a comical worm likeness. A purple bruise was blooming on her left cheek.

J.P. glanced at the ceiling. "Good one, God. Why *her*?"

CHAPTER 11

"PUT ME THROUGH TO the Governor, now," Clancy barked. "Thank you for taking my call, George. Let's schedule a face-to-face session to discuss the illegal immigration policy. We'll both be in Orange County on the morning of the fourth. We should have all other leaders and cabinet members attend. That way, we can adopt the policy right away."

"Hold your horses. I haven't signed your appointment order yet," the Governor pointed out. "This was a very unexpected and unpleasant surprise for me."

"We both know that's a mere formality, George," Clancy interrupted. "I want to show my appreciation and support. We should avoid embarrassing moments with the press."

"Stay out of sight for now." The Governor sounded tired, worried, and annoyed by Clancy's repeated use of his first name. "You'll have your shot."

"Sound advice, George. No reason for me to keep bumping into the press hyenas."

"I'll see when I am available to meet with you," Hunter replied. He felt cornered and annoyed with himself for allowing Clancy's manipulation. However, he knew there was no other way if he wished to run for reelection in the fall.

"I'll start on drafts of the plan to discuss with the cabinet. It's imperative, George. Illegal immigration will cripple California and eventually the entire country."

"Do that. Have a wonderful weekend." Hunter dismissed him.

"You too, George. I'll wait for your call. Meanwhile, I will set up the meeting for the fourth." He clicked off and leaned back on the comfortable seat of the limo.

He dialed Purcell's number. "Status report," Clancy shouted.

"I have transferred everything to Site C. Security system is up and running. I posted Wallace and Bonds. We cleaned all traces at Site A," Purcell reported in one breath.

"What about the sand coons and the spics?" Clancy probed.

"Warden Spears moved them off premises earlier today," Purcell answered.

"So much for anticipating everything. Stupid law of unintended consequences nearly nailed us. Great job getting the train wreck back on tracks. You proved to be a powerful leader."

"Thank you, sir. We believe in the cause," Purcell replied. "All of us."

"Good to hear. I am on my way to Site C to check it out for myself. Leaving Sac as we speak. I'll be there in sixty minutes. Meet me there with the master plans. I would like to make some minor modifications."

CHAPTER 12

"OOPS. CARRY ON, PLEASE," J.P. addressed *Fireplug.* "This is all in the law enforcement family. *Who am I to judge?*" He lifted *Rail* by the neck to wobbly feet.

"I can't allow you to walk out of here alive," *Fireplug* reacted, turning off the music. "Even if you don't know it yet, you learned too much." He glanced at his own gun holster hanging from the top bed.

J.P. smirked. "If you're like me, you can resist anything but temptation."

J.P. wondered what he had learned that could justify *Fireplug's* statement. Two crooked cops kidnapped and tried to rape a woman—a woman he would not mind seeing dead on the side of the road. Hell, he might even run over her a few times himself to make sure she did not get up. Something did not add up, and J.P. could not stand unexplained riddles.

"Morgan, if you leave me here, I'll have you brought up on charges." Lisa shouted. She rubbed her mask off, letting it hang from one ear.

No matter how distressed she was, J.P. had a hard time keeping his eyes off her. He contemplated she was one of God's loveliest creations. Except for her attitude.

"It'll be my life's mission to see you pay for it. You, miserable bastard," Lisa wheezed.

"Anything new in your repertoire?" J.P. asked. "We have been down this road."

"This is your payback, Morgan?" She spat every word laced with venom.

J.P. ignored her outburst. He had stumbled onto something big, but he had a hard time putting the pieces together. "I will go with the option to leave you here, Ms. Jensen. Have a lousy rest of your life, all two or three hours of it. Ta-ta." He waved the Berretta.

"Calm down. Neither of you is going anywhere," *Fireplug* stated in a certain tone.

"John Paul Morgan, you help get me out of here this instant, or so help me God..."

"When, or I should say *if*, you get away, you can ensure I get the needle and the gas chamber. For good measure." J.P. gazed into Lisa's eyes. "They seem confident you will not see the sunrise. I am better off leaving your sorry ass in their hands. You guys, are competent enough, right?" J.P. stepped backward, dragging *Rail* whose legs buckled under him.

"Please, don't leave me here," Jensen pleaded. "I'm scared. They'll kill me. They think I know something about Anna's death. Morgan, even you can't be that cruel." Her eyes softened up, and tears left wide streaks through her light makeup.

"Refresh my memory," J.P. shot back. "Why not?"

"You were an officer and a gentleman once." Jensen displayed a mix of panic and bewilderment. "Honor, duty, protecting those in need? Any of that ring a bell?"

"Damn it," conceded J.P. "Blame my mother. I could never abandon a damsel in distress, even if it is you." He waved the gun, pointing first at *Rail* and then at *Fireplug*. "What do you propose we do with them?"

Jensen twitched her nose and shrugged.

"The old fart seems to know me, but I do not remember him. Can you introduce us?"

"I don't know who he is, either, or why he abducted me." Lisa shook her head.

"Would you enlighten me, sir?" J.P. asked in a mock-polite tone, pointing the Beretta at *Fireplug*. "I feel at a disadvantage here."

"You never saw me back then." *Fireplug* squatted. His hand slid with his falling pants.

J.P. tracked the motion with his gun, bemused, like an adult humoring a child.

Fireplug stood, aimed a short-barreled revolver at Lisa's head and buried the tip of the pistol in her ear. "Let my partner go, or I'll shoot her. What would your mother say then?"

"Do you believe I care about what happens to her? Ha, ha, ha!" J.P. broke into a full-blown laugh, tightening his grip on *Rail*'s throat. *Rail*'s eyes bulged out under the pressure.

"Jerk. Have you no honor?" Lisa hissed, leaning away from the gun barrel.

"This is your last warning!" bellowed *Fireplug*. "Let him go and you surrender to me."

"Not a chance. The line about my mother was just smoke, so she would calm down while I got out of here." J.P. said. "You know both of us, so you know our history."

"You're making a grave mistake. Let's talk this over." *Fireplug* switched on the charm.

"Story of my life," declared J.P. "Let's summarize the situation for those a little slow on the uptake." J.P. knocked on *Rail*'s bulletproof vest, looking at the revolver in *Fireplug*'s hand. His expression turned soft, and he let out a "phew." Then he shifted his gaze to the Berretta in his hand. His eyes opened wide with mock amazement. "Wow."

"Morgan, stop screwing around." Jensen attempted to control her faltering voice. New tears grew in the corners of her eyes. She fought hard to hold them back and lost.

"Keep your panties on." J.P.'s voice stayed calm, crisp, and in full command.

"Screw you!" exclaimed *Fireplug*.

J.P. felt *Rail* wince. Then *Rail*'s body sagged against J.P.'s chest.

Fireplug fired twice. The first bullet hit *Rail* in the chest, on the edge of his vest. The second one whizzed over J.P.'s head as he squatted with *Rail*'s falling body.

J.P. double-tapped *Fireplug*'s body armor. The shots catapulted *Fireplug* atop Jensen.

The shots reverberated like cannon blasts and the aroma of cordite filled the room.

Then everything turned tomblike quiet.

CHAPTER 13

THE SILENCE LASTED ONLY seconds. Lisa let out a piercing scream, struggling to push *Fireplug*'s body away. Morgan allowed *Rail*'s body to slide to the floor and then pistol-whipped him. He stuck the Beretta in his belt, dragged the wheezing *Fireplug* off the hysterical Jensen, and then handcuffed him, securing his arms through the welded corners of the lower bunk beds. J.P. retrieved *Fireplug*'s gun, clubbed him with it, and shoved it at the small of his own back. *Fireplug* slumped forward, his head lolling into unconsciousness.

J.P. hauled *Rail* to another pair of bunk beds and secured him the same way, and then he collected both cops' backups. He removed all the rounds from the back-up guns and then threw everything under the desks covered in laptops.

"I will release you when you stop screaming." J.P. turned to Lisa.

"I promise to be quiet. Just untie me," she panted hard.

J.P. recognized that *killer-shark-disguised-as-fluffy-kitten* grin on Lisa's face. He had seen it before, followed by the big bite out of the unsuspecting prey's hide. *How can something so beautiful be this malicious? Think coral snakes. Mother Nature can be exceedingly cruel.*

With expert moves, J.P. cut the bindings, freeing Lisa's ankles and wrists.

"No macho comment? 'Come with me if you want to live'? Or something along those lines? This is your big chance." She rubbed her wrists and scowled.

J.P. took two steps away from her and kept quiet.

"I am scared, and I don't know what's happening." Lisa adopted a sheepish tone. "You're a known criminal, and you're involved with the people who kidnapped me."

"No time to debate your flawed assumptions." J.P. raised a finger. "Had I known they wrapped you up in that rug, I would have stayed out of it. Apparently, I know less than you."

"You can't know less. I know nothing." Jensen was adamant about her innocence. "I do not understand why they kidnapped me or what they want."

"I think we should make ourselves scarce before their reinforcements arrive."

"There are more of these freaks? I don't buy it, you just waltzed in here, not with your past." Her demeanor changed. Her body shuddered less, and she started regaining control. Her eyes examined the floor. "This involves you, somehow."

"I would love to compare notes, maybe put together a nice collage." J.P. sighed. "Let's get out of here while we can."

"Why? They're your cronies," she accused him. "They wouldn't hurt you."

"Right." His voice dripped sarcasm. "That is why the fat guy wanted to kill both of us. I set off a million alarms getting in here to save your ungrateful ass."

Lisa stared at J.P., challenging him. She could put to shame any dog with a bone.

"This is unproductive." J.P. shrugged. "You stay. Blame everything on me. You are an expert at that. I will check around, and then I am leaving. Please stay out of my way." He propped the door open with a chair. "See you around, lady. It has been a real displeasure seeing you again. Let's avoid that in the future."

"Stop calling me 'lady.' My name is Amelia Elizabeth Jensen, or Lisa Jensen for short. Actually, to you, it's *Ms. Jensen*. You can't leave. Your friends kidnapped an Assistant DA."

"Oh boy," snorted J.P. "Earth to Ms. Jensen. Give it a rest, will you?"

"Why were you at Anna's home? How much do you know?" The lawyer in Lisa hoped to contain the situation. Morgan was a very dangerous loose end for her and Phil.

"I was out of the country. I could not risk of checking my voice mail. Anna left this message on Tuesday afternoon."

He activated the speaker on his phone. Anna's voice filled the room, vibrating with enthusiasm. "J.P., I got it. Undeniable proof, the Holy Grail of evidence. Oh. My. God. You'll never believe it, even if you see it with your own eyes. Drop whatever or whoever," she giggled like a schoolchild, "you're doing and come see me. Right now. It will be worth it, I promise."

Anna's voice sounded coy. She always turned everything into a joke, a riddle, or a puzzle. She claimed it kept her mind sharp and entertained. It had gotten her in trouble more times than anyone could count in Court, but all judges still liked her.

J.P. paused the message, and Lisa's gaze fell to the floor.

He resumed playing the voice mail message. "Bring a case of champagne. We'll drink every drop. I promise. Thank God for sunny days. See you soon, babe. Run, don't walk."

Lisa kept her gaze glued to her bare feet for a while and then looked away. Liquid crystals enriched her eyes again. J.P. perceived contrition and wondered what she was hiding.

CHAPTER 14

J.P. SEARCHED THE UNCONSCIOUS men. An LAPD badge identified *Rail* as Officer James Smythe. *Fireplug's* brand new, shiny CDoHP badge decreed him Special Agent Jon Sadowsky. "I thought I knew all the cop shops. What the hell is CDoHP?" he inquired, and Lisa shrugged. He scanned the card. "California Department of Homeland Protection."

J.P. retrieved a large pen out of his pocket and set it in a penholder on a desk. "Do you know what Anna found? I do not believe she killed herself."

"I have no idea. How would I know what she found? She called you." Lisa let it all out in a rapid-fire sequence. Her strained voice and increasing delivery pitch snatched J.P.'s attention. He did not have the time to explore whatever she was concealing. He knew Lisa was skilled at compartmentalizing and burying information.

"I am leaving," said J.P.

"We wait right here, together." She poked him in the chest. Lisa explored the room. She lunged under the conference table and retrieved Smythe's automatic and magazine. She slammed the clip and yanked the slide. The sound of the round entering the chamber rivaled a small detonation. She aimed at J.P., struggling to cover the mild shaking of her hands. "Throw down your gun and put your hands up. You're under arrest."

Morgan sported the look of a parent spotting a child break a vase. He pulled Wallace's Berretta out of his belt in slow motion. "Correct me if I am wrong, *lady*. I just saved your sorry ass." J.P. pointed his gun at Smythe and Sadowsky, then stowed it at the small of his back.

He stepped closer to her and adopted a defiant stance. "Your move. Do you?"

"Do I... what?" Lisa asked, baffled.

"Hate me enough to shoot me? You want to make up for failing to convict me?" He lifted his hands to the sides at shoulder height, palms forward, mimicking Christ the Redeemer.

"Drop your gun and lock your fingers behind your head." Lisa's face flushed. Her hands shook harder from overexertion and adrenaline rush.

"OK, you win." J.P. reached behind his back and pulled Wallace's Beretta out with two fingers. He threw it on the floor and stepped closer to her. He retrieved Sadowsky's automatic and held it with two fingers at arm's length between them. "Pay attention next time. I had two guns on me. A mistake like this could cost you your life."

He dangled the weapon, making sure her eyes followed it. With a flick of his wrist, he tossed it at her feet. The pistol hit her left ankle and bounced onto her right foot. She winced and looked down, startled by the pain. J.P. twisted Smythe's firearm out of her hands. He set the safety to ON and handed her back the gun — butt first. She took it with an automatic gesture.

J.P. turned his back on her and retrieved the badge wallets confiscated from the four unconscious men. He lined them up and took several pictures. "There will be plenty of issues to explain when their friends show up. I plan to forget this happened," J.P. said.

Lisa walked over to Sadowsky. She spat on him, kicked him in the ribs twice, and hopped around on one foot, holding her toes. "Damn it, that hurts. I should wear pointy steel-toed boots." She delivered a powerful soccer-style strike to Sadowsky's balls.

J.P. cringed and shuddered, imagining Sadowsky's pain when he did wake up.

Lisa sat on the bed and lowered her head in her hands. "What do you propose we do?"

Noticing that Lisa's body trembled again, J.P. took the gun out of her hands and set it down on the bed. "I know you want answers. God knows, so do I. We must get out of here. The adrenaline rush is wearing off, and your body needs to rest. If you do not allow your body to recover, it will not be pretty."

"Stop handling me," Lisa snapped.

"I do not plan to spend another eighteen months in lockup for this. Cops stick together." J.P. tossed his hands up in surrender and then picked Wallace's and Sadowsky's automatic weapons, and a set of keys from the pile on the floor. "I am sure these are your keys. Your car is downstairs. It was the most disagreeable experience running into you. I hope to never see you again in this lifetime."

CHAPTER 15

STANDING ON THE CATWALK, J.P. inventoried the warehouse. He turned on all the lights and spent several minutes taking pictures. A massive device caught his attention. It resembled a cross between a cement truck mixer and a gigantic plastic clothes dryer.

Lisa joined him as he marched back to the improvised security office. "What's all this?" Jensen asked, pointing at the equipment in the warehouse.

"No idea."

"You're familiar with military gear."

"Let's not rehash the past." J.P. said.

He sauntered to the first Humvee, snapped pictures, and attempted to open the metallic box painted dull military-style green with Cyrillic external markings. He turned toward the security office and bumped into Lisa, who attempted to cut him off. The collision knocked her off her feet, and he caught her just before she hit the ground. "Get into your car and leave now," he said, helping her back on her feet.

J.P. left Lisa standing, reentered the security office, and shook Bonds awake.

"Where are the keys to the boxes in the Humvees?"

"The boss keeps them with him," Bonds replied, still groggy.

"Where would I get a hold of this boss?" asked J.P. "Sounds like a fun guy to meet, you know, for a beer, maybe an afternoon lynching and stuff."

"Go fuck yourself," Bonds retorted. "Mr. Clancy will hang you by the balls. You cannot even understand who you're messing with, asshole."

"Have it your way." J.P. coldcocked Bonds.

In for a penny, in for a pound. Who am I kidding? This smells like several million pounds, judging by this warehouse alone.

"Why are you taking pictures?" Lisa waved Smythe's gun.

"Insurance." J.P. trudged away from her.

"That sounds suspiciously like intent to blackmail."

"I am only responsible for what I say, not for what you hear," J.P. shot back.

He resumed inspecting the crate in the Humvee. Using a small pick, he opened the locks and peered inside. The box, lined with thick bluish gray metal sheets, held a single dull, faded green trunk with a worn out red star on its lid. A vanishing symbol for nuclear radiation was still visible. He rested his forehead on the edge of the open lid and sighed.

He had experienced plenty of days full of surprises in his life. Tonight, without a doubt, took the cake and all the ribbons. His pulse sped up, and a rush of heat brought color to his cheeks. He opened the lid of the oversized suitcase and photographed its content. He examined the two nearest Humvees, finding and photographing the two identical trunks in lined crates.

The remaining Humvees held BioHazard suits, weapons, and ammunition. The trucks held boxes marked with various stamps and warnings; Skull and Crossbones, Biohazard, Toxic. J.P. inventoried and photographed everything.

The last of the trucks held four pallets, covered with brand-new camo tarps. The load on pallets comprised money, $20 and $100 bills shrink-wrapped in cubes about one foot on each side, then stacked four by five and six high. He uncovered all the pallets and took several pictures, making sure he got all four pallets in each frame. He took multiple close-ups of each one of them.

J.P. retrieved a stack of twenties and one of hundreds from the nearest pallets. He photographed the money and then removed several bills from each stack and pocketed them. He estimated the total to be over $300 million, maybe more than $400 million.

That is a lot of money, except it is useless.

"Are you robbing the place now?" Every one of Lisa's words dripped vitriol. "I couldn't help but notice your excessive familiarity with picking locks. For a criminal of your caliber, petty theft is quite a few steps down, don't you think?"

J.P. removed a bill from each of the stacks on the floor and offered them to Lisa with an exaggerated bow. She flipped them over twice, shrugged, and handed them back.

"You want me to be your accomplice? Nice try."

"You might need gas money for the trip home," he replied. He snagged the bills, held them up to the light, flicked them, and passed them back. "Fakes. Finest quality. They probably used actual US currency paper and plates, but the embedded strip is wrong. Blank. They would most likely pass a cursory pen inspection at the local corner store or gas station."

He left her squinting at the fake currency, extracted two more notes and then placed the stacks of money back on the pallets. He covered them up with shrink-wrap, smoothed the plastic over the corners, and then tied the tarps back in place.

Lisa watched him in silence. Not sure of what to do with the counterfeit bills, she stuffed them in her bra. "Do you know how much money that is? What's in those boxes in the Humvees? What's all that stuff in the other trucks?" Lisa fired question after question.

J.P. sported a preoccupied expression, ignoring Lisa's incensed queries.

"You do not get it, do you?" he asked. "This is a private mercenary group, most or maybe all of them, active law enforcement. This stash is off the books. They will not hesitate to eliminate anyone who learns about it. I could not care less about immunity or whatever else you think will protect us. If we survive the night, that is."

"Oh, quit being so melodramatic," Lisa shouted. "This is America, not some banana republic."

J.P. walked away. "Before Trump, I would have agreed with you."

CHAPTER 16

J.P. RETRIEVED WALLACE'S BERETTA and shot every server three times, making sure he destroyed all hard drives. Lisa jumped with every round, covering her ears. She caught herself admiring his thoroughness and calm demeanor.

Satisfied with the damage inflicted, J.P. turned to Lisa. "I am not involved in this. I wish I never knew about it. I suggest you forget everything you saw tonight."

"We wait for the authorities. If it does not involve you, you talk with them and get to go home or wherever it is you live nowadays—cave, sewer."

"My, oh my. Hasty trip back to your vicious old self. Wait a second. I believe there is a rule preventing prosecutors from asking the accused questions outside the presence of defense counsel. I heard it could lead to disbarment." J.P. sauntered away without waiting for her to answer.

"Yes, there is. It only applies when formal charges have been filed, or when the suspect is in custody, or subject to interrogation. Why?"

"I was hoping we did not have to talk anymore."

"Hilarious, Morgan." Lisa blocked his path to the stairs. "Anna was my friend, too. I always admired her judgment, unless she defended a jerk like you."

"I cannot offer a valid argument, Counselor," J.P. said. "It was a losing proposition from the get-go, yet somehow, she pulled a miracle the size of Mount Everest."

"You got that right. Without her magic, you would no longer be with us." Lisa let it all out in a hissed whisper. "Not that I or anyone else would ever miss you, freaking *Butcher*."

"Thank you for your sincerity. It is such a rare trait these days," J.P. taunted her.

They climbed the stairs back to the multi-purpose room. Sadowsky's phone chirped. Lisa jumped, startled by it. She fished the device out of the pile on the floor and answered it.

J.P. snatched the phone out of her hand and ended the call. "You have a death wish?"

The phone rang again. Lisa grabbed it from J.P.'s hand, stomped over to the nearest chair, and answered while flipping J.P. the bird. "Hello?" Her voice was steady. She held the phone away from her ear, her exquisite face showing signs of deepening crow's feet.

"Who are you? Why did you hang up?" The caller was loud and annoyed.

"This is Orange County ADA, Lisa Jensen. Who is this?"

"Ms. Jensen, what is your location?" An unfamiliar voice asked with authority.

Lisa sat up straight as J.P. signaled her to hang up. "I am in a warehouse, location unknown. The owner of this phone and his partner kidnapped me and brought me here against my will." She switched tactics midstream. "Who am I speaking with?"

"What is the status of the men who... brought you there, Ms. Jensen?" The man's voice was hard as forged steel.

"They are... incapacitated. I was about to call the police. I intend to press charges and pursue this matter to the fullest extent of the law. These two animals are not fit to be law enforcement. They belong in the darkest prison."

"Incapacitated?" The voice asked. "How did that happen?"

J.P. seized the phone, ended the call, and hurled it on the bed. "Are you out of your mind? Whoever it was, he called the man who wanted to rape you." He grabbed her left wrist and dragged her toward the door. "We are leaving. In the morning, go to your boss, and tell him the story. Hell, wake his ass up tonight. I do not care. Just leave me out of it for now."

Lisa shook free of J.P.'s grasp. "I'm not going anywhere. I'll wait here for the police. I'll have these animals arrested and prosecuted. If you have nothing to hide, stay with me." Lisa dialed 911 on the desk phone. She identified herself and requested to speak to the police.

Sadowsky's phone chirped again. Lisa darted to the bed and answered it. "Hello." She returned to the desk and lifted the receiver, holding one phone at each ear.

"We located your signal," the 911 operator informed her. "A patrol car will be there in a few minutes. Will you be safe until the officers arrive?"

"I think so," replied Lisa. She replaced the desk phone receiver back in its cradle and returned to Sadowsky's phone. "OK, who are you?"

"Is there anyone else with you? How did you incapacitate them?" The man on the mobile phone continued his inquiry as if nothing had happened.

"I kicked them in the balls," Lisa hissed. "Very hard."

J.P. seized the phone, ended the call, and pitched it against the wall. "You are suicidal. What possessed you to answer?"

"The police are coming." Lisa's eyes sparkled with rage.

"Who will they side with when they find their own guys tied up?" J.P. quizzed. "Best way to sort this out is from afar. Australia far. Let's go. We go to the police on our own terms."

"I can't let you go." Lisa lifted the gun and pointed it at J.P.'s wide chest.

"You want to stop me, shoot me. If you fire at me, shoot to kill. Otherwise, I will return fire, and I do not take prisoners. Force of habit."

"We need to talk. There are things you don't know about Anna's death." Lisa said.

J.P. stopped in the doorway, studying her through narrowed eyes. He wanted to ask her about so many things, but this was not the time nor the place. "I appreciate your newfound concern for the truth and my well-being. Given our history, I am sure you do not mind if I skip your funeral or do not send flowers. OK, maybe I will attend your funeral, that is — to make sure it is for real." He nodded a mock salute and left.

As he crossed the doorframe, a bullet tore into it. He winced and kept walking. She had in it her to fire—at the woodwork, not at him.

J.P. descended the stairs three at a time and pushed the button marked Roll-up Gate. The giant door vibrated and ascended at a turtle's pace, screeching in protest. Outside, he heard the familiar whining of approaching police sirens. The flashing lights reflected in the windows of the surrounding buildings announced the cruisers were only seconds away.

CHAPTER 17

J.P. CROSSED THE RAILROAD tracks and turned into a Park-and-Ride less than a hundred yards from the warehouse. He cut the engine, climbed in the back, and activated more recording equipment and monitors. On the screen, he observed Lisa gesticulating at two uniformed cops, a man, and a woman. Both police officers had their guns trained on her.

He wanted to see if Ms. ADA could talk her way out of this mess. In his opinion, she was way out of her depth. He verified that the system recorded and uploaded to his website. The miniature camera pen he had planted on the desk captured most of the room, Lisa, and the unconscious Smythe and Sadowsky. The uniformed cops exhibited anger. They insisted she needed to surrender her weapon. Lisa gave up the gun, and the police handcuffed her.

J.P. donned a wireless headset, covering only one ear. He fiddled with the controls to improve the sound quality and then retrieved a water bottle from the mini-fridge. J.P. thanked God the real cops had shown up first. He muttered, "Let's see what breed of fuzzy critters live in your hat, Ms. Jensen. This allows me to appraise the situation properly."

Clancy walked in, dressed in the same expensive tailored suit he wore at the press conference. Four burly men followed him. Their outfits were of lower quality. The bulges at their sides and underarms suggested multiple weapons. They had the stiff body, upright posture and demeanor characteristic of bodyguards and people trained in lethal hand-to-hand combat.

"This show should prove informative and entertaining," J.P. quipped at the monitor.

Clancy shoved his badge in the local cops' faces. The policewoman gestured toward Lisa, but Clancy cut her off and ordered them both out of the room.

"Are you Ms. Jensen?" Clancy pivoted toward Lisa. "My associate who spoke with you earlier said you incapacitated our men. Hold on a moment." Clancy raised his hand. "A few details first. Afterward, we'll have some time to ourselves."

Clancy spun to his entourage and issued orders in a low voice. One man turned on his heels and marched out of the picture. "Secure the premises," Clancy addressed the remaining men. "Thank local law enforcement for their help and dismiss them. They must not file a report about responding to her call, this place, or our presence here. Clear?"

"Yes, sir." The lingering three bodyguards nodded in unison.

"Review the security tapes. Assess the situation. See if she was alone."

The three men disappeared as if ghosts chased after them.

Lisa stood. "I'm the victim here. I resent being treated like a criminal."

"We haven't determined that. Stay put. I have some questions for you."

"You can't detain me." Lisa's face reddened. "I demand you identify yourself. They kidnapped me, almost raped, and killed by these scumbags. What else do you need to know?"

Clancy pushed her down on the bed. "Cooperate, and everything will go much faster." He returned with a roll of duct tape. He reached down and removed her shoes.

"You wouldn't dare!" she cried.

"Yes, I would." Clancy tore a piece of tape and stepped over Lisa's legs, locking them between his knees. With great pleasure, he applied several layers of tape over her mouth and around her wrists. All the while, she struggled in vain. Clancy stepped back, admiring his handiwork, and rubbed his palms together. "Now sit there quietly while I piece this together, or I will knock you out. You turned out to be a rather hefty inconvenience, and I don't have time for this."

CHAPTER 18

J.P. CONSIDERED THAT LISA bit off more than she could chew. He might need to help her. Professionally, he hated her guts, yet he could not allow her to get hurt. He watched the scene, trying to wrap his head around Clancy's order that the local cops file no report.

From the corner of his eye, J.P. noticed the local police cruisers drive away. *Now it is only Reedy Guy and his cronies. He chased away the locals, and they did not put up a fight.*

J.P. devoted his full attention to the screen, watching Lisa scream and kick. Then he saw Purcell enter the room and report to Clancy, "Premises secure. Duty officers are conscious. No signs of a break-in. All servers shot to hell. No surveillance footage. Simpson says it's beyond anyone's ability to retrieve it. The online backup was not active yet."

"Smart rats, these perps of yours," Clancy interrupted him.

"Yes, sir. They covered their tracks very well. Nobody else is on the premises. At first inspection, nothing appears to be missing."

"We don't know who broke in, how they did it, or what they learned. Am I right?" Clancy demanded. "How did they even know about this place?"

"We interview the men downstairs and these two... idiots," Purcell gestured toward Smythe and Sadowsky, "and we'll find out, sir. Until then, it would all be sheer speculation."

"Wake up this slob." Clancy pointed to Sadowsky. "I want to question him first."

Purcell lumbered over to Sadowsky and reached for the handcuffs.

"I didn't give you permission to remove his cuffs," Clancy barked.

Puzzled, Purcell nodded and then slapped Sadowsky.

Sadowsky's eyes popped open and focused on Purcell. He struggled to stand, but his handcuffed hands prevented it. He settled on the bed, leaning forward, reaching for his crotch.

"Take these off me," Sadowsky grunted, tightening his thighs around his genitals.

Clancy stepped into Sadowsky's view. "How the hell did you let this happen? Start at the beginning and leave nothing out. I'm interested who knows about this place, unless the four of you, geniuses, tripped over one another and handcuffed yourselves."

Sadowsky began, "Jamie and I went to monitor that lawyer's house, Anna Richter, see who showed up, if they suspected anything about her death."

"Why were you at her place if she's dead?" Clancy asked. "I am not aware of this. Who was, this Anna Richter? How is any of this relevant to our operation?"

"Because of the item..." Sadowsky searched for words, stealing a look at Lisa.

"Don't concern yourself with her." Clancy motioned at him to continue.

J.P. perked up. Either she was in with them or Clancy had already decided she would not survive the night. His money was on the second possibility. He felt a pang of guilt for allowing her to stay behind. Whatever she did, she did not deserve to die like this. Nobody did.

"Can you take the cuffs off me, so I can sit up right?" Sadowsky inquired.

Purcell looked at Clancy, who made a dismissive hand gesture.

Sadowsky stretched and then sat next to Lisa, rubbing his wrists. "Motherfucker, I swear I will kill him this time."

"Who?" Clancy queried.

"Morgan. John Paul Morgan. A real piece of shit from the past," grimaced Sadowsky.

Lisa retreated from Sadowsky in disgust. She scrubbed her face on the wall, removing the duct tape from her mouth. "I demand you place this filthy pig under arrest," she yelled.

Clancy faced Purcell. "Make sure she does not interrupt again."

Purcell placed Lisa face down on the bed and wrapped tape over her mouth until the roll ran out. Then he used the handcuffs he had taken off Sadowsky to bind Lisa's ankles. "Stay put, and you may survive the night," Purcell whispered in her ear.

"Now, where were we?" Clancy returned his attention to Sadowsky. "Oh, yeah, we were talking about Richter's house and Morgan. Please continue."

"Richter was a two-bit lawyer." Sadowsky resumed. "We learned she received the item twenty-four hours before we eliminated her. We had to know if she shared the information."

Lisa wriggled in protest upon hearing the unfair characterization of her friend.

Clancy pointed at her with one finger, his gaze locked on Sadowsky. "What info?"

"She waltzed in like she owned the place," Sadowsky sidetracked. "We identified ourselves and attempted to interview her. She was most unhelpful and belligerent, as you can see. We had to knock her out and bring her here. It is imperative we find out what she knows."

"What's this 'item,' and why is that information so important that you found it necessary to kidnap an Assistant DA and get this Morgan character involved?" Clancy asked, shifting his gaze to Lisa. "I'm not aware of anything that warrants that."

Lisa grew restless, attempting to remove the tape from her mouth again.

"We didn't know about this bastard's involvement until he walked through that door." Sadowsky pointed behind Clancy. "We thought he was dead, or he ran away years ago. I think you need clearance for that part, sir. With all due respect, of course, sir." Sadowsky shuddered, attempting to get rid of the sweat beads trickling from his brows into his eyes.

"Who should clear me for this?" Clancy paced around the room in random patterns with his hands clasped behind his back.

"The Big Man. It's his deal, sir." Sadowsky whispered.

"The Big Man," parroted Clancy. "Should I call him right now and share the details of our current situation before I ask him for clearance?" Clancy produced a mobile phone.

"We can clear it with him later." Sadowsky backpedaled.

CHAPTER 19

"**Y**EARS AGO, LONG BEFORE** this op, there was a botched operation. They hired us to scare Hunter. He was the OC DA. Our client needed him to drop the charges against the client's son. The Big Man lost it, and then the whole thing turned into a royal fuck-up."

J.P. choked on the gulp of water, dropped the bottle, stood up and hit his head on the roof. His intuition screamed that he had just learned why they had killed Anna. She found out who had murdered his family and got evidence that exonerated him.

J.P.'s mind raced at the speed of light, connecting the dots from Anna's death back to George Hunter and the brutal homicides of J.P.'s pregnant wife and their nephew. Realization lit up his face.

Could this be it? Could I be that lucky? Oh, Anna, why did you not wait for me?

"The client demanded we videotape the op," Sadowsky continued. "Then everything went to hell. Later, the tape disappeared. Until Tuesday, when the Richter woman got hold of it. The Big Man instructed us to take any steps necessary to keep it a secret."

Lisa arched her body, eyeing Sadowsky with pure hatred and terror.

"What is on this tape?" asked Clancy.

"You must ask The Big Man, sir. I already said too much. You know how he is." Sadowsky's neck veins pulsated faster. "Also, with Morgan, sir... it's personal for him."

"You bet I will ask him," shot Clancy, fuming. He did not press further.

J.P. concluded they would kill Lisa. It defied his moral code to let her die, regardless of what she had done to him in the past. Yet, the odds of a one-man rescue operation were zero.

He decided it was time to call the cavalry and let them sort it out. He retrieved one of the untraceable mobile phones he kept in the SUV and dialed 911 but did not push TALK. A statement rattled around in his mind. J.P. focused on what stopped him from calling the police.

Sadowsky said they still needed to interrogate her. I have some time.

Clancy whistled, pondering the facts revealed by Sadowsky. "How does Morgan fit in? Is he trying to save the little Miss ADA in distress?"

"I doubt that," Sadowsky snickered. "Morgan got charged with those murders, and she was the second chair prosecutor. How did he get involved? Richter called someone about the tape, but I never dreamed it would be this asshole. The number was untraceable."

"That should have been your first clue trouble was coming." Clancy whipped around, putting his face so close to Sadowsky that he could smell the flavor of the gum in Clancy's mouth. "How can you be so stupid? When we are this close to our ultimate objective?"

"When he barged in here, he did not know who I was," Sadowsky continued. "After the Richter woman got him off on the murder charges, he fell clean off the face of the Earth."

Clancy wigwagged with both hands Italian style, summoning Sadowsky to speed it up.

"We first tried to take him out back then. The Big Man labeled him a threat, though Morgan didn't know a thing. We intercepted him the night his wife died. We drugged him and pushed his car off the road. Somehow, the fucker survived. After the trial, we couldn't find him. The matter became less pressing until we forgot all about it. My guess is that he was watching Richter's place tonight. Or maybe he followed her." Sadowsky gestured toward Lisa.

"Why would he watch Richter's home?" Clancy asked.

"Only a guess. He tailed from somewhere. For the life of me, I can't figure out how he got past the duty officers. When Morgan barged in, armed, we didn't stand a chance."

"Maybe you should have asked him." Clancy screamed. "Nice try to change the subject and shift the blame onto Wallace and Bonds. I'll deal with them. The bigger problem we face is that your stupidity and incompetence compromised our operational security. A dangerous, resourceful individual penetrated our lines. He now knows about us."

"He's just one guy, for God's sake." Sadowsky jumped to his feet. "He's a giant fuck-up, a has-been Navy desk jockey. Some analyst. He got lucky tonight. That's all."

"I beg to differ." Clancy cut him off, poking him in the chest.

Sadowsky lost his balance and fell backward on the bed.

"He tailed you here unnoticed." Clancy cut off Sadowsky's protests with a horizontal hand chop. "He infiltrated our home, neutralized four trained and armed officers, supposed to be the *crème de la crème*, and made his exit clean. If he hadn't tied you morons like hogs, we might not know he was here. I'd say that shows he's exceptionally skilled. Lethal even."

Clancy pivoted to Purcell. "Get Simpson up here to report directly to me. Expand the security perimeter and find Morgan now." He stepped away from his men. "On second thought, bring everybody up here on the double. We need to deal with this disruption first."

He turned back to Sadowsky. "We have a significant security breach. This is not the time to make mistakes. You should have briefed me about that fiasco long ago."

Sadowsky objected again, and Clancy signaled him not to interrupt.

"I'll let the Big Man know what I think of the way he does things and the quality of people he lent us for this mission. You are a complete disgrace. This warehouse and this operation must remain a secret even after the *True Patriot Day*. No one can know about it. The public could never understand what it takes to assume this kind of leadership and make history happen. You almost screwed everything up tonight."

CHAPTER 20

CLANCY PACED LIKE A caged animal, treading each step. With his face locked in a grimace, he eyed Smythe. "Wake up this other slob," he ordered Sadowsky.

Sadowsky shook Smythe's shoulders until his eyes opened. He unlocked and yanked the handcuffs off his partner's wrists and then jerked him to his feet.

J.P. counted nine men as they filed in. He could feel anxiety in the room rising with each of Sadowsky's colleagues. They all stood with squared shoulders, hands clasped behind their backs, and their gazes riveted on Clancy. Wallace and Bonds stood aside by themselves, examining their boots with undue interest.

Clancy stopped in front of each man and then stepped back, facing his troops. "I don't have to paint you a picture of what's going on. These two idiots," he pointed to Smythe and Sadowsky, "allowed John Paul Morgan, an unknown quantity, to follow them here. Morgan penetrated our defenses, disarmed, and incapacitated the two dim-witted guards on duty. To say that he compromised our operational security, and this thing could blow up in our faces, is the understatement of the century. Can anyone explain to me why you became so blasé? So careless? Do you understand what's at stake here?"

Clancy resumed walking in front of the men who remained at attention, still as statues. "Do you comprehend the importance of this operation? Do you know what will happen if we fail?" Clancy bellowed, stomping his feet. "This Morgan now represents a clear and present danger to our mission and our goals. Go get him!"

"Yes, sir," the men answered in unison.

Curiosity started mounting in J.P.'s mind. *Dictators were all short people—Napoleon, Hitler, Stalin, to name just a few. What is up with this pompous jerk? He walks and talks as if he were the second coming of Jesus Christ himself and the last best hope for humankind.*

If J.P. would help Lisa, this would be the time. Everyone was in the upstairs briefing room. He got in the front seat, started the engine, and drove out of the Park-and-Ride. He reached for the untraceable phone again. He started planning to keep everyone busy in the room upstairs until the local police arrived and then turn the show over to them.

Clancy approached Sadowsky, almost touching noses. "As the senior officer, it was your responsibility to ensure operational security. Your carelessness compromised our sanctuary. This campaign is in jeopardy because of your lack of discipline and commitment."

Sadowsky raised his hands in protest.

"You exposed our mission to this Morgan character. Our plans must remain secret. This operation has extraordinary importance for our country. Your stupidity compromised it."

Clancy pivoted and roared, "Gentlemen, do not kid yourselves! We are at war. We fight for the survival of this great country! This failure mandates only one penalty—death!"

J.P. skidded the SUV to a stop. His eyes darted back to the recording equipment. *Could this prick be for real? Death? As in battlefield-style summary execution? Where did he think he was? Nah, he could not be serious. He was trying to scare the Bejesus out of his men. However, if he would execute one of his men, they would sacrifice the local cops on sight.*

"Get me a weapon," Clancy ordered Purcell.

Purcell handed his sidearm to Clancy, butt first.

"Not yours, moron. One of theirs." He pointed to Sadowsky and Smythe.

Purcell tendered Smythe's gun.

Clancy took it as if white-hot, pulled the slide, and confronted Sadowsky.

Sadowsky backed away until his spine pressed against the beds. "Wait," he begged. "We couldn't know that prig followed us." He glanced at Smythe for support.

Smythe opened his mouth, yet no sounds came out. Behind them, Lisa's face mirrored Smythe's terror. The air in the room became too thick for anyone to breathe.

Clancy aimed at Sadowsky's forehead. Sadowsky attempted another step back, but the bunk beds pinned his shoulders. "Wait. Wait." He raised his shaky hands and whimpered. "I can find and eliminate Morgan. Then everything will be OK. He's the only breach. Please."

Clancy relaxed his arm. The barrel pointed a few degrees up, away from Sadowsky's dripping forehead. Clancy straightened out the gun, and his expression hardened. "What about her?" On the verge of exploding, Clancy pointed the gun at Lisa.

"We take care of her after we find out what she knows. Chances are she'd be dead in a few days, anyway. What does it matter now?" Sadowsky's voice gained volume.

"That's not the point. You failed miserably. You endangered our lives, our plans, and years of hard work." Clancy seemed to reconsider and lowered the gun. "Unfortunately, you are a senior leader, with great responsibilities. Also, you're not one of my men. You're one of *his*." Clancy's lower lip quivered with. "It seems I cannot adequately punish you just yet."

Sadowsky breathed out and wiped thick perspiration off his forehead. His legs buckled, and he lowered himself on the bed next to Lisa, who had twisted herself into a good approximation of a pretzel. Lisa pushed away from him until bedrails hurt her shoulders.

"There is another party, equally responsible for this, who is not a senior person in the operation, and one of mine," Clancy declared in an ominous tone. He turned, faced Smythe, raised the gun, and shot him between the eyes.

CHAPTER 21

THE BACK OF SMYTHE'S head burst in a shower of blood, brains, and bone shards that landed on the beds, covering Lisa and Sadowsky. Smythe's body came to rest on Lisa's legs, sending her into a squirming frenzy. She stared at Clancy with sheer terror.

"Sorry, Jamie." Clancy lowered the gun. "You should have paid better attention in class." He faced the rest of the men and raised his voice. "Let this be a lesson for all of you. Our mission is too important. No more failures. Clear?"

He waited for the "yes, sir," chorus with a frozen frown and then resumed, "Do you have second thoughts about what we have set out to accomplish? What will happen to our country if we fail? Do you think those Washington politicos will solve any problems? They are too busy blaming one another while this great country is speeding toward hell."

"No, sir," the men responded as one. The quick turn of events had stunned them, but like all obedient soldiers, they had no intentions to challenge Clancy's actions or authority.

Sadowsky sat in shock, staring at his red hands. Smythe's blood and brains continued to dribble down his forehead, streaking down his face, dripping onto his upturned palms.

"If you fail me again, *I will* replace you." Clancy bellowed.

Sadowsky nodded. His body vibrated with a fear he had never learned, even in combat.

"Make sure they find Morgan's prints." Clancy handed Purcell the gun. "Put out an APB. Armed and extremely dangerous. Cop killer. Shoot on sight. Take Jamie and Ms. Jensen to that lawyer's place and torch it."

"Yes, sir." Purcell's trained-soldier discipline took over.

"Make it look like Ms. Jensen helped Morgan kill Jamie and cover up his murder. In case Richter made copies, torch the house then her office." He paced, turning on his heel with the precision of a Swiss clock to face his troops. "Find this Morgan jackass now. I want him tonight. Dead or alive, I don't care. This breach ends here and now. Dismissed."

The men scrambled in utter silence to execute his orders.

Lisa curled up, stifling her sobs. This was it. This was how she would go out. All dreams of making a difference would die here, and she did not understand why.

Lisa had pushed Smythe's corpse off the bed and stopped wriggling. Curled into a ball, she no longer shivered. She had guts. She stared up at Clancy, this time with a serene face. She had made her peace with it. She had no way of knowing, nor did she ever imagine that J.P. still had something to say about the whole thing.

J.P. reckoned it was time to put some distance between himself and Clancy's goons and loony toons. Jesus, Clancy executed a man for a minor transgression. J.P. saw no reason to make it easy for the lunatics to find him. He needed to capture and interrogate one of them.

Half serious, J.P. considered he might need to find a quiet corner of the Australian desert. First, he must find this Big Man and thank him in person. Sadowsky admitted they had set J.P. up for murder and tried to kill him. It was time J.P. had a talk with him and learned about the fiasco that had cost him his family, his friends, ten years of his life—and now Anna.

"I deeply regret this, Ms. Jensen." Clancy stopped pacing and looked at Lisa with the concentration of a predator contemplating dinner. "If there's any consolation, your death will not be in vain. You'll be a martyr, and your demise will contribute to the birth of a new nation."

That was no consolation to her, Lisa's eyes conveyed.

Purcell, Sadowsky, and Allen—a tall, slim young redheaded man— walked back in.

"Clean up this mess," Clancy repeated his orders. "Then take Ms. Jensen and Jamie's body to Richter's house. Make sure there's nothing left to identify or collect as evidence."

Clancy sat at the desk behind the camera pen. "Change of plans. The gun and the bullet go with them to the scene. Label Morgan mentally unstable. I don't want anybody trying to take him alive and talk to him." Clancy resumed staring at Lisa, whose eyes shot daggers back.

"Sir, we should interrogate her," Sadowsky said. "She may know where Morgan is."

Clancy tapped his fingers on the desk, absentminded. "No need. If she prosecuted Morgan back then, slim chance he told her anything. With her and Richter dead, you need only concern yourself with Morgan, unless you don't think you can find him, Mr. Sadowsky. We are only providing you the entire law enforcement community as backup."

"He's so dead." Sadowsky spat his words out. "That asshole got the drop on me—on us, I mean. It'll not happen again. His ass is mine. I intend to kick it out of this world."

"Save it for someone who cares. That attitude would have served you better before Morgan got the drop on you. If Richter spoke to anyone else about what she learned, you would know about it by now. It doesn't sound like anyone would sit on this stuff, unless they're neck-deep in it." Clancy looked away, shaking his head in disgust.

Sadowsky and Allen scooped up brain matter from the wall and the bed. They wrapped the remains with Smythe's body. Sadowsky strode to a cabinet and retrieved a large syringe. He seized Lisa by the back of her neck and forced her face down on the bed.

"Just in case," he gloated. Letting out a moan of pure sexual pleasure, he plunged the needle above Lisa's hairline. The duct tape muffled Lisa's yelp. Her body became limp like a rag doll and her eyes rolled up in her head.

Sadowsky dragged her inert body to the floor and wrapped it in a camouflage tarp.

CHAPTER 22

ALLEN AND SADOWSKY BROUGHT their cars to an abrupt stop in front of Anna's home. They carried Smythe's rug-wrapped body and dumped it in the living room. Then they repeated the procedure with the still-unconscious Lisa.

"Park the cars away from here. I'll get started." Sadowsky took charge.

Allen retrieved two canisters and a box from the trunk of the cruiser and concealed them in the shadow, inside the low fence. He moved the Honda and the Charger down the street and then walked back with long strides, eager to put the mess behind him. He resented having his evening plans ruined and daydreamed about the hot date he had planned with the glorious young blonde, Stacie, "with *ie, not a y*." But work had to intrude. There would be many girls, especially after *True Patriot Day*. His mind filled with fantasies about the women he would woo in just a few short days with his new position and authority.

Allen picked up the canisters, placed the box under his arm, and pushed open the front door. He froze, unable to make sense of the tableau in front of him. Smythe's dead body lay on top of the blue rug. Sadowsky, handcuffed, mouth and ankles covered in duct tape, looked up at him in terror from the floor. Between them lay Lisa, unconscious, rolled-up in the tarp.

Allen dropped the incendiary materials, reaching for his sidearm. The unmistakable shape of a gun barrel touched the back of his head. "I had a terrible day," J.P. said in a baritone, almost melodic voice. "You know the drill."

Allen complied, staring into Sadowsky's fearful eyes. "Mother-fucking idiot. He got the drop on you twice in one night. You are a disgrace. I wish it was you who died, not Jamie. You think you are so much better than we are? I hope you rot in hell. I'll volunteer to shoot you for this." Allen stepped forward and kicked Sadowsky in the chest, and the sickening sounds of cracking ribs filled the living room.

Sadowsky curled up in a fetal position, screaming in agony behind the duct tape.

J.P. grabbed Allen by his neck, pulling him off-balance, then handcuffed him. "As much as I would love to let you go on with it, I need the idiot alive, so he can answer some questions. God knows I waited long enough."

Allen nodded, turned, and sized up J.P., assessing weight, height, and the distance between them. He tested the handcuffs behind his back. "You must be Morgan. I'm impressed. Let me go. Have fun with this idiot." Allen felt the weight of his backup piece snuggling against his bony ankle, and his confidence kept him eye to eye with Morgan. *Chance favors the prepared mind*" Allen recalled his former drill sergeant's motto. Apprehending Morgan would earn the undying appreciation and admiration of the group and Clancy's personal gratitude.

"My momma raised no fools, and I am an only child." Morgan motioned with the gun for Allen to lie down next to Sadowsky.

Allen held his gaze, then settled face up with bent knees, observing J.P.'s every move.

"Still playing the dutiful little soldier, Allen." J.P. said. "Please, save it. I am too tired, pissed off, and bored with all of you."

Allen rolled over with reluctance. J.P. kneeled on Allen's back, taped his mouth, retrieved the backup piece, and then bound his feet together. J.P. spun Allen on his back, unwrapped Lisa from the tarp, positioned her to face the front door, and then took pictures. "That should do it as evidence," said J.P. "Let's hope it will not come to that, but it seems one can never have enough insurance. I will be damned if I will take this lying down, so to speak."

J.P. dragged Sadowsky to Anna's home office, where he cuffed his hands through the computer cable hole cut in the antique wooden desk. J.P. pulled the door shut behind him, giving the dead bolt a hard twist. The click of the lock felt final and sent a chill up his spine as he recalled the times the sound of a falling prison latch had changed his life.

He pocketed the office key, marched Allen to the half-wall between the living room and the kitchen. J.P. cuffed Allen behind his back, with his arms around the pillar. "I always thought it messed up the flow of the room, but it comes in handy. Do not scratch the paint."

Allen cursed under the duct tape, straining his hands against the pillar.

J.P. smacked him upside the head. "Be cool. I have nothing against you. I want answers from your friend. I promise I will not hurt you."

Satisfied that he had Allen and Sadowsky secured, J.P. kneeled next to Lisa. He removed her arm and leg bindings and then the adhesive strip around her mouth. Lisa twitched and stirred as the duct tape pulled at her hair, but the drugs had a firm hold on her.

J.P. used a damp towel to wipe duct tape residue from Lisa's face, then scooped her up with great care. Her body was heavier and more muscled than he had expected. He felt her warm breath on his neck as he lowered her onto the couch and tucked a pillow under her head.

"Wait a minute, will you? It is time for me to get some long-overdue answers."

CHAPTER 23

"**T**HE BOSS IS BACK**,**" Purcell announced walking into the security office.

"Son of a bitch." Simpson slammed his fist on the desk. "I got him." He added in a somber voice, "But there is a problem. I know the boss won't like it."

"What is it?" Purcell strived to maintain his image of the eternally prepared soldier. *"Let no one see weakness. The less they know, the more you are in control"*—a motto he had built his career on. A flashback brought the two most influential people to mind—his wife, Amanda, and his baby brother, Calvin. Both taken so early from him.

Purcell allowed himself a rare moment of reminiscence. There was no one prouder or more devoted the day Calvin got his Border Patrol Agent badge. Cal beamed with youth and confidence, full of dreams and promise. He had become a protector of the country he loved to the point of obsession. A few short years later, a *coyote* evading capture gunned him down like an animal and left him to die at the mercy of Southern California desert predators.

The *coyote* ratted out his competition and disclosed ingress routes and tunnels. To add insult to injury, the government pussies offered the *coyote* an inexcusable lenient sentence. Every single one of those corrupt politicians was nothing but a spineless, self-serving piece of garbage. He and Clancy would change all that soon enough.

"I retraced Sadowsky's route." Simpson interrupted Purcell's reverie. "This Expedition is always five to ten seconds behind. It has to be Morgan. I lost him when he got here. I've been trying to reacquire him." Simpson switched windows on the screen. "Now look at the security camera at the Park-and-Ride across the tracks. There is the black Expedition pulling in after The Big Man talked to Jensen, the same time the local cops arrived. Now watch closely." Simpson fast-forwarded the recording. "Can't see the plates, but nobody comes out. Nobody gets in. It just sat there, with its lights off, until two minutes before Jamie died."

Simpson trimmed the recording speed. "The lights come on and it takes off in a hurry. First, it crosses the tracks. Maybe he thought of coming here. Then it got back on the 5, heading south, and I lost it again." Simpson sighed. "I'll need some time to pull the feeds from the freeway cameras to find out where he went, but I can venture a guess."

"What's the bad news?"

"I bet he planted something upstairs to listen or perhaps watch. Why else would he wait around? I bet he knows about the plans for Richter's place, and he's going to ambush Sadowsky again. We have to warn him and Allen. Man, the boss will be furious." Simpson knocked on the screen, tapping the SUV's image with his finger. "This guy is a serious heap of trouble."

"I'll tell the boss. Find whatever this asswipe left behind. Hold off on calling Sadowsky or Allen until we find it. We don't want to tip our hand." *The KISS rule, "Keep it simple, stupid!"* was another motto Purcell had built his career on. This way, Sadowsky may get what he deserved. Losing Allen would not go well with the boss, though.

Simpson produced a handheld scanning device. He switched it on. "If it's transmitting, I'll find it. It's fascinating that it didn't show up on our scanners, though. Most likely, it's upstairs. That's where I would have left it."

"What's going on?" Clancy asked, passing by Purcell without breaking stride.

"We identified Morgan's SUV." Purcell ran behind, reporting in a rapid-fire manner.

Clancy halted outside the briefing room. Purcell stepped closer and whispered in Clancy's ear. "Morgan left something behind, like a bug. Simpson is searching for it. Morgan parked across the tracks and listened in." Having finished his report, he backed away, standing at a respectful distance, knowing Clancy's temper could be uncontrollable.

"This unforeseen pebble in my shoe feels more like a giant boulder." Clancy rubbed his chin and paced, stomping every step. He pulled Purcell further on the walkway and continued in a conspiratorial whisper. "As of right now, finding Morgan is the highest priority. He knows about this place and everything we have here. We cannot allow him to live."

As Purcell walked away, Clancy grabbed his arm and pulled him back. "If he listened in, he may have recorded everything. We don't need that complication. Find him. Find out what he knows, recover the recordings, and get rid of him. Check on Sadowsky and Allen. He may have gone to Richter's house to ambush them. Make sure if they pick him up, or he contacts law enforcement, no one, and I mean absolutely no one, talks to him. Request to hold him completely isolated and incommunicado. Then you bring him to me."

"Yes, sir." Purcell felt he dodged a bullet. Clancy was famous for shooting the proverbial messengers.

Simpson's device beeped faster as he approached the metal desks. He plucked the pen and held it up, triumphant. "I got it, boss." He disassembled the pen and showed them the parts.

Clancy screamed and kicked the desk, then flung a chair at the wall.

"My, my," whistled Simpson. "This is the latest generation spy-pen, high-def camera, Hi-Fi sound, records internally, and broadcasts in the 5.8 GHz band. This is not your average toy that our regular scans could find. I saw prototypes at the spy tech show a few months back, but I didn't think they were available. This beauty cost a fortune." Noticing Clancy and Purcell's somber faces, he stopped. "He's got it all, I'm afraid."

"This changes everything," Clancy resumed pacing. "Wake everyone up. I want this place packed and cleaned up within the hour. Move everything to Site B. Last thing we need is a showdown with the Feds or God knows who else. Assume he has intercepted Allen and Sadowsky, he commandeered a radio, and he is listening in. Everyone uses only the new encrypted radios we ordered for CDoHP. Absent those, use the encrypted mobile phones only. This is a nightmare we don't need when we are so close. So goddamn close!"

Simpson and Purcell scrambled in complete silence to carry out the order.

CHAPTER 24

J.P. SET THE DRY towel down next to the duct tape roll. He lifted a cushion from the office sofa and placed it on Sadowsky's knee. He aimed Sadowsky's own gun at the knee, resting it on the cushion. J.P. cut the tape around Sadowsky's mouth.

"I despise violence and torture. However, this seems to be the language you understand. I want only answers to my inquiries, or I pull the trigger every time to deviate. We do this until you bleed to death, or I run out of bullets. Clear so far?"

Sadowsky nodded, then shook droplets of sweat from his forehead and brows.

"First question." J.P. started. "Who is 'The Big Man'?"

"I can't tell you that. He'll kill me." Sadowsky's eyes doubled in size, and more sweat beads materialized on his creased forehead.

"I represent a more pressing issue. I am not in the mood for games."

"You got here ahead of us. You must know what the boss did to Jamie," Sadowsky crumpled into a heap of defeat. "He was one of us, for God's sake. The boss is a mellow kitten by comparison. The Big Man will kill me and then my family. Ask anything else."

"OK. We will come back to that one. Why?"

Sadowsky studied him for a long time. "Why... what?"

"If you try that again, get used to flying a wheelchair for the rest of your life. Why were and your Big Man blackmailing George Hunter? How did my family factor in?" J.P. demanded.

"I can't tell you that," Sadowsky sobbed. "Shoot me. If I talk, he'll torture my family in unimaginable ways. He enjoys that stuff. He's not right in the head, you know."

J.P. pulled back the hammer and pushed harder against the cushion. His left hand moved the towel over Sadowsky's mouth. "Are you sure? I am here. He is not. I will turn you into a cripple. How can you justify what he did to my family?"

Sadowsky peppered his sobs with uncontrollable hiccups. "I just can't tell you. If you kill me, maybe he'll let my sister and niece live. Maybe."

"How touching. Where was that concern when you murdered my family and my friend Anna?" J.P. asked. "Nothing to say equals no use to me. Reconsider?"

Sadowsky's eyes begged for the mercy he knew would not be forthcoming.

"Who murdered Alice and Artie? You were there. You tried to kill me after you framed me for their deaths. I could not even attend their funeral."

Sadowsky's face turned bright red, and his breathing faltered. He did not move or speak for a long time, choosing to study the wall behind J.P.

J.P. shoved the towel in Sadowsky's mouth, then changed the angle of the barrel and fired. The bullet grazed Sadowsky's thigh. Sadowsky squealed, and his eyes welled up with tears. J.P. yanked the towel out of Sadowsky's mouth.

"I'll tell you this and only this. You know him very well, and you think he's dead. Hell, everyone thinks he's dead. However, he's very much alive, and he's one sick, sick puppy. He doesn't care about anyone or anything that gets in his way. All he loves is money and power." Sadowsky clenched his jaw and stuck his chin out like a stubborn child.

"We have time to get acquainted. You will talk," snorted J.P.

"I'm sorry for the family. It was collateral damage. Kill me or let me go. I'm done talking." The light in Sadowsky's eyes dimmed.

"You mean my family?" Dark clouds formed around J.P.'s forehead.

"Go fuck yourself," Sadowsky's labored breath and sweat stunk up the small room.

"You need time to think things over." J.P. had no intention to kill or inflict serious injuries. He planned to debrief Sadowsky, then hand him to the local cops for Anna's murder.

J.P. wrapped the towel around the leg wound and secured it with duct tape. Then he covered Sadowsky's mouth, wrapping the tape around his head several times. "First bullet was an intentional flesh-grazing wound, so you may still walk after I get my answers. Next shots will not be. Compared to what you did to my family, it will still be too little."

J.P. loped out of the office and locked the door behind him. He walked over to Allen, who had slumped against the restraints on the pillar. J.P. checked on Lisa, who continued to sleep off the heavy drugs.

J.P. rummaged through Allen's pockets until he located the Honda keys. He checked the restraints, noticed the wear markings on the pillar, and frowned. "You had to scratch the paint. I will make sure Anna's mom sends you the repair bill. Now, sit here causing no further damage, or I will knock you out."

He reflected on how innocent she looked, then marched out the front door. He knew Lisa was a brilliant lawyer who lost her humanity in pursuit of court victories.

CHAPTER 25

ELLIOT PARKER WAS GETTING comfortable with a novel in his brand-new Sleep Number bed. Purcell's name on his mobile phone caused him to jump to his feet. Purcell was the leader of his "Special Action Unit," as they had grown fond of calling themselves.

"This is of the utmost importance. I need you to take care of it, posthaste, with no mistakes." Purcell relayed Anna's home and office addresses, along with the instructions.

Parker hung up and then pressed the speed dial key reserved for his companion, Ryder. "Five minutes. We've got wet work orders." Parker skipped niceties.

Parker scurried out of his apartment, carrying a small duffel bag. He took the stairs to the parking garage and started the engine of his cruiser.

Ryder, attired in black and hoisting an identical bag, got out of the elevator six minutes later. Ryder climbed into the passenger seat of the black Dodge Charger R/T.

"We've been best buds longer than I care to remember. Would it kill you to give a sleeping man a chance to get out of bed before you bark orders?" Ryder asked.

"In twenty-odd years, were you ever on time for anything?" Parker replied.

"Ouch. What crawled up your butt, bud?" Ryder feigned pain.

The two of them met at Army boot camp. A drill sergeant with a sense of humor paired them later. Parker and Ryder. They had been at each other's side ever since, through more missions, troubles, and life-defining events than either of them cared to remember.

"When they offered us the opportunity to get out of those dead-end CHP jobs, you jumped on it as if there was no tomorrow. Now you're back to your old crap."

"Back the truck up. What happened?" Ryder counteracted Parker's outburst.

"We got the call. This is our best chance to prove ourselves. You start by being late."

"All right, all right." Ryder put his hands up in mock surrender. "What's the mission?"

"Locate and eliminate several people. The primary mission is to capture a guy, John Paul Morgan. Alive, if possible. Here's his picture." He held his phone for Ryder to inspect it.

"Sounds like something went seriously wrong," Ryder squeezed in.

"You betcha. The directive is to execute all of them with extreme prejudice. If capturing Morgan alive is not possible, he must disappear without a trace. Whatever breach happened, we must contain it and tie up all loose ends tonight. Failure is not a way of life I enjoy."

The two professional soldiers traveled in silence the rest of the way to Anna Richter's home, going to do a job they believed to be necessary for the future of their country, the same way they had done many times in the past across the globe.

CHAPTER 26

J **.P. BACKED LISA'S HONDA** in the driveway and opened a rear door. He scooped Lisa up with the pillow, her shoes, and her purse. He placed her with care in the backseat then parked half a mile away, concealing the Honda behind a dusty U-Haul. J.P. turned off the ignition, cracked the front windows, locked the doors, and dropped the keys inside.

J.P. walked at a normal pace. He did not want to tangle with the police. He had Sadowsky's recently fired automatic tucked in his belt. He noticed a shadow at the opposite end of the park, advancing with moves characteristic of Special Forces–trained soldiers—the deliberate, slightly crouched stance, gun trusted forward, sweeping the area in front of him.

J.P. glued himself to the fence and glanced around the corner, searching for anything else out of the ordinary. A second silhouette crept, with similar movements, from the other side of the park. The coordinated, dance-like search for a target was hard to miss. Silenced guns meant professional soldiers, or mercenaries, on a hunting mission. J.P. wondered how they had arrived so fast. They could not have come from the same place he had broken into. They were local talent, dispatched after the people at the warehouse discovered the camera pen he had left behind. He knew the *Shadows*, as he thought of them, were hunting for him.

Sitting in the dark triangle by the fence, J.P. calculated his next move. He had to hand it to these guys. They had resources, recovered quickly from setbacks, and moved fast. He wondered about his, and Lisa's, actual chances of survival. Time for a new strategy. He realized he was flying purblind into a shit storm, with no instruments, driven by curiosity, fueled by revenge, so far protected only by dumb luck. A dangerous thing under any conditions.

The *Shadows* made their soundless approach. J.P. winced when he saw an old man walking a rat-sized dog. The man was oblivious of the soldiers, despite the mutt's tense yelps. One *Shadow* alerted his partner to the old man. The other stopped and gave the all clear signal.

The *Shadows* synchronized their arrival on Anna's front lawn. They glided in eerie silence with a liquid economy of moves, a sign they had worked together before and knew how to cover each other's back. They climbed the stairs as if they were two choreographed dancers, one facing the house, the other the park. They stopped at the door and listened. One of them climbed down the stairs and disappeared in the backyard. The other stayed behind and scanned the street. The front door opened, and the second Shadow vanished inside.

Holding Sadowsky's gun flush against his thigh, J.P. reached Anna's front lawn. He did not have a plan. He circled the house and halted by the French doors opening to the backyard. The living room lights afforded him an unobstructed view inside, while the curtains concealed his presence. One *Shadow* had dragged Sadowsky into the living room without removing his bindings. The *Shadow* cut the tape from Sadowsky's mouth with one swift move.

That is not a good sign for Sadowsky. Damn it. I wish I had more time with him.

The two *Shadows* stood to the side, facing Sadowsky and Allen. Smythe's dead body in the middle of the living room separated the two pairs of men like a bad omen. J.P. strained to hear what they discussed, filling in most of the blanks. He could hear Sadowsky pleadings and Allen snorting one-word, annoyed answers. The *Shadows* exchanged a meaningful glance. One ambled to the front door. The second one retreated to the corner formed by the foyer and the kitchen wall.

Parker called Purcell, spoke a few words, listened for a long time, and ended the call with, "Done, sir." He nodded to his partner, who picked up a cushion.

Sadowsky got up clumsily and hopped kangaroo-style, attempting to run nowhere. He fell and then crawled backward on the floor, flopping like a fish on the dock. "No. No. You can't kill us. We are indispensable. Call back and ask for the boss. He'll tell you. Call him!"

Allen slumped, silent, resigned. Ryder ripped the towel from Sadowsky's bleeding leg and forced it in his mouth. He pointed with one finger, an unmistakable order to be quiet.

Standing outside the French doors, J.P. calculated the chances of neutralizing both *Shadows* before they fired back. He had to shoot through the double pane doors at an angle. That would alter the rounds' trajectories. Both *Shadows* wore bulletproof vests. That meant he had to go for head shots. Tall order under the best circumstances, using a familiar gun. He had someone else's weapon and needed to fire at moving targets. It was unsafe. The heavily populated neighborhood also presented an opportunity for collateral damage from stray bullets. He also debated whether he was ready to kill people who had done nothing to him. Yet.

J.P. wanted Sadowsky alive to answer his questions and pay for Anna's murder. The *Shadows* could find Lisa if they looked for her. It was more important to cover her for now.

J.P. dialed 911 on the untraceable phone. He placed a voice-altering device over the microphone and reported seeing men fighting inside Anna's house. He suggested multiple units responded without lights or sirens and surrounded the house before going in. He turned the phone off, removed the battery and SIM card, and returned everything to his pockets.

On the opposite side of the park, a single police cruiser flashed its lights as it approached at breakneck speed. J.P. sped up and attempted to intercept the unsuspecting cops before they walked into an epic ambush. The cruiser screeched to a halt in front of Anna's driveway, and the police officers vaulted out of their seats and climbed the stairs in a hurry.

CHAPTER 27

PARKER REDIALED PURCELL'S NUMBER. He relayed Sadowsky's claim.

"Hold one," Purcell replied.

Parker noticed the lights of the cruiser approaching the house and pressed the MUTE button. He signaled Ryder, and they took positions flanking the front door.

The two uniformed young cops ignored J.P.'s attempts to get their attention, fixating on Anna's front door and windows. They knocked on the door, waited for a while, and then knocked again. They glanced at each other, pushed the door open, and walked into the house, guns drawn, announcing themselves.

Parker and Ryder disarmed and handcuffed the officers on the floor within seconds of entering. Ryder slammed the front door shut and dragged the young cops into the living room next to their other captives.

J.P. sprinted up the steps, cursed at the closing door, and then rushed to the back doors. He heard Parker speak. "Sir, we have an extra complication," Parker reported, then waited for a full minute. "Yes, sir. Consider it done." Parker glanced up at his partner and nodded like married couples and long-term partners communicate their intentions.

Parker trotted to the sofa, picked up a throw pillow, and motioned to Ryder, who lifted the padding closest to him. Using one gun seized from the uniformed officers, Parker shot Sadowsky, before he moved on to Allen. He covered Allen's face with the smoking cushion and shot him between the eyes. Ryder finished the Irvine cops using the other weapon confiscated from them. The Shadows discarded the cushions and pistols on top of the bodies.

Ryder collected Allen and Sadowsky's wallets and badges but left the uniformed cops' shields. He emptied the canisters on the five bodies.

Parker tore the stove gas line and then sprinted into the garage. He tore the water heater feeding gas line and pointed the hissing metal hose toward the house. Then he propped the garage door open. Each man took a small device from the box Allen had brought.

"Three minutes," said Parker, setting the timer. Ryder nodded. They yanked the safety pins, placed the devices on the floor and strolled out the front door, then across the park. Parker kept the vehicle under the speed limit, like a man on a Sunday drive, showing no emotion or concern. They had completed a job. Nothing to it, really.

"Too bad for the Irvine unis. Unavoidable collateral damage. Necessary for the greater good." Ryder sighed.

Parker nodded with empathy.

"We have one more job to complete our mission tonight. The sooner we get it over with, the better. I'm sick and tired of the status quo."

"Amen, brother," was the only reply Ryder found in his vocabulary.

CHAPTER 28

WHEN PURCELL REPORTED SADOWSKY'S newest failure, Clancy threw a fit much worse than usual. He tossed things at the walls and screamed like an overgrown child who broke his favorite toy. "I should shoot you where you stand and then move on to your band of bumbling idiots. How the hell did I get involved with such inept people?"

Purcell stood at attention, stiff as a board. He concealed his anger under a rock-hard expression. The embodiment of the obedient soldier who listened to his superior vent.

Clancy calmed down. "How long until we move out?" he asked.

"We will load everything within the hour, sir. In less than two hours, we will be out of here and all traces erased."

"Still too long," Clancy growled. "We could have unwanted visitors. I'm tired of surprises, Purcell. What happened to our well-oiled machine? Until tonight, we had nothing but brilliant planning and beautiful implementation. Are we going to blow it during the last three days? Go make sure nothing else happens, or I will hold you personally accountable."

"Yes, sir."

"Did the APB go out?" Clancy asked as Purcell opened the door to leave.

"Not yet. We've been waiting for Sadowsky to report when finished."

"Stop making excuses. It's a terrific thing, actually. Include details about Morgan's connection to a massive video and currency counterfeiting operation and add to it information about murdering our men and the two Irvine PD officers. No one can question him before we do. I want him dead, or I want him quiet. Release the APB as soon as you leave these premises."

"Yes, sir!"

"Burn this place to the ground and make sure nothing links it to us."

"May I suggest we just clean it up? We haven't been here that long. There's not much to erase. A fire will attract too much attention," Purcell said.

"You're right," Clancy conceded. "I'll be at Site B. Straighten this mess up. Now!"

CHAPTER 29

J.P. WAITED FOR THE *Shadows* to leave, then broke through the French doors. He checked for survivors, knowing there would be none. The smell of gasoline fumes and gas build-up overwhelmed him. Once again, he had to postpone searching Anna's house. He inspected the timed incendiary devices. Not enough time to disarm them both. He opened the front door, ran down the stairs, and hurled both contraptions to the middle of the park.

The explosions erupted a second apart, rocking the otherwise quiet neighborhood. Dozens of lights turned on in unison. J.P. cursed and walked to his SUV before the neighbors started coming out. Irvine PD and the Fire Department would arrive at the scene, and then he would get stuck there. Lisa Jensen was still out there alone, fast asleep and vulnerable.

He raced his SUV to Lisa's hidden car. He waited to see if the *Shadows* would attempt to locate and eliminate her. He decided against another call to 911 that would send first responders to Anna's office, the undeniable target of the *Shadows*. He did not want more innocent officers or firefighters in harm's way.

The massive detonation rocked the entire neighborhood. He watched the ball of fire and fragments of Anna's home ascend in the night sky. For a moment, it drowned the wailing sirens of approaching emergency vehicles. J.P. cursed again. *Darn pilot light.*

Satisfied that Lisa was safe for the moment, he took off towards Anna's office, hoping for a chance to search it before its inevitable destruction planned by the *Shadows*. He was two blocks away when the blast of windows and the sounds of twirling flames engulfing what used to be Anna's quaint little law office.

It was as if they had erased all traces of Anna's life in less than one hour.

He expected Anna had remembered his tedious advice to store important documents and evidence somewhere else, not in her house or office. The question was, did she listen, and where did she hide them this time?

He knew the cops would drag him into the mess when Lisa Jensen woke up. For now, he needed to put the whole thing in his rearview mirror and sort through it overnight. Or with a clear head in the morning when he predicted the proverbial shit would hit all the fans at once.

He had an extensive set of pictures, video and audio recordings captured that night. He had enough to bargain with the cops.

PART TWO

July 2

CHAPTER 30

T HE TRILLING OF HIS private phone jolted J.P. from a restless sleep. He felt his body bathed in sweat and kicked the bunched sheets. He read Candy's name on the screen and let his head drop on the pillow with a loud, painful groan. He turned the handset off, reassembled the phone used the night before to call 911 and then dialed Candy's home number.

"J.P.? Thank God I found you. I've been calling for two days. I'm in trouble and need your help. Are you there?" Candy Richter, Anna's mother, was frantic, talking up a storm.

His eyes darted to the alarm clock—6:41 A.M. He needed a solid week, not only three hours of sleep. That was the problem with bad guys. They had no respect for other people's needs or schedules, or the victims' families. "Good morning. Please calm down," J.P. replied.

"J.P.? Did you hear about Annie?" Candy asked.

J.P. felt her pain over the phone. "Yes, Candy. You have my most heartfelt condolences." He wondered for a moment what had happened to the eternally happy hippie, Candy Richter, the woman whose effervescent spirit was omnipresent and inextinguishable. He struggled with the feelings of guilt, debating how much he should tell Candy.

"She didn't kill herself. A mother knows." Candy's voice dropped an octave.

"I know that, too." His voice echoed the hurt he felt. He did not want to scare her by sharing he knew who killed Anna. That he needed to do in person. "What kind of trouble?"

"You know Annie didn't commit suicide?" Candy caught the nuance in his statement. "What do you know, J.P.? Tell me. I'm going through hell. My baby girl is dead, and I do not understand why."

Damn. She knows me so well.

"Not on the phone. What kind of trouble?"

"The police called. Someone set Annie's home and office on fire last night. The police say it was arson. They're asking if I know who might have done that and why. How could I possibly know? They asked me to go to Irvine to give a statement. I need someone to go with me," Candy said, letting the questions and demands tumble out of her mouth.

"Candy! Stop, please," J.P. interjected. "Anna was an attorney. She had lawyer friends. You will be better off with one of them. Given my history with Irvine PD, if I go with you, I am bound to cause more harm than good. Let's meet and talk, and then I will help you find someone to go with you. It will be safer that way."

"J.P., I want you to go with me. Annie trusted you the most. I don't know any of her lawyer friends the way I know you. Annie needs you, too. Help me clear her name." Candy's rapid-fire style rattled J.P.'s nerves.

Oh, the guilt knife. Mothers know how to twist it so effectively.

"I will pick you up at eight thirty, the usual way. Let's talk in person. After I share with you what I learned last night, we go to the police." Would she want to take chances with their lives afterward? Where was that damn *pitcher* of espresso when he most needed it?

"OK," Candy resigned. She knew arguing with J.P. was akin to shouting at the storm.

After a turbo version of the morning's routine, J.P. drove to his usual coffee shop. He ordered the customary *six-shot large white chocolate mocha, skim milk, no whipped cream*, that always invited the young baristas to chuckle and tease him.

He winked at Carla, the freckled blond teenager who tended to him today. Sensing something different about him, she locked her bright green eyes onto his, quizzing.

"Here you go, J.P. Rocket fuel reinforced with nuclear juice." She relied on their standing joke. "I hope it helps launch your day into a pleasant orbit." Carla giggled. She always made it a point to brush her hand over his when she passed him the cup. He rewarded the gesture by squeezing it between his index and middle fingers. It was their ritual, an innocent moment of flirtation both knew would go no further, but it brightened their day. This morning's gentle touch set off warm sensations in J.P.'s heart. He flashed a sad smile.

At the door, he glanced over his shoulder at Carla. *I hope you will not miss me, should this be my last cup of Joe. Take care, kiddo.*

He drained the last drop from the java cup as he reached Candy's home. J.P. was half an hour early as signaled with the phrase, "the usual way." Candy had been ready and emerged with her shoulder bag in hand. She locked the door, tried the handle a few times, and rushed to J.P.'s SUV. She slid in and fastened her seat belt.

"May I have your phone?" J.P. asked.

Candy's eyebrows arched, but she handed it to him without question.

He turned it off and removed the battery and SIM card. J.P. said, "I hope I am paranoid, but if I were them, I would trace your phone today. Let's go before they figure out that I got here early." Pulling away from the curb, he continued, "Before I tell you anything, I must warn you it will put you in grave danger. The people who did this will have no qualms about killing us to keep their secrets. Are you sure you want to know?"

"Did you kill my daughter?" Candy asked point-blank. "Is that what you're saying?"

"God, no, Candy. However, she died because of me."

"So, you didn't kill her yourself, but you got her killed? Is that it?" Candy started weeping softly, wringing her hands.

"It is a long story related to Alice's death. It seems history has a way of catching up to us. I regret that you and Anna had to pay the price, too."

"OK. Tell me everything. I don't have anyone else left in my life, J.P. I want to clear Annie's name, so she and I can rest in peace. That's all that matters to me now, and I'm requesting your help. You are free to say no, of course."

Like the moon is free to break from Earth's orbit.

"I will tell you what I can. It is my fault Anna is dead. I know why she died and who assassinated her. The same group executed her killers last night."

"Good." Candy leaned against the door. She watched J.P. with love, pride, and sorrow.

"Here goes nothing." J.P. recounted some events from the previous night. "I left out a few minor things. I did not want you jumping out on the freeway." J.P. attempted to brighten the mood. He felt spent. They were in Lake Elsinore, heading south in morning light gridlock on the 15 Freeway. J.P. spotted a restaurant and headed for it in search of breakfast and more coffee.

CHAPTER 31

ISA WOKE UP DISORINTED, with a stiff neck and a throbbing headache. She sat up, wondering how she ended up sleeping in her car, in the backseat with a pillow she did not recognize. Holding her head with both hands, she examined the area outside the window. "Where am I? What am I doing here?" She struggled to trigger recollections of the night before. Her mind drew blank after blank, fueling the increasing feelings of frustration and irritation. She tried the door and found it locked. She thanked God for having enough common sense left.

She searched for her keys. She saw them on the driver's floor mat. She climbed into the driver's seat, fished out her mobile phone from the purse, and turned it on. She reflected that she never turned the darn thing off. She read her phone display: 8:50 A.M., July 2. OK, it was a start. July 2? Next thought was that she would be late for work.

She chuckled, reflecting on the irony of the situation. She did not know where she was, yet she worried about being late for work. Phil would be proud of her.

Lisa lowered the sun visor and studied her face in the mirror. Shock set in as the reflection stared back. Her hair was in a state of bedlam, and thin creases covered her face. A large purplish yellow bruise adorned her left cheek. She ran her fingertips over it, probing for pain. How did she get it? Did she give better than she got?

"What happened last night? The Hangover Part 7?"

Unable to answer any of her own questions, she examined the stained blouse and torn bra strap. Lisa straightened out her clothing the best she could. She removed the ruined stockings, ignoring the small dark stains. Then she ran a hairbrush through her hair.

She started the car and drove off, looking for a landmark to help get her bearings. She regretted declining the GPS option for her car. Next car will have it for sure. The street names were English, and the signs had the familiar Orange County look. At least, she did not wake up in some godforsaken Mexican town, sleeping off too much tequila—again.

She arrived at a STOP sign and recognized Anna's street. She took a second to get her bearings. On instinct, she turned toward Anna's place. Her heart beat faster, and a light sweat trickled down her neck. She squeezed the steering wheel with renewed hope that Anna might shed some light on the previous evening. Maybe they went on a binge and had too many 'ritas. That would not explain the black eye and torn clothing, but it was a start.

Lisa's chest tightened at the sight of Anna's home ruins and her breathing quickened. Her optimism scattered, witnessing the intricate dance of smoke wisps rising in the warm morning air. Her heart sank a little more with every yard she got closer to the disaster.

"What happened here? Where is Anna? Is she hurt?" she murmured.

Two fire trucks with flashing lights guarded the smoking remnants. A dozen firefighters gathered their hoses. Police cars blocked the street at both ends. A charred Irvine PD cruiser stood like a barricade between the park and the heap of rubbish that used to be Anna's home.

Lisa sighed with relief. None of the vehicles at the scene belonged to Anna. The usual onlooker crowd had gathered outside the police barriers, talking and taking pictures. Lisa parked by the Crime Lab van, donned her jacket and shoes, and then sprinted toward the house.

The nearby cruiser's passenger door flew open, and the cop spilled out in a hurry, blocking Lisa's path. "You can't go in there, madam. It's a crime scene."

Lisa tried to circumvent him. He grabbed her arm as she passed him. She shot him a scowling look. "I'm an Orange County Assistant DA, for God's sake. Let me through."

"I know who you are, madam. It's too dangerous. The fire could reignite any time. You could get hurt and contaminate the crime scene."

Cooper guided her away from the house and steered her towards the Honda. The shock of his statement made Lisa docile for a moment. The second cop got out and leaned against the trunk, watching with a curious expression.

"My friend Anna, the owner of the house, is she OK? She lived alone. How did the fire start?" Lisa asked the questions machine-gun-style.

"Slow down, miss. We know nothing yet. You must wait patiently with the rest of us. It may be awhile before this case makes its way to your office for prosecution." Cooper clutched Lisa's arm to prevent her from running toward the house again.

"How do you know it will require prosecution?" Lisa wriggled her arm free.

"I probably shouldn't tell you this, but you'll find out, eventually."

"Just tell me." Lisa felt her body tremble and fought to conceal the shaking.

"Last night, nine-one-one got an anonymous call about men fighting inside. Dispatch sent a patrol car to investigate. The officers never returned, nor did they contact the station again. That's their burned cruiser." He pointed at the heap of scorched metal. "Nobody's heard from them. The fire started around 2:00 A.M. Still, that's not the weirdest thing here."

"What is the weirdest thing then?" Lisa fought the desire to grab him and shake the information out of him all at once.

"May I see your ADA ID, miss? To make sure we're on the same page." The second cop stepped in, thumbs hooked in his belt, inches away from his gun holster and cuffs.

"Lisa Jensen, OC DA's office. I'm a friend of Anna Richter, the home's owner," Lisa replied, pointing to the smoldering remains. Her eyes locked briefly on the twirling columns of smoke. She prayed in silence that Anna was not hurt.

"I didn't ask who you were. I asked to see your identification," the officer repeated. He kept his gaze trained on Lisa, assessing her. He took in the details of her torn clothing and her disheveled appearance.

"Officer... Sparks," Lisa said, reading his nametag. "I don't know you, but your partner and I know each other. That should be enough."

"I still need to see your identification. Or I'll arrest you now for interfering with this investigation." Sparks seized Lisa's other elbow.

"Have you ever heard of probable cause, *Officer Sparkey*?" Lisa growled.

"Have you looked in the mirror lately?" he shot back. "I have five dead bodies in there, and you look like you went ten rounds with Mike Tyson. You do the math, Counselor." He advanced toward her, their bodies almost touching.

Lisa stomped back to her car and retrieved her credentials. "Happy now?" Returning her attention to the younger cop, she asked, "Officer Cooper, what is the weirdest thing?"

"Well, madam, when the call came in last night, we had this house already sealed as a crime scene. The house is a crime scene and IPD did not allow people to be there."

"Crime scene? Why?" Lisa pivoted toward the fuming ruins.

"If you are such a good friend of the deceased, madam..." Cooper started.

"Deceased?" Lisa's voice turned shrill. Hope that Anna was OK diminished with every passing second, floating away intertwined with the smoke. She wanted to get a grip on the situation, yet she could not remember a thing. She needed a foothold to get her balance back and stop the world from spinning out of control.

CHAPTER 32

"**M**AYBE I SHOULD GO** to Irvine PD alone," Candy said. "They could wait to arrest or shoot you. You're better off staying away for now."

Candy and J.P. had exchanged very few words after food arrived.

"I do not want you dealing with the Irvine PD alone. I am painfully aware of all the unpleasant possibilities," replied J.P.

"I lost everyone else in my life—Tom, may God protect his soul, and now Annie, may she rest in peace. My parents and my brother went long ago. You're all the family I have left. I cannot bear to lose you too." She placed her hand over his.

J.P. remained silent, allowing her to finish.

"Don't worry about Annie's name. I know, you know, and God knows she didn't kill herself. That's good enough for us. I can handle the police. You take care of yourself and Max." She took a deep breath and sipped some coffee. "Give me copies of everything. I'll take them to Lisa Jensen. I know Lisa. She will see that these people answer for what they did."

"What about you? Will you be OK with that?"

"Annie would want us to celebrate her life and remember her in the most positive way. I taught her that since she was a toddler."

"She told me a thousand times if she died before me, I had to make sure you never grieved more than five minutes. She only allowed me two."

"No reason to let anguish ruin our lives, too. The past belongs in the past. Let's focus on what we can change and make sure whatever these people planned does not come to fruition. I know Annie would consider that a worthy memorial service." Candy stood and pointed to the door. "It's time to take care of it."

J.P. waited outside the restaurant while Candy used the bathroom. He allowed the warm morning sun to soak in and pondered how many more sunrises he would see.

Candy walked up and hugged him. "I need to thank you for avenging Annie."

"What are you talking about? I have done nothing." He studied her face. "Quite the opposite. I am sure they murdered her because—"

Candy put her hand on J.P.'s lips, silencing him. "You said last night their own people shot Annie's killers. Because you followed them and put a dent in their plans."

"That is a long stretch of the imagination, Candy."

"The murderers are dead. That's all that matters."

"No, no, no, Candy. I see what you are doing." J.P. broke away.

"J.P., don't be an idiot. Let Annie rest in peace. Her killers are dead. Call it divine justice. Your conscience is clear. God and the people who truly matter know the truth."

"Nice try, Candy. Did you think it would be that easy?"

"I had to give it a shot. You're all I have left, my son."

"Thank you. I appreciate it. I still have a debt of honor to repay. I could never live with myself if I walked from this fight and they got away with everything. Not when I am this close to learning what happened to Alice and Artie."

Candy took his face between her palms with a mother's gentleness. A tear streaked down her cheek. J.P. wiped it with his finger.

"Candy, these are evil people. They have wicked plans. Nobody in their right mind executes five, no, make that six, people purely for kicks. They assassinated Anna for what she found out. Somehow, that made her a threat to their sinister plot. I cannot and will not let them get away with it, if it is the last thing I do on this Earth."

"Well, then. Let's go get them." Candy hooked J.P.'s arm. "Let's go see Lisa Jensen and let's..." She sang a parody of Pink's *"Get the Party Started."*

"I created a monster like that Stallone movie, *'Stop! Or My Mom Will Shoot.'*"

Candy placed her hand over her heart, faking a fainting spell against the SUV.

CHAPTER 33

LISA PERCIEVED COOPER'S INTERNAL deliberation. She appeared as if she had slept in her clothes several nights — hair all over the place, an enormous bruise on her cheek. Most of all, she realized she must seem not to be all there mentally. To top it all off, she was wobbly, and not only on her feet. She recalled Cooper liked her in and out of the courtroom, and he had even asked her out twice.

"Ms. Jensen, I think we should get you to the hospital. Have someone check you out. Make sure you're OK. Right, Randy?" Cooper engaged his partner.

"Get your own ass out of trouble. She could be a suspect. Did you stop to think about that? Fire Department said there were cops' badges on those bodies. We could have dead cops. If we screw this one up, we'll never live it down," Sparks answered.

"A suspect in what?" Lisa slammed her hands on her hips, and standing on her toes, she got in his face. She glanced at the smoking remains, thinking it was obvious this was a much bigger deal than she had figured. She kept pushing, hoping everything would fall into place. She wanted to ask the right questions, regain control somehow.

"Lady, you could use some mouthwash." Sparks backed off, waving his hand in front of his nose. He reached in his pocket for a pack of gum, offering it to Lisa.

"Who's dead? What aren't you telling me?" Lisa took a stick and started chewing.

"If you're a close friend of Ms. Richter, you know she committed suicide two days ago. Two of our own are missing. Their half-burned patrol car is out front, and there are five dead bodies in that house. Do you see the problem here?"

Did she see the problem? By God, was Mount Everest tall? Was the pope Catholic? What did she just walk into? What had happened there?

"Anna didn't commit suicide. She couldn't have. Two days ago? Today is Friday. She died on Wednesday." Lisa's voice faded. "What happened to the world? Why doesn't anything make sense anymore?" The harder she tried to hold on, the more the world whirled around.

She recalled prosecuting a man once for aggravated assault on his wife. As his sole defense, he claimed no memory of the days leading to the event. He pleaded and swore on his children's lives he could not remember a single thing. Throughout the trial, Lisa had ridiculed him and called him "a coward who refused to take responsibility for his actions." A sudden twinge of guilt overtook her. Was it possible he had been telling the truth? Was that how he felt? No time for that. She resolved to snap out of it and focus on the giant problem at hand.

Sparks noticed the dark stains on the back of Lisa's jacket. He stepped forward and confronted her. "What is that on the back of your coat, miss? Is that blood?"

"I don't know." Lisa tugged at her clothes. She removed her jacket and studied the big dark smear surrounded by several smaller ones. She forced herself to think, to remember how the stains got there. It was as if the last few days never happened. The last thing she recalled was a party at the office. Big drug case conviction. The office shut down one hour early on Friday afternoon to celebrate. That was June 25. June 25! What happened since then?

Panic set in. She did her best not to lose it in front of the cops. She focused on the jacket and examined the smallest stains. "This is high-velocity blood spatter. How did all this blood get on me?" Her brain shifted into overdrive, and she felt like a freight train going down a steep slope with faulty brakes. "Anna committed suicide? No way. On Wednesday? What was I doing on Wednesday? On Tuesday? What was I doing yesterday? How did I get here?"

Lisa felt woozy. She ambled away and lost her footing. Cooper leaped and caught her just before she hit the ground.

Sparks keyed his lapel mike. "Dispatch, Adam Two-Niner requesting an ambulance and a unit to replace us at the scene. Request Sergeant Crawford and someone from the DA's office to meet us at UCI Medical Center. We have ADA Lisa Jensen at the scene in need of medical assistance." He released the mike key and shook his head. "OK, Coopernova, you know how to make them fall at your feet. Let's see if you can sweet talk Ms. Jensen into telling us what she knows. Because it involves her. She's in it up to her pretty eyebrows."

CHAPTER 34

THE BRIEFING ROOM AT Site B had the feel of a salty steam bath. Smells of sweat, gun oil, tobacco, and testosterone lingered in the thick air. Clancy turned off the big-screen TV behind him, ending the video conference. He looked worse for the wear as he let his eyes roam the room. Two dozen hard, determined faces stared back at him.

"We've been up all night, and we're all tired, but we will not fail. This is the last lap. In two days, we'll sprint across the finish line. Number one priority remains apprehending or neutralizing Morgan."

The men in the room nodded or grunted, and several pounded their fists on the table.

"Gentlemen, you're the inner group. You're familiar with all details of our operation. We chose you to help lead this country into the greatest battle for its existence." He stood, leaned forward, and yelled, "For a new California, a new America, and the new world!"

"America for Americans!" the men roared in unison, slamming fists over their hearts.

"Trident Security will provide some assets. The entire law enforcement community is on the lookout for Morgan. I need to focus on the preparations for the *True Patriot Day*. Whoever gets Morgan will have our sincere gratitude and my personal appreciation. Happy hunting! Don't come back without his head for me to mount on my wall."

"Yes, sir. Thank you, sir!" The group's answer shook the walls and the furniture.

"We now begin the public relations phase of this operation. We must bring the masses to our side. Our cause is just, and we will prevail. Dismissed."

"I thought you would reveal all the details," Purcell said once they were alone.

"Purcell, only you and the Big Man are privy to all aspects. We cannot trust anyone else with the specifics of our plans for California, or the plans for the entire country."

"Do you think Morgan will be a problem, sir? Can he prevent *True Patriot Day?*"

"No one can stop us now. In hindsight, I should have never joined forces with The Big Man and his thugs. Most of them have serious mental problems and too many skeletons in their closets. Yet without him, we wouldn't have the money and trustworthy personnel needed to succeed in California. Keep this between us, Purcell. No need to create discord."

"If Morgan shows up on the radar of law enforcement, they'll arrest or shoot on sight," offered Purcell. "We could try to recruit him. He's been wronged big time by the Navy. His official file doesn't say how, but I can smell it. He stood trial for the double murder, we know he didn't commit. Headed for death row. He's got to be one angry cat and must have some serious beef with the establishment. A man so resourceful would be useful to our cause."

"Not if he heard Sadowsky spill the beans. Catch him first. I'm not concerned about the law enforcement community. I worry about him going to the goddamn media. The whores masquerading as journalists nowadays will twist the truth and pervert our agenda for the sake of ratings. We need to get him first. Go take care of it, Purcell."

CHAPTER 35

"WE NEED HER CLOTHING** preserved for evidence. Keep her isolated until we can interview her." Sparks attempted to control of the situation. His intuition and experience, as a cop and Army MP, told him Jensen held the keys to the nefarious events unfolding.

"First, we need to figure out what's going on with her. Make sure she's OK, don't you think?" ER Head Nurse Clarion pushed past him with a scowl.

"She is a witness to multiple homicides. She fainted at the sight of blood." Sparks said.

"Well, *Officer Doctor*, or is it *Doctor Officer?*" The head nurse stepped into his path. "Why did you bring her to us if you diagnosed her all by yourself? You could have saved everyone's time. I could be resting my feet on my desk, enjoying my third cup of coffee."

Sparks wished it was not so hot in the ER. "I meant nothing by it. We were talking to her. When I pointed out the blood on her jacket, she collapsed." Sparks tried to save face. He opened another button on his shirt.

Clarion inserted her body between Sparks and the gurney. "Then maybe you will allow us to examine her and see what's going on, us being medical professionals and all."

"Thank you, madam," intervened Cooper. "Let's go, Randy."

"These fine gentlemen will be out of our way as soon as you get them Ms. Jensen's personal effects." Nurse Clarion directed her staff. Back to Sparks and Cooper, "Now just for you guys, we have a cafeteria in the basement where the doughnuts are out of this world."

Sparks protested. Cooper grabbed hold of his arm and led him away. "Let's go, Randy. Let them do their jobs. Have a little patience."

Sparks freed himself from Cooper's grasp. "She seemed disoriented and had a hard time remembering things, like the fact that her friend committed suicide. That's important."

Cooper guided him out. "They'll figure it out. We'll talk with her when she wakes up." Cooper smiled back at the head nurse. "You didn't have to castrate him in front of everyone."

"I'll let your mother know what company you keep, Stevie." Nurse Clarion gave them a dirty look, then her rotund face broke into a broad smile as she tussled his hair.

"She knows your mother?" Sparks jiggled his arm free.

"Of course. She's known me since I was born. You could have handled it with some tact. This is still the same-old Irvine. The more things change, the more they stay the same. You remember that?"

"I wanted to make sure we preserved the evidence. Ms. Jensen knows what happened in that house last night." Sparks defended his position, convinced time was of essence. "I can taste it in my mouth."

"C'mon, pardner. Buy you a cup o' coffee and one of 'em fat-free, suga'-free, taste-free doughnuts," said Cooper in a cartoon character's voice. He pushed open the swinging cafeteria doors, allowing Sparks to go in first.

CHAPTER 36

"I LOVE THIS ROAD, with its majestic landscapes and its sharp curves. It helps me relax and think while I drive." J.P. cut through the marvelous wilderness of the Cleveland National Forest.

"After what happened to you here?" Candy asked.

"I admit Ortega Highway poses personal dilemmas for me."

"You never talked about that," Candy probed.

"Maybe it is time," answered J.P. "This is the spot where I went down that night."

He pulled into a turnout area. They crossed the road and walked to the edge of the ravine. "I woke up down there." J.P. pointed to a rock formation, two hundred feet below them. "It is a miracle the car did not explode. I wonder why I survived. Probably just to deal with the guilt and the pain."

Candy smacked the back of his head. She stared at him with a defiant gaze. "You are never to think trash like that. I'm your mother now, and I forbid it."

"Yes, Mom," retorted J.P. "I dragged myself up to the road and hitchhiked to Irvine. When I got home, there were cops everywhere. The second story had burned out, and the roof had collapsed. I vaguely remember a cop telling me about Alice. Later, they said I broke his jaw, and it took five officers to subdue me." A tear trickled down his left cheek. He wiped his face with the back of his hand and resumed. "Next thing I know, I was in jail, charged with the murders. I still cannot recall the few days before Alice died. I tried drugs, hypnotherapy, everything I could think of. An entire week wiped clean as if it never happened."

"You still carry all that guilt. It's not good for your soul," Candy stated. "I worry about you. You need to forgive yourself, J.P. You said you learned last night the men who killed Annie were after George Hunter, not you."

"I need to know for sure whether Alice and Artie died because of something I did or who I was back then. The police report said Alice, and I fought that morning before I left for San Diego. Sometimes we did that for fun. It was never serious stuff. She always said makeup sex was her favorite. Alice would pick a small fight now and then, just for kicks. I knew it, and she knew I knew it. We playacted. God, I loved her so much." J.P. allowed his gaze to drift across the canyon. "And I miss her like California deserts miss the rain."

"If it's any consolation to you, I know you didn't kill them. At first, I thought you did, like everyone else. I was so mad at Annie when she asked me to take you in and take care of you after the deadlocked jury. I was furious with her. I threatened to disown her and never speak with her again. She was relentless. When I got to know you, the man I met during those ten weeks could not have done those horrible things." Candy hugged him.

"You think so? I was not sure about it myself."

"J.P., you have a gentle, beautiful soul. You are the most patient and loving man I ever met, bar my late husband."

"Sh. Keep a lid on that. I need to preserve my image." J.P. smirked.

"What are you afraid of? People might see through your BS and actually like you?"

"Something like that," he replied. "Nostalgia time over."

CHAPTER 37

DR. SYLVAN WAS A petite, attractive Indian woman with dark eyes and a mane of raven hair free flowing over her shoulders. She examined Lisa's body and sighed with relief. The only visible sign of injury was the yellowish-purple swelling on Lisa's left cheek. Dr. Sylvan gently probed the bruise with the tip of her gloved finger.

Lisa fretted, and her eyes popped open. She sat up with a jolt, startling the doctor and the nurses. The sheet fell off her body, leaving her exposed. The room felt chilly and outlandish to her. Lisa shivered and glanced down, discovering her own naked body. Self-conscious, she enfolded her arms around herself. A nurse held out a hospital gown, which Lisa wrapped around her quivering body.

"Where am I? What happened? Dr. Sylvan? What's going on?" Lisa thought her instincts betrayed her. She shivered and scanned the room and the medical personnel's faces.

"Lisa, you are safe," Dr. Sylvan reassured her friend. "We are at the UCI Medical Center, in the ER. Irvine PD brought you from a crime scene. You are OK physically, except for the bruise on your cheek. You'll look like a raccoon for a few days, then you'll be good as new. I will order more tests to confirm..."

Lisa waved a hand, while holding on for dear life to the thin fabric around her body. She needed some quiet time to think.

"Can we get you anything? Food? Water? Pain meds?" Dr. Sylvan asked.

"I'm starving. I don't seem to recall anything after last Friday afternoon." Her eyes continued to explore the room. She continued in a tentative voice. "It's still July 2nd, right?"

The doctor nodded, scribbled on Lisa's chart, and handed it to the nearest nurse. "Run these tests. Call for a psych and neurological consults. She may have suffered a concussion, or, maybe, the memory loss has a different cause."

The nurses rushed out of the room.

"I will be blunt with you, Lisa. You're with the DA. I know you've had your share of cases like this. We believe someone may have drugged and possibly sexually assaulted you. It would account for the memory loss. I would like to order a sexual assault kit. I cannot force you to undergo an exam, but I think you should."

Lisa blushed. She sensed her face turned red, and she became even more self-conscious. She had had her share of cases where the rape victims would rather let the attacker go free than endure the demeaning examination and the ensuing public humiliation of a trial. She wanted to pull the sheets over her head and cry.

"Yes." Her DA training kicked in. "Drugs and sexual assault would account for the torn clothes, the bruise, memory loss, everything." She lay back on the bed. Lisa recalled with another pang of guilt the times she had been the one questioning a young woman after a rape, pushing her, refusing to take no for an answer. She told the poor girl there was nothing to be ashamed of or scared about. Here she was, unable to look her doctor, her *friend*, in the eye.

"I'll leave you alone. If you'd like someone to be with you, I'll send a nurse. To keep you updated, they will take blood and collect evidence for an SAK, and someone from the psych department will come by and talk to you. Would you like to call anyone? Maybe Victim Counseling Services?" Dr. Sylvan touched Lisa's hand and held it for a moment.

"No. Please allow me some time alone to gather my thoughts." Her eyes implored the doctor to return a shred of her dignity, which she knew was slipping away.

CHAPTER 38

"PURCELL?" SIMPSON WAS WORRIED**, yet he had to share the information.

Purcell stirred awake, opened one disapproving eye, and then turned to face the wall. He had been dreaming of Joanne, his late wife, and had the urge to return to that blissful fantasy. In it, she was alive, vibrant, and ready to share the world with him. She had died from complications due to pregnancy at a San Diego ER, where she waited for six long hours. The doctors tended to a group of illegal immigrants injured when their beat-up van rolled over during a hot pursuit by Border Patrol Agents. Had they tended to her earlier... If only.

Purcell relived the gut-wrenching pain, and the visceral hollowing caused by the news of her death. He was serving his country overseas. She stayed behind, with no one to protect her. Worse still, she was pregnant with their first child, the result of their last night together before he shipped out for his fourth tour of duty overseas. The plague of illegal immigration claimed the lives of his brother, his wife, and his unborn child. Weak politicians allowed the responsible parties to escape prosecution and punishment. All that was about to change.

"Hear this." Simpson gave him a gentle shake. "It's urgent."

Purcell knew Simpson would not go away. He was acting on Purcell's instructions to relay news. He rolled to face Simpson and propped his head, yawning. "Simpson. What is it?"

"We intercepted a request made by an Irvine patrol car an hour ago."

"An hour ago?" Purcell's eyes opened wide, and he sat up on the cot with a jolt.

"There are only two of us. We need more techs. With the move, having to set up again, it's hard to monitor everything." Simpson had the excuse ready. Purcell waved him on.

"We were not tracking Jensen's phone. We didn't know she got away last night. She turned the phone on at 8:50 A.M. somewhere in Irvine and made a beeline for Richter's house. I already sent Coldwell and Maxwell to intercept and report on the situation."

"Good thinking. I should have told you she was alive," conceded Purcell.

"Irvine PD officers at the scene requested an ambulance, the investigator assigned to Richter's case, and an ADA to meet with Lisa Jensen at the UCI Medical Center. I came up here as soon as I heard it. Jensen is alive and talking," Simpson concluded.

Fully awake, Purcell walked away from the bed. Compartmentalization was another of his firm beliefs. Everyone should only learn what they needed to know to get the job done, nothing more. Too much information confused the mind. However, sometimes that backfired. "No worries about Jensen. Sadowsky gave her one of Doc Death Jones's knock out cocktails. She'll be lucky to remember her own name this morning."

"She asked for the investigator assigned to Richter's death investigation and someone from the DA's office." Simpson voiced his doubt.

"How do you know she asked for them?"

"I heard the Irvine cops at the scene request the investigator and the ADA..."

"So, we don't know *she* asked for them. You know about assuming."

"Yes, sir. You make an ass...," Simpson started.

"... out of you and me." Both finished the sentence, laughing at the stale joke.

"Leave it to me. Any news on Morgan?" inquired Purcell, hoping for something positive he could report to Clancy.

"Nothing concrete, but hear this. Irvine PD called Anna Richter's mother at 6:30 A.M., asking about the fires at her daughter's home and office."

"So? What's that got to do with anything?" Purcell showed his annoyance. The lack of sleep and the added stress of the last sixteen hours wore his patience thin.

"Wait. We tracked her after Sadowsky and Jamie killed her daughter. The Big Man requested it as insurance. As soon as she got off the phone with Irvine PD, she called a number that we could not trace. It's a complete dead end any which way we tried."

"Spare me the technobabble," pleaded Purcell.

"The phone rang twice before they turned it off, so we couldn't pinpoint it. Are you ready for this? That number appears in both Richter women's phone records."

"Big deal," Purcell snorted.

"Wait. Another call originated from an untraceable phone in Trabuco Canyon a few seconds later. It went to the mother's landline."

"Make it snappy." Purcell tensed up.

"We had some trouble with the local cable company granting us unrestricted access to their phone service records. We have no assets out there. We don't know what they discussed. We cross-referenced the phone that called her house today and guess what?"

"What, Simpson, what!"

"It's the same phone that called Irvine 911 last night. That call got the two uniforms sent to investigate." Simpson glowed. "A buck gets you ten that it belongs to Morgan."

"Couldn't you have told me only that?" Purcell knew he could not go back to sleep.

"Wait. There's more." Simpson held his palm up.

"If you say 'wait' one more time, I'll strangle you. Very slowly." Purcell's eyes narrowed. He felt steam building inside his skull, ready to blow through his nose and ears.

"This is pretty cool stuff. We traced the call—"

"Simpson." Purcell stomped his foot.

"We found Morgan's home area. We're not sure which house is his yet. We sent two teams out there. First, we sent a team to Candace Richter's place to follow her. They missed her this morning. We rerouted them to Irvine. She will show up there any time now. Then we dispatched Corelli and Timmons to Trabuco Canyon to investigate that call that originated from there this morning. We cross-referenced the tax records—"

"Simpson, stop!" cried Purcell. "I know you're proud of this crap, but I don't have the time for it, nor do I care. Just give me info I need to know."

"We narrowed it down to about forty homes. I got a glimpse of his SUV going up there last night, but I don't know where exactly. We'll have Morgan's home address in no time. We wait for him to show up at Irvine PD or at home, problem solved." Simpson waited for Purcell to take it all in and decide. Simpson did not want to become the lightning rod for Clancy's tantrums. Better Purcell than him.

"Great job, Simpson. You have all this info written somewhere?"

Simpson handed Purcell several printed sheets inside a folder.

"Excellent." Purcell dismissed him. As Simpson walked out of the room, Purcell muttered to himself, "Techies. Can't live with them, can't kill them. What's a poor soldier to do?" He reached inside his jacket, pulled out his secure phone, and dialed Parker's number.

"Lisa Jensen resurfaced at UCI Medical Center. Sadowsky gave her a drug cocktail that should erase the memory of a herd of elephants. But I don't want to take any chances. Eliminate her and anyone who had contact with her since last night. It's possible Morgan is there or will show up." Purcell added, "He's like a bad penny. Detain him if you can. Otherwise, eradicate with prejudice. All of them."

CHAPTER 39

"**P**LEASE, CALL ONE OF Anna's friends to go in with me. Someone we can trust," Candy pleaded as they approached the 5 Freeway.

"You should go see Lisa Jensen and ask her to help you navigate the red tape and BS at the Irvine PD. Ask her to please leave my name out for now. After you get done with Irvine PD, Ms. Jensen and I will meet to discuss last night's events and how to handle it."

"Can you call her?"

"Do you think that is a good idea?" argued J.P.

"You're right. Can I have my phone?"

"Leave your mobile off. I suspect they may track it." He handed Candy a Ziploc bag containing handset parts. "Put it together and use this one."

"I'm an old woman, J.P."

"So, you say. I know you can still kick ass when it counts." J.P. smirked.

"Thanks. I was talking about my memory. I have Lisa's number in my phone. You wouldn't know it by heart, would you?"

"Not if she was the last woman on Earth. I would cut out that part of my brain." J.P. shuddered as if he had just stepped into a freezer.

Candy jiggled her finger. "Be nice, J.P."

"Call 411. I bet she lists her mobile. If it is not, try the DA's office."

"Her phone is off. It went straight to voice mail," Candy reported and then called 411 again and asked for the number to the Orange County DA's office.

"May I please speak with Lisa Jensen?" Candy asked.

"No." The responder's tone was abrupt, downright hostile. "Who is this?"

"Something's wrong." Candy covered the phone. "She is very discourteous."

"What do you want with Lisa?" The voice became even more antagonistic.

"Lisa and my daughter were friends. My name is Candy Richter."

"Oh my God, you're Anna's mother. I'm so sorry, Mrs. Richter. I knew your daughter. It's been such a shock for all of us. We cannot believe it. There is something strange going on here that involves Lisa and arson cases at your daughter's home and office. We are all on edge and apprehensive about unidentified callers."

"Oh," managed Candy amid the verbal avalanche.

"I guess I can tell *you*. Lisa is in the hospital. She fainted earlier at your daughter's home. I heard it burned to the ground."

Candy seized the chance to take control of the conversation. "Which hospital?"

"UCI Medical Center."

"Can I get in touch with her or send her a message?" asked Candy.

"We can take one for her. One of our attorneys is on her way to the hospital now. Lisa asked for someone from our office and for the investigator handling your daughter's suicide case. Oh, darn. I'm so sorry. I meant the inquiry into your daughter's death. The rumor is Lisa remembers nothing. Someone slipped her a mickey and, maybe, date-raped last night."

Candy thanked the woman and hung up.

"Time to reconsider our strategy," Candy said. "Lisa is at the hospital. She asked to speak with the investigator in Annie's case and someone from her own office. We should go to the hospital. She may need your help."

"I have no intention of showing up at a hospital crawling with Irvine cops. Not for Lisa Jensen, while there is a 'shoot on sight' warrant attached to my name. Just think of all those Irvine PD score settlers and their itchy trigger fingers." J.P. twitched his nose in protest.

"I'll go in alone. Then she'll grant you safe passage, so you can talk to the police."

"It does not feel right. Something else is wrong here. I can feel it."

"I promise you that Lisa is a reasonable person."

"It is not Lisa Jensen I am worried about. She and I hate each other's guts, but we handled it OK last night. She did not shoot me. She did not scratch my eyes out. I did not wring her neck." J.P. rubbed his belly with an unconscious gesture. "I have this sickening feeling in the pit of my stomach that something is terribly wrong."

"Then I guess you will not like this. The woman said something strange. Rumor is that someone slipped Lisa drugs and date-raped her last night. She remembers nothing."

J.P.'s smacked the steering wheel, laughing. "Damn it. Of course, this is just my luck. It would only make sense to drug her if they would let her live. They were clear about killing her and framing both of us for the mess at Anna's place."

"This is only a rumor at the DA's office."

"You are right. Let's deal with the facts. You talk to Ms. Jensen. I will be right outside the hospital if you need anything." They pulled up at UCI Medical Center. "Keep that phone on at all times. If she says it is OK for me to show up, call this number." J.P. handed her a jet-black business card. The glossy side had only a phone number printed in raised, shimmering gold. "I will be up there." J.P. pointed across the street to the overflow parking lot.

While waiting, he downloaded the photos he had taken and the video and audio recording of the previous night's events onto several flash drives.

CHAPTER 40

T HE CONFERENCE ROOM IN the hospital basement, next to the cafeteria, had the feeling of a tropical island. The air was heavy and sticky. The hospital had turned off the air-conditioning in unused areas. Even though it was back on, the A/C unit had not made a dent yet. Cooper and Sparks joined Dr. Sylvan, Sergeant Crawford, a fifty something black man with a shaved head and piercing brown eyes, and ADA Arlene Spike, a slightly overweight brunette with an infectious smile and hair cropped short, well above her shoulders.

Dr. Sylvan perused Lisa's file. Her expression vacillated between anger and confusion. "I don't know what's weirder, so I'll go over the results. It'll be your job to interpret them. She tested positive for a cocktail of drugs, including a derivative of Rohypnol, the date-rape drug. It's something our lab techs have never seen. Their best guess is 'synthetic designer drugs engineered to induce a coma like state and wipe out someone's recent or short-term memory.'"

"What does that mean, Doctor? How was it administered?" asked Arlene Spike.

"The techs are researching the drugs. It fascinates them. The cocktail was too strong for a quickie. They used the words 'multiple elephant doses,' and not in a funny way. It's a wonder her systems didn't shut down. We think she should be in a coma." Sylvan pushed her chair under the air-conditioning vent.

"You mean she's lucky to be awake or alive?" Arlene probed.

"We don't know. Nobody has ever seen these drugs. However, we agree about the dosage. Way, way too high. When we know more, you'll know. The lab guys will dig something up." She wiped her face, waving the file to create a light breeze.

"Do you think it was the perp's intention to kill her?" Sparks cut in.

Dr. Sylvan shrugged. "I just don't know enough about the drugs to form an opinion."

"What else we got?" Arlene pushed. "Is she OK?"

"The SAK was negative," Dr. Sylvan added with a broad smile. "Thank God."

"Are you sure?" Arlene leaned forward on the edge of her seat.

"The SAK results revealed no recent sexual activity. That's consistent with the lab findings. Most likely, they drugged her to cause her to forget something else."

"Like what?" asked Crawford, who kept scrupulous notes and recorded the meeting.

"Your guess is as good as anyone's," replied the doctor. "All I can offer you are facts and test results. She has a bruise, resulting from a hard punch, most likely from a man, given the size and depth. Her clothing and personal effects are waiting for you to take custody."

"Thank God. Can I see her now?" Arlene asked, her fingers mimicking a snake pit.

"One more thing." Dr. Sylvan reached into the bag with Lisa's effects and pulled out two glassine envelopes, one holding a hundred-dollar bill and the other a twenty-dollar bill. "The nurse who found them in Ms. Jensen's bra thinks they're counterfeit."

Everyone perked up. Sparks lifted the envelopes to the fluorescent light.

"Your nurse has outstanding eyes. There is no print on the embedded strip the Treasury puts in for authentication," Sparks exclaimed, passing the envelopes to Cooper.

Cooper studied the bills and then tossed them to Crawford.

"It looks like Ms. Jensen may be involved in a counterfeiter ring investigation. They couldn't afford to kill her, so they drugged her to wipe out the memory of whatever she discovered. Arlene, do you know what she'd been working on?" Crawford asked.

"I do not know," Arlene shrugged. "I'll call Phil. He would have approved it."

"That's all I have for now." Dr. Sylvan rose to her feet. She looked at Arlene. "I don't see why you couldn't visit with her. However, I want to caution you that Lisa is in a fragile state. A chemically wiped-out memory is a serious condition. She cannot provide much information about the last few days. It's as if they never happened for her."

A chorus of "Thank you, Doctor" ensued, and Dr. Sylvan left the room with haste.

"We have nothing to contradict the findings in Ms. Richter's case, so my job here is done. I see no reason to torture Ms. Jensen further. If you uncover anything worth mentioning, you will call me, right?" Crawford shook hands with Cooper and Sparks. "Always a pleasure, Counselor. I am glad your friend is OK. Go talk to her. If she knows anything about my case, please let me know." Crawford picked up his notebook and marched out.

"I should talk to her first," Arlene said. "You can wait outside. Lisa suffered enough trauma. She needs a friendly face, not two male cops interrogating her."

"You're right, Counselor. We'll wait for you to let us know about your progress." Cooper stood and seized Sparks's elbow, speaking in one of his cartoon voices, "Let's go, pardner. Got us a fair maiden to watch over."

"You drive me nuts with your cartoon voices," muttered Sparks, grabbing the bag with Lisa's effects. "Sometimes I want to shoot you myself just to shut you up." Sparks stopped in his tracks and turned on a dime. Arlene collided with him. "Ask if she will see a hypnotherapist. We need something, anything, to help with the investigation into those five dead bodies."

"Even with hypnotherapy, she might remember nothing," Arlene said.

"I'll take anything I can get right about now," replied Sparks. "Coop, you go with her and watch the door. I have to check in at the shop and send these bills to the lab. Maybe we get a lead. I'm itching for some good news."

119

CHAPTER 41

ARLENE SPRINTED TO THE bed and hugged Lisa. They both broke into tears.

"How are you, girl? How are you holding up?" Arlene brushed Lisa's hair with the gentleness of a mother comforting her distressed child.

"They say I'm OK, but I feel lost. I remember nothing since last Friday." Lisa talked in a faltering voice, holding on to Arlene's arms as if they were lifelines.

"They found enough drugs in your system to knock out a herd of elephants, honey. The theory is that the drugs wiped your short-term memory. On the bright side, you weren't raped. Other than this rather sexy bruise on your cheek, you're A-OK."

"Sexy, my ass. You still don't know how to lie." Lisa managed a weak smile.

"We'll get through this. 'It's nothing but a thing.' That's our motto." Arlene retrieved a compact makeup case. "Let me take a stab at that bruise."

"Yeah, that's it. It's nothing but a thing, a lump in the road, not even big enough to be a speed bump." Lisa smiled and offered her cheek, still holding on to Arlene's forearm.

"That's my girl." Arlene wiped Lisa's tears and dabbed at the shiner. "Honey, we have to talk about what you remember. The nurses found counterfeit money in your bra. Good quality, I wouldn't have given them a second look. Does it mean anything to you?"

"Not a thing. I recall nothing at all, useful or not, after the party last Friday. I hoped you might fill the gaps, trigger something."

"Sure, honey, if you think it will help. We need to know what happened last night at Anna's place. The Fire Department found five dead bodies, and everyone is on edge."

"Why does everyone assume I know anything at all about what happened at Anna's place last night? The dead bodies could be drug dealers using the house for a deal that went south. I don't know. There could be a million other explanations that do not involve me."

Even as she argued the case, Lisa's inner voice kept asking the tough questions. What was she doing there last night, sleeping in the backseat only a few blocks away? How did she get that black eye? Whose blood smeared her clothes?

"Because, honey, you popped up at that scene, looking like hell, pumped full of designer drugs, carrying counterfeit currency, and you have amnesia. Something drew you there. You're a lawyer. Think like one. How does it all tie together?" Arlene's voice returned to the professional ADA tone, and she switched on a digital recorder.

"Arlene, I know nothing. I didn't even know Anna was dead. All I remember is waking up in my car this morning." Between tears and hiccups, Lisa recounted what she remembered.

Arlene finished covering up the contusion. She switched off the recorder. "I'm so sorry. I'm here for you, anything you need. We'll get through this. The most important thing is that you're OK." She flashed a conspiratorial smile. "Need be, we'll make up some fun memories. You and a sexy hunk of a movie star stranded on a deserted island."

"Can you help me get out of here?" Lisa chuckled and punched Arlene in the arm. "I feel like a stranger in my own body. Being here is so depressing. I need to get back to work. Do something useful before I drive myself crazy trying to remember this last week."

"Take it easy, hon," Arlene pushed Lisa's hair behind her ears. "Work will still be there when you get better. The bad guys always find substitutes, no matter how many you put away."

Lisa sighed and said, "I don't know any other way to get my mind off this. If there is nothing wrong with me physically, I should be able to go, right?"

"Listen. About that," Arlene saw an opening and took it. "Maybe you should talk to a hypnotherapist. They can help with those repressed memories."

"My friend Arlene asking? Or ADA Spikes?"

"Both, honey, both," admitted Arlene. "I want all of you back."

A loud argument erupted in the hallway. Arlene opened the door with care. Officer Cooper was engaged in an animated dispute with an elderly woman. The woman seemed familiar, but Arlene had a hard time placing her. The woman held a large shoulder bag behind her back, looking ready to swing it at Cooper. Cooper had his left arm out, attempting to keep the woman at a distance, while his right hand rested on the butt of his holstered gun.

"Officer Cooper, what's going on?" inquired Arlene.

"This woman threatened to hit me if I didn't allow her to see Ms. Jensen. She refuses to tell me who she is," Cooper answered, gaze trained on the woman.

"Madam, the officer is right. Ms. Jensen is in a delicate state, and she cannot have visitors," Arlene asserted.

"What are you doing in there?" Candy jutted her chin out, bag ready to strike.

"I'm with the District Attorney's office. We are investigating several murder cases, and Ms. Jensen has pertinent information."

"That's not true," said Candy. "I heard she has amnesia."

Cooper and Arlene exchanged baffled looks. Both their jaws dropped in sync.

"How do you know that?" Cooper recovered first.

Candy pressed her lips tighter together, drawing an imaginary zipper over them.

Cooper and Arlene both took a simultaneous step toward her. Candy stood her ground.

Intrigued by the quarrel, Lisa stepped out of the room.

"Hello, Mrs. Richter. Arlene, leave her alone. This is Anna's mom. Mrs. Richter, please come in. I'm so sorry about Anna." Lisa held out a hand reaching to Candy.

"It's OK, Officer. She is the mother of the woman who committed—I mean, who died Wednesday. Her daughter owned the home that burned down last night," Arlene offered.

Cooper removed his hand from his gun. "What a relief. The entire Irvine PD is looking for you, madam. I'll notify the investigators you are safe. They want to talk to you."

"Can I spend a few minutes with my daughter's friend first, Officer? She is in dire straits and I'm here to offer her my support." Candy's voice evoked melted butter.

"If that's OK with them." He gestured toward Lisa and Arlene.

They both nodded in agreement, and the three women disappeared into the room.

"Crazy old bat. I almost shot her." Cooper sat down and took several long breaths, shaking his head.

CHAPTER 42

FROM HIS SURVEILLANCE POST, J.P. scanned the UCI parking lot. His body had tensed up for a reason he had yet to fathom. He sighed and let his fingers drum on the steering wheel. His unconscious mind had registered something that had put him on high alert. His conscious mind was still struggling to figure it out.

His gaze locked on two black-clad men walking in step through the hospital door. He recognized that ballet like synchronization. J.P. identified the *Shadows*, the assassins who showed up at Anna's place the night before. He grabbed Sadowsky's gun and sprinted across the road, avoiding skidding cars, ignoring angry horns and expletives shouted by the motorists.

J.P. climbed the stairs three at a time. He braked on the reception counter with his arms and asked for Jensen's room. The volunteer asked his relation to the patient. J.P. waved the gun, and the old woman almost passed out. "Room number and location. Now!" yelled J.P.

"Room 326. Take the elevator and then down the hall and to the right toward the end," the volunteer replied in a meek voice, pointing to the elevator bank.

J.P. broke into a full run for the stairway, knocking over the security guard attempting to stop him.

CHAPTER 43

"ARE YOU READY FOR an actual bomb?" the duty sergeant, Pearce, asked.

Sparks tried to make sense of Pearce's somber voice. He groaned, "No more bad news, Sarge. I've had enough today, and it's not even noon."

"This is good news," replied Pearce. "Remember John Paul Morgan?"

"Who can forget him? The fucking *Butcher of Irvine*." Sparks grunted louder.

"We got an updated APB. Morgan shot an LAPD cop, and he is the prime suspect in killing everyone found at the Richter house. He's been running a counterfeiting ring. He is, I quote, 'mentally unstable, armed and extremely dangerous.' Wanted dead or alive." Pearce's voice switched to jubilant. "My gut says the emphasis is on 'dead.'"

"That's something you don't hear every day. Counterfeiting, huh? I'll keep my eyes open, Sarge. Check out those fake bills Ms. Jensen had on her. Maybe he's behind all this." Sparks whistled in surprise. He walked with a renewed spring in his step.

From the corner of his eye, Sparks noticed a blur of movement outside the hospital. His jaw hit the floor when he saw Morgan running at full speed toward the main entrance, gun in hand. Sparks made the connection between the APB on Morgan and Lisa Jensen being in the hospital. He broke into a full run, screaming into his lapel mike.

"Attention, all available units! Officer needs assistance at UCI Medical Center. Suspect John Paul Morgan sighted at main entrance carrying a weapon. I say again. All available units to UCI Medical Center. Suspect John Paul Morgan spotted carrying a handgun."

Sparks ran like an Olympic sprinter toward the main hospital elevator bank.

The volunteer at the front desk had just sat down to catch her breath after giving J.P. Lisa's room number. She picked up the phone to alert the other security guards, when Sparks crashed into her station, wielding his handgun.

"Where did he go?" Sparks yelled between heavy breaths.

No clarification needed, but she required a few seconds to find her words. "Room 326."

Sparks ran to the open elevator, determined to make sure Morgan did not get to Lisa Jensen, and that Morgan did not get away this time. It was time for him to pay for everything. The murder charges he skated on, the embarrassment he caused the Irvine PD, for the countless other victims who, without a doubt, suffered at his hands afterwards.

CHAPTER 44

COOPER HEARD HIS PARTNER'S radio call and jumped to his feet, pushing the chair back with a loud scrape. He retrieved his gun and held it along his thigh, sprinting to the T end of the empty hallway. "Talk to me, Randy. Where is the son of a bitch? Is he coming my way?" He noticed Parker and Ryder. They walked toward him in an odd, harmonized manner, mirrored aviator shades scanning their surroundings in sync. Cooper let go of the button on his lapel mike. "May I—"

Parker lifted his arm, and Cooper's eyes locked on the strange object pointing at him. Before his brain identified the silencer, the bullet had already entered his forehead. Cooper fell backward like a broken life-size doll, legs akimbo, partially blocking the hallway. The sound of the falling body was louder than the report of the gun. Parker and Ryder never broke stride.

They stepped over Cooper's body, avoiding the pooling blood, and continued to Lisa's room.

CHAPTER 45

J.P. REACHED THE THIRD floor and crashed through the stairs door into a deserted hallway. He noticed a pair of legs on the floor, bent at an odd angle. He dashed to the T junction and saw Cooper's body, complete with the third eye. He peeked around the corner. The *Shadows* walked past the halfway point of the passage. J.P. lifted his gun, aiming in their general direction, and sauntered behind them, careful to avoid alerting them.

Sparks squeezed between the elevator doors before they opened all the way. He saw the pair of legs sticking out from the hallway. He realized they belonged to his partner, and a black fog settled over his brain. Sparks rushed to the corridor, focusing on the hole in Cooper's forehead. He tried to shove down his rage, and he spun around, glimpsing Morgan tiptoeing down the hallway, away from Cooper's fresh corpse.

Sparks adopted a shooter's stance and pointed his gun at Morgan's back. "Freeze, Morgan. Police. Drop your gun and keep your hands where I can see them."

J.P. halted and lifted his arms in slow motion. Parker and Ryder spun in unison, both their guns coming up midway through the turn. They fired a mere millisecond apart. J.P.'s lizard brain reacted first, and he crashed through the door on his right.

The two silenced bullets passed through the space where J.P.'s chest had been and hit Sparks. First round pierced his left shoulder, one inch above his bulletproof vest. The second connected with his body armor, knocking him off his feet. Sparks's head flopped backward and smashed against the wall. His gun clattered on the polished tile. His eyes closed in slow motion as blood seeped into an octopus-shaped crimson puddle under his body.

Arlene stepped into the hallway. Her gaze followed the corridor. First, she noticed Parker and Ryder's backs, dressed in black tactical gear. Then she perceived the uniformed cops lying at the end of the hallway in separate, expanding scarlet pools. "What's going on?"

Ryder turned. Arlene focused on the silencer. She attempted to rush back into the room. The round pierced her temple, thrusting her and pieces of her skull and gray matter against the doorframe. She was dead long before her body had finished sliding to the stone floor, where it settled in a shapeless heap.

Inside the room, Lisa and Candy yelped and jumped to their feet, like two squirrels ready to scramble up a tree in search of safety.

J.P. collected himself off the floor. He ignored the shrieking woman and smashed the mirror with the pistol grip, picked a sliver, and crouched by the main door, sticking his left hand out into the hallway. He saw the two Shadows, one facing him, the other the opposite end of the hallway. Beyond them, he noticed a woman's body slumped in a doorway, half in, half out of the room. Nobody else ventured out into the hallway.

J.P. read the number on the door above him: 320. The room with the body in the doorway had to be 326. *Candy?* J.P. sighed with relief upon realizing that clothing did not match. It could have been Lisa Jensen. He experienced a brief pang of satisfaction at the thought. Then his inner voice admonished him. Not even Lisa Jensen deserved to die like that.

In the mirror shard, he observed the Shadow facing him raise his weapon. J.P. withdrew his hand just as the bullet bounced off the tile floor. The slug ricocheted along the hallway, passed through Sparks's right foot, and then came to rest in the growing pool of his blood.

Behind J.P., the woman screamed like a banshee but did not dare move. J.P. shoved his left hand out, holding the mirror fragment, and assessed the situation. Both killers faced toward him, advancing with their guns at the ready. J.P. stood, faced the wall, and exchanged the gun and the mirror in his hands. He raised his left hand above his head and then reached out into the corridor. He pointed in a slight downward angle and fired two rounds. The deafening report of his gun reverberated off the walls for several seconds, as if a giant wrecking ball had struck the building.

J.P. heard with satisfaction the stomach-turning crunch of a bone shattered by the bullet. The surprised cry coming from one killer brought a sly smile to his face.

Gotcha, bastard. That is for interfering with my chance to interrogate Sadowsky.

Shuffling sounds filtered from the hallway. J.P. heard a door kicked open, followed by dragging sounds, a couple of shouts, and then silence.

J.P. swapped the gun and mirror shard and then ventured another quick peek down the empty passage. A trail of blood led into room 324. He glided in silence toward room 326. A soft moan drew his attention to Sparks, slumped in an awkward position against the wall behind him, in the middle of two pools of blood.

J.P. returned to the T junction. Cooper's forehead showed there was nothing J.P. could do for him. He collected the cops' firearms and hauled Sparks into the closest available room by the back of his bulletproof vest. He gave the injured cop a cursory examination, taking in the details of each wound.

"Through-and-through wound," he muttered, dropping the guns in the nightstand's top drawer. He noticed the second bullet embedded in the body armor. "This is your lucky day, pal. You wore your vest to work." J.P.'s eyes dropped to Sparks's bloody foot. The shoe had a through-and-through bullet hole. "No dancing for a while, but at least you are alive, Officer Sparks. You are a very lucky man. These guys are bad news."

He shoved one towel under the front and back of the vest, covering the shoulder wound. He removed Sparks's shoe and wrapped the second towel around the injured foot. He called the switchboard, requested a trauma team to tend to Sparks, and then hurried down the hall.

J.P. entered the deserted room 326. He checked the bathroom — vacant. He noticed the window with the broken pane. Below lay the adjacent building's second-story roof. He stepped out, looked around for Candy, then ventured to room 324. He peeked inside just in time to see two women cowering in their beds and one Shadow executing his wounded partner. The women's terrified eyes resembled ping-pong balls, barely visible above the blankets.

J.P. had a hard time accepting the psychotic behavior he witnessed. These maniacs executed people as if they were in a video game, one equipped with a RESET button. J.P. pinched himself to make sure he was not dreaming.

Parker, standing at attention, saluted Ryder's dead body and then collected the silenced weapon and dog tags. He glanced out the window. Seeing J.P.'s face, Parker's features contorted like a Francis Bacon portrait. He lifted his arm and shot twice. J.P. was already on the move back to room 326. Parker stormed out of the room and ran down the hallway past Cooper's dead body. He turned the corner and disappeared through the staircase door.

J.P. exited room 326 with caution into the deserted corridor, save for Cooper's dead body. He entered room 324 with his gun leveled in front of him. Both women pointed to the door, shaking like leaves in the wind. He kicked the wall in anger and walked over to Cooper's body. The bullet hole was still there in the officer's forehead.

J.P. bowed his head. *So young. I will get them, kid. I promise.*

J.P. reentered the room where he had left Sparks. He squeezed Sparks's injured shoulder. Sparks's eyes fluttered open. His mien darkened and warped with fury.

"Morgan, you son of a bitch. You are under arrest."

"I admire your spirit, Officer Sparks. Now, listen, because I do not have a lot of time, and you want to hear everything I have to say."

Sparks attempted to stand, but the pain in his foot was excruciating. J.P. helped him to a comfortable position, lifted the injured foot and placed a pillow under it. "Listen carefully. In room 324, there is a body. He is one of the two guys who shot you and your partner." J.P. laid it all out in Reader's Digest format about Lisa's kidnapping and the murders at Anna's home. Sparks listened with clenched teeth, fighting in vain to gain control over Morgan.

Outside the hospital, police sirens grew louder.

The trauma team rushed from the elevator, amidst rattling gurney and equipment.

"The cavalry is here. Time for me to move on," said J.P.

"That is heavy stuff. Morgan, let me take you in right now. I guarantee your safety, and I'll help you through this," Sparks pleaded.

"Tempting, Officer Sparks. I still have bitter memories of my last encounter with Irvine PD. If I live through this, I will turn myself in with all the evidence. I have to take care of an old friend who just lost her daughter. These maniacs murdered Anna Richter too. Sadowsky and Smythe did it, and I have evidence implicating the people who ordered it. Set the record straight. It would mean the world to her mother." J.P. dashed out of the room.

"Who are Sadowsky and Smythe again?" Sparks attempted to delay J.P. He struggled to stand, but the pain and loss of blood caused him to fall back. He rallied and hopped to the door, yelling after Morgan to stop.

CHAPTER 46

"CANDY, ARE YOU OK?"** J.P. sighed with the force of a small tornado.

"J.P., thank God. We're OK. Are you OK? Where are you? We've been looking all over for you. God, I thought I lost you too." Candy's voice warmed J.P.'s heart.

"Do not worry about me. The two killers were there for Lisa Jensen. One of them is dead, the other still on the loose. Stay out of sight. Where are you?"

"We're leaning against your truck. You didn't lock it, but we didn't know what to do. Inside it's even hotter than outside," Candy replied.

"Just push the START button. The key is inside. Keep out of sight and wait for me to call you when I am ready," J.P. instructed her.

"How long will it be?" Candy's voice faltered with anxiety.

"A while. I am in surgery right now," J.P. stunned her.

"Real pandemonium down there," observed Candy, taking it all in. The hospital parking lot swarmed with cops, patients, and medical personnel. Police cars with wide-open doors laid abandoned everywhere like butterflies that crashed into the ground. Most cruisers still had the roof racks lit. Two fire engines added color to the living, moving landscape.

Twenty minutes later, the phone chirped and Candy snatched on the first ring.

"This is J.P. Morgan, calling for a pickup." J.P. attempted to sound chipper. "I am at the gas station on University by the south on-ramp."

"Oh yeah, I know it," said Candy. "We'll be there in two minutes."

"Who is 'we'?" J.P. wondered aloud. "That is the third time she said 'we.'"

CHAPTER 47

T HE SUV SKIDDED TO a stop, and J.P.'s eyes bulged out. Candy drove, and Lisa Jensen sat in the passenger seat, wrapped in J.P.'s blanket, sporting a dark scowling look. Candy squeezed between seats onto the back chair. J.P. slipped into the driver's seat, ignoring Lisa's glare. He drove south onto the 405 Freeway and took the next exit, then headed east.

Lisa retreated and flattened herself against the passenger door.

"I would introduce you, but it's rather obvious you already know each other. Play nice, both of you." Candy stuck her face between the seats.

"I'm here because you said the *Butcher* has a recording that proves what happened to me last night. I don't have to pretend to enjoy this. Let's see it," Lisa shot back.

J.P. scanned the surroundings, his eyes bouncing like a spectator's at a tennis match.

"Now is an excellent time. The shorter this encounter is, the better." Lisa grimaced.

"You have a point there," J.P. conceded. He turned right, then right, and right again, arriving back at Sand Canyon Avenue. He stopped at the red light, preparing to turn left, back toward the freeway. He turned to Candy. "What did you tell her?"

"Not much. Just that you knew what happened to her last night and have recordings of the events. Then all hell broke loose. Someone shot that charming girl, Arlene. Lisa had to break the window, and we skipped out of there, scurrying like roadrunners on the roof. At my age!" Candy ended in a shriek, throwing her hands up in the air.

"I am sorry about your friend," J.P. said, stealing a sideways look at Lisa. "Those two were pros. She should have stayed inside the room."

"I'm sure you are sorry. I think you killed her. We didn't see any other shooters, did we, Mrs. Richter? Are you now coming after me, Morgan? Huh?" Lisa demanded.

"We talked enough. Let's try silence for a long while. Then we can watch the recordings. I will give you some context information and copies, and then we go our separate ways. God knows I can barely stand being this close to you." J.P.'s voice sounded like icebergs bouncing off each other.

"Fine. The less time we spend together, the shorter the shower I'll need," Lisa replied.

J.P. focused on the traffic on Sand Canyon. He noticed a black Chrysler 300 blowing through the intersection at high speed and then braking hard and sliding into a sudden U-turn with no regard for the oncoming vehicles. J.P. checked his rearview mirrors. In the passenger-side mirror, he detected part of the front grille of a Ford Explorer, two cars behind him in the next lane. Behind the plastic lattice, almost invisible, was a blue lamp.

"Damn it. How did they find us?" He glanced at Lisa and then at Candy. Puzzled, he scanned the interior of the SUV and then assessed the traffic on both sides of Sand Canyon.

CHAPTER 48

"**WHO FOUND US?**" Candy and Lisa asked in concert, craning their heads.

J.P. did not answer. He concentrated on the Chrysler headed their way. He slammed his foot on the gas, ignoring the red light, and crossed four lanes of traffic without colliding with anyone. Amid angry horn beeps, sending a slew of cars sideways into the opposing traffic lanes, he turned left into the freeway-bound lanes.

The Explorer flashed its under-the-grille lights and turned on the siren. The Chrysler performed an elaborate slalom, avoiding cars that crossed its path, aiming for J.P.'s Expedition.

The Explorer broke free from the pack of vehicles at the red light and joined the pursuit. J.P. held the gas pedal to the floor, heading toward the freeway. The powerful V8 responded, and they gained on their pursuers. The Chrysler and Explorer gave chase, with lights flashing and sirens wailing, ignoring the other cars in the road.

"Are you insane? You want to get us killed?" cried Lisa. "Pull over this instant. Those are police officers in pursuit. You must obey them."

"So were the guys who kidnapped your prissy ass last night," J.P. retorted. "I bet the killers who showed up at the hospital this morning, with orders to eliminate you, were Law Enforcement Officers as well. Come to think about it; they probably had an appointment; you just forgot about it. Amnesia and all."

Lisa shot him a dirty look, clutched the armrest, and closed her eyes in prayer.

"Now sit there, hold on for dear life, and let me see if I can get us out in one piece. And maybe, just maybe, we live to see the sunset tonight."
Not together, I hope.

J.P. turned on two wheels, passed on the shoulder, disregarding the red light at the end of the on-ramp, and joined the northbound traffic on the freeway, at over eighty miles per hour.

"Let me have that phone." J.P. stuck his hand out to Candy. They were now traveling at over 100 mph, creating quite a stir in their wake. He dialed and pushed TALK.

Lisa opened her eyes, saw the phone in his hand, and exploded. "You are completely mad. Pull over, now." She reached for the steering wheel. J.P. slapped her hand away.

"Fred! Kill all the cameras for two miles around the office. Now. Get out and stay mobile. I will call you shortly." J.P. ended the call and then shot across two lanes of traffic, aiming for the Jamboree Road exit. He left the freeway at 90 mph, performing a daredevil's slalom through the slowing traffic and on the shoulder, earning himself another throng of angry horn toots and flashing headlights. He headed east on Jamboree and moved to the far-left lane.

The Chrysler remained glued to his rear bumper. The Explorer followed close behind. J.P. slowed down as he approached the intersection with Barranca Parkway.

Lisa stared at him as the blood drained from her face and knuckles. The red light ahead sent chills up and down her spine, and she braced for dear life. She watched mesmerized as J.P. lowered the visor and revealed a traffic preemptive device, the kind emergency vehicles used to manipulate traffic lights. Still concentrating on the rearview mirror, J.P. pushed the button and then slammed the brakes, sending the SUV in a violent skid.

The Chrysler crashed into them. Everything not secured sailed forward toward the windshield. Candy's purse smashed into the windshield and then bounced into Lisa's lap. Lisa, Candy, and J.P. slumped forward violently and then rebounded in their seats. The Explorer rear-ended the Chrysler and propelled it into J.P.'s SUV's trailer hitch. The hitch went through the radiator of the Chrysler and cracked its engine block.

J.P. pushed the gas to the floor, and the SUV sprung forward, with the Chrysler still attached to the hook. He drove through the intersection as the light turned green. At the last moment, he jerked the steering wheel to the left. The large vehicle groaned in protest but turned on two wheels, causing the Chrysler to detach and continue its sideways journey into the Jamboree Road pedestrian refuge. The Chrysler's passenger-side wheels hit the curb surrounding the median strip, flipped over, and came to rest on its roof in the flower bed.

J.P. sped off on Barranca toward MacArthur.

Behind them, the impaired Explorer attempted to keep up. The damaged front fender rubbed on the Explorer's front wheels, and its busted radiator whistled, sending up angry clouds of steam. Coldwell gave up. He pulled over, jumped out, and shot an entire clip at J.P.'s SUV that was getting away.

One bullet hit the cracked rear window, shattering it, and the flying shards of glass peppered the interior of the Expedition.

Enraged by the failure, Coldwell kicked the Explorer's front tire, flailing his arms and screaming like a small boy who had lost his favorite toy. Maxwell, his partner, removed the gun from his trembling hands and forced him to sit on the sidewalk.

CHAPTER 49

"**T**HAT WAS EASIER THAN I expected," muttered J.P. "Is everyone OK?"

Lisa pummeled him with both fists, her fury in crescendo mode stressed by small spitballs. "You could have killed us. You are insane. Let me out of this car this instant."

J.P. did his best to protect himself. Keeping the vehicle steady on the road proved to be a hard task while enduring Lisa's violent pounding. The blanket bunched around Lisa's waist as she punched his shoulder without restraint, grunting louder with every hit.

"Nice breasts. Mother Nature or man-made?" J.P. asked.

Disoriented, Lisa ceased her assault. She looked down at the flimsy gown covering her chest and retreated. She pulled the blanket tighter around her slender, shivering frame.

"Thank you," smirked J.P. "Where can I drop you off, Ms. Jensen? Obviously, you are not grateful about my saving your life. Again. Have it your way. I give you four hours."

"Four hours for what?" Lisa spat back, poised to strike like a cobra.

"Before they find and kill you. Last night, I watched them slay three of their own, along with two of Irvine's finest. One assassin who came after you at the hospital today, *executed* his wounded partner in room 324. I am sure you will be dead inside of two hours. Four is a safer choice. I do not take sucker bets. Where would you like me to drop you off?"

"J.P., be serious. You can't abandon her." Candy gripped his shoulder.

He turned on a side street and pulled over in front of a squat, gray, single-story office building. "Goodbye, Ms. Jensen. It was a true displeasure seeing you again. Let's not make a habit of meeting this often. My poor heart can only take so much."

"Maniac." Lisa's voice quivered. "You evaded police officers. All they wanted was to talk, probably ask questions about what happened at the hospital today."

"I'm sure you are right," countered J.P. "Wait. I know this one. They wrote their questions on the bullets. They intended us to catch the slugs and answer their queries at our earliest convenience. They did not want us to get bored at the morgue while we waited for our autopsies. How considerate."

Lisa pounded the dashboard with both fists and let out a frustrated scream. She stepped out of the car, slamming the door, and then strode ahead, with no idea where she was going.

J.P. drove up to her, lowered the passenger window, and asked, "May I have my blanket back, Ms. Jensen? It gets cold at night."

"Get another one, freak. Better yet, go to hell. You won't need it there."

J.P. displayed his best pretend-hurt look, placing his hand over his heart. "Been there, more times than you can imagine. It is not as warm and cozy as you may think." Then he shrugged and drove away.

The head slap surprised J.P., causing him to brake violently. His nose collided with the steering wheel. Candy's voice amazed him. "Knock it off this instant. That poor girl is in danger. I know you don't mean this. Stop the car, let her back in, and let's go figure this out."

Lisa could not resist smiling. The 5'-3" frail old woman smacking the 6'-5", bear-sized fellow around—now that was a show worth watching. And she had front row tickets.

"Yes, Mom," answered J.P. in a mocking tone. He turned to the rolled-down window. "Ms. Jensen, can you find it in your heart to forgive my temporary lapse in manners?"

Lisa struggled to avoid laughing. Despite everything she had experienced, the situation was funny. Watching Morgan squirm brought a cheerful grin to her face. She looked very much like a girl expecting a tasty treat at the county fair. "Only if you promise it'll never happen again." She folded her arms across her chest.

"Scout's honor, Ms. Jensen." J.P. lifted two fingers to his eyebrow. "Please get back in before we draw attention to ourselves."

"Lisa, get back in the car. Despite his bravado, all the crap he spews out is just that. Crap. He has a heart of gold, and he would never allow you to get hurt," Candy pleaded.

"More like a heart of gold... stone. I saw what he did to his wife and nephew. Those images still haunt my dreams to this day." Lisa quavered, closing the passenger door.

CHAPTER 50

"**I**F WE ARE DOING this, I need something from you, Ms. Jensen," J.P. said.

"*You* need something from *me?*" She braced her back against the passenger door and then re-crossed her arms over her chest, clutching the blanket, her newfound shield.

"You will not make this easy." J.P. sighed.

"I won't agree to do anything to help you. You ran from the police, endangered lives, destroyed two police vehicles, hurt, maybe even killed several peace officers. You want something from me, an Assistant DA. If you expect immunity for what happened, forget it. I will gladly testify against you at the trial. I hope they put you in the ground or in a dark cage for the rest of your miserable life."

"Is she always like this?" J.P. looked back at Candy. "I am doing my best to help her when every fiber of my body wants to kick her to the curb."

"Lisa, keep quiet, please. I want him to help you. They murdered my Annie. They would have killed you and me, too, if it wasn't for J.P." Candy stated.

"Ms. Jensen, I need your word that whatever you learn until we resolve this situation stays with you. You cannot use the information against me, and you definitely cannot use it against any of my friends. You are an attorney, so you know about keeping secrets."

"I'm not your attorney," she spewed back.

J.P. reached into his pocket, pulled out a money clip, and selected a dollar bill. Then he leaned over and stuck it behind the blanket at the base of Lisa's neck. "Now you are."

"What is this? Do you think I'm that cheap?"

"I retained you as my lawyer. Remember *The Client,* when Susan Sarandon asks the boy to give her a dollar and tells him she is his attorney?"

"Are you out of your mind?" Lisa's head bobbed back and forth from J.P. to Candy.

"I retain you temporarily as my lawyer. You must observe attorney-client privilege. You can never mention what you see, hear, or learn about my life and my friends. In return, I offer to keep you alive, at least until this is over. Afterward, the status quo can resume."

"It's a fantastic deal, Lisa. If there's anyone who will do the impossible to keep you out of harm's way, it's J.P., no matter how he claims to feel about you," Candy urged.

"You understand I cannot be a party to concealing anything illegal or help in the commission of any crimes. I could lose my license, my job, everything."

"You forgot your life," J.P. said.

"What about my life?" Lisa's voice trembled again.

"You forgot the chance to lose your life. I say, do not take the deal. Go on your merry way. By 5:00 p.m., your coworkers, friends, and family will start making funeral arrangements for you. I plan to attend it, to make sure it is for real."

"You are serious, aren't you?" Lisa asked. J.P.'s words sounded like an ominous thunder in her mind. She knew she did not have all the facts. Something just beyond her conscious grasp told her she should trust him, against her better judgment.

"They found *me* today. I am hard to find. They *pinpointed* us on a road I had no intention of taking until I turned on it. You know what those odds are? Winning the Powerball and MegaMillions jackpots in the same week has better odds."

Lisa dismissed him with a hand gesture but said nothing. He sounded sure of himself, and she had no information to disprove his case.

"The two assassins who came after you this morning executed everyone at Anna's home last night. Two of the murdered men were—let's leave this for later. I will wager everything I have you will not make it to sunset on your own. Even standing in the middle of the DA's office or a fully staffed police station." J.P. finished with a scoff.

"My God, you have information about last night's killings? We have to go to the police right now and tell them everything you know." Lisa reached again for the ADA hat.

"That was the plan before the party poopers showed up at the hospital. There is an APB on me. Some people hope, others pray, that I meet at least one bullet head-on. You get why I feel apprehensive about walking into any cop shop."

"Why would the police shoot you?" His comment baffled Lisa.

"Because the guys I rescued you from last night accused me of shooting a cop."

"Did you?" Lisa inquired.

"Did I... what?"

"Shoot the cop," Lisa said, twirling a loose hair strand.

"No. Their boss executed Officer Jamie Smythe for allowing me to tail him and his partner back to their nest after they—" J.P. stopped in mid-sentence. "It seems such a minor offense, but there you have it. He got shot between the eyes, and I recorded it. Then I went to Anna's home and recorded all the execution-style murders that took place there."

"After they..." Lisa latched on his unfinished statement. "What are you hiding?"

"Not relevant. At the hospital, I gave Officer Sparks of Irvine PD an informal statement. I told him most of what I learned. When this is over, I will go to the cops. Right now, I do not know what I know."

"What kind of BS is that? You 'don't know what you know?'" parroted Lisa.

"No time to explain it all right now. Please accept my proposition. Later, I will share with you everything I discovered last night. Baby steps."

"So, if I don't take this deal of yours, you won't tell me anything, and I'm doomed to die before sunset, is that it?" Lisa raised her eyebrows, batting her eyelashes.

"If you agree, you can keep the dollar."

"Lisa, it's pucker time. With the damaged car, we're bound to attract unwanted attention." Candy reached out and touched Lisa's shoulder.

"OK. I'll take the deal, with some conditions."

"Oh, Lisa, come on!" exclaimed Candy.

"No, Candy, it is perfectly OK," said J.P. "Ms. Jensen, I accept all your conditions. Let's get moving." He shifted into DRIVE and pulled away from the curb.

"That's preposterous," cried Lisa. "You can't accept all my conditions without hearing them first."

"I do not need to know your pre-requisites. All I ask is that you respect my friends' privacy and do not use something you may learn against me or them. That is the deal."

Lisa found herself speechless. She kept thinking of a comeback while J.P. drove into the parking lot of a small warehouse park. He pushed a button on the SUV's HomeLink, and one door rolled up. J.P. pulled inside, cut the engine, and stepped out. The giant door squeaked its way down.

CHAPTER **51**

"GODDAMN. MOTHERFUCKING. ASSSHOLE. That Morgan!" Purcell hung up. He imagined how rewarding it would be to kick a guest chair. He dreamed with satisfaction of sending it across the room to crash the glass doors to Clancy's fancy bookshelves.

Clancy watched silently, waiting for the actual news. They were in the private office Clancy kept for himself at Site B. Site B was a mirror image of the warehouse dubbed Site C, except for Clancy's private space carved out of the second-floor briefing room. Site B became overcrowded with the people and materials moved from the abandoned Sites A & C. Clancy stayed in the safety of his own office to avoid questions from his troops with tempers as heated as the air both inside and outside.

"He got away again. He disabled both cars we sent after him. They lost him near John Wayne Airport. We're checking traffic cameras to reacquire him. Timmons and Corelli rolled over in pursuit. It's a colossal mess. Cruiser is a total loss. They got away with just cuts and bruises. But Irvine PD is asking questions about our officers operating in their territory without IPD knowledge. They are holding our guys unofficially for now." Purcell spat it all out.

"You keep underestimating this Morgan character. It seems he's a one-man demolition crew, hell-bent on screwing up our well-laid plans. What will it take for you and your alleged *exceptionally trained* men to deal with him once and for all?" Clancy demanded.

"He got lucky once more, sir. It will not happen again. I'll make sure we deal with him." Purcell snapped to attention. "I'll rip his heart out with my own two hands. In my entire career, I never felt so humiliated and annoyed by a trash bug like him."

Clancy watched, amused, as Purcell regressed to his military days. "Purcell, you better remove this Morgan thorn from our side. I think it's time we paid attention to the final details of our operation. Our country's future demands it." Clancy enjoyed putting the screws to his men when he could. He believed it kept them focused and sharp.

"Yes, sir! Anything else, sir?" Purcell barked, still standing at attention.

"Get the Irvine chief of police on the phone. I'll sort it out. When all those idiots who lost Morgan get back, I want a word with them in person. Same for Parker. I want to hear from his own mouth how Ryder died, how they messed up this simple task. All they had to do was eliminate an unarmed woman who doesn't remember a thing and had no reason to fear them."

"Yes, sir, right away." Purcell executed a full turn.

"Purcell, get me the file on Morgan," added Clancy as an afterthought.

"The file, sir?" Purcell froze in his tracks. "What file?"

"The one that starts with the name of the doctor who assisted his bitch mother in the delivery room and ends with what he had for dinner last night, just before he decided to screw with our plans!" Clancy screamed, whacking the desk with both fists. "That file."

"Coming right up, sir."

Clancy's desk phone rang a minute later.

"Thank you for taking my call, Chief. I'm sure you are busy there today. I've been monitoring your situation."

CHAPTER 52

L ISA CLIMBED OUT AND helped Candy exit from the back of
the SUV.

J.P. had parked next to another Expedition EL. This one was
silver, otherwise a replica of the black one. A midnight blue Toyota
Avalon completed the mini fleet. The warehouse looked like any other
rented by contractors, tile setters, or local printers. An electric charge
filled the air, the kind encountered around power lines or transformers.

Most of the place was empty, save for stacks of unmarked boxes
lined up against the far wall. Two state-of-the-art electronic banks of
computers, monitors, and communications equipment filled the left
wall. On the right and entrance sides were three offices and a large
conference room with eight high-back leather chairs surrounding a pool
table. The three-piece mahogany conference tabletop rested against a
wall, and a cue lay on the table. It looked as if someone was coming
right back to finish the game.

On the far wall of the conference room, there were nine triangular
casings, six holding folded US flags. The other three held French, UK,
and Australian banners.

Lisa wondered about the flags. They gave those to the families of
people fallen in the line of duty. To the best of her knowledge, J.P. did
not have any fallen heroes in his family.

J.P. returned with women's clothes and running shoes. "I have no
underwear or bra handy." He handed Lisa the apparel, who accepted
it with a gratified expression. She was pleased to have real clothes. She
examined the space and turned to J.P. with an inquisitive glare. His
pose put any mime to shame.

"Where can I change?" Lisa asked.

"Right here is fine by me," replied J.P.

"J.P. Morgan," Candy exclaimed. "You had better behave."

"You cannot blame a guy for trying." J.P. put his hands up in mock surrender, with a smirk worthy of any kid eyeing an ice cream cone. "There is a bathroom behind the offices. The door is just out of sight."

"Why do you keep doing this, J.P.?" asked Candy when they were alone.

"She had her fun all those years ago. A little payback will not hurt her."

"J.P., you are better than this petty crap. Focus on the task in front of us. There are bad people trying to kill that girl. They already killed my Annie. Knock it off, will you? Help her out now, and she may return the favor one day." Candy shook her head and her finger in unison as if admonishing a misbehaving teenager.

"Yes, *Mom*. Right now, I would settle for getting away from her. Forever." J.P. started transferring everything from the damaged black SUV into its silver twin. He added some equipment bags and several aluminum cases.

Lisa returned wearing a black T-shirt and a pair of jeans that were tight and long on her. She rolled up the bottom of the jeans' legs. She still looked striking, despite her mangled hair and the makeup-covered bruise.

"Everything to your liking?" asked J.P.

"It will do for now. Shoes are two or three sizes too big," quipped Lisa, shaking her left foot for effect. The running shoe almost fell off. She reached down and straightened it.

"It is all we have in stock. Well, I can offer you a pair of men's shoes, size 15 wide. You could stick both your feet in each shoe."

J.P. turned to Candy and handed her a credit card with a picture of tropical fish.

"Ms. Jensen, this warehouse and everything you learn while you are a guest here is part of our deal. Are we clear on that?" J.P. slapped his hands together.

Annoyed, Lisa stuck her tongue out and then nodded with reluctance.

"We cannot use our credit or debit cards, none of the usual stuff. This is for unavoidable emergencies only. The pin is 9642. That spells 'yoga,' thanks to Anna. You can withdraw up to $1,500 a day at ATMs, especially on casino floors. Use it at gas stations or any places with automated pay options. You may use it at restaurants or online. Everywhere else, they may ask for ID, and things could get dicey."

"You said we couldn't use credit cards." Lisa rested her hands on her hips.

"Yes, I did. They will trace ours," replied J.P.

"Why are you giving it to her then?" Lisa asked. "Is it stolen? Counterfeit?"

"Lisa Jensen, ladies and gentlemen, 100 percent DA, 100 percent of the time. Come and get yours while supplies last." J.P. shook his head in mock disbelief, gesturing with both arms like a show host introducing a guest. "This is a special, almost magical card, untraceable to us."

"Bullshit. There is no such thing. Every time you swipe a card, it leaves an electronic trace. Even fifth graders know that." Lisa kept at it.

"That is true, Ms. Jensen. I said, '*untraceable to us*.' What makes a card conspicuous is where the paper trail points. This card's path does not lead anywhere near us."

"Huh?"

CHAPTER 53

"**N**O WONDER CROOKS STAY** ahead of you. This one was for Anna, in case she ever needed to leave no paper trail. It is a corporate card in her name. However, no one can tie Anna's name to this corporation under any circumstances." He handed it over to Lisa.

The card read *A. Richter*, and under the name was an enigmatic corporation name.

"Isn't it illegal to use a corporate credit card without being an officer of, or at least associated with, the corporation?"

"There you go with the legal and illegal crap. The incorporators empowered certain individuals to execute financial agreements on behalf of the corporation."

"I went to law school. Skip this stuff. Get to what makes this card so remarkable."

"I just told you. Nobody can tie the corporation and the card to Anna." J.P. shrugged.

"How can she have a corporate card then?" Lisa became more frustrated.

"The treasurer of the corporation can establish a company credit card account. The treasurer then can request cards for authorized users, without providing additional information. The corporation assumes complete liability for the account. The banks are happy to provide the cards. More fees for the bank."

"Oh, I get it. What happens if the authorized user uses the card for illegal purposes? The corporation and its treasurer get stuck with the liability. All banks require the identity of each individual card user for their records and for government reporting."

"Not all banks need to do that. I guess the treasurer must trust those users implicitly." J.P. assumed a candid expression, like a mischievous child daring a sibling.

"Who is the treasurer in this case?" Lisa continued her cross-examination.

"A friend of mine." J.P.'s smirk reflected his delight.

"How come this friend of yours trusts Anna?" Lisa stayed on track with the relentless obsession of the lawyer seeking the end of the thread during cross-examination.

"He doesn't even know Anna. He knows of her, but never met her," J.P. answered.

"Why did he get a card in her name?" Lisa asked.

"I asked him to. Very nicely, I may add." J.P. did his best not to laugh. Lisa's mind amused him. It worked only in terms of black and white, legal and illegal.

"You are impossible. Are you going to tell me, or do I have to drag it out of you one question at a time for the next five hours?"

"I thought you enjoyed twenty-question games, grilling an uncooperative witness. I am sure you have done that before." He broke into a short laugh, wondering if she could ever drop the consummate Assistant District Attorney hat, or think in shades of gray.

"Can you get to the point? This must stop. You promised." Candy stepped in.

"What has to stop?" Lisa caught the bone in midair and latched on to it.

J.P. looked at Candy with an expression that begged her not to answer.

"That he would stop toying with you as payback for the things you said and did when you prosecuted him," Candy answered anyway, waving a finger at Morgan.

"Is that what you're doing? Blaming me for doing my job?" Lisa placed her hands on her hips and took two steps forward, getting under J.P.'s face.

"You could have done your job with less enthusiasm and more concern for the truth and facts. The things you pushed on the jury and the media were conjecture, speculation, and biased interpretation. The attacks were personal. We both know it."

"That was me doing my job. I saw what you did to that poor woman and that little boy. I had to be passionate about it. I had to make it personal for every juror in that box. I had to make sure they saw you for who you are, and that justice was served." Lisa stood on her toes, still several inches short of being nose to nose with J.P. Her lithe body shuddered with fury.

"What happened to 'innocent until proven guilty'? You could not know I did it. Even *I did not know.* You wanted to make a name for yourself. You drew erroneous conclusions from other people's work, who presented only the info they wanted, so you would prosecute." J.P. probed, trying to learn what made her tick and how she reacted under pressure.

"I had to convince myself before I ever set foot in the courtroom. Otherwise, I could never persuade the jury. That was my job. If you blame me for doing it well, screw you."

"There is a slight error in your statement," he pointed out in a calm voice. He knew she had reached the breaking point. He liked the fact that, right or wrong, she stood by her actions.

"Do tell. I had no doubt about your guilt. I still don't. I did my job the best way I knew how. And I don't deserve this crap from you."

One more flick, and over the proverbial edge she goes. I wonder if she may need a parachute. Well, let's see. J.P. was pushing the envelope too far, but he needed to know.

"Did your job include sleeping with your boss and doing his dirty work at my trial?"

CHAPTER 54

SPARKS'S EXTEDED FAMILY, COPS and their families filled the emotionally charged waiting room beyond capacity. Almost forty people held their collective breath, waiting to hear the surgery results. The surgeon walked in, then stopped when faced with the sudden surge of human bodies. He removed his mask and smiled with practiced reassurance.

"Everything went great. He is out of danger. We'll keep him here for a few days for observation and recovery, and then you can have him back, good as new. Now if I could speak privately to Officer Sparks's family, please."

Cheers erupted from around the room, followed by a flurry of phones whipped out to share the blissful news. Sparks's father, an Irvine police lieutenant himself, broke off his wife's hug and stepped toward the surgeon, accompanied by his daughter-in-law, who leaned on him for the few steps needed to reach the doctor. Old Man Sparks assumed the lead. They carried a quiet conversation, and then the doctor retreated.

Old Man Sparks, holding on to his daughter-in-law, raised his voice to overcome the myriad of excited conversations in the room. His voice faltered a bit from the emotion.

"Everyone, if I could have your attention for one moment. Thank you for being at our side in this time of need. Randy is doing terrific. He is out of surgery, and he is conscious. The wounds are not life-threatening. He was wearing his vest, which saved his life today—a lesson for all of you out there. You know who you are, those who still think vests are optional."

A few light chuckles followed from the room, accompanied by sighs of relief and a few stifled sobs. The crowd sensed the wave of reprieve sweeping over.

"They will allow family only to see him today. Check in tomorrow to find out if he can have visitors. You don't have to go home. You just can't stay here any longer. Those on city time, get out of here before I take names," Old Man Sparks finished with a smile.

CHAPTER 55

LISA TOOK A STEP BACK, lowered herself on her feet, then retreated further. She looked at J.P. with a mixture of emotions flittering across her face. Horror, guilt, shame, rage, and hatred found their way in the rotation. "How dare you? I did no such thing. What are you insinuating? Is that your way of trying to win the argument? It's a lousy way, Morgan."

J.P. stood his ground, watching her with the intensity of a jungle cat.

"Is that the best you've got?" Lisa rocked on her feet.

Candy stepped closer. Keeping his gaze fixed on Lisa's eyes, J.P. held up a finger. "Candy, stay out of it." He stared Lisa down and continued. "If I cannot trust you to tell the truth, how can I keep you safe? How do you expect me to keep you alive?"

"What does that have to do with what's going on now? I see no connection. My private life is just that, my private life. It does not concern you."

"It puts me in the line of fire. I need to know that I can trust you. I am not judging you. I just wanted to see if you had the courage and integrity to admit it."

"I still see no relation." Her eyes shot daggers, and she chewed on her lower lip.

"If you trust me with your life, trust me to know how to protect it. I do not know where the next threat comes from, unless you tell me the truth every single time I ask. I do not care about interpretations or perceived morality. This was a test, and you failed miserably. Next time, the price could be your life."

Lisa rocked on the balls of her feet, bit her lower lip again, stomped the ground a few times, and decided. "I got seduced by his mind. He is extremely bright, you know. We worked together for long hours. One thing led to another. How did you know? I never told my best friend. Our careers would have been over."

"What do you think I was doing in court?" Morgan questioned her.

"I have no idea." Lisa's shoulders and eyebrows went up in concert.

"I was studying you. I found it odd to see a young girl, two, three years out of law school second-chair one of the most notorious murder cases. Either the DA considered it a slam dunk, and you were on the fast track, or something else was going on. I have known George since I was a kid. I bet it was Tomlinson who wanted you to be his second chair."

"Oh, so now you are questioning my professional abilities? Are you insinuating I slept my way to the top? Is that it?" She rebounded and proceeded on the retaliation path.

"Not at all. I am summarizing my thought process. Anyway, I needed a distraction from the boring long days of legal maneuvering. All that back-and-forth arguing about how to interpret every little detail in six different ways drove me insane. I admit, sometimes I fantasized about you strutting naked around the courtroom on those high heels you like."

Lisa regained her footing and expanded her counteroffensive. "You are an obnoxious pig. On trial for your wife's murder..."

J.P. waved her to be quiet. "There is a method to my madness. Return the courtesy and listen without judgment. Doing my best to stay awake, I saw Tomlinson, your boss, looking at you the same way. One difference, though. On his face, you could read the satisfied look of someone who did not have to imagine it. *He knew* what you looked like naked on those heels."

"You are a sick man, Morgan. I'm done here. I don't have to listen to this crap. I'd rather take my chances with the killers only you believe to exist." Lisa stalked to the rolling door. "Let me out of here, Morgan, or I'll accuse you of kidnapping."

"You may go anytime. The clothes have to stay, though," quipped J.P.

That earned him another smack to the back of the head from Candy. "Don't let him get under your skin, honey. He's just acting stupid, like a little boy. He is an overgrown teddy bear. With issues, it seems." Candy hooked Lisa's arm and walked her back. "J.P., this is the last time I will say it. Knock. It. Off. Leave the poor girl alone. She's been through enough."

"I apologize for this. I need to know I can trust you."

"It's a screwed-up way of or earning someone's trust." Lisa was not ready to forgive.

"That is what they tell me."

"Are you ever going to tell me what makes that card untraceable, or are you stalling because it's baloney?" Lisa resumed the interrogation.

"I told you everything. To be fair, I should add that the corporation and the bank are in a tax haven, and the treasurer owes me big-time. My friend transfers the funds from the corporate account to the bank credit card. Loop closed. Everyone is happy."

"How does he take it out of your account without a trail?"

"First, someone who wanted to track us would have to know where to search. Believe me, nobody has a clue where to look in this case. Second, he owns the bank."

CHAPTER 56

"**OK. I'M OFFICIALLY IMPRESSED.** Can I get one of those cards?"

"Unless I vouch for you, it will never happen, lady."

"Don't call me 'lady,'" Lisa retorted, showing some teeth.

"Yeah, what's up with that? Last night, you yelled at me for that."

"You and I spoke last night?" Lisa's eyes widened in surprise. She pivoted toward Candy. "You never mentioned that."

Candy shrugged. She enjoyed seeing the two of them work together for a change.

"We shared... Well, sort of romantic evening. You mimicked a Gordian knot, promised to give me the needle, then swore to send me to the gas chamber afterward, for good measure. The lighting was dim, like at a posh restaurant on Valentine's Day. Does that count?"

"We spoke last night? You know what happened to me for the past week. I need to know. Morgan, tell me," Lisa pleaded.

"Not for the past week, only since seven thirty last night, when you went to Anna's and let yourself in like you owned the place. Where did you get the keys? Candy and I found that interesting. What were you doing there? We are curious about that, too."

"I was at Anna's place last night? I don't remember a thing. I don't have keys to her place. She wouldn't give me copies. She always joked that if I ran into her secret lover, I may not approve of her choice." Her face lit up. "Oh, my God. She meant you."

"Anna and I were like brother and sister. I watched you let yourself in her home, as if it was the most natural thing. What were you looking for?"

159

"I don't appreciate being interrogated. I remember nothing for the past week, and I have no idea why, or if, I went to Anna's place last night."

"We have to work together, not against each other. We should get something to eat before we tear each other apart," Candy, the peacemaker, stepped in.

"OK. We will table this for now. Let's get out of here." J.P. strode to his office.

Lisa blocked his path. "Not before I see that recording. It's the only reason I came to meet you. Otherwise, I would be at the hospital talking to the police."

"You would be at the hospital, all right. Instead of talking to the police, you would be cooling your heels off at the morgue, awaiting autopsy." J.P. sidestepped her.

"You are so sure. Show me the tape." Lisa quivered.

"Safety first, entertainment later. Fasten your seat belts. The movie starts after we reach cruising altitude. It is time we got out of here. We are safe, but it still bugs me they pinpointed us today. I feel like I am missing something important here."

J.P. pulled two sets of keys and handed one to Candy. "These are for the condo in Vegas. The Avalon's navigation system has the address pre-programmed. The security code is 9642, just like the PIN for the card. Anna, again. Your prints are still active in the security system, so you will have full access to everything."

J.P. pointed the key fob at the Avalon. The Avalon beeped and blinked in response. He handed Lisa the second set of keys. "Please, go to Vegas with Candy. Keep a low profile. Wait for me to call. Do not touch the security system until you have your fingerprints scanned in."

Lisa nodded and accepted the keys with an instinctive motion.

"Use this first." J.P. retrieved two bundles of cash from the attaché case and waved them at Candy. "You need to get groceries on the way there. Nobody has been there in over three months. Please keep away from big chain establishments, any places where they have too many security cameras. Big sunglasses, hats. Blend in."

Candy raised the money above her head and let out a half-hearted "whoopsiiieeeee." She pretended to dance for a moment and then settled for a sad smile instead. "Vegas, baby. Here we come. If Annie could go with us." Tears formed in the corners of her eyes, and her face locked up in a mask of deep pain and sorrow. "Oh, Annie."

"Is that how you plan to keep me alive? Ship me to Vegas? What if something goes wrong, or you don't call?" Lisa confronted J.P. again.

"I gave you a bundle of cash, and I am sending you to Las Vegas—Sin City. I am providing first-class transportation and luxurious accommodations. Just wait until you see the place where you will be staying. Most women would hop with joy," deflected J.P.

CHAPTER 57

S PARKS GREW TIRED OF the hugs, congratulations, and reassurances. He wanted to address a serious problem. "Dad, I need to talk to you alone. Tell them I need to rest."

Old Man Sparks nodded and turned, facing the family. After another long round of hugs, reassurances, and best wishes, father and son were alone at last.

"Dad, who can we trust in the department? Who will keep quiet no matter what and help us with something quite odd?" asked Sparks.

"Define 'odd,'" Old Man Sparks requested.

"I will tell you what happened this morning. I can't wrap my head around it yet. Then I will ask you to help me do something unusual."

"Son, you got shot. The shock, the pain, you just got out of surgery. It may be some time before you make sense of it. You need to rest. Let us catch Morgan and deal with him."

"Twelve years between Irvine PD and being an MP taught me more than just being a cop. Don't patronize me, please. That's just it. Morgan didn't shoot me. I don't think he shot Coop either. Hard to believe, but I think he was there to help ADA Jensen."

"Nope, I checked. Hell hasn't frozen over yet."

"He told me things I didn't know. He shared information he knew we didn't have, and it would take us a long time to uncover, if ever."

"You spoke to him? Why didn't you arrest him? Better yet, why didn't you shoot the son of a bitch between the eyes? Son, he killed your partner, Arlene Spike, and a visitor." The concerned father stepped closer to the bed.

"Dad, stop and listen to me. The IA pricks will be here soon, and I can't tell them this. Not yet, anyway. I have to make sense of it first. I need you to trust me and help me."

"It hurts to see you in that bed. I'd trade places with you in a heartbeat. I don't know what you saw. However, Morgan trying to help Lisa Jensen? I'll never buy that."

"Look at me." Sparks attempted to sit up. He winced in pain and gave up. "This is your son in this bed, and he needs your help. Do I have to ask someone else, *Lieutenant* Sparks?"

"OK, I'll listen." Randy's plea got his father's attention.

"First, I need you to buy me some time with Internal Affairs. Tell them anything you can think of to delay them for a day or two, maybe until after the weekend."

"A day or two? You know the pressure we face to close this case."

"I know what I'm asking. There is something else entirely going on here. We need to figure that out first. Let the IA boys cry foul play. I'll talk to them, just not today."

"You should tell IA about all this and let them churn it out."

"Here's a test, Dad. Cop to cop. What would you do to the guy who shot me?"

"I would put a bullet between the bastard's eyes. No questions asked."

"Fair enough. You know for sure who shot me?"

"That piece of crap Morgan, the biggest embarrassment—"

"Absolutely sure? No doubt?" Sparks leaned on his elbows, flinching in pain.

"Yes, of course!" shouted Old Man Sparks, taking a step back.

"You failed, Lieutenant. You just murdered an innocent man," Sparks exclaimed.

"No way is that bastard—"

"He may have committed other crimes. I'll give you that. But he did not shoot me, and I have a hunch he did not kill Coop either."

"It's my turn to ask you if you're absolutely sure."

"About Coop, no. I wasn't there. I know for sure Morgan didn't shoot me. I had him in my sights, and I was ready to fire. He was walking away from me. There is no way he turned around and got off two shots before I did. By God, I wanted an excuse to empty my clip into him. After I saw Coop lying there, I lost it. That was my mistake. I focused only on Morgan and avenging Coop. I didn't consider any other possibilities. Another thing. I didn't hear the shots that hit me. I only felt them. Morgan carried a regular automatic."

CHAPTER 58

"**I**'M NOT MOST WOMEN**. I want to see that tape, then I'll take it to the police, and we'll be done." Lisa cocked her head to one side.

"We cannot do that yet. If you recall, I said the group that kidnapped you last night, and everyone involved in the murders at Anna's place, they seem to be cops."

"Say you. Just because you have a grudge against law enforcement, it doesn't mean the bad guys are all police officers or all cops are crooks."

"No, say their badges. Tonight, I will call and tell you how to access the recordings and the other evidence from last night. There is a laptop there. I will walk you through it. Now, I need you somewhere safe. I need to move fast and do things you may disagree with."

"Nice try, Morgan. I'm not going anywhere. We made a deal. I'm not letting you out of my sight until this is over." Lisa blocked his path again.

"That will not work. I need to move fast—"

"And you need to do things I may object to," she taunted him.

"Our deal was that I keep you alive and safe, not that you go everywhere with me."

"You should have listened to my conditions before agreeing to them. One of them was 'I don't let you out of my sight until this is over.' How do you like them apples?"

"Oh, that is so low. Even for you, Ms. Jensen, that is so low. Low, low, low." J.P. locked eyes with Lisa. "I propose a cease-fire, so to speak. Until this is over, we set all our differences aside. We work together for the greater good. I promise to have faith in your intentions. If we act friendly and trust each other, we will avoid tons of trouble."

"You've got yourself a deal." Lisa stuck her hand out. "Just so we're clear, when this is over, I'll no longer pretend to trust or like you."

Candy cut in. "Why do I have to go to Vegas? I doubt anyone's after me."

"They may think Anna left copies with you. They will not take chances," replied J.P.

"We can go to my friend's house in Palm Springs. She lives in a gated community. She has email and Internet access for when her grandkids visit," Candy pleaded her case.

"Candy, I appreciate the offer. I have no intention to hide. I want to keep you and Ms. Jensen out of harm's way while I take care of this. I know the condo in Vegas is safe. Nobody can link it to me, you, Anna, or Ms. Jensen. When I figure it out, I will come and get you."

Lisa stood on her toes under J.P.'s nose and crossed her arms over her chest. "Like hell you will. Let Mrs. Richter go alone. I'll stick with you, watch the famous tape, maybe roast some marshmallows!" Lisa exclaimed. "Then we go to the police and put this behind us."

"Yeah, that's a splendid idea. Get rid of the old bag. The cable's on, right? I wouldn't want to miss my favorite cooking shows. Don't worry about my dead daughter and the funeral arrangements I have to make."

J.P. clenched his teeth, then said, "OK. Candy, you go to Vegas alone. It would mean the world to me if I did not have to worry about you, too. Ms. Jensen and I will sort this out, and then we will help you with the details for Anna's funeral and memorial service."

"I'll go. You worry too much. I love you, J.P. Take care of yourself and look after her." Candy hugged him and gestured toward Lisa. "She may act all tough, but she's a softie, just like you." She squeezed and patted Morgan's cheek and then embraced Lisa. "Don't let the big guy get under your skin. He's a terrific friend to have in a pinch, and he likes you. I can tell."

"Yeah, right," scoffed Lisa, holding on to Candy. She felt the need for human contact.

"The more a boy likes a girl, the more he picks on her," Candy whispered in her ear. "One other thing about J.P. If he makes a lot of noise and flails his arms, he's harmless. When he becomes silent, calm, and intent, run like hell. That's when he turns deadly, and anything standing in his way is going up in smoke." She let go of Lisa, executed a perfect a pirouette, holding the cash above her head, and sang in a sad voice, "Vegas, here I come. God, how I miss my little girl. You two take care of each other. Go get them and show them no mercy."

"After last year's trip, I promised Anna I would never allow you near a slot machine. Ever. Again. Keep that promise for me, will you?" Morgan said.

"What happens in Vegas stays in Vegas." Candy stuck her head out of the car and winked at them. "Let's do this and then throw Annie the goodbye party she deserves."

"You are incorrigible, but I love you!" yelled J.P. over the sound of the engine starting. He reached inside the silver SUV and hit the HomeLink button.

The warehouse door rolled up with a light squeak. Lisa and J.P. stood and watched in silence as Candy drove out of the building, blew them a kiss, and sped away. The door tumbled back down with an impending sense of doom.

CHAPTER 59

"RANDY, I'M NOT SURE** why, but I want to believe you. All witnesses in that wing reported hearing only two gunshots, it seems Morgan's." Lieutenant Sparks let his voice trail off. Something about the silenced shots got his attention. The Crime Scene Unit found more than just two spent shell casings at the hospital. They shot Randy Sparks three times and the stranger twice. The forensics team uncovered two shots at a window. Someone had shot Arlene Spikes and Cooper once each. Yet everyone reported only two gunshots during the incident.

"Dad, I had time to reflect on this. Last thing I remember before I blacked out was Morgan leaping out of the way. There were two dark silhouettes farther down. I was so intent on avenging Coop that I didn't take the time to assess the situation. Hell, I didn't even focus on anything else. Then blam, blam, lights out."

"We didn't see anyone else. Morgan shot Cooper and then you and Arlene. He may have killed an innocent bystander too," the father insisted. "We haven't identified him yet."

"Room 324. Shot in one leg and killed execution style with a single bullet to the head?"

"Yes. How did you know this?" Old Man Sparks took another step back, as if his son's statement hit him in the chest.

"Morgan told me."

"He admitted to you?"

"No. He said we'd find him. He left his gun behind to run ballistics and said we'd be able to match the bullet from his weapon to the leg wound. The head shot would be from a different gun. That one will match rounds I got shot with."

"What do you need, Randy? I'll give you the benefit of the doubt. I'll never understand why you would stick your neck out for Morgan, of all people."

"You taught me that sometimes you must stand up even if it's not the popular choice."

"You're convinced Morgan didn't shoot you. You want to stop us from killing him in a standoff. You know about the APB and the other cops he murdered in cold blood?"

"Yes, Dad. Though I hated him with every fiber of my being, something in his eyes, his voice, the way he said it, the things he revealed to me, I got this feeling he was telling the truth. He wanted someone to know in case he didn't make it. He promised that, when it was all over, he would surrender to us and bring the proof he had."

"What do you need?" Old Man Sparks nodded. He knew his son well, and once he had decided, there was not much left to do except help him and see where it went.

"People able to think outside the proverbial box. We must figure out this riddle before more people die. I believe Morgan is trying to prevent more bloodshed. Bring the reports of the fire and the shootings at the Richter place, and the incident at the hospital today."

"Will do. Anything else?"

"Check on those fake bills Lisa Jensen had on her. Bring her, too, although if she recalls nothing that happened before today, she might not be much help. Find us a conference room here with some privacy. I'll brief everyone on what I learned from Morgan today. Dad, get me a darn wheelchair because I don't think I can walk on my own yet."

"Consider it done. One hour." The father in him wanted his son to rest. The cop in him wanted the information. Knowing Randy, the father knew he would not get a word out of him unless he did what the son had asked. He was proud that his son would put himself on the line for what he believed to be right, to prevent further loss of life.

"Dad, one more thing. Handle it quietly. We don't want to set off any alarms in case Morgan's telling the truth."

"OK. Let's hear it."

"Morgan thinks they already moved out. Check on it anyway. I don't like the fact Morgan was so sure they were cops from so many outfits. But we cannot afford to write it off." Sparks repeated the address of the warehouse in Florence.

"I'll have it checked out right now."

"Keep Mom and Wendy away. I need some room to move, without having to fight for every step I take... or for every roll of the wheelchair." He laughed at his own joke. "Now all I've got to do is convince the nurses to cut my meds, so I can stay awake and think clearly. Where's my gun when I really need it?" Sparks muttered.

CHAPTER 60

"**I MUST ADMIT, ONCE** I got to know you a little, you're different from the monster I envisioned. What's next?" Lisa asked.

Her new attitude surprised J.P. He could sense something shifted. She seemed ready to listen from a unique perspective. "How are you with a handgun?" he inquired.

"I hate them. I see every day the terrible things guns do." Lisa grimaced.

"Normally, I would agree with you. Well, I do not hate guns. They serve a purpose. In the wrong hands, they can be dangerous. However, the question was not how you feel about them. Will you shoot your toes off as soon as you get a chance?"

"You, condescending SOB. I'll have you know I am a decent shot."

"We will see," he said. "Just a piece of advice: if you shoot at the bad guys, empty your clip. Otherwise, an overzealous prosecutor may challenge your story of fearing for your life."

"You are an arrogant, murderous son of a bitch." She fumed.

"Auto or revolver?" he insisted.

"Either, I guess."

"Don't guess. If we do this together, you may have to defend yourself. I need you to be self-sufficient, not freeze when it counts, trying to figure out how to work the gun."

"Mr. Big Macho Man has issues with protecting the innocent little village girl." Lisa toyed with him, batting her eyelashes. "Scared she might get hurt on his watch?"

"Exigent circumstances call for exceptional measures and actions, Ms. Jensen."

"Call me, Lisa."

"Huh?"

"We'll be working together for a while, having to trust each other. We might as well use our first names. I prefer Lisa." She thrust her hand out.

"John Paul, but then you know that. My friends call me J.P." He took her hand with considerable care as if fearing it would break in his grasp like a twig.

"Does that make me your friend?" she asked, playing the precious card, complete with fluttering eyelashes and head cocked to one side.

"Do not push it." He let go of her delicate fingers and reached inside the safe for body armor. He chose one, checked the tag, and handed it to Lisa. "Wear this all the time, please."

The front read *MPIS*. Above that stood a smiling golden bear with its front paws wide open. The back, it read, *Stop! Save Bullets!* She chuckled and set the body armor on the table.

"Does it work?" She pointed to the directive on the back of the vest.

J.P. picked up the vest with a childish smirk and flipped it twice, giving it a cursory examination. "Do you see any holes in it?"

"Hardy, har, har."

Lisa watched as he loaded the guns she had chosen and then picked out four more SIGs. He added magazines and speed loaders for all weapons.

"Six guns? Between us, we only have four hands." Lisa arched her eyebrows.

"Yeah, but I can shoot with my toes, too," quipped J.P. He closed the lids on the two cases and pulled out a duffel bag. He grabbed another bulletproof vest from the wall safe, same size as the one in Lisa's hands, and then loaded boxes of ammo in a duffel bag.

"I wonder how you will fit your immense chest in that tiny body armor. Maybe it stretches out, like spandex. That would be fun to watch."

"You never know until you do." J.P. switched to an enigmatic grin.

"Are we planning to start a war? That's over two thousand rounds."

"I have my version of the Boy Scouts' motto. 'Better to have it and not need it, than to need it and wish you had it.' Believe me. I have been there, more than once."

"Sir, yes, sir." Lisa mock saluted him and broke into a hearty laugh. "You suddenly look so serious after you picked on me all day."

J.P. carried the duffel bag and gun cases to the silver Ford. Behind him, the wall safe closed like magic. He returned to the office and brought out two more bags, which he loaded with various equipment, binoculars, electronic gear, and items that looked alien to Lisa. J.P. loaded everything in the silver SUV and opened the passenger door for her. She climbed in. He seized the attaché case off the hood, slid into the driver's seat, and drove away.

CHAPTER 61

THOUGH THERE WERE MORE traffic cameras, J.P. chose surface streets, relying on the fact they had changed cars.

Lisa was deep in thought, looking out the window, seeing nothing. "I need clothes and shoes that fit. Can we get something to eat? Hospital food only feeds baby chickens."

"What would you like?"

"Something good, comfort food and a cold beer. I crave protein. The beer is optional."

"I know just the place."

They first stopped at a sporting goods store. They bought makeup, giant sunglasses to cover Lisa's bruise, undergarments, two changes of clothes, and a pair of sneakers in Lisa's size. After that, Morgan pulled into a parking lot next to a franchise burger joint.

"Fast food is gross," complained Lisa.

"Have faith, Ms. Jensen. It is all about trust."

Lisa climbed out, mumbling under her breath. To her surprise, J.P. headed away from the fast-food place toward a small side door accessing the building next door. A sign showed a mom-and-pop grocery store with a German name. Curious, Lisa followed him.

The deli store had a sandwich counter packed with people. The store's A/C unit worked overtime. Coming in from the outside heat, Lisa shivered. In a reflex move, she snuggled up to J.P. like a baby bird seeking a parent's body heat and protection.

I must admit. She feels wonderful. John Paul Morgan, you are losing it. This woman is the devil incarnate, and you know it. Maybe that is why she feels warm.

"For here or to go?" He pointed at the menu on the wall.

Lisa surveyed the store and found it too crowded. "To go. Maybe we can find a nice place to eat in peace. I want a pastrami sandwich with everything. I'll get the chips," she said, noticing the aisles overloaded with goodies. She picked the largest bag of BBQ potato chips.

"This is not your last meal," he jested. "Save room for a few calories later, the big holiday weekend coming up and all."

"I could make up for starving the entire week." Lisa gazed up to him. "Is this OK? I seldom buy them. Today, I crave chips. They are part of my comfort food group."

He placed the order, took the ticket, and then checked the refrigerators by the front door. He settled for two half-liter bottles of beer and water. Lisa did not recognize the brands.

J.P. pulled into the Irvine Lake Park. Lisa hugged the bag of chips as if they were the source of life itself. They found a picnic table under an oak tree. The deserted park offered an unspoiled landscape, a view of the lake and enjoyable silence. Hundreds of birds chirped, and the soft wind unsettled tree branches and produced small waves that lapped at the lakeshore.

J.P. set the food and the bottles of beer and water on the table between them.

A cloud of small white butterflies swooped by, fluttering around them. Lisa tittered like a happy schoolgirl at recess and unwrapped her sandwich.

"Wow," Lisa said between large bites of the sandwich, her gaze following the butterfly cloud. "This park is fabulous. I never knew it existed." Another big bite of the sandwich followed by a handful of chips shoved in her mouth. "I could live like this. Better than the cramped place I have in Newport." She stopped, aware she gave away too much information.

Lisa continued to eat as if food was going out of style. She sipped from the beer. "This is uncommonly tasty beer. I've never seen it before. What is it?"

"They make it at a boutique brewery outside of Munich. It only gets imported in small quantities by stores like the one we just left."

"How come the big boys are not importing it?" Lisa took another swig from her bottle. "They could make a killing with it. Beats any of the beer commercially available around here."

"I have known the owners of the deli store for years. From time to time, they regale me with stories about Germany. The recipes go back generations in the family, and the brewers have no interest in making and exporting it in large quantities." J.P. played with his water bottle, looking at the lake. "I guess they have a different value system over there."

"Level with me, Morgan. What's going on? You haven't touched your food," Lisa inquired. She set her sandwich on the table, drank more beer, and stared J.P. in the eyes.

"Last night, I saw and heard things I was not supposed to. I do not know what to make of it. The more I think about the whole thing, the less it makes sense," J.P. said in a gentle tone, as if he feared she might bolt. "Things any sane mind cannot explain."

"Are you trying to scare me, Morgan? I asked you to be straight with me."

"Quite the opposite, I am holding back a lot. I do not want you to call for a quick haul to the loony bin. You saw it too, but you do not remember."

"You mean I saw all of this too? Is that why they drugged me, to wipe all of it from my memory? What did I see, Morgan?" she pleaded.

"I do not know why they drugged you. I guess we will have to ask them when we catch them. I promise you. We will get them."

"Let me finish eating. Show me the evidence you've been teasing me with all day and then tell me everything from the beginning. Leave nothing out." She picked up the sandwich and continued in a half-hearted voice. "I'm a big girl. I can deal with it, whatever it is."

"OK. While you eat, is there anyone we need to contact for you?"

"Like, who?" Lisa's eyebrows arched like Roman bridges.

"Any immediate family members, relatives, close friends, boyfriend, fiancé."

"You could just ask me if I have a boyfriend or a fiancé, Morgan. No need to beat around the bush like that," Lisa quipped, flashing a mischievous smile. She enjoyed paying him back a little while she found her solid footing, which had eluded her the entire day.

"Do not flatter yourself," J.P. replied. "It is a simple threat and loose ends assessment."

"Fine, be that way," she retorted. "Parents died when I was in law school. I met Mrs. Richter going with Anna on holidays. No boyfriend, no fiancé, no siblings on the West Coast."

"Siblings. Where?"

"A sister, married to an investment banker, who transferred to New York. We hardly keep in touch. No kids either. I never found Mr. Right Guy. Mostly, they were Mr. Right Now." She chuckled at the old joke and continued, "I don't have anyone they can use. Outside of work, there is nobody." She became introspective, reflecting on how empty her life must have looked to an outsider. "All I've been doing for the past, well, all my life, is work, work, and then work some more. I hardly have anyone in my life I can even turn to for help. Pretty sad."

J.P. nodded. Feeling the need to break the silence, Lisa said, "For whatever it's worth, I think you are a true gentleman. I don't know what happened last night, but the way you came to our rescue today, the way you handled everything, I am impressed. I wish there was a different history between us. I see now why Anna defended you all these years."

J.P. nodded and kept quiet. His eyes shifted to the mirror surface of the lake. Anna had been the little sister he never had. After he had lost Alice, she kept him from going insane. She had defended him and had saved his life. J.P. was sure she had also died protecting him.

CHAPTER **62**

"**P**URCELL, GET THE MASTER** plan maps for me," Clancy ordered.

"Sure thing, sir. May I ask if you intend to change anything? You need me in here?"

"No. I need to be alone for a while," replied Clancy without looking up.

"Theoretically, changes are possible. Practically, they would be near impossible. We are at T-42 hours and counting."

"Thank you for the reminder. Just get me the plan maps."

"I'll go about the business of apprehending Morgan." Purcell left the room, puzzled.

His portable radio hissed, "Purcell, you need to come down stat."

He strolled to the security office. Simpson pointed to the digital map on his laptop. "That dot, that's Morgan, Jensen, and Richter's mother. The bug stopped transmitting after Corelli crashed into Morgan's SUV by the John Wayne Airport. It just came back on a minute ago. We sent the reactivation signal every ten minutes, just in case."

"You're sure about this?" Purcell fretted with anticipation.

"As sure I as I can be without eyes on it. We lost them in Santa Ana. Traffic cameras were down, so we don't know which way they went. It's been about three hours, consistent with the distance from Orange County, factoring in holiday weekend road conditions."

"Don't lose them again." Purcell touched his finger to the pulsating dot. "Gotcha, asshole. I'm coming for you." He summoned a chopper to pick him up, and then he summoned Parker. He strode into the warehouse and pointed at the first two officers there. "You and you, get your gear, and bring a sniper rifle. Be ready to go in two minutes."

"They may have changed cars, sir. We need visual confirmation," Simpson whispered.

Purcell climbed the stairs two at a time to Clancy's office. "We found Morgan. I'll lead a unit and eliminate them."

"Them?" Clancy asked.

"Lisa Jensen and Anna Richter's mother were with him in Irvine," Purcell clarified. "It stands to reason; they are fleeing together." Getting all three at once would be a blessing and end the breach at the same time.

"It's about damn time. Report as soon as you dealt with him. Then let's concentrate on getting our plan in motion."

Purcell skipped the stairs three at a time going down. Parker and the two men he had drafted for the job were already waiting in the car with the passenger door open. Purcell addressed the men in the car. "This looks like a piece of cake. It's time to clear it up because I'm tired of this dickhead making us look incompetent."

Simpson called Purcell fifteen minutes later.

"Our guys have a positive location on Morgan's house. What are your instructions?"

"How many assets we have chasing after Morgan?" asked Purcell.

"Four officers at his place, two more at the older Richter woman's place, and two on standby at Irvine PD to pick up Corelli's team of four. Two more casing Lisa Jensen's condo and four to cover the other women, in case he shows up there."

Simpson's report brought a grimace to Purcell's face. He cursed aloud. "Sixteen people out of commission because of this asshat. Two more are in Corona. Three—no, make that four officers dead in the past twenty-four hours, two cars destroyed, operational security compromised. Five men in this chopper and one helicopter much-needed somewhere else tied up in pursuit. What a goddamn waste of resources. All this because one little pissant couldn't mind his own business." The men listened and watched in silence, sharing his pain.

"Sir, the men at Morgan's place, what should they do?" Simpson's voice fetched Purcell back to reality.

"Go through it. Grab anything that might be of any use later and then burn it. Make sure Irvine PD releases our men right away. I don't care what you have to do. Call Mr. Clancy if you need to. Get everybody back to base ASAP. We've got more important things to worry about. Let's end this once and for all."

CHAPTER 63

J.P. TOOK A SIP of water. He admired the majestic beauty of the park, the peacefulness of the lake. His eyes followed the kaleidoscope of butterflies plummeting toward the water, and he envied them with all his heart. The breeze had died away, and the surface of the water reflected everything like a polished mirror.

"How did you know about this place and about the deli store? This is excellent food. Outstanding choice." Lisa followed his gaze, mesmerized by the butterfly swarm.

"I live nearby."

"How close?"

"A couple of miles. We need to stop by my place next."

"Really? You want to take me home already?" Lisa's face became a mask of outrage.

"What?!"

"I'm not the type you can take home and have your way with her after just one sandwich and a beer. Good sandwich and beer, I grant you that." She no longer could keep the straight face and broke into a full body laugh. "I got you!"

"Seeing how you eat, I had to give it a shot." J.P. played along. He understood her need for some relief. She had been through a lot since the night before, even if she did not remember.

"So that's how it will be? OK, we're even." She pushed away the rest of her sandwich, then stood and stretched. "I'm done."

There was something about her now that she had trusted him. She was a striking woman, witty, playful, intelligent. J.P. stood, picking everything off the table.

Another place, another lifetime. Maybe, just maybe.

"You still haven't touched your food or beer. What's going on, Morgan?"

"I thought we were calling each other by our first names."

"Shields up! Red alert. Deflect, deflect," she quipped. "Level with me, J.P."

"I will save it for later. I should not take any chances driving under the influence with an ADA in the car." He ignored Lisa's sideways glance and headed back to the SUV.

"I wish we—I could stay here forever," Lisa chanted. She twirled around a few times, lost a shoe, got it back, and hopping on one leg closed the distance.

"I'll change into the new clothes at your place, if that's OK."

"Watch out for the hidden cameras."

"Do you ever take anything seriously?" Lisa asked. "Bullets are flying, crazed killers pursue us, yet you never lost your composure. You're cracking jokes, and it rubs off on me."

"Life is too short," retorted J.P., walking around her.

"So?" Lisa blinked a few times, alternating glances between J.P. and the lake.

"I do my best thinking under intense pressure. I ask myself, 'If this was a sitcom, what would be the most outrageous solution?' I just pick the answer farthest out in the cornfields. It turns out nobody predicts those. Implementing them turns out to be a lot of fun."

"I still don't get you," she insisted, searching for something.

J.P. recited,

"If you can keep your head when all about you
Are losing theirs and blaming it on you;
If you can trust yourself when all men doubt you,
But make allowance for their doubting too;
If you can wait and not be tired by waiting,
Or, being lied about, don't deal in lies,
Or, being hated, don't give way to hating,
And yet don't look too good, nor talk too wise."

"What is that?" Lisa asked.

"A poem," he smiled. "*If* by Rudyard Kipling. It is full of wisdom and advice. I always have trouble applying that last verse to my life, though."

"Rudyard Kipling as in *The Jungle Book?*"

"The same." J.P. opened the door for her.

"You are something else. I'll give you that," Lisa conceded. "Yet as strange as this may sound, I feel safe with you. That's odd, considering your history."

An alarm sounded from the equipment in the back of the SUV.

"Oh, no. No," murmured J.P.

"What is it?" Lisa glanced over the interior of the SUV for the source of the noise.

He turned on a monitor. The nine-split image of a home security system showed three men, guns held in front, searching the place. A fourth one stood guard outside the front door. In the circular driveway, there were two Dodge Chargers with their front doors open.

"The surveillance system at my place. They are in my home right now," he answered.

"We can't go there." She tried a smart-aleck comment. "You were saying?"

"I am not accustomed to self-doubt. They found me on the move today. They found my home, a place I kept secret for years. It is like they have a line inside my head."

"If they are LEOs, they have a great deal of resources," Lisa offered.

"I kept my life and home concealed from the *government* all these years."

"Oops, now the establishment knows," wisecracked Lisa. "How did you manage that? In today's world of electronic records, that is almost impossible."

"I spell that word a little different."

"Huh?"

"I spell it *'I'm possible,'*" he answered. "Just not today, it seems."

"What does that mean?" Lisa inquired.

"Some other time, Ms. Jensen," he whispered. "Banker, get out. Get out now!" J.P. switched off the monitors and climbed into the driver's seat.

"What banker? Who's at your place?" Lisa questioned him.

"My indolent cat. Well, he is a cross between a mountain lion and a pig," replied J.P. He backed the SUV out of the parking spot without offering additional information.

"What does that mean?" Lisa drew closer to exasperation.

"He is the size of a small mountain lion, and he eats like a pig. He is the laziest, fattest cat on the planet, hence the nickname *Banker Cat*. He puts Garfield to shame. He knows how to take care of himself, though. The local dogs, hell, even the coyotes respect him."

"I'm officially impressed. I never believed that you could care about anything with a pulse. After I saw those pictures, your reputation as the *Butcher of Irvine*—"

"Can you drop the whole thing, please? I need to think," J.P. snapped.

"No need to bite my head off." Lisa took a defensive posture. "Where are we going?"

"Running for the hills. Well, mountains. May I please have some peace and quiet?"

Lisa pouted, examining the scenery outside the window. J.P. was oblivious to her reactions. Annoyed, she reached in the backseat and grabbed her new shoes.

CHAPTER 64

THE SIZZLING AIR SMELLED of medicine, gun oil, sweat, and testosterone. Tempers flared higher than the room temperature. The conference room's maximum occupancy was eight people. Ten Irvine PD officers watched Lieutenant Sparks push his son's wheelchair. Sparks guided the IV tree, with four lines running into his veins. Every cop nodded in acknowledgment at the father and son, and then they scrambled to their seats.

"Before we start, you have one last chance to walk out. No hard feelings," Sparks began. "What I am about to ask will go against deep-rooted opinions and beliefs most of us have. It could spell serious trouble, too." Sparks surveyed his brethren. The officers exchanged inquisitive looks and conceding nods followed. Old Man Sparks locked the door.

"From this moment forward, we are all in. This is an unofficial task force. Its purpose is to neutralize a threat we know very little about. Allow me to finish before you ask questions. Then let's review each report, every single question, no matter how long it takes. I feel it in my bones this is important." Sparks's ominous tone sent chills down the group's spines.

"There is no recording of today's incident at the hospital," stated Old Man Sparks. "Someone deactivated the entire surveillance system remotely, using manufacturer-embedded codes. The hospital security didn't even know the codes existed. We need to reconstruct the events from scraps of information and witness statements. Randy's account will prove crucial."

Sparks narrated his encounter with Morgan. His friends scribbled copious notes and compared information in the reports with their own knowledge. Sparks mentioned the names of the cops killed in Anna Richter's home. Lieutenant Baker, the lead investigator on the case, phoned them in. The dispatcher confirmed the identities, and the room erupted. They agreed. That information could only mean either Morgan was the shooter, or he had witnessed it all.

"My son asked me to check on a warehouse in Florence." Old Man Sparks picked the ball up. "I asked a friend of mine to do some snooping. The place is vacant, tighter than a drum, swept clean, and ready to rent. He asked around, and an off-duty night watchman remembered a flurry of activity around three o'clock last night. They moved in yesterday and out overnight."

"For all we know, it could have been a legit operation," remarked Sergeant Stonehill.

"How many legitimate businesses move everything out of a warehouse in the middle of the night?" Old Man Sparks asked. "Less than twenty-four hours after moving in, no less."

"I still don't see the relevance," Stonehill added.

"That's not the odd part. My friend said they dispatched two patrols in response to a 911 call. It was the only call involving a warehouse. There is no record of it in the logs. In the morning, the chief called a meeting. Patrol officers, desk sergeant, dispatcher, all of them."

"More baloney. How can there be a call they did not log? I never heard of that," Stonehill said, relentless in defending his point of view.

"Someone turned off remotely the security system at UCI Medical Center. We had eight murders in less than a week?" Old Man Sparks stopped, realizing he made his point.

"I met a different man today," Sparks seized the conversation, "the opposite of the image I had. I'm convinced Morgan pulled me out of the line of fire. He could have killed me a hundred times. He had my gun, Coop's, and his own. We were alone for minutes. He knew about the APB. He knew every cop in California was after him, yet he took the time to stop the bleeding and call a medical team for me. He stayed with me until they arrived." He stopped to catch his breath. "This getting-shot thing, I don't recommend it."

Everybody laughed at the joke, dissipating some tension in the room.

"Instead of running, he passed on information we didn't have. I have a confession to make. I've been a police officer for twelve years. I've been a cop's son all my life. Today, I finally grasped the full depth and value of 'innocent until proven guilty'. For years, I hated Morgan. Hatred blinded me today, and I never stopped to assess the situation. I paid for that by catching three bullets. The man I met today couldn't have done any of that stuff to his family. Maybe we missed something crucial, back then and now."

"Like what?" Stonehill scoffed. "Morgan killed his wife and nephew. The end."

"I always wondered about the money transfer the day his wife died. He claimed he didn't know about it. If he moved that money out of the country, and he was gone all night, why come back? He could live the good life in a country with no extradition. However, he's here. He was here the day after the murders, and he is still here today. Why?"

Lieutenant Simon's phone rang. Simon headed the investigation of the incident at the UCI Medical Center. He walked out and returned with a few sheets of paper. "Fingerprints and ballistics reports came in. Morgan's fingerprints were on Officer Cooper's weapon, though they were not in a position showing he fired it. The direction of prints showed he handled it. Same for Randy's gun. Ballistics confirmed at least five slugs had been fired from weapons with silencers. Get this, Morgan's gun belongs to a State Trooper, Sadowsky."

All eyes shifted to Sparks, who sat quietly, watching and listening with unmatched intensity. Simon continued reading the reports.

"This sounds exactly like Randy's account of Morgan's story. In official format!" Lieutenant Baker exclaimed when Simon finished the summary.

"We have to find Morgan first. We all know what that means," Sparks concluded.

CHAPTER 65

THE FREEWAY BENT LEFT and descended. Candy spotted ahead the town of Primm. It was the first settlement in Nevada, just over the border. She recalled when there was only a sign, welcoming travelers to the Silver State. First, a gas station, then Whiskey Pete's Hotel and Casino came up. After that, it was a virtual explosion of buildings, like drawings in a cartoon. Overnight, Primm became a respectable border town with a large outlet mall, several hotels and casinos, a roller coaster, an amusement park, and so much more. After the recessions and COVID-19 pandemic, the town was catching its breath, and started growing again.

Candy hoped she could make it to Vegas before she had to stop again for a bathroom break. She had decided already. She would go to the Venetian, her favorite casino on the Strip, and drown her sorrow on the slots. She thought J.P. worried too much, and she needed a distraction from all this. She felt a twinge of guilt, knowing Anna was dead. However, she knew that, with Lisa and J.P.'s help, she could handle all the arrangements.

"Who would recognize me in Vegas, the city with the largest influx of tourists in the world?" she said out loud. "What happens in Vegas must stay in Vegas." She passed Primm and then realized she could not make it to Vegas. She had to find a bathroom—soon.

CHAPTER 66

PURCELL AND HIS TEAM scanned the northbound freeway traffic below.

"Simpson, I don't see any black Ford SUVs. Are you sure they are here?" Purcell's irritation grew more unmanageable by the minute. He left on the wild-goose chase convinced of its success, but now he considered Morgan may have misled them.

"They have to be there. They could have changed cars before they left Santa Ana. Coldwell shot the back window of Morgan's SUV, and the stunt he pulled crumpled the rear of the SUV..." Simpson did not finish his sentence.

"Well, it isn't a damn Ford Expedition. They probably changed cars or something." Purcell's annoyed answer rang loud enough to hear over the engine noise. "Or they found your stupid bug, planted it on someone else, and I'm out here chasing ghosts." He had an idea. "I'm going to have the pilot fly low above traffic. Let us know when we are on top of them. Check for reports of stolen vehicles close to John Wayne Airport."

"Already did, sir," Simpson replied. "No stolen vehicles in the area before they left. The theft may not be reported yet, or they could have had another vehicle stashed away. I can tell you for sure it did not belong to either of the Richter women or Jensen. We accounted for those. I'm not able to find any vehicles registered to Morgan or at his home address."

Purcell instructed the pilot to position the aircraft over the highway traffic. The pilot argued safety and Nevada's regulations. Purcell cut him off and ordered him to do it anyway, claiming he would assume responsibility. The pilot shrugged and descended to one hundred feet alongside the freeway.

"About as low as I can," the pilot said, settling 10 mph faster than the vehicles below.

"They're slowing way down, and... They just left the freeway. They are on the off-ramp now." Simpson's excited voice resumed as the helicopter approached the town of Jean.

The entire crew watched the only vehicle leaving the freeway, a blue Toyota Avalon taking the off-ramp, heading to a small roadside diner.

"That's our target!" yelled Purcell and instructed the pilot to climb, knowing that they would attract attention no matter what. He hoped Morgan would not be sure the chopper was following him. The helicopter climbed to five hundred feet and crossed to the western side of the freeway. Purcell trained his binoculars on the Avalon. He watched with suppressed anger as Candy stepped out of the driver's seat, activated the alarm, and headed into the restaurant.

The car's lights flashed twice.

"Oh no! We just wasted God only knows how many hours!" shouted Parker.

Purcell ordered the pilot to hover south of the small hotel cluster. He kept the binoculars trained on the car but saw no movement inside. Could they be hunkering down out of sight? Purcell ordered the pilot to keep the vehicle in sight at all times. They watched Candy return to the Avalon and resume her trip toward Vegas. Purcell removed his headgear and slammed it on his knee. His cheeks developed crimson blotches.

"Simpson, arrange a rental car to meet us at McCarran." Purcell put his headgear back on. The pilot pointed to the fuel gauge. "We also need fuel. Ten, fifteen minutes max. Get to it." He did not wait for an acknowledgment before he switched to the cabin system. "Parker and I will RTB You two get the rental and coordinate with Simpson. Intercept that woman and make her tell you where Morgan is. The entire operation is in jeopardy. You get that information by any means necessary and cover your tracks. Clear?"

"Crystal, sir," replied the two men.

Purcell's sigh overpowered the engine noise. He leaned back against his seat and closed his eyes. They were so close to the conclusion of their mission, and many other things needed immediate attention. Instead, he found himself in the middle of nowhere, chasing an asshole who proved to be more elusive and resourceful than they had anticipated.

"Even the best conceived plans do not survive contact with the enemy," went the adage. In Purcell's mind, Morgan became the mortal enemy of their operation, ideals, and way of life. Purcell renewed his commitment to hunt Morgan down and eliminate him. He opened his eyes when they touched down on the tarmac at the Las Vegas International Airport. The sight of the rental car waiting for them on the tarmac, right beside the fuel truck, reignited his faith.

"Morgan is nothing but a bump in the road He can't stop progress. Happy hunting, boys," he wished the officers, who had already jumped out of their seats.

CHAPTER 67

THEY ARRIVED IN THE town of Lake Arrowhead as J.P. finished recounting the events. He stopped at a locally owned grocery store. They drank in the clean, crisp mountain air. Lisa twirled around, taking in the majesty of the massifs around. She gulped the fresh air with delight, unable to get enough. She looked like a carefree teenager on her summer break.

"What exactly are we doing here?" she asked with slight apprehension.

"We enjoy unpolluted air and the serenity of nature. Later, we cook, eat, feed the bears, regroup, and rethink our strategy. Think of it as a short boot camp for the mind."

They bought steaks, potatoes, tomatoes, vegetables, lettuce, eggs, milk, cereal, and warm bread from the store's own bakery. Lisa carried a *Death-by-Chocolate* cake she had eyed for a minute before J.P. caught on and placed it in the cart along with a pack of bear claws.

"Keep in mind I don't cook," Lisa quipped back in the car. "Why six jumbo steaks? Are we feeding your private army? How many people are coming?"

"Just Fred."

"Just Fred. He must be another giant. Who's this Fred?" Lisa had never been this irritated interrogating anyone else in her life, except for Morgan ten years before.

"Fred is, well, just Fred." J.P.'s face broadened into a proud grin.

"Why are we here? I'm not complaining, mind you. But, according to you, a zombie army up to no good is on our tails. Hardly the time for a vacation."

"They are not zombies. They are flesh and blood, with appalling ideas and the funding they need to put them into practice. That is scarier in my book."

"That's your point of view. No offense, I can see how years on the run can turn you into a conspiracy theory nut, with a side dish of paranoia."

"Why would I take offense to that? For the record, I have not been on the run. I have been right here, making a living, and searching for the answer to what happened to my family."

"It didn't come out right. You know what I mean." Lisa backpedaled.

"I know what I saw last night, and I know what I heard. I do not need speculative interpretation. What I need is accurate information."

"You're impossible. What's with the bear claws? Everything else is on the healthy side. More or less. Those things literally have a ton of sugar and fat, each."

"Bits of wisdom from the girl hogging the chocolate cake. Obviously, they are for the bears." He shrugged. "Let's go to the cabin. Fred will be along soon. We have dinner, watch the feature presentation, and make alternative plans. They may include moving to Australia. The idea crept into my mind after I watched last night's executions, live and in color."

After climbing through the picturesque streets of Lake Arrowhead, they took a lateral forest road and arrived at a closed gate. On the gate hung a large sign: "*Government notice: No trespassing. Unauthorized persons will be prosecuted.*" J.P. unlocked the padlock, drove through, and then locked the gate behind them.

"Breaking into a government facility? That's your idea of lying low."

"What makes you believe that?"

"The sign back there." Lisa pointed behind them with a hooked thumb.

"Which government is that?"

"What do you mean? Does it matter?"

"Not really. What government owns the property? Who will prosecute us?"

"The sign only says, '*Government Notice.*'" Lisa recalled the sign. The lawyer saw the flaw in her own logic. "The sign is fake."

"Yet you would never consider driving beyond that gate," stated J.P.

"Darn. You are something else. Everything about you is just smoke and mirrors. Maybe that's why you got away..."

"You said that last night, too. You promised to stop those comments. At least while we are fighting this thing together."

"I remember nothing. You could make it all up."

"I could."

The road brought them to a small clearing, revealing a cabin standing in the middle of the dense forest. The trees provided almost complete cover, making the home invisible from more than a hundred feet. The effect of the setup astonished Lisa.

"Wow. Cool trick, Morgan. What's next? Rabbits out of a hat?"

"Bears out of the woods. Give me a hand with the groceries, please."

"Enough with the bears already." Lisa pouted, scanning their surroundings with apprehension, half-expecting a gigantic bear to charge them and take their provisions. "I'm a city girl. I don't like wild animals, except at the zoo."

Lisa stood in the middle of the first floor, grocery bags in hand, taking it all in.

J.P. gave her the quick rundown. "Make yourself at home. The guest room down here is yours. It has its own bathroom, but we use it as the service bathroom. I hope it does not bother you. I will start the BBQ," he said as he disappeared through the side door.

The extensively remodeled cabin had a two-story cathedral architecture crowned by an exposed beam ceiling. The first floor consisted in part of a large space; the living, sitting, and dining areas. A guest room, a bathroom, and a storage closet, tucked under the stairs, formed one side of the first floor, the kitchen the opposite side.

The cabin was luxuriously furnished and appointed yet understated. A beautiful hand-carved dining table for six stood next to the kitchen wall. Overstuffed sofa and matching love seat and armchair surrounded a hand-carved coffee table depicting a bear on its back with an enormous etched crystal on its paws. The detail was marvelous, giving the impression that the bear could drop the glass top any minute and run out the door to play in the forest.

The second floor extended atop the wraparound porches on the first floor. Above the kitchen was a sitting area, furnished with overstuffed couches and a large sofa, surrounding another handcrafted table depicting a family of does. A T-shaped bridge connected the two master bedrooms and the sitting area to the wide staircase. Fireplaces in the living room and upstairs enhanced the charming ambiance. Paintings on the walls, soft oil colors, portraits and landscapes reflected a woman's touch.

No photographs of any kind, though.

The interior was refreshing and smelled of fresh pine and cinnamon. On the wall next to the front door were nine triangular casings holding folded US flags and the French, UK, and Australian banners, same as at the warehouse. Lisa bit her lip to stop herself from asking the obvious question. She could not recall another day so filled with excitement and danger. She wondered whether her life had become mundane.

"Very cozy, Morgan—I mean, J.P. It will take time getting used to this after being in the city for so long." Lisa headed for the kitchen to drop the grocery bags on the counter.

CHAPTER 68

"**W**HAT THE HELL IS happening?" Sergeant Pearce jumped in. "This took place on my watch, and we get the best info from a civilian, a man we all want dead?"

"That SOB was right on the money. This stinks to high heaven." Simon looked around the room. Everyone was considering the implications of everything they had just heard.

Sergeant Pearce broke the silence. "If I subscribed to conspiracy theories, I might think someone dispatched an assassination team to eliminate Lisa Jensen. Morgan foiled their plan and wounded one of them. The other one executed his partner to prevent us from interrogating him. Nothing like this has ever happened throughout the history of Irvine."

"I have to admit. It raises a few questions," Lieutenant Baker put in.

"Here is another thing that will send your head spinning." Sergeant Pearce shuffled through papers and picked up one sheet. "I've been trying to figure this one out for the past fifteen minutes. I hoped it was a mix-up, but I don't think so. This is hard for me, as you know. Governor Hunter is my little girls' godfather. When his daughter died, man, I wanted to obliterate that SOB Morgan myself. I am getting on his bandwagon now." Several nods around the room assured him the others shared his feelings.

"APB on Morgan came in before 5:00 A.M. No name of the officer shot by Morgan, and it listed Ms. Jensen as a possible casualty. Because it was incomplete, Stampler classified as a low priority. He requested clarification, and the name of the officer killed. Crossing T's and dotting I's The name was not available to us."

"I never heard of something like that," put in Officer Collony who had kept quiet.

"When Ms. Jensen showed up alive, Stampler insisted on getting a name. At 9:00 A.M., the issuing entity provided the identity of the cop Morgan supposedly killed, James Smythe, LAPD. Morgan told Randy that Smythe was one of the five dead bodies. We got their IDs confirmed, what, a half-hour ago? Smythe is one of the DBs in the Richter home."

"They didn't have his body. How did they issue the APB hours before we found it?" Old Man Sparks asked the obvious questions. The silence in the room was deafening.

"Morgan could have dragged the dead body there. I admit. It sounds far-fetched. So, what do we do now? We throw the son of a bitch a hero's welcome parade?" Collony surmised.

"How about just being courteous and not shoot him on sight? Try to listen to what he has to say? Like true, professional police officers?" Lieutenant Baker shot back.

"I don't know about a parade, but he should get something. Morgan just made my life a lot harder," Crawford intervened. "There I was, all done typing the report on Anna Richter's death. Now, I have to reopen the investigation because Morgan says they have murdered her. I want to know the truth, damn it. That girl deserves it. Her family, too."

"Gentlemen, set your feelings aside. We have an enormous problem on our hands. I feel sick to my stomach knowing that fellow cops tried to manipulate us into what amounts to an execution or an assassination. I don't enjoy being someone's cat paw, doing their dirty work." Old Man Sparks stood. "Everyone gets an assignment. We will reconvene at oh seven hundred tomorrow before our official shift to compare notes. Pass the word to everyone else. We want Morgan alive, unharmed if possible. I, for one, want to hear what he has to say."

CHAPTER 69

LISA HAD SHOWERED AND changed into the new clothes. She studied her reflection in the full-length mirror, taking in the soothing music emanating from hidden speakers. Music appeases the savage beast. She only knew Morgan as the *Butcher of Irvine*.

J.P. walked in through the side door, headed for the kitchen.

"Can I help with anything?" Lisa asked.

"You are a guest for the first twenty-four hours. After that, since you do not cook, we will have you on dishwashing detail to earn your keep," he joked. "The steaks will be ready shortly. Would you like a glass of wine?" Lisa declined, saying she would save it for dinner.

He strode into the kitchen, picked up a platter, and vanished outside.

Not knowing what else to do, Lisa sat on the couch, away from the light. She hugged an oversized pillow and closed her eyes, reflecting on the events of the day. She considered she felt so off balance, unaware, owing Morgan her life, seeing him in such a different light. She could not recall the last time she felt this out of control.

The front door burst open, and a young woman stormed in.

Lisa froze, taken by surprise, and studied the new arrival with interest. The girl wore a motorcycle helmet, a light leather jacket, and shorts revealing exquisitely long legs. She removed a heavy backpack, her helmet, and her coat and then dropped them on the floor.

Left standing was a magnificent creature. Lisa experienced threats at the intruder's beauty and sexual magnetism. Lisa realized her vocabulary lacked the words to offer a proper description, and she felt her body temperature rising along with her pulse.

Lisa knew she was attractive, but this girl made her reinterpret the lyrics of a country song that went, *"They love their women one beat shy of a heart attack."* This young lady belonged on the cover of magazines, of all the magazines. She had to hand it to Morgan. He had an excellent taste in women. His wife had been a knockout, but this girl was in a class of her own, and she defied depiction by mere mortals.

What did they call him at Annapolis? *"J.P. Morgan chase anything in a skirt."* However, tiny shorts were acceptable whenever the situation dictated. Lisa had not felt such jealousy with a side of insecurity in a long time, not since high school.

Lisa worked herself into resenting the girl to an extent she had not thought possible. She observed in silence, unable to control her emotions.

The young woman shook her long, curly, fire-engine-red hair, creating a true flare-up.

"Hoooooney, I'm hoooome!" the young beauty announced at the top of her lungs, in a decent impression of Ricky Ricardo. She waited, listened, then scanned the room, and noticed Lisa in the shadows. Lifting her left eyebrow, the girl turned to face Lisa.

J.P. ambled in, and the young woman pivoted toward him and leaped in his arms, wrapping herself all around him—arms, legs, head—like a small child.

"Or a monkey," muttered Lisa to herself.

J.P. enveloped the girl in a bear hug and buried his face in her tresses. They stood while he brushed away her locks with gentle strokes to kiss her temple. The porcelain skin contrasted with her vibrant hair, creating a hallucinogenic effect.

Lisa watched, mesmerized, incapable of breaking the spell. Another pang of jealousy probed Lisa at the sight of the intimate embrace and true, unadulterated love for each other. She could not recall the last time someone had held or loved her like that.

No wonder he murdered his wife. A wife gets in the way. A wife and a child would hinder him even more.

The girl climbed down, kissed his cheek, and examined Lisa from head to toe. "Papa Bear got a playmate." She adopted a childish tone. "She's cute. Can we keep her?"

"Max, behave. This is Lisa Jensen. Lisa, this is Max." J.P. stepped between them. He clapped his hands together. "Now that Max is here, we can eat. It is a marvelous thing because I am starving. Max, would you take your stuff upstairs and then join us for dinner?"

Max ignored him and cocked her head to one side. She fluttered her impossibly long eyelashes, causing Lisa to fluster again with resentment. The vibrant emeralds adorning the angelic face kept throwing Lisa off balance.

"Lisa Jensen... Lisa Jensen. Why do I know that name?" She thought hard, then twitched her nose. Her head straightened out with a snap. She twisted to face J.P. with the fury of a brewing storm. "Not *that* Lisa Jensen, right?"

"Actually, she is that Lisa Jensen," J.P. replied in the calmest voice possible.

(

CHAPTER 70

"**A**RE YOU OUT OF your damn mind? J.P. Morgan, you are the biggest idiot I ever met." Max turned on the fury of a full-blown hurricane. She berated him for an entire minute.

Lisa backed up, startled by the ferocity of Max's reaction.

J.P. endured it in silence. Max took a breath, and J.P. took advantage of the break. "She is in mortal danger. She needs help."

"So, what! She can be in mortal danger somewhere else. She's an ADA. She has a thousand cops itching to protect her. Why is it your obligation? How did this happen? How did you hook up with her?" Typhoon Max continued to blow with gale force.

"If I may..." Lisa stepped closer.

Cyclone Max twirled around to face Lisa and unleashed a newfound fierceness. "No, you may not. Stay out of this. I'm talking to him."

Max's demeanor stopped Lisa dead in her tracks and prompted her to rethink her approach. There was something uncontrollable, almost animalistic, in Max's wrath. Max toned it down to tornado level and crossed her arms over her chest. "This ought to be good. Explain."

"Please, go upstairs, and freshen up. Calm down, please. Dinner is ready. Lisa and I will set the table." J.P. attempted to restore the peace.

"'Lisa and I will set the table,'" Max mimicked him in her childlike manner. "So, it's '*Lisa and I now*'? What are you on? Did you hit your head?" She moved closer, checked his head for bumps, and lifted one of his eyelids and then the other, examining his eyes. "Hmm. No concussion. He seems lucid. It must be a new drug that causes temporary insanity."

"We can discuss it at dinner." J.P. put his arm around Max and led her to the stairs. He scooped up the backpack and handed it to her. "Just have a little patience and faith in me."

As she reached the landing halfway up the staircase, Max shot another murderous look, locking eyes with Lisa. Max continued clomping all the way and disappeared in her bedroom. She slammed the door so hard the cabin walls shook, and windows rattled. Lisa believed she heard roof tiles sliding and paint chips falling.

"That went better than I expected," whispered J.P. "I apologize for her outburst. She is not a fan of yours, as you can imagine. All is well when it ends well. Let's set the table."

"That went better than you expected. What was that? She went from a playful kitten to *ultra-bitch* in a nanosecond. I never saw anything like it." Lisa needed to unleash her own frustration, and J.P. seemed the perfect target.

"By 'better' I meant no broken skulls, bones, windows, dishes. Everyone still has all eyes and teeth. The cabin is not on fire. Yeah, I expected much worse."

"You could have warned me. Who is she? How dare she call me a playmate? I don't have to put up with this. I don't need your help that bad." Lisa leaped on the high horse and proceeded straight to gallop, ignoring J.P.'s discomfort. "She thinks she's some goddess deciding if you can help me. Who is she? I thought you said only Fred was coming."

"Max is Fred."

"What? What kind of name is Fred for a girl?" Lisa felt the urge to return to being herself. She needed to be in charge, the one asking the right questions and calling the shots.

"Something for you to bond over during dinner. Can you please help me set the table?"

"I want no connection with that... crazy woman. I'm not even hungry anymore. How can you think about food after that?"

"I skipped lunch, remember?" He hooked Lisa's elbow as if leading her to a gala. "Come on. You will be great friends, I can tell." J.P. flashed an innocent, disarming smile.

"We will be great friends? Where were you for the past few minutes?"

"Max does not hide her emotions well, the result of a traumatic childhood and a medical condition called Asperger's Syndrome. She will tell you more about herself. If she likes you."

"I bet she's just another poor, beautiful little girl with titanic daddy issues, and you are this fabulous guy helping her get over them," Lisa mocked. "Morgan—I mean, J.P., I have to ask. Are you out of your mind? We've been through some hair-raising scary moments today. Yet you're still cracking jokes as if we watched a 3-D movie. Are you really this cool under pressure? Do you ever take anything seriously?"

"Asked and answered, Counselor. I think of it this way. If I die, I might as well know I enjoyed living and pass on to the great beyond with a smile on my lips." He paused and examined her bewildered face. "I have the advantage of being most creative under tremendous pressure. It could be a character flaw, unnerving for others. It works for me."

"You bet your ass it's a character flaw," Lisa scoffed. "What gets me is that after hating everything about you for ten years, you tore down my defenses in a matter of hours."

CHAPTER 71

LISA WAS STILL SORTING her feelings when Max climbed down the stairs. Focusing her squinting eyes on Lisa, she stomped outside without a word. Max returned with a dusty bottle of red wine, grabbed a corkscrew, keeping her intent gaze trained on Lisa. "I need a drink or two, maybe three entire bottles," Max announced.

"Are we contributing to the delinquency of a minor?" Lisa shot J.P. a cruel look, wasting no time in sharpening her words.

"Ladies, behave," interceded J.P. "Let's have a civilized dinner. There will be plenty to be angry about soon enough. No need to waste your energy taking it out on each other."

They took their seats at the table. Max, making a spectacle, sat next to J.P., forcing Lisa to take a seat across from them. J.P. uncovered the platter with the cooked steaks, and the irresistible aroma filled the room. Lisa noticed only three steaks on the platter. She recalled Morgan carrying out all six of them, uncooked. J.P. served Lisa, Max, then took the last piece.

"This is great. How did you know how I take my steak?" Lisa asked, savoring the first bite, her eyes half open.

"During one session that ran late, the DA's team ordered lunch in. You ordered your steak medium rare."

"That was more than a decade ago. My tastes could have changed. How did you remember that, anyway? Have you been stalking me?" Lisa became livid.

"Many tastes change in life, not the way we eat steak. Until last night, I had not seen you since that last day in court, except TV, but I always changed the channel immediately."

"How did you remember it?" Lisa ignored the TV comment.

"I am cursed with a photographic or eidetic memory, and I used to—."

"OK, forget I asked." Lisa signaled the end of the conversation, turning red.

"I want to hear it." Max leaned forward.

"No, you do not." J.P. recognized an imminent Titanic-sized disaster in the making.

"Are you kidding me? Now I must hear it." She rested her elbows on the table, closer to Lisa. "OK, dish it out. What doesn't Papa Bear want me to know?"

"Max, leave it alone," J.P. muttered between clenched teeth.

"The suspense is killing me." Max leaned further into the table, fanning her napkin.

Lisa went for broke. "Today he admitted that during his trial, he used to fantasize about me walking naked through the courtroom."

"*Strutting* is the term I used," J.P. hissed, his teeth still clenched, shooting Lisa a disapproving look. "You had to get her started."

Max slammed both hands on the table and let out a belly laugh that sounded like wind chimes. She leaned forward further, almost touching noses with Lisa. "Honey, I'll let you in on a secret. He's a man. He can't help it," Max stated in a conspiratorial whisper.

Lisa waited for more and then caught on and burst into laughter.

"You know, Max," retorted J.P., "I thought I was getting myself a cute sex slave. Instead, you turned out to be more trouble than I ever imagined—a daughter, a wife, and a mother-in-law all rolled into one. Had I known then what I know now..."

"Yeah, yeah," Max waved her hand. "They wrote a country song about it. Get over it. This is fun."

"You have his number. What kind of name is Fred?" Lisa asked.

"My parents couldn't agree on a name. They settled on Frederica Maxine. After I met Papa Bear, I stopped using Frederica, shortened Maxine to Max. It sounds more intimidating and keeps the boys off-balance." She laughed like a child with no worries in her life.

She had an irresistible, infectious personality, and she was quite a young woman. Lisa saw why Morgan liked Max. It was hard not to adore her once she calmed down.

"'Fred' is a code word between us. It's our way of signaling mortal danger." Max continued. "We must obey without question whatever instructions follow 'Fred.' We never had to use it before today, except for the drills. This morning, I almost hung up on him. Luckily, I recognized his voice."

They ate and talked at length about the events of the past day. J.P. brought up a second bottle of wine. "For the entertainment portion of our evening, we can have dessert and coffee on the couch, watching tonight's featured horror flick." J.P. stood and carried his plate.

"Finally!" exclaimed Lisa. "I've been waiting all day. It seemed as if you wanted to do anything but show me this video or tackle the bad guys."

"You will understand why in a minute. May I remind you of the hospital episode and the freeway chase? One of my personal philosophy cornerstones is 'Never engage the enemy unless you know strength, position, tactics, and weak spots.' A solid exit strategy is a big plus."

"Let's assume for a moment you're right. Why didn't we go to the authorities outside the state? Like DC, for instance? Let them figure it out." Lisa stuck to the law-and-order track. She had a hard time changing the tune, and the wine was not helping.

"They may be renegades, but they are still active law enforcement. If I oversaw that operation, I would set fail-safes to alert me if anyone got wise. I dislike surprises. Neither does their boss, I can assure you." J.P. poured the last of the wine and then continued. "Are you certain they limited it to California?" His face was as serious as Lisa had ever seen it.

"You mean they're doing this all over the country?" Lisa's eyes widened.

"The main platform I heard last night was, 'America for Americans.' I think they intend to get rid of the illegal immigrants, blah, blah, blah. You know about illegal immigration issues. The entire border with Mexico is almost a war zone. They seem to hate everyone. I just do not know for sure what we are facing. What I know is that we only have one shot at solving this mystery. 'When hunting with one bullet, you wait for the clean shot' goes the old saying."

Lisa reflected he was right, in part, at least. She knew nothing about the people who chased after her. She and Max cleared up the table and loaded the dishwasher, all the while chatting up a storm. J.P. brought in a laptop and connected it to the TV in the living room.

"I think I need a few minutes outside to clear my head. I drank that wine way too fast," announced Lisa, wobbling a little as she returned from the kitchen.

"Papa Bear, are you trying to get her drunk and take advantage of her? Care to share?" Max chuckled in her playful, childish way, slapping J.P.'s shoulder.

"Max, behave, please," J.P. said, exasperated.

Max blew raspberries and returned to the kitchen. Lisa sauntered to the side door.

J.P. gripped her elbow. "Lisa, wait."

"You guys can have the room. I'm not staying in here. I'm not some plaything, you know." She shook free of his grasp, baring her teeth at him.

"Lisa, wait, that's not it." J.P. attempted to stop her again. She swatted his hand away and then continued stomping to the side door. She flung the door open and found herself face to face with a giant bear standing on its hind legs, teeth bared, front paws extended wide.

CHAPTER 72

CLANCY DREW ON HIS Cuban cigar, savoring his favorite eighteen-year-old scotch. Circles of smoke formed an ever-expanding, an almost perfect cone. He allowed himself a moment of reverie while he contemplated the thrilling days ahead. He finished dinner. The most expensive sushi money could buy brought in from Sasaki. He might as well enjoy it; in a few days, they would stop serving, along with thousands of other restaurants.

His phone chirped. He grimaced. "It's the famous Big Freaking Man himself," Clancy said to no one. He was one of a handful of people who knew the Big Man's actual identity and the depth of his involvement in their operation. He was also a childhood friend. When he needed help with his grand plan, Clancy knew the right psychopath to call on.

"What's this crap I hear about Morgan crashing the party and getting away? Is it true that you abandoned Site C? What happened to my men? I'm unable to get in touch with Sadowsky." The Big Man wasted no time with niceties.

At times like this, Clancy wished he never collaborated with him. But, better the devil you know... "I don't know where you got your info," Clancy interrupted. The politician went to work. "Morgan followed your idiot Sadowsky, who was conducting unauthorized—"

"I allowed him," the Big Man cut in. His labored wheezing sounded like a hair dryer.

"Nobody told me or Purcell. They acted without permission. We are so close to the final chapter. All our assets have to be—"

"You did not have clearance for that part," the Big Man butted in again, his voice loaded with contempt. He despised having to justify himself to anyone.

"This is my operation," Clancy burst in. "Sadowsky went off the reservation and murdered that lawyer. He and Smythe kidnapped an ADA to cover up your screw-up."

Clancy realized that chasing his ultimate dreams had taken him on a path of incredible allowances and sacrifices. Lately, everything the Big Man did seemed to be the work of a true sociopath. With a side of a mass murderer.

"That thing with Hunter's daughter was an unfortunate accident." The Big Man adopted a defensive position, working hard to conceal his genuine feelings. He loathed being exposed, even though he knew there was no danger from Clancy.

"Vice President Cheney's shooting that guy in the woods might have been 'an unfortunate accident.'" Clancy stood up to him for once.

"We have bigger fish to fry," the Big Man deflected.

"You're damn right. Four of our operatives are dead. I have over twenty assets scattered all over California and a helicopter with five men aboard in Nevada chasing after Morgan. This prick seems to be a ghost. All we ever find is a cold trail."

"That Irvine mess that's all over the news, that was you? And Morgan?"

"We had to improvise and clean up after that imbecile, Sadowsky. He brought the abducted ADA back to Site C before the dust had settled on the move. Morgan waltzed in and out, neutralized four of our men. We had no clue he'd been there. God only knows what he learned while he was there."

"What does he know?" The Big Man switched to damage control mode.

"I bet Morgan is after you, even if he doesn't specifically know it." Clancy saw no reason to share that Sadowsky had spilled his guts and that Morgan got it all on tape.

"We covered it up. Don't worry. The trail doesn't lead to us."

"If you covered it up so well, why is it blowing up in our faces?" asked Clancy.

"Four of your guys, huh?" The Big Man changed subjects with the grace of a bull chasing a red banner. "He rescued the DA woman? Hot damn. He hasn't lost his touch." His tone reflected a weird admiration the Big Man had never shown before toward anyone.

"We caught a break. She was part of the team that prosecuted Morgan. She stayed behind, and we dealt with her," Clancy proclaimed, proud of his achievement.

"How did you deal with her?" The Big Man disliked what he had heard.

"We administered one of Doc Death Jones's memory eraser cocktails. I ordered Sadowsky to take her back to Irvine, set Richter's house on fire with her inside, and frame her and Morgan for the arson." Clancy got it all out in one breath.

"They found five male bodies." The Big Man's voice got more worried.

"She should have died in that blaze. Morgan beat Sadowsky and Allen there, ambushed them, and rescued her. Purcell took care of the rest."

"What was Allen doing there? I paired Sadowsky to work with Smythe," the Big Man snapped. The constant surprises and the need to learn about the facts by dragging the information out of Clancy wore his patience very thin.

"Jamie suffered a tragic accident. His body went to Richter's place. We blamed it on Morgan and used his death to augment the APB. I had to pair Sadowsky with someone else. Allen had orders to watch him," Clancy said, aggravated by the need to explain himself.

"What kind of 'tragic accident' are you talking about?" The Big Man laughed in his customary sinister manner, sensing there was more to the story.

"I had to set an example to avoid further failures and breaches in security," Clancy replied, evasive on purpose.

"You executed Smythe as a morale booster? *Governor*, I'm impressed. You're finally growing a pair," the Big Man said, and then let out another ominous chuckle.

"Don't call me that. Yet. Let's drop this fiasco of a conversation. Our people are working on finding Morgan. They assure me he's as good as dead."

"I'll believe that when I see it. You know, although he cost me a very comfortable career and broke my nose, jaw, and three ribs, I still respect the son of a bitch. I admit, I always admired him a little. He'd surprise us and put things together out of thin air—"

"You know Morgan personally? You need to help us with insights about the way he thinks," Clancy interrupted, his voice climbing in response to the shock of the revelation.

"Nobody knows how that SOB's mind works. He's one of those creative thinker shitheads whose brains jump all over the map like crazy jackrabbits. You can never follow his reasoning or anticipate what he'll do next. I'll give him that. He's still a force to reckon with, if he's got your panties bunched up. Son of a bitch, Morgan. Who knew he was still alive? Life's full of surprises. Not all of them pleasant," the Big Man hooted.

Clancy moved the phone away from his ear in disgust.

CHAPTER 73

LISA SHIVERED WHILE HER mind reacted in alcohol-delayed mode. She had seen that bear before. Her reptile brain registered the danger, but she remained frozen in shock.

The bear stepped forward, its front paws reaching for her. Lisa shrieked loud enough to shake the cabin off its foundation. She ran for dear life to the opposite side of the room, her feet barely touching the floor and couch. She stopped atop the side table in the corner, holding a cushion in front, her heart in her throat; and she stuttered, trying to catch her breath.

"B-b-b-b-bear! It... It... It's a b-b-bear! Help! Help! Somebody, help!" Lisa shouted. Her heart throbbed, and her entire body felt on the verge of collapsing.

The bear grumbled, dropped to all four paws, and meandered into the living room, bobbing its head. The complaining animal made a beeline for the sofa and lay down on it, letting out what sounded like a sigh of disappointment. The couch groaned under the bear's weight.

Lisa screamed louder, standing on the tips of her toes. She waved the cushion, eager to scare the beast. Every single hair on the back of her neck stood at attention, and her skin swelled up with peanut-sized goose bumps. She felt trapped with her back glued to the corner and pushed further up the wall, upright on her toes in a position any ballerina would have envied. In full panic mode, sporting a mask of wild terror, she scanned the room for an exit, any escape path, like a cornered rabbit. She found no escape route.

Max wandered in from the kitchen, studied the scene, strode over to the couch, and smacked the bear on its hind leg. "Marie, get off the sofa. You know better than that."

The bear growled and attempted a playful swipe at Max, who continued to stand with a stern expression, pointing at the floor. Eventually, Marie stirred her limbs in slow motion and raised one leg at a time, protesting every move. Marie ambled to the rug in front of the fireplace where she plopped her massive body, settling face down—a three-dimensional, living, breathing bear rug. Max followed her and lay on top, rifling through Marie's fur. Max spoke in a soft, singsong voice, lost in a world of her own.

Lisa watched the entire incident with growing skepticism. She understood there was no threat from that bear. She dropped to her feet atop the table, exploring the room. She located Morgan leaning against the guest bedroom door, one leg bent, foot planted against the door frame, arms crossed in front of his chest, laughing his head off.

Shaking like a leaf, Lisa threw the cushion at him and missed. "You jerk. You think this is funny. That's a real bear. I almost had a heart attack and wet my pants at the same time. You're laughing like a nincompoop." Her face was flustered, and her heart portended to fly out of her chest. However, she had never felt more alive and alert.

"I tried to tell you. When I got the equipment, I heard Marie outside. We have this little routine when we come up here. She shows up at the back door and knocks in her own way. We open the door, and she rewards us with a welcoming bear hug. Then we feed her. We play with her. Think of her as an overgrown house cat." J.P. shrugged, amused.

"Overgrown house cat?" Lisa shouted in disbelief, mimicking a leaf in a storm. "That's a thousand-pound, lean, mean killing machine." She sensed her heart slowing down, and her voice dropped an octave. She recognized she missed the rush of the experience, though.

"Sh." Max raised her head, scowling at Lisa. "She's not quite 400 pounds. She weighs maybe 370. She can understand you, and she has feelings, you know."

"You people are insane. I need some air." Lisa stomped both feet and headed toward the door. She changed her mind in mid-stride. "I'll just go to my room and open a window." She attempted to get her breathing under control. "Any more surprises out there? Maybe an elephant, a tiger, a giant snake, anything else I need to worry about?"

J.P. and Max exchanged a quick glance and burst into laughter.

"No. Maybe mosquitoes," Max teased her, alluding to J.P.'s disdain for them.

"Why worry about the bad guys trying to kill me? I'll be lucky to survive these two lunatics." Lisa turned to Max. "You couldn't warn me you had a pet bear?"

Max shrugged, not knowing what to say, and queried J.P. with her eyes.

He delivered the line flat, with laser-guided precision. "I did. Several times actually."

Lisa cocked her head, waiting for something to follow. The smirk on J.P.'s face widened. Lisa threw her hands up in a sign of both surrender and supreme frustration and then trudged into the guest bedroom, slamming the door.

CHAPTER 74

HAVING REGAINED HER COMPOSURE, Lisa returned to the living room. She felt foolish, aware now that she was never in any danger. Marie acted like a house pet. Lisa had to admit that it must have been hilarious to watch her scramble to the perceived safety of an end table, ready to take on a full-grown bear armed with a sofa cushion. She stared at Max, who fed the bear a sandwich, half a loaf of bread and a full piece of cooked steak.

"That's why he bought six! 'Here, we feed the bears.' Oh, that bastard!" cried Lisa.

Max invited Lisa closer. Lisa signaled with her head, 'No.' Max chuckled and laughed like a child who never grew up. Lisa examined the surrealistic tableau, her heart still pounding and hair standing on the back of her neck. Astonishing beauty feeding the tamed beast.

Max grabbed Lisa's hand and walked her to the fireplace. Marie rolled on one side, observing with childish curiosity, mouth half open, awaiting the next bite. Lisa resisted at first and then moved closer, every inch causing her to become more skittish. Max led her to the bear. They kneeled, and Max guided Lisa's hand into petting Marie, who seemed to have ascended to bear heaven. Max leaned over and handed the last sandwich to Lisa. "She's hungrier than usual. Feed her. You'll make a loyal friend for life."

Lisa's eyes widened in terror, and she waved her hands.

"Come on. Marie's a blast. Maybe we'll have time tomorrow to play with her." Max's voice trailed off. She seemed to recall happier times when she and Marie romped in the forest, two cubs without a worry in the world.

"My heart is still in my throat, pounding like a jackhammer. I've never been this close to a live bear, not even at the zoo." Lisa's voice betrayed fear and awe.

"Think of Marie as the first exhibit for our own petting zoo," Max punned. She shoved the sandwich in Lisa's hands. "Now, feed her before she gets it herself."

Lisa's eyes expanded with renewed shock. Reassured by Max's smile, she edged the food closer to Marie's mouth. Marie kept still, and then in one swift move, she took a huge bite, scaring Lisa half to death. Both women giggled, and Lisa leaned into Max as if they were old friends. Lisa reached out with her other hand and petted Marie. The coarse fur felt warm, pleasant to the touch. Marie took one more bite, then Lisa dropped the leftovers in Max's lap.

"It's too close. You finish feeding it." Lisa retreated to the perceived safety of the sofa. Seeing Max's dirty look, she added, "I mean her. Thank you."

Max fed Marie the last piece of the steak sandwich and motioned for Marie to get up. She headed toward the kitchen. "I'll let J.P. know you're ready." Max smiled, seeing the alarm in Lisa's eyes. "Relax. It's time for her to go outside, anyway. Come on, Marie."

"How long have you been together?" Lisa asked, causing Max to stop on a dime and spin around like a whirlwind.

"Do you mean Marie and us or just J.P. and me? It's been the same, eight and a half years." Max walked into the kitchen, leaving a stunned Lisa attempting to come to grips with the answer. Max returned with the tray of bear claws and ripped the cover.

"*Obviously, they are for the bears.*" Lisa recalled J.P.'s statement. Son of a bitch set her up from the get-go. Oh, how she despised him. She absolutely hated him for it. However, as practical jokes go, it was a good one. Bastard!

Marie's ears perked up, and she leaped without effort onto all fours, following Max to the side door. Max strolled out with Marie in tow and returned within a minute. "J.P. will be right in. I had to get Marie out with the bear claws. Otherwise, we would scrub the cabin for a month. She absolutely adores those things."

216

"Eight and a half years? That would mean you were, what, fifteen at the time?" Lisa reverted to the previous conversation.

"You're in the ballpark," Max answered.

"You two got together when you were fifteen?" Lisa's face turned red with rage. Her heart banged harder against her rib cage, and she felt her head temperature rising.

"Yep."

"That's statutory rape!" she cried, clenching her fists. She wanted to storm outside, beat Morgan to a pulp, and then hang him from the tallest tree. Upside down.

"Nah. Believe me, I tried. Very hard. He wouldn't go for it." A mischievous smile changed Max's features, reminiscent of an adolescent prankster.

CHAPTER 75

"**H**E PROVED TO BE** one hell of a surprise. We wasted precious resources on him. Tell me everything about him," Clancy demanded, leaving no room for argument.

The Big Man stopped laughing, drew on his own Cuban cigar, blew out the smoke in slow motion, and sipped from the glass of twenty-five-year-old single malt. His reply came out in a staccato rhythm, punctuated by heavy breathing. "He worked for me in Naval Intelligence. He was the most creative SOB we had. He could put things together like nobody's business. Technically, he was an analyst, but he did fieldwork. We tolerated his quirks because he was good, and he could think on his feet. He foiled dozens of plots to hurt our troops overseas. In his spare time, he, George Hunter's son Jack, and some jarhead—I don't recall his name—spent a lot of time with this crusty old Marine gunnery sergeant, Solomon. The gunny was an instructor at Camp Pendleton, an elite sniper who won every shooting competition there is. Word is that Morgan, Jack Hunter, and the jarhead were pretty good with guns themselves."

"I don't care about his achievements," Clancy cried. "He did great things for this country. Send flowers to his funeral. Write his eulogy. I don't care. I need to catch him. Why did he leave the Navy? His file said he quit, forfeited all benefits but gave no explanation."

"He left because he attacked me," the Big Man explained. "One day, he picked a fight with me over some crap intel. Bullshit. He was trying to cover his ass by blaming me. He got in my face, ambushed me, broke my nose, jaw, and three ribs before they pulled him off me. Naturally,

I pressed charges. I wanted him court-martialed. The bleeding-heart SECNAV cut him a deal, allowed him to resign instead. Pussy."

"Something doesn't fit with what I read about him, but I'm not interested in that. Tell me how to catch him." Clancy's tone grew more concerned.

"I don't have the faintest idea. The one thing that would get him out of hiding is if a person he cares about was in danger. If we grab someone important to him, he'll show up. His parents passed away. He has no siblings. His wife is dead, no children. After the trial, all his friends disavowed him. I don't think he has anybody we can apply pressure to smoke him out. Too bad the lawyer who defended him is not available for this exercise." The Big Man sniggered. "I honestly didn't think he was alive anymore," the Big Man concluded. "After his trial, he just disappeared. We wanted to tie up our loose ends but couldn't find him. For a while, I thought Hunter, or his family, took care of him. I'll let you know if I can think of something."

"What was that botched thing involving Hunter?"

"I told you, it was an unfortunate accident," the Big Man barked, angry. "It has nothing to do with our operation now. Anyway, I'll level with you. We needed to soften George Hunter up. A client was desperate to get his son acquitted and released from jail. Junior got himself nabbed with a lot of drugs and guns on the boat he kept at the Newport Beach marina. He was looking at a long stay in a state-run Hotel California."

"OK, enough stories. Can you help us catch Morgan or not?" demanded Clancy, rapping his fingers on the table. He regretted even more his association with the Big Man.

"Relax, Governor. It's too late for anyone to stop us now. FYI, tonight I'm going ahead with the backup option we discussed aimed at convincing our current Governor to see things our way. Just in case the primary option doesn't work out as planned." The Big Man issued a maniacal laugh. "Great thinking with the counterfeit story. I might just use that to set Morgan up for it." His disturbing hoot sounded like a bellow before he clicked off.

CHAPTER 76

"WHAT DO YOU MEAN? What's going on here?" Lisa leaned forward, stunned and flabbergasted. "Who are you?" The lawyer in her took over.

"That's just like him. What did he tell you?" Max threw her head back, slapping her thigh, all the while giggling like a schoolgirl.

"Nothing. I know he called you twice, called you 'Fred,' and spoke cryptically to you both times. Then he told me you would join us for dinner."

"That's my J.P., all right. I can guess why he doesn't like you enough to talk about the two of us. Well, we're the closest thing we both have for a family. He's the best father any girl could have. I'm the most rebellious and ungrateful surrogate daughter there is."

"What about the 'sex slave' comment and your 'thing together'?"

"That has to do with how we met. Let me tell you the story, since J.P. would rather have all his teeth pulled without anesthesia." Max smiled. They got comfortable on the couch, facing each other. "I once had a picture-perfect childhood. I grew up in Santa Monica, a few blocks from the beach. After my eleventh birthday, my mom died of breast cancer. Less than six months from diagnosis to the coffin. My dad took it the hardest. He had loved her so much, and he was lost without her. First came the heavy drinking, then the inability to concentrate at work. Eventually, he got fired. We lost the house, ended up in the less wealthy part of town."

Max paused as she struggled to come with grips with her emotions. "Then it was drugs and dealing them to sustain his habit. He shacked up with this woman, Carmen, a prostitute working the Sunset Strip. He dragged me along for the ride. I was thirteen when Dad was arrested for possession with intent to sell for, like, the hundredth time. This time, he got five years, and he left me with Carmen. She took 'calls' at our apartment. It was tiny. I had to wait in the living room while she and her 'guests' were busy in the bedroom."

Lisa's eyes reflected the fire she felt inside, and her nails cut into her palms.

"One day, another disaster. Carmen got an STD, and she couldn't work. One of her Johns was so horny that he offered her double for me. She asked for triple. They settled." Max's eyes became hollow, and their usual spark vanished. She aged ten years in an instant. Her voice and her body trembled from emotional overload.

"Oh, my God. Tell me you didn't," Lisa muttered.

"I was thirteen. I said no. I tried to run. They drugged me. I was so out of it that, when it finally happened, I didn't care. I don't remember it. Shortly after that, I dropped out of school. I was so ashamed and disgusted with myself. Carmen drugged me out of my skull most of the time. She rented me to whoever paid the premium rates. That lasted over a year."

Lisa sensed her mouth drying and realized her jaw was hanging open. She tightened her lips, wondering whether she looked as incensed as she felt. She wanted to reach out and comfort Max but did not know how.

Max continued, reliving every moment, oblivious to Lisa's struggle. "One night, Carmen and I are doing our thing. Here comes Papa Bear. He was tracking a runaway. He sees me, and he talks to Carmen for a while. He leaves and returns ten minutes later. He gives Carmen a fat envelope, and she makes me get into his car. Back then, I was a zombie. No soul left, just something men used and discarded. I probably had more heavy drugs in my system than blood cells. Carmen told me to go with him and do whatever he asked, seeing how he paid her top dollar for the privilege."

Lisa clasped her hands in front of her mouth, listening in a trance, ignoring her tears.

221

"I found out a few years later from Carmen. Papa Bear negotiated a sale price for me. He bought me for $15,000. Pretty cheap, come to think of it." Max flashed a sad smile. "Carmen was high as a kite, and she sold me to him to do with me as he pleased, his 'personal sex slave.' It became our private joke. I don't know why he did it. I had never seen him before. He just drove by that evening, and it turned out to be the luckiest night of my life."

"Oh no," Lisa uttered, causing Max to snap out of her reverie.

"Relax, Counselor. I'm here, aren't I? It was a blessed night. I've been thanking God and my lucky stars every day." Max took Lisa's hand and held it as if Lisa needed comforting. "That was the first time I tried to, you know, in the car, on the way from Santa Monica to our house in Trabuco Canyon. He fought me hard, told me to wait until we got home. It was pretty funny, come to think of it."

"How is that funny?" Lisa straightened out, searching for a handle on the situation.

"You had to be there, I guess. No other man ever said no to me, especially one who had paid for it. First, he tried to detox me at home. Every day, one of his clients, a doctor, came by to check up on me. About a week into it, I needed drugs, and I had exhausted all my tricks. Papa Bear still wouldn't let me touch him or get drugs. I offered to let him do anything he could imagine just so I could get a fix. I was burning up from the inside. I had one thing on my mind: 'I need a fix. NOW!' And I was ready to do anything to get it. And I mean anything."

Lisa rearranged her legs under her and ended up closer to Max, who reached out and placed a hand on her shoulder, triggering Lisa's need for human contact. "I came up with a plan." Max resumed. "I stole a few heavy-duty sleeping pills from the doctor's bag. I acted mellow and submissive all day. I crushed the meds in his food. That night, I sneaked into his room and stabbed him in the back as he slept. I stole his motorcycle, ran to the first crack house I could find, and resumed my previous lifestyle. I didn't have any money, so I started trading sex for drugs. I don't know why he didn't bleed to death in his sleep. Sheer luck, I guess. Another thing I thank God for every single day." Max raised her eyes in prayer.

Lisa reached out and hugged her. They sat, crying softly, locked in an embrace they both needed. Max pulled back and continued, "He tracked me down a few days later. When he found me, I was so high and I was sure he would kill me, and I didn't give a damn. Instead, he brought me straight up here, where we spent the next three months, just the two of us. Marie showed up at some point, but I'll tell you about her later. I asked him a thousand times why he didn't wring my neck. He said he was protecting his investment. That's Papa Bear for you."

"I have a hard time with this entire story," Lisa began.

Max placed her fingers on Lisa's lips. "He took care of me, fed me, held me, talked to me, and went through hell with me. I did everything in my power to hurt him. He never hit me or yelled at me, not once. OK, he yelled a few times. The doc came up twice a week to check on me and bring meds. Nobody had cared about me that much, not since my mom died."

"John Paul Morgan did all that?" Lisa struggled hard to reconcile her experience of the man. She felt woozy from wine and the mixture of emotions evoked by Max's story.

"He's quite a guy once you get to know him," Max answered, daydreaming. "Since they murdered his wife, I don't think he's been with anyone else, definitely not for as long as I've known him. He made up some convoluted thing about being his fault she's dead. It's a twisted guilt trip he lives through every single day. All he ever does is work, research, take care of me." She wiped tears. "We didn't own the cabin back then. He rented it from a local booze head. We bought it as a place to get away from it all, started renovating it, added on to it. Oh my God, when we first got here, it had these horrible orange cabinets everywhere. I guess the previous owner used some leftover *Caltrans* paint. It was just scary, Halloween scary. We spent an entire week stripping the paint to re-stain them. We settled in to remodel it bit by bit. One day, Marie showed up. I had novel ways to fill my days, and soon, I was over the withdrawal. I still recall that first day when I woke up, and I did not feel the sweltering need to have a fix. At first, it was like a dull pain, then it subsided, and then it disappeared."

Max stood, got bottles of water for both, then resumed. "J.P. Morgan decided to rescue someone, and he picked me. Why me? I guess we'll never know. I asked a million times. He always says I saved him more than he saved me. I love him more than life itself. Without him, I wouldn't be alive today. I know that. Do you think we can suggest his name for sainthood?" Max asked in her childish manner, trying to lighten up the mood.

"What? I'm sorry. I got distracted for a moment. J.P. Morgan, the *Butcher of Irvine*, who would have ever thought?" Lisa snapped back to reality, fighting contradictory feelings.

"I was right about you." Max shoved Lisa away hard and jumped to her feet. "He should have left you to fend for yourself or go to your cop friends for help. You don't deserve him—his help." Max's jaw quivered. She clenched her fists, ready to pummel the snot out of Lisa.

"What?" Max's explosion took Lisa by surprise. Reviewing what she said, she added, "Oh, Max, I'm sorry. I didn't mean it. Just reflecting aloud. I meant it as a compliment."

"If that's your idea of a compliment, don't waste any of them on me." Max backed away, holding her hands in front of her as if repelling Lisa with her entire being.

CHAPTER 77

J.P. AMBLED IN CARRYING a toolbox. "Why the standoff and horse faces?"

"You're such an idiot. You had no right to bring this cold, heartless bitch into our lives. Not up here." Max unleashed her rage on J.P. She pummeled his chest and shoulder. "This is our place. This is our life, moron. Ours."

J.P. winced and accepted the thumping without protest. "I leave you alone for five minutes, and you are at it again? What do I have to do, lock you up in separate rooms? We have much bigger issues to deal with right now."

"I must apologize deeply to both of you. I made an inappropriate remark," Lisa offered, imploring forgiveness with soft sapphire eyes. "I called you the *Butcher of Irvine*. She is right. I wasn't thinking. I was just reflecting how different my perception of you is than the man in Max's story, her savior."

J.P. lifted his palm toward Lisa and turned to Max. "What have you been telling her?"

"She asked how long we've been together. I told her how we met."

"Why, Max? She does not need to know that. Nobody needs to learn about it. That is your story and mine, baby. Let's keep it that way." He pulled Max into his arms.

"Why not, Morgan? Are you scared that someone might learn you are not the crusty, son-of-a-bitch mur... I mean, we all thought you were? It's a wonderful thing you did for her." Lisa's words fell out of her mouth, not quite as she intended them to.

"You never made an impulse buy? I find that hard to believe." J.P. tried to derail the conversation pile-up away from Max's story.

"She's not a pair of shoes or a purse you cannot afford. We're talking about a human being. She's right. You are a giant moron."

J.P. held Max close to him and glared at Lisa, "Do not kid yourself, Ms. Jensen. Nothing can alter your perception of me. If anyone can make this thing seem wrong, it will be government drones like you, who think in terms of legal, illegal, 'can I get a conviction,' or 'should I pass on prosecuting it.'"

"That's so not fair." Lisa protested.

"Maybe it is not reasonable. However, it is what it is. I am not interested in changing your opinion of me. You and I have a business deal. When this is over, I will continue to do what I do. You will go back to prosecuting criminals and convicting the occasional innocent person. That maintains the public's trust in law and order and wins elections. Life goes on. Until then, please let's attempt some civility among ourselves."

"Is that why you think I do what I do? Then you know nothing about me." Lisa stood her ground and returned J.P.'s intense stare, feeling the volcano building up inside her.

"If I want to know something, I will ask," J.P. slammed her. "Hopefully, you will answer truthfully this time." He returned his attention to Max. "You, young lady, need to learn to be less volatile. Other people can have separate opinions about me. You cannot go around smacking everyone until they embrace yours."

"Why not? If people knew the real you, they wouldn't say the things she did and said during the trial," Max countered.

"Max, what is this really about?"

"How can you protect her? She calls you the *Butcher of Irvine*. You're ready to lay your life on the line for her." Max crossed her arms on her chest and cocked her head.

"You don't have to agree, but I ask that you respect my decision. When someone is in mortal danger, you put petty differences aside and help. When the peril has passed, you both reassess the relationship. That is how I do things."

"I don't refer to you as the *Butcher...* I'm sorry. I should have been more careful. Today has been a stressful day for me. I'm running for my life, and I don't know why. I'm in danger for seeing something I don't recall. I'm forced to accept help from a man I never thought I could stand being in the same room with, let alone work with," Lisa pleaded, hoping to reestablish the fragile peace of the dinner table conversation.

"Your point?" Max tapped her toes, pressing her lips in a tight line.

CHAPTER 78

"MAX, BEHAVE, PLEASE.** Let her finish. I would like you both to watch the recordings of last night's events. It will provide answers for Ms. Jensen and plenty of information for you. I have been thinking about this all day. Maybe you two can see it from a different angle, provide some insights, or point out stuff I missed." J.P. clutched Max's hand and guided her back to the sofa while petting her tresses. Max almost purred under his touch.

"I apologize again. From the bottom of my heart. I'll watch what I say around you. Truce?" Lisa raised her arms, signaling surrender. She extended her hand to Max, who took it with significant reluctance. "Now let's watch that darn video. I would like to see if I can figure out what I have been doing for the past few days," Lisa said.

The image shook, then it focused on Smythe and Sadowsky at the top of Anna's front steps. From inside the rug on Smythe's shoulder, a red shoe dropped. Sadowsky scooped it up before it settled on the ground.

"What's this?" asked Max. "Can you at least give us some context?"

"That is Lisa wrapped in Anna's rug," replied J.P.

"You are positive I was inside it?" Lisa inquired.

"Just watch. Here comes the unceremonious dump in the trunk of your own car. You entered Anna's home at 7:35 p.m., followed by those two. Next time I saw you, you were doing a decent impersonation of a pretzel in their warehouse in South LA. If you were not in that rug, how did you get there? Nifty trick."

"You know where they took me. Why didn't you call the cops?"

"You called the cops last night. They came, and then Reedy Guy—" J.P. began.

"Excuse me, Reedy Guy who?" Lisa interrupted.

"Their boss, Clancy. Keep watching. He will show up soon enough. When I do not know their names, I nickname. That way, I track them, like characters in a play. He showed up, badged the local cops, and kicked them off the scene. They left without argument, so he must be some heavy hitter in the law enforcement community."

"Why didn't you call the Feds, DHS, someone? I don't like that you ran. It makes me feel that you have something to hide."

J.P. decided against engaging in the debate. "They are highly mobile. As soon as they figured I recorded everything, they moved out. The Feds would have found an empty building."

"That's not true. They could have followed up on the leads," Lisa insisted.

"Lisa, think about it. You still consider me the *Butcher of Irvine*—"

"I apologized for it already." Lisa pouted, throwing her hands up in the air.

"I am talking about credibility, not to mention there is a 'shoot on sight' warrant out there with my name on it." He twisted, attempting to see the back of his shirt while tugging at it. "I can feel the bull's eye burning a hole in my back."

"I see what you mean," Lisa conceded. "Still—"

"Kids, settle down. Otherwise, I'll turn off the TV and send you to bed. I'm terribly cranky without popcorn and dessert." Max mocked them in a motherly tone.

They returned their attention to the TV. J.P. skipped through the drive to Florence.

Without warning, the front door crashed open. Two men leaped inside, silenced guns in hand, and their eyes swept the cabin in search of a threat.

"Nobody moves! Police! Hands where we can see them!" the tall one roared.

CHAPTER 79

"**HOW THE HELL DID** you find us?" J.P. removed his feet off the coffee table.

"Wouldn't you like to know, asshole! Your time of causing trouble is over. Sit tight so we don't have to shoot you yet." The taller of the self-professed cops closed the front door and beamed a vicious smile. He was lean, sported a shiny shaved head and a blond goatee.

Lisa felt shaken to her core. She glanced back and forth from Max to J.P. Max appeared baffled by the intrusion. J.P.'s face remained an impenetrable mask. His eyes darted around, taking everything in. She considered what J.P. would nickname him and gave it a shot. *Tall Stick* seemed appropriate. The short one, a foot shorter than his partner, had a mop of light brown hair, and short, skinny arms. *Short Stick*. The *Sticks* patted them down for weapons, keeping everyone in sight and the entire cabin in their crossfire fields with practiced efficiency.

"Anyone else here, dickhead?" inquired *Tall Stick*.

"Only the three of us." Lisa broke the silence.

"Is that so, asshole? Answer me." *Tall Stick* demanded J.P.'s response. He took a menacing step forward, thrusting his gun in J.P.'s face, and then slammed the laptop shut.

"There is a platoon of Marines upstairs and a squad of hungry bears outside. They are waiting for us to feed them. You should take over host duties. Set out plenty of food because they need to eat." J.P.'s voice was loud and had a high pitch, as if scared.

The *Sticks* exchanged a quizzical look, and then *Short Stick* climbed the stairs.

Lisa shot J.P. an inquisitive look. J.P. kept his eyes on *Tall Stick*. Lisa turned to Max, who monitored Short Stick's movements.

Lisa addressed *Tall Stick*. "What's going on here?"

"Shut up. I'm not asking again." *Tall Stick* pointed his gun at Lisa.

Short Stick checked the upstairs areas, then the kitchen and downstairs bedroom. "All clear. We can call it in." *Short Stick* posed himself in a shooter's stance in front of Max.

Tall Stick spoke into a two-way radio, making no attempt to hide his satisfaction. "Beta Six to Site B. We have a progress report."

"Go ahead, Beta Six," Simpson replied.

"Beta Six to Site B. We have Morgan and Jensen in custody. We apprehended a third suspect, female, mid-twenties, identity unknown. This Morgan guy isn't so tough up close."

"Congratulations, Beta Six. You earned our lifelong admiration and gratitude. Locate and retrieve all recordings and documents, whether or not they relate to our operations. Do not take any chances. Report when finished," Simpson instructed professionally, though his voice burst with excitement.

"Consider it done." *Tall Stick* hooked the radio on his belt. "I wish we could spend more time getting to know each other."

That earned him disgusted looks from Max and Lisa.

Unfazed, *Tall Stick* pointed at the TV. "Unfortunately, work must intrude. Is that the illegal recording made at our classified facility? Are there any other copies?"

J.P. impersonated a sculpture. His eyes were the only sign he was alive.

"I asked you a question, jackass!" Tall Stick yelled, waving the gun. Then he shot the couch, about six inches from J.P.'s shoulder. "Answer me."

"What?" J.P. flinched and looked at him as if he had just come out of a trance.

"Our big fucking hero is shell-shocked." *Tall Stick* made a repulsed face and advanced closer to J.P., stopping only inches on the opposite side of the coffee table. He leaned in and continued as if talking to a retarded person. "I asked if there are any other copies."

Lisa's anxiety level tripled. What the hell? Morgan did not scare that easy. She read his file. She saw him in action. However, here he was, sitting like a deer in the headlights.

Max seemed to be in a trance of her own, which added to Lisa's mounting concern. She alternated looks between them, then settled her gaze on *Tall Stick*.

Short Stick displayed the eager look of someone who had somewhere else to be.

A light crashing noise outside the side door got everyone's attention.

"Check it out." *Tall Stick* ordered his partner.

Short Stick leveled his gun and threw the door open. Marie stood in the doorframe, on her hind legs, front paws spread wide, looking for her hug. "Shiiiitttt!" *Short Stick* panicked and retreated. Marie followed, bobbing her head as if surprised by his reaction. *Short Stick* fired twice into Marie's chest.

Marie let out a howl and leaped, knocking the gun out of *Short Stick*'s hand.

"Noooooo!" Max screamed and leaped off the sofa.

Short Stick crashed backward. *Tall Stick* turned his head to inspect the commotion.

J.P. grabbed the lamp from the end table and arched its base into *Tall Stick*'s temple. *Tall Stick* moaned and piled on the floor. J.P. dived over the coffee table and scooped his gun. He rolled, landing on *Short Stick*, who sat shell-shocked, petrified eyes locked on Marie.

Max flung herself at *Short Stick*'s gun and aimed it at him. "Just flinch, asshole."

Short Stick's terror-filled eyes continued to focus on Marie, who grumbled three feet away. J.P. handcuffed him. *Short Stick*'s gaze shifted from the injured bear to Max while the veins on his temples resembled clogged cartoon pipes.

"I got this one." Max nodded toward *Short Stick*. Her face flushed with anger and agony, not knowing how severe Marie's wounds were. She maintained her position.

J.P. flipped *Tall Stick*, handcuffed him, and dragged him next to his partner. He checked *Tall Stick*'s gun for a chambered round and then handed it to Lisa. "Every inch one of them moves earns them a bullet each. Start with the knees. It makes for a powerful statement. Family jewels are more entertaining. Messier but definitely more fun."

Short Stick's eyes widened, and his body shook like a small tree in a hurricane. His breathing became labored and sweat started rolling freely from his hairline.

Marie thrashed, attempting to get up on all her fours. J.P. helped her sit, leaning her against the open side door like a heavy person. "She'll be OK," J.P. said after a cursory examination of Marie's chest wounds. "The bullets are under her shoulder blade. We need to get her down to Dr. Wilson's shop to have them removed, but she'll be OK."

Max sighed relief and wiped free-flowing tears from her cheeks. Lisa's legs gathered the strength to support her. She came to J.P.'s side, keeping a respectful distance from Marie.

"There is a First-Aid Kit in the guest bathroom." J.P. directed Lisa. "We need to clean this wound and stop the bleeding. It's a long way down the mountain." He retrieved the gun from Max's hands. "Max, give Marie something to sedate her. Otherwise, she will be a handful. She needs to hold until we get her to Dr. Wilson's."

J.P. dragged the two *Sticks* away from Max and Marie. "I do not think you want to be this close to Marie when she gets over the shock. She might not need food for a month."

"Please don't let the bear get me. I have kids," *Short Stick* pleaded.

"What do you know? He worries about his kids." J.P. shook his head. "Yet you didn't hesitate to barge in here to execute us. Where was your concern for your kids then?"

J.P. handed Lisa the gun he had taken from Max. "One inch, one bullet each. Do not worry about saving ammo. Blow off some steam while you are at it. I will make sure they came alone," said J.P. He checked the captives' pockets and retrieved a set of car keys.

CHAPTER 80

LISA LIFTED BOTH GUNS and slipped into a new persona. She interpreted J.P.'s comments as the preamble to some form of mind games or psychological warfare. She knew it would come in handy when the questioning started, and she could hardly wait to get some answers for herself. "Talk fast because I am *soooo* tired of being used for target practice. One of the side effects is that my trigger finger gets uncontrollably twitchy."

"I don't know anything. I was just following orders." *Short Stick* bobbed his head.

"Where did I hear that excuse before?" Lisa pretended to be deep in thought and then leaned forward, mustering all the venom she was capable of. "Oh, yeah. The Nuremberg Trials. All the *innocent* Nazis, who did not understand they were doing anything wrong. Now talk."

"I don't know anything. Please don't shoot me. We had instructions to arrest Morgan." A thicker layer of sweat formed on *Short Stick*'s forehead, dripping into his eyes.

"You don't know anything. How many kids did you say?" Lisa mocked him.

"Two," *Short Stick* answered.

"Either way, if the wife wants more kids, she's going to have to turn to someone else. Start talking, or I'll test the messier but more fun theory." She pointed the gun at his privates.

"Please, lady. I don't know anything. We had orders to capture Morgan. And you."

"First mistake." Lisa smirked. "Never call me 'lady.'" She mimicked shooting both guns at his private area in an alternate motion and then blew imaginary smoke from the barrels.

Tall Stick stirred and moaned. *Short Stick* went into a full-blown panic mode. "Creighton, stop moving. They'll shoot us."

Creighton opened his eyes and tried to sit up. Lisa shoved him back down with her foot. "You should listen to your partner. Stay down."

"Take these things off me. We are police officers. You're making things worse, Ms. Jensen." Creighton pulled against the cuffs, his malicious eyes assessing the situation.

"What offense did I commit, Officer Creighton?" asked Lisa.

Creighton replied, "You are Morgan's accomplice. That's enough."

"And what crime did Mr. Morgan commit, Officer Creighton? What crime am I an accomplice to?" Lisa adopted a courtroom manner.

"You and Morgan infiltrated a classified site. You stole confidential documents and information vital to national security. Then you and Morgan killed five police officers."

"Wow!" exclaimed Lisa. "You said that with a straight face. Very convenient, don't you think, Officer Creighton? Let's say you're right. How does that explain the silenced guns?" Lisa waited for an answer. With nothing forthcoming, she continued. "Let me guess. You wanted to avoid disturbing the wildlife when you assassinated us. How considerate of you."

"Our weapons don't concern you. We identified ourselves. We are police officers. There is a valid APB and a warrant for Morgan's arrest, along with his accomplices."

"Here I was, watching this video depicting how your friends kidnapped and took me against my will to this 'classified facility.' Then you two break in and pretend to arrest me for being Mr. Morgan's co-conspirator. See, that is not how I remember last night's events at all."

Max finished patching up Marie and took one gun from Lisa's hands. "Yeah, I could use some enlightening. What gives?"

Creighton attempted to sit up again. Max propelled him down with her heel, bouncing his head on the floor. "What did J.P. say? For every inch they move, one bullet each?"

"Something like that, but I think it was more of a loose guideline. He said we should have fun with it and blow off some steam. Where should we start?" Lisa directed the gun at Creighton's crotch and then at his knee, oscillating. "Officer Creighton, anything?" Lisa asked, aiming the gun to his nether area. "My trigger finger is getting itchy, very itchy."

The two prisoners remained quiet, Creighton calculating his next move, *Short Stick* fidgeting, unable to concentrate on anything else.

"Well then, Officer Creighton, let me tell you how I recall last night's events after your cohorts abducted me." Lisa paused, allowing Creighton to add something. "I recall minding my business when your cronies kidnapped me—"

"You shouldn't be able to remember anything," *Short Stick* blurted.

Lisa and Max both broke into hearty laughter. "That's right. I'm not supposed to remember anything because your goons drugged me. If you know nothing, how did you know that?" Lisa said between laughs, concentrating for clues on Creighton's cruel face.

"You Nimrod, I had this, and you blew it. She knew nothing for sure until you opened your stupid big mouth. When we get out of here, I'll shoot you myself, you imbecile. There is no room for the likes of you on our team, in our new world." Creighton spat words like arrows. If looks could kill, *Short Stick* would have turned to minced meat.

CHAPTER 81

A QUICK RAP AT the door got their attention. Lisa shifted her gun. Seeing J.P., she lowered it and let out a sigh, rivaling a gust of wind. "Knock louder and wait for an invitation."

"This is my cabin." J.P. replied. He strode over to Marie and checked Max's patchwork. "It looks good. Let's get her to Dr. Wilson's."

"Yeah." Max buried her head in Marie's shoulder, comforting her beloved companion.

"This cabin is compromised. I brought their car up front. It was just beyond the gate. They had accurate intel about our security measures. I wonder how. We will load Marie in the Expedition and put these two in the trunk of their own car."

"Wait a minute. We just started asking questions," Lisa complained. "We need some answers. Maybe shoot off some *huevos* first."

"We will interview them. I would love nothing better right now. Somehow, we are not safe here. Marie needs medical attention. She is a house cat when she wants to play, but she is an injured wild animal. We never shot her before. It was hard sometimes, believe me."

Max rolled her eyes, petting Marie's head.

"I don't know how she will react when the sedative wears off, but she'll be a handful. She will want to eat these two. I am worried about Max, too," J.P. winked. "When she figures out they hurt Marie, she will go postal. Nobody hurts Marie and gets away with it."

"OK." Lisa nodded.

"Before the night is over, I want to hurt some animal abusers. These two pieces of shit will do, for starters. Just try to stop me," Max joined the ruse.

"You will get your chance. Let's get out before reinforcements arrive," J.P. urged them.

"You think more jerks will come looking for their comrades?" Lisa asked. "What is this, a bad video game? The more zombies you kill, the more show up to replace them?"

"They made critical, costly mistakes," answered J.P. "You escaped. They did not finish the frame-up job at Anna's place, lost three men and executed two Irvine cops to cover it up. These two rushed up here, but I bet backup is on the way. They may be bad guys, but they are not all stupid. Somebody has to have some brains to have put this shenanigan together."

"Then, let's shoot them here and save ourselves the effort," Lisa scoffed.

Lisa's comment brought a renewed wave of terror to Short Stick's face.

J.P. smiled and whispered in Lisa's ear, loud enough for everyone to hear him. "I do not want to clean up. No worries. Clancy does not tolerate failure. These two earned a summary execution and a quick burial in these woods. Their only chance is to talk to us."

The two prisoners exchanged worried looks, the bravado in their eyes replaced by distress. They knew what had happened to Jamie Smythe and Clancy's reputation.

J.P. removed the chair/cot to make room for Marie and then appropriated a box from the Sticks' cruiser—a flare gun and six flare cartridges; several flash bangs, both full and training size, two MP5Ns, extra ammo. He kept one radio and threw the other in the box.

Max perp-walked the captives to the cruiser and motioned for them to get into the trunk. Creighton complied, resigned. *Short Stick* dropped to the ground, pleading, "Please don't do this. I have two kids. They need me."

Max whistled for J.P., who strode over, picked up *Short Stick* by the belt, and dropped him in the trunk atop Creighton. "Stop whining." J.P. tore off the trunk safety lever, pitched it in the thick brushes lining the driveway, and then slammed the lid.

Max and J.P. brought Marie out on a furniture dolly. Marie was semiconscious, and her head lolled from side to side, eyes half open, drool dripping from her mouth.

"We have to get her in." J.P. scratched his head. "I could use the winch, but she will get mad, and she may take it out on us."

Max rushed into the cabin and returned with Lisa's chocolate cake. She pulled on Marie's ear. Marie grumbled louder and opened her eyes. Max jumped in the SUV and removed the lid. "Come on, baby bear. Come to Maxie. Chocolate cake."

Marie caught a whiff and perked up. She yelped in pain as she stood on shaky legs. With one hop, she was in the SUV in pursuit of the treat. Max forced her to sit down. "Like giving candy to a baby... bear," Max quipped, petting Marie, who settled to munch, making a chocolaty mess. "Don't worry, Marie. We'll clean it up, girl. Enjoy."

Lisa watched in amazement, then she clicked. "Hey, that's my cake." She turned toward the cruiser's trunk. "That short guy gets his balls shot off tonight. The bear's eating *my cake*."

J.P. pitched Lisa the Expedition keys. "You drive Max and Marie. Follow me."

"No way. I'm not getting in the car with that—with Marie. You go with them." Lisa studied the keys in her hand and shook her head.

"Fine." J.P. reached for the keys. "You drive the car with the two psycho killers. They will probably ride quietly and will not try to escape and fulfill their mission."

"Why can't Max drive the SUV, and I'll ride with you and the two psychos?" Lisa continued to seek solutions to her dilemma.

"Who will keep Marie calm in the back of the truck while Max drives?" J.P. quizzed.

Lisa realized there were no other viable options. She twitched her nose. "OK. But if that bear makes one wrong move, I'm jumping out."

CHAPTER 82

THE SMALL CONVOY STOPPED in the parking lot of the local Animal Hospital. J.P. waited for Lisa to back up to the ramp and then opened the back gate.

Marie leaped out and howled when she hit the ground. She was distressed and in obvious pain. Whatever Max had administered at the cabin had worn off.

Doc Wilson and Chris, his assistant, both in green overalls, beelined for Marie.

"Jesus! Who did this?" asked Chris, her eyes darting furiously from Max to J.P. "If I get my hands on the son of a bitch, he'll wish he was never born."

"We have them in here, Chris." J.P. banged on the trunk of the cruiser. "I plan on interrogating them myself, maybe hurt them a little. You could join in."

Chris gripped Marie's ear and started pulling her toward the office. "Let us tend to Marie first. Don't you dare leave before I have a talk with them."

J.P. mock-saluted Chris. Marie followed Chris and Dr. Wilson, shuffling her feet and complaining all the way.

J.P. dragged Short Stick out by the belt, letting him drop. *Short Stick* hit the ground with a loud thump. J.P. repeated the procedure with Creighton, getting another loud thud, followed by a moan. J.P. handed Lisa and Max flashlights then he goaded the two prisoners into the thick forest extending behind the clinic. Max went to the backyard of the small veterinary hospital.

They walked a quarter of a mile to a small clearing. J.P. motioned for the captives to stop. Max joined them, carrying two shovels she had borrowed from the vet's office.

J.P. explained. "First one to talk gets to go home. The other one gets shot in the gut and stays here in the forest at the mercy of the wildlife. Or, I can hand you over to Clancy."

"You wouldn't dare to kill us. We're cops," Creighton called his bluff.

"I am already wanted for allegedly murdering five police officers. What are they going to do, fry me twice? Ha, ha! I said shoot, not kill. The coyotes, the mountain lions, and the bears will take care of the rest. It is more fun that way. For me, of course."

"You are dead anyway," Creighton taunted J.P. "I'll see to it myself."

"Do either of you have any idea what it is like for wild animals to eat you alive? Oh, the excruciating pain, the incredible agony, and the sickening feeling when the flesh tears off your bones." J.P. shivered. "Brrrrr."

"I don't know anything. If I did, I'd tell you. I have two kids, and my wife is pregnant with our third." *Short Stick* expanded his repertoire.

Lisa caught on and went along for the ride. "Now she's pregnant with their third. That's new," Lisa said. "I'll make sure she gets help from the local psycho association to raise your children in the proper environment. Your maniac bosses offer survivor benefits, right?"

"Shut up, you moron. They cannot kill us. We are police officers. People know where we are. They are bluffing," Creighton declared, scanning J.P.'s face for a sign.

"Wrong," J.P. exclaimed and smacked Creighton across the face with the butt of his gun. Creighton tripped over a stump and fell backward in the grass, his nose and upper lip bleeding. J.P. wrapped several layers of tape over Creighton's mouth, then turned to Lisa and pointed to *Short Stick*. "Escort him to the trunk of the cruiser, please. Max and I will take care of Officer Creighton, who thinks I'm joking." He shoved *Short Stick* in Lisa's direction. "Officer Creighton wants to stay here and dance with the wolves. Say goodbye, now."

J.P. passed Lisa the silenced gun and ushered her away.

Lisa contemplated she was not ready to leave the *Butcher of Irvine* alone in the forest with a man he had threatened to kill—a police officer, no less.

"Go on," J.P. urged. "We still have to get out of here tonight before the reinforcements show up. Time is a wasting. Soften him up. Be creative. He is no good to us, unless he talks."

Lisa glanced at the pistol in her hand, uncertain what to do.

J.P. stared at *Short Stick*, who waited with visible apprehension for the next part. "Say 'thank you.' I am not sending the crazy redhead with you. She might kill you before you get back to the car. You hurt her bear, dumbass," snorted J.P.

"Go on, sunshine. We don't have time to waste." Max grabbed *Short Stick* by the back of his shirt and lifted him to his wobbly feet. "J.P. and I will be along in no time."

Lisa beckoned for *Short Stick* to walk toward the vet's office. He tripped, looking back to his partner, before he got his legs under him. Lisa pushed the silencer behind his ear. "Turn again, and you may accidentally run into a bullet."

Short Stick acknowledged and kept going.

J.P. waited until Lisa and her charge were about a hundred feet away in the woods. J.P. kicked Creighton in the ribs and fired two silenced bullets. Creighton yelped in pain.

Max sniffed and shouted louder than necessary, stifling a laugh. "Phew. Gross! Did he just shit his pants, or is that the smell of spilled intestines? He's gonna stink up the woods."

Short Stick tried to glance back. His ear met the cold silencer of the weapon in Lisa's hand, and he picked up the pace, whimpering like a small animal caught in a trap.

CHAPTER 83

LISA FOUGT AN INNER BATTLE. She wanted to make sure Morgan and Max did not kill Creighton. Bad cop or not, he was a police officer and a human being. Today, she saw a new side of Morgan. He could have shot the two men a thousand times. However, he allowed them to live, resorting to phony threats, playing into their preconceived notions about him to assuage them. She bit her lower lip, not daring to turn her head. Those were empty threats, right? He wouldn't kill these people out here, would he?

Lisa and *Short Stick* reached the parking lot, where Chris waited by the cruiser.

"Is he the shithead who hurt Marie?" Chris advanced to meet them.

"Yes. All she wanted was a hug, and he shot her in cold blood. Twice."

Chris kicked *Short Stick* in the groin, soccer-player-striker-style, and then stepped back, admiring her work with supreme satisfaction. She did not tolerate animals being abused.

Short Stick gasped for air, then doubled in pain, and tumbled to his knees. Eventually, he landed face first on the crushed rock and sobbed, wheezing and panting.

Lisa opened the trunk and motioned for Chris to help lift him. The two women dropped *Short Stick* in, closed the lid, and exchanged high fives. Chris pulled a pack of cigarettes, offering one to Lisa, who refused. They walked to the building's designated smoking area.

"Marie's OK. Dr. Wilson got the bullets out. Thank God, no fragmentation. He sedated her, and he'll keep her overnight. She's tough, young, and healthy. She'll be running back into the woods, wreaking havoc again in no time," reported Chris, pulling out a cigarette.

"I haven't had a cigarette in many, many years, but tonight I need one." Lisa reached out. "Last cigarette I smoked was when I prosecuted Morgan for murder. My friend, his defense attorney, bet me that if I lost, I had to quit smoking forever. I was so sure of myself that I took the bet on a dare. It goes to show you. Life has some weird things in store for us."

"You prosecuted J.P. for that thing with his wife?" Chris shot her a puzzled look. "What is he doing with you? The stories he and Max told about you, well, mostly Max." She took another drag. Her head snapped up. "Does Max know who you are?"

"Yes, she does." Lisa nodded. "Interesting girl, Max. What's her story?"

"Max hasn't gouged your eyes or twisted your neck yet? Wow! This is getting better and better." Chris pulled on her cigarette, ignoring Lisa's question.

"She almost scratched my eyes out tonight. Why is she so overprotective of Morgan? I mean, she acts as if she is both his wife and his mother."

"Max is a gifted child with severe social adjustment issues. Her IQ is north of 180, or something like that. She has an autism disorder, Asperger's, but she's the sweetest girl you will ever know. I met her when they brought Marie in for the first time. Max was seriously screwed up back then. She shared pieces of her story with us. What that child went through, I don't wish on anyone." Chris inhaled and blew the smoke out in slow, ascending circles.

Max and J.P. emerged from the darkness. Lisa's eyes inquired with doubt and fear.

"Gagged and bound to a tree," reported Max in a whisper. Lisa blew a sigh of relief.

J.P. shook his head and, without a word, strode to the cruiser. He opened the trunk and pitched in the two shovels, making sure some fresh dirt hit Short Stick's face. "Chris, we need to hold on to the shovels a little while longer." He pointed to *Short Stick*. "Did you have your talk with him yet?"

Chris nodded with satisfaction. "I wouldn't mind another go at it."

J.P. smiled and closed the lid. Inside the trunk, *Short Stick* let out a muffled cry and resumed sobbing. Chris led the way into the vet's office, followed by Lisa, Max, and J.P. Dr. Wilson assured them Marie was OK, sleeping off the anesthesia. Dr. Wilson promised Max to release Marie as soon as she could take care of herself. They left the vet's office with a lighter heart, knowing the animal that saved their lives did not suffer permanent damage.

"Officer Creighton was not cooperative. Let's hope his partner is, or his interview will be also short." J.P. stressed his words with bangs on the trunk lid. "Max, take him up to our favorite picnic area. I will get coffee and meet you there. We could be up for a long time, if he talks." He reached inside the SUV and brought out two SIGs, which he exchanged for the silenced guns Lisa and Max carried.

Max got behind the wheel of the cruiser, waited for Lisa to get in the passenger seat, and peeled off in a storm of dust, crushed rock, and pebbles.

J.P. watched them leave, then crossed the road, heading for the twenty-four-hour diner.

CHAPTER 84

"**J**ESSIE, HONEY, CAN YOU** get me four large coffees to go, please?" J.P. stopped at the counter, scanning the diner. He added, "Do you have any chocolate cake?" Seeing Jessie's look, he held his hands up. "It is not for me. I promise. Put a fork with it, please."

Jessie nodded, making an elaborate show of her disbelief.

J.P. sauntered to a booth occupied by two park rangers and two Sheriff's deputies. He dragged a chair, straddled it at the end of the booth, leaning over its back. "Howdy, boys."

They measured him up and down and replied with *howdy's* and "How are you, J.P.?"

Deputy Carlston, a giant black man, more muscles than anything, pulled out a sheet of paper, unfolded it, and handed it to J.P. "Care to explain this first?"

"How long have you known me?" J.P. scanned it and handed it back.

"Since my Navy days when you saved my bacon from that undeserved Court Martial. I still owe you. What are you doing this time?" queried Carlston.

"Did you ever know me to be that stupid?" J.P. asked.

"Is that a trick question?" retorted Carlston.

J.P. surveyed the faces around the table, looked each one in the eyes, and was about to answer when all four busted out laughing. One of the park rangers reached out and patted J.P.'s shoulder. "Every redneck with a badge is after you, and you call a meeting with the cops? Vintage Morgan. What did you do now?" he inquired between laughs.

246

"I pissed off an anal-attentive guy with nasty plans. I do not know what they are, but it is bad, bad news for all of us. I just stumbled onto it. Mostly crooked cops from various outfits, hence the APB. I have a few favors to ask. You can arrest me or shoot me later. If I live." J.P. waited for an answer but got nothing out loud.

"What was that commotion in Doc Wilson's lot? Was that your bear girlfriend you guys brought in?" Carlston jabbed J.P., and everyone chuckled. "It looks like you drove in a police issue Crown Vic, and I saw you take two people into the woods, but only one of them made it back. It reminds me of those hunter stories I heard as a child."

"A quarter of a mile from Dr. Wilson's shop is an oval-shaped clearing." J.P. looked at the park rangers. They acknowledged they knew it. "I gagged and tied Officer Creighton to a tree." J.P. continued. "Please take him into custody. About an hour ago, he and his partner tried to kill me, Max, and Assistant DA Lisa Jensen from Orange County."

"Attempted murder on you won't stick because of the warrant," Nate Francis, the second deputy Sheriff, added. "You know that, J.P."

"Charge them with poaching." J.P. chuckled. "They shot Marie."

The men hooted. J.P. always found novel ways to surprise them.

"I need you to hold him and his partner for as long as you can. I do not care what you do. Lose their paperwork, drug them, whatever. Just buy me some time before their backup shows up here to get them. These are evil, vicious people. I promise you."

"OK, J.P., let's say they shot Marie, tried to kill you, and all that. I have two questions. One, where is his partner now? Two, how the hell do we justify detaining two LEOs, who will claim they were executing a lawful warrant?" Carlston laid it out.

"Show me your weapons." J.P. stunned all of them with the request. The four officers exchanged puzzled looks and laid their service weapons on the table. J.P. handed the Sheriff's deputies the guns seized from Creighton and his partner. "Do you notice any differences?"

Carlston used napkins to pick up both guns, unscrewed and studied the silencers, and then whistled. "Professional stuff. We have rotten apples in the bushel. I'll figure it out for tonight. When Jasper arrives, all bets are off. It'll be up to him, you know." Jasper, the local Sheriff, did not like nor trusted Morgan as much as his friends.

"What do you want us to do with them? You still haven't told me where the partner is. It would be stupid for him to show up dead somewhere, and it turns out we've been sitting here twiddling our thumbs, chewing the fat with you," Deputy Nate Francis put in.

"I will interrogate him. You can listen in." J.P. placed a small device on the table. "I'll drop him off at the station when I am done. One more thing." He produced a plastic envelope from his shirt pocket. "These are the bullets Dr. Wilson pulled out of Marie. They came out of one of those silenced guns. Evidence of poaching."

"We should interrogate them if we want it to hold up in court," Francis said.

"This will never make it to court. I cannot have you guys involved in this." J.P. waved him off. "They murdered five cops to keep this thing under wraps. Did you hear about the bloodbath and arson in Irvine? What you do not know is that it happened at Anna's house."

"Is Anna OK?" Nate asked, alarmed.

"They killed her on Wednesday and made it look that she jumped off a bridge. I am sorry, Nate. I know you liked her," Morgan reported with his hand on Nate's shoulder.

"Damn them." Nate smashed his fist on the table, drawing scolding looks from Jessie.

"You have my word everything I told you is true. I cannot promise the other one will spill the beans. We screwed with his mind. He believes we executed Creighton and left him in the woods for the wild animals to snack on. I think he will talk. I do not know whom I can trust in the law enforcement world. Neither should you. Watch your backs. All of you."

"That's good enough for me. Don't do anything crazy or stupid, OK? If things get too complicated, let us handle it." Nate looked around the table, inviting them to back him up.

"Me, do something stupid?" J.P. faked hurt feelings. "Have I ever?"

"Where do we start, and how long do we have?" Carlston asked, laughing. He got nods all around. "Keep it clean. Don't do anything we might all regret."

"Thank you for your trust. Please watch your backs. I mean it. These people are bad news. They will show up eventually, looking for me and the poachers."

J.P. walked to the counter to pick up the coffees and the piece of cake. "Thanks, sweetie." He patted his back pocket then said, "Darn. My wallet is in the truck. Put it on Carlston's bill, please." He winked at Jessie and strolled out.

CHAPTER 85

"DID BETA SIX CONFIRM** ending their mission?" Purcell barked at his radio.

"No, sir," replied Simpson. "They are overdue for a sitrep."

"Verify!" Purcell growled. "I want validation now." He paced, another lousy habit he had picked up from Clancy. "Good riddance, Morgan. No one can or should stand in our way."

"We cannot contact Beta Six, sir." Simpson's hesitant voice cut in.

"Say again!" Purcell felt hot under the collar.

"Sir, we cannot raise Team Beta Six." Simpson's voice faltered.

"That's what I thought you said." Purcell snarled. "What the hell does that mean?"

"We tried all available means, sir." Simpson's voice still trembled. "No luck."

"Send a freaking carrier pigeon and two snap turtles, I don't care. Confirm they completed their mission. First, what's your assessment?" Purcell asked the dreaded question.

"We have to assume Morgan may have neutralized Team Beta Six, or, at the very least, delayed them, sir," Simpson replied.

"I see. What contingency plan do we have?"

"Team Alpha Four's ETA is forty minutes to Beta Six's last location, outside Lake Arrowhead, two miles from the highway. We'll know within forty-five minutes, sir."

"Too long," muttered Purcell. "Keep me posted. Anything at all, you hear?"

"Yes, sir."

250

Purcell set the radio down and banged both fists on his thighs. "Who is this Goddamn Morgan? Everyone I sent after him failed. How did we miss him recruiting him?"

Purcell composed himself, then walked to Clancy's office. "We lost contact with the team that apprehended Morgan in Lake Arrowhead." Purcell stood at attention, biting the inside of his cheek. His sixth sense told him there were plenty of good reasons to worry.

"How did you manage that?" Clancy shot him a disappointed look, equating Purcell with a bothersome gnat.

"No excuse, sir. We acquired the intel, and we acted on it immediately. Beta Six was the only team in the area. They caught Morgan." Purcell dumped it all out in one breath.

"You sent them in alone?" Clancy stood. "You know how cunning this Morgan is."

"We don't have assets in the San Bernardino Mountains. I advised them to proceed with caution and wait for reinforcements if they could not control the situation. This may be a case of equipment or signal failure. They are deep in the mountains."

"Then why run and tell me about it? Why do you need to cover your ass? I'm fed up with problems, failures, and excuses. We spent two years planning, setting up this operation. During that time, we had fewer mistakes combined than we did in the past twenty-four hours."

Purcell knew better than to answer. This was a no-win situation, if he ever saw one. He stood at attention, waiting for Clancy to calm down.

"You think you're ready to be the head honcho of the top law enforcement agency in the land? Do you have the stones to be the second most powerful man in California?" Clancy approached Purcell and stopped an inch from his nose, flooding Purcell's nostrils with the smell of cologne and the flavor of the mint gum he always seemed to chew. "One guy had you and all of your elite teams running around in circles, endangering this mission, getting our people killed, exposing our men and our plans. Have I left anything out? Oh, yeah, you didn't answer my question. Do you think you're qualified to run the new CDoHP, Purcell?"

"Yes, sir, I am."

"Prove it. Get rid of this pain in the ass called Morgan before I offer him the job." Clancy's spit hit Purcell's face, who continued to stand at attention without flinching.

"Yes, sir!" Purcell screamed back, snapping his heels, which reminded him of his boot camp experience more years ago than he cared to recall. He ran to the security office.

"I need a status report on our available teams and all current intel on Morgan. Right now. Move, people!" Purcell yelled. The four people on duty scrambled.

Purcell listened to the reports, scanning the paperwork. "Get me detailed info about Beta Six's movements since we dispatched them to intercept Morgan—every stop they made, every piss they took—on a map," Purcell demanded.

Christina Dole sprang into action and handed him a stack of papers, still warm from the laser printer. Purcell scanned them. "What time did they report apprehending Morgan?"

"Nine forty-six, sir," replied Simpson.

"They stopped here at 9:23 p.m.," Purcell muttered. "Their car sat until 10:04 p.m., then went deeper into the forest. It sat there for twenty-two minutes, then went back into town. It stopped in the middle of the town for forty-six minutes, and then it moved up the highway and left the main road. It's been sitting here, in the forest, ever since." He pointed at the papers in his hand. "Am I reading this right?" Several apprehensive nods met his penetrating gaze.

"It's possible they had to dispose of the bodies first, sir," Simpson said.

"Or Morgan is disposing of them and their cruiser," retorted Purcell. "Get a chopper to pick me up ASAP. Have a team of seasoned SWAT officers, the best we have, in full combat gear, meet me at the helo pad in five minutes. I'm going out there myself. This time, I intend to bring that asshole's heart with me. He won't need it after tonight."

CHAPTER 86

J.P. MANEUVERED THE SUV to catch the trio square in its headlights. Max and Lisa were on the near side of the picnic table. Their trembling captive sat alone on the opposite side. J.P. handed Lisa the small box with the chocolate cake and set the coffees on the table.

"Your pal, Officer Creighton, wanted you to know you don't have to talk to us. He said hell is a warm, cozy place, and he is eager for you to join him. He saved you a primo seat by the hot coals pool." J.P. shifted his eyes to Max. "Has he told you anything useful?"

"Only that his name is Powell." Max shook her head. "He acts tough. Then he cries about his kids and pregnant wife. He claims he'd rather die than betray his comrades and their cause. My vote is to shoot him in the belly and leave him for the bears, wolves, and mountain lions. They will get him before he bleeds to death. We don't need to waste time burying him."

"Yeah, blast him, and let's go before some local Johnny Law shows up." Lisa joined in. "I can only hope his brethren will take care of his poor wife and children." She pointed the gun at Powell. "Nice knowing you, dirtbag. Say hello to Creighton for me." She cocked the SIG. In the night's quiet air, the hammer sounded like a church bell ringing grim news.

"Wait. I'll tell you everything I know." Powell tried to stand, tripped, and fell backward, legs flailing, bringing smiles to everyone's faces.

"Too late," wisecracked Lisa. She pointed at Max. "Stand him up, so I can shoot him. Stupid SOB can't even stand up and take it like a real man." She looked at Powell. "You insist you know nothing, so there is nothing you can tell us."

"Don't kill me. Please. My kids need their father." Powell burst into tears.

J.P. struggled to keep a straight face. Lisa had taken on the part, and she played it with gusto, impersonating a warrior princess on a vengeance mission. "It is getting rather chilly out here." J.P. shivered, though the temperature was in the seventies. "Let's go back to the cabin. We can interrogate them there. Then we can shoot them and leave them in the woods. Let's make sure the wildlife has something to snack on tomorrow."

J.P. released the Transmit button of the radio on his belt, then dropped the device in the tall dry grass with no one being the wiser. He ignored Max and Lisa mouthing in silence the question "them?" and dragged Powell shoving him in the back of the SUV.

Max peeled off, leaving a cloud of smoke behind.

"Head back to Orange County. We need another vehicle." J.P. twirled his finger in front of his chest, concealing the gesture from Powell. J.P. settled on the floor and ignored Powell.

J.P. pretended to turn off the equipment. "Should we interrogate him now?" J.P. asked. "I do not want to waste time dragging him to OC. He may know nothing. It is much harder to get rid of a body in OC. Too many people, not enough wildlife to take care of the remains."

Max and Lisa nodded their eager approval in unison.

"Convince us why we should let you live. You are not going to OC." J.P. pushed the Record and Transmit buttons on the remote device he had palmed earlier.

"I'll tell you everything I know, I promise," Powell shrieked. "The bosses keep the info compartmentalized for security. It's a very professional organization. Each one of us knows our small part. That way, the bosses can train and integrate replacements in a short time. I was in the Army for eight years. I did two tours of duty in Iraq and Afghanistan, mostly supply chain work, no combat. When I returned home, I had nothing. My old job, gone. A fucking Mexican or Guatemalan worked there for half the pay. I couldn't find any work, and my wife was pregnant with our second child. That was at the height of the pandemic crisis. There were no jobs, and those of us who served overseas, we had it even worse. Nobody wanted us."

"I am not interested in your personal history. Life is hard. You got more trouble than your fair share. I want to know about the guys you work for," said J.P.

"I was getting there. The one thing I regret is that I did not take part in the Insurrection when President Trump called us to action, to march to the Capitol and take back our country. We have to be strong if we want to have a country to call our own."

"Cut to the chase. The only reason you are alive is to provide information."

"OK, OK. I caught a break. A buddy of mine and I went to the police academy as a last resort. There, I met this intense tactical combat instructor, Purcell. He was ex-military, Special Forces, a sharp and tough guy. Out of the blue, Purcell calls and asks me to meet with him. I said sure. I mean, he was an instructor, and I needed to support my family."

"I am getting bored here. If I fall asleep, shoot him and dump him on the side of the road." J.P. yawned, getting more comfortable on the floor behind Lisa's seat.

"Wait, wait. Purcell asked me if I wanted to be a part of something big, an operation that would change this country forever and give it back to the Americans. There was a good job and significant money in it for me. They paid for training, a few hours a week at first. I could keep my current job with Riverside PD. I'm a patrolman there."

J.P. faked disinterest and yawned, motioning for Powell to speed it up.

"We started training a few hours a week, then it was an entire weekend and so on."

"Training for what? What are you supposed to do for that money?"

"We just finished preparations for *True Patriot Day*. After we clean California, we rid the entire country of all the fucking illegal immigrants, and we put the inferior races in their place. We give our country, and the jobs, back to Americans, and stop wasting our resources taking care of the inferiors and their fucking children."

Morgan pretended to fall asleep and snorted, sending Powell into a frenzy.

"Listen," Powell shouted. "Do you know how much we spent taking care of illegals? Trillions. I can't get a raise because of budget shortages. We pay for their children to go to college, while my kids have to share books at school. Budget shortages. Their children get free health care, my kids starve and share clothes. Screw them illegals. Our country borrowed trillions of dollars to spend on them, and we work our asses off to pay for it."

"Sounds reasonable. Why all the secrecy? Why not tell John Q. Public what you are doing?" J.P. stretched his arms.

"I said that too. Mr. Clancy doesn't want to expose the entire plan. Look at what they put Donald Trump through. He is this country's greatest patriot, who had the courage to take on the issues and bring giant injustices to light. All he got in return was the criticism from all the News Fakers, the Anti-Trump media, especially the Criminals and Negrolovers Network."

CHAPTER 87

"**OH, I SEE,**" **SAID J.P.** in a flat tone. "You figured you can do much better than Trump if you keep it secret and spring it on the unsuspecting people."

"Again, look at what they did to President Trump. Even the broken clock is right twice a day, but to listen to the Fake News, he did absolutely nothing right his entire time in office."

"I am no big supporter of Trump, but I will give you that one," J.P. sneered.

"The Fake News media and the swamp creatures blamed him for everything, including the COVID pandemic, and gave him no credit for developing the vaccines that later the Democrats distributed mostly to inferior races. We are going to restore this country to its greatness. That starts when we reinstate the one true President. Donald John Trump." Powell beamed. "He had the courage and foresight to do what no spineless politician in Washington ever did. Stop the invasion of illegals, inferior races, criminals, and drugs into this country."

J.P. sighed, "You think that only non-whites, and non-Trump supporters caused everything that is wrong with our country."

"That's right, all the blacks, criminals, even the Jews who set fires to profit from our misery. Come to think of it, even the Coronavirus knows the difference between good, God-fearing, white American folks and the black and brown parasites who bleed this country dry."

"Jesus Christ," exclaimed Lisa. "You cannot be serious. Hundreds of thousands of Americans died, not only blacks and Latinos, or illegal immigrants."

"But they died three times as many," Powell announced in a triumphant voice. "Filthy, disgusting leeches taking everything from hard-working Americans. They deserved that. Look at the waste they caused our country since they stole the election from us, true American patriots. The Great Old Pussies rewarded President Trump's heroism by betraying him."

"OK, back on topic," said J.P. "What makes you think nobody will care?"

"Who? The clueless lawyers?" Powell continued in a crescendo voice. "The ACLU, the bleeding-heart liberal pricks, all would say it's unconstitutional and shit. Protecting those fuckers who invade our country in drones, form caravan after caravan to assault our borders. We should have never helped them with health care and vaccines. The true, deserving American patriots should have received proper care and vaccines first. Natural selection would have taken care of the inferior races plaguing our country."

"Hmm. So, you and your buddies will protect the country from them forever?"

"Yes," Powell exclaimed. "On the fourth, a new era begins. America for Americans. My kids will grow up in the Great America envisioned by President Trump when he will take his rightful place and lead us to the promised land. Money spent on our kids, in our schools, in our communities, jobs and programs to benefit true Americans. The world will, again, tremble when America speaks. We will, again, be the ones who will dictate world policy and make sure the American way prevails. No more of this pussyfooting around, political correctness bullshit."

"Oh, on the Fourth of July. Symbolic." J.P. caught the ball and tossed it, not wanting to tip Powell off. His senses were all on high alert. His body felt like a piano chord zinging with anticipation. "What is going to happen on the fourth? Where is this going to take place?"

"I don't know for sure. It's all hush-hush. We're ready to implement the plan as soon as we get the go-ahead." Powell boasted as if he was talking about some noble act of valor. "When our bosses led by President Trump will issue the call, we'll answer, armed and ready to get rid of all those corrupt politicians who care only about lining their pockets."

"So, you do not know squat. I could have learned all that from the Internet."

"It'll happen in the Bay Area, Los Angeles, and somewhere in Orange County. Those are the opening events. The rest of California will also play a part. Everything's in place. Nothing can stop the rebirth of California and soon of this great nation. I can hardly wait for the rightful people to run this country and make sure that only true Americans benefit from our sweat and tears. Good riddance to all those illegals, blacks, browns, yellows, and any other blood sucking races." He trumpeted the information, his smile growing wider, giving him the look of an oaf.

"What is your mission?" J.P. turned his face.

"As soon as we reinstate President Trump, I'll liaise with the LE agencies in Riverside County and provide guidance and clarity during the transition," Powell proclaimed his answer.

"Why are the Riverside County law enforcement agencies going to need guidance and clarity?" *From you, no less*, J.P. did not add.

"I don't know. We'll receive our instructions from Mr. Purcell and Mr. Clancy, who get their orders from the President, and we'll coordinate with the locals. We have to be in position, ready to go into action on the Fourth of July," he explained.

"Who is your boss?" J.P. resumed. "Where does he come from, and what is his angle?"

"Mr. Richard Clancy. He's a true American who works in Sacramento and has all the right connections." Powell studied his knees, avoiding J.P.'s gaze, despite the darkness.

"What's the Big Man got to do with all this, and who is he?" J.P. switched tactics.

Powell hesitated. "Nobody knows who he is. He runs Golden Trident Security. They provide support, logistics, and personnel when we need it. Their officers are all former SEALs, Rangers, Special Forces. All 100 percent Americans." Powell's upper body straightened out.

"No one knows who he is? It doesn't bother you?" J.P. probed.

"No. After the spineless politicians unjustly prosecuted all the true patriots who supported President Trump during the 2021 insurrection, operational security and confidentiality are a must. Our comrades spilled their true American hero blood to protect democracy everywhere, and the traitors in Washington squashed here, in America. They stole the presidency from us, from our hero, President Trump."

"OK, get off that high horse," countered J.P. "I want to know about The Big Man."

"He's not involved in the everyday operations. He handles the money, and I hear he's a freak about it. He always talks about getting his billions. His company set up private prison camps in the desert. After the *True Patriot Day*, we are going to ship the illegals there to sort them before we kick them back to Mexico or whatever bumfuck country they came from. Good riddance. That way, my kids can grow up in a better country."

"Oh, you mean prisoner camps like the ones built by Trump's administration. Or like the health clubs the Germans built during WWII? *'Arbeit macht frei'*?"

"J.P. Morgan, that's so inappropriate," snapped Lisa, outraged.

"We'd all be in danger if this got exposed," Powell offered the party line, filling in the awkward silence after Lisa's intervention. "As soon as they stole the election from our President, the fucking Democrats canceled all contracts with Private Prisons, putting thousands of true Americans out of work, while they flooded the streets with illegals and criminals."

J.P. ignored Powell's rant, and asked, "What would happen? The illegals would get together with pitchforks and axes and topple your ivory tower? Let's talk about the CDoHP. What rank do you hold?"

"I'll be a Special Protection Agent in Charge, running my squad. I'll supervise Riverside first, then San Bernardino County," Powell answered with pride.

"Will be? What rank do you hold now?"

"Nothing yet. Mr. Clancy will official announce the CDoHP on *True Patriot Day*. It will be the top law enforcement agency in California. We'll oversee all other government agencies and the efforts to rid this state of illegals and put the inferior races where they belong. I'm proud to be a part of that."

"I see. What are the nukes for?" J.P. delivered the proverbial bomb in a flat tone.

CHAPTER 88

"**S**IR, WE GOT A SHORT transmission from Beta Six," Simpson's voice sounded upbeat. "Morgan somehow turned the table on Beta Six and is taking them to a cabin, probably the same cabin where our team caught them. I'm sending your pilot the exact coordinates."

"We have to figure out how to avoid the trap, since we can't ignore the tip. We have nothing else to go on." Purcell addressed the men in the chopper. "Are you up for the task?"

Four SWAT officers nodded with eager looks on their hard, resolute faces. They all felt the pain and fatigue brought on by the stress caused by Morgan, but would not show it.

Purcell ordered the pilot to fly high above the coordinates of Morgan's cabin and switch on the IR viewer. They passed over the cabin twice.

"There's nobody there. The only warm sources are mechanical. We can fly all night, and we'll never find them. It's a wild-goose chase." The pilot craned his neck to see Purcell.

"Land at the closest pad and maintain radio silence until we get there. I still haven't figured out how Morgan stays a step ahead of us all the time," concluded Purcell.

"The closest landing pad is at the Lake Arrowhead hospital, next to the Sheriff's Station," the pilot reported. "We'll land in three minutes, sir."

"Tell Alpha Four to stay out of sight until we arrive." He addressed the team. "Be ready for anything. We cannot let Morgan get away again. He's close. I can smell him."

261

Purcell vaulted out of the chopper before it set down. Team Alpha Four was waiting by the helipad, and they joined the SWAT officers to follow Purcell.

Four deputies, two park rangers, and the night dispatcher clustered around a desk at the Sheriff's Station. They listened to a device, ignoring Purcell and his men as they entered.

"Can you believe that? This is serious shit." Carlston pushed from the table. He noticed Purcell's group. "What can we do for you, gentlemen?"

"We're here about Morgan," Purcell offered. "He called us." He strained to hear over the excited chatter. What had captured everyone's interest? "What is that you're listening to, Deputy... Carlston?"

"Oh, J.P. called you to get the poachers," Carlston reasoned. "Creighton is in holding. J.P. is interviewing the second man, Powell, right now. We're listening in. When done, he'll drop him off here. Then you can have them." Carlston walked back to the table.

Purcell had to fight hard to keep from betraying his surprise. Did he hear right? Morgan interrogated Beta Six? Broadcasting it to these rednecks? What a clusterfuck.

"I know that voice, sir," a SWAT member whispered, pointing to the table. "That's Powell, sir. He's talking." Purcell nodded and signaled his team to deploy around him.

The six men fanned out around the room.

"Where is this interview taking place?" Purcell approached the table.

Seven faces looked up at him. Seven shrugs ensued.

"This suspect is being interviewed right now, and you don't know where he is? Who is conducting the interview? Are you recording this?"

"We are." Nate spoke first, pointing to the receiver and recorder on the table. "This stuff is incredible. *True Patriot Day*? What kind of crap is that? Getting rid of the illegals? God knows I agree with some of it, but I don't get the—" He froze mid-sentence.

They heard J.P. ask about nukes. The Sheriff's deputies and the park rangers all stood at once, pushing chairs back with long scraping noises.

CHAPTER 89

"WHAT NUKES?" POWELL ASKED,** squirming while his eyes bulged out.

"Nukes?" Max's and Lisa's heads snapped back in harmony.

"Nukes? What nukes? What are you talking about, man? I know nothing about no nukes." Powell's voice cracked with alarm. "I never saw nukes."

"These morons are playing with nuclear bombs? Morgan, are you freaking insane?" Lisa recovered first. "You can't keep this information to yourself. We have to go to the authorities." Her shrill voice filled the SUV's cabin with anxiety.

Max struggled with the steering wheel and eventually settled the truck on the road.

J.P. patted Powell down, retrieved his badge. "I *am* talking to the authorities. Meet Officer Powell, Riverside PD." He held the badge for Lisa to see. "Officer Powell, I would like to make a report that your band of lunatics possess three portable, tactical nuclear weapons, origin and purpose unknown. I verify the weapons are real and—"

"You know what I mean," Lisa barked. "The *proper* authorities."

"Where are these 'proper authorities' you speak of? Who can we trust? Pretty much every cop I ran into in the past two days seems connected to them. And the ones who were not, ended up dead. How many more innocent people do you want to throw in their path?"

"You've got to believe me. I know they have this cuckoo doctor, Doc Jones. They call him *Doctor Death Jones* behind his back. He can make weird chemical shit, untraceable concoctions and poisons. But nukes? I've got kids, man. I would never mess with that," Powell whimpered.

They all noticed Powell's attempt at detaching himself from the group and their actions. J.P. waited, hoping for Powell to share something else he may have perceived.

"All I want is to follow my President in his efforts to make America great again, provide jobs and benefits to us, the true Americans who have somehow become slaves to the Jews, the criminals and illegals. We have to be strong and take our country back. That's all."

"What about the pallets of shrink-wrapped fake money? What is it for, and where does it come from?" J.P. capitalized on Powell's fear.

"Pallets of money? I don't know anything about that or the nukes. Please, man, believe me. I swear on my children's lives." Powell started sweating rivers.

J.P. thought Powell was an insignificant pawn with no strategic value, a simple kid who fell for promises of master manipulators and did not have a clue. "Max, let's go back to the Sheriff's station. We will drop Officer Powell off to share the cell with his pal, Creighton. They can explain the silenced weapons, their mission, and shooting Marie to the proper authorities in the morning. If they live that long."

"You didn't kill Creighton? All this was a trick?" Powell wailed.

"Do not believe everything you hear," snorted J.P. "I never killed a cop. I am not about to start now. Even dirty cops are law enforcement, which means the death penalty. You need to learn to think for yourself." He pushed Powell with disgust to the back of the SUV.

CHAPTER 90

PURCELL DREW HIS SIDEARM. The SWAT team aimed their MP5s at the cluster of people around the table. Team Alpha Four covered the entrance.

"That is extremely sensitive classified information. It falls within the purview of national security." Purcell said. "I need to know I can trust you with it."

"You're with *them*. The guys J.P. warned us about." Carlston got angry, overwhelmed with shock. "What are you up to? You know we can't keep it quiet. If the nukes exist—"

Purcell shot him in the forehead. Carlston dropped like a giant sack of potatoes. The SWAT team opened fire. It was over before the deputies or rangers reached for their guns.

"This should have never happened. That jerk is screwing everything up," Purcell muttered in frustration. He turned toward his men. "Take positions outside and wait for him to return with Powell. We'll end this. Nobody else gets in or out of this station. Clear?"

The SWAT officers scrambled outside.

Purcell stopped Team Alpha 4. "Find the surveillance system." He sauntered to Nate's body, retrieved his service weapon, and walked not to the holding cells area.

"How did you screw this up?" Purcell snapped at Creighton.

Creighton recounted in rapid-fire fashion the bear incident and the ensuing events. Purcell lifted Nate's gun, shot Creighton, and then shook his head in disgust. "Good help is so hard to find." He shot the sleeping drunk too, cursing under his breath.

He walked back to the front room, wiped the gun with a handkerchief, wrapped Nate's hand around it, and placed it back in the holster, then sat down at the table.

CHAPTER 91

J.P. CHURNED THE INFORMATION they had learned from Powell, staring out the window as they approached the Sheriff's station. His intuition rang a five bells alarm. Something was wrong. His eyes focused on the helipad. "Helicopter. Keep going, Max."

Max complied. As they drove past the Sheriff's station, J.P. and Lisa craned their necks, trying to glimpse something. J.P. turned on his personal phone and dialed Carlston's number. He waited for the answer and listened without a single word.

"Hey, Morgan. Are you coming back with the guy?" Purcell asked in a neutral voice.

I heard that voice last night. Purcell?

"Howdy, partner. Yes, I am bringing him in. Did you enjoy the show? What a trip." J.P. continued, "Listen. We are down the street. Be there in a minute, but I cannot stay. Come out to get Powell. We have to keep moving."

"OK." Purcell's voice revealed he allowed himself a moment of hope.

"Hey, buddy, bring that twenty you owe me for the coffees tonight," J.P. said.

"Sure thing, buddy," answered Purcell.

"Nice try," chuckled J.P. "Carlston never calls me 'Morgan'. He paid for the coffees, not the other way around. Who are you, and why do you have his phone?"

"Oh, sorry, Morgan." Purcell scanned the dead bodies. "This is Deputy Francis. Carlston went to the little boys' room and left his phone. He asked me to answer if you called."

"You get points for perseverance. Carlston takes his phone everywhere. Even in the shower. Deputy Francis's name is Nate. Now, who are you?"

"Seriously, Morgan, this is Nate, good buddy. Come on over. Bring that prisoner to us. I'll go tell Carlston to hurry it up in there."

Max stopped in a parking lot a quarter mile past the station on the other side of the road. They could see the Sheriff's station and the helicopter on the pad but no activity.

J.P. rolled the dice. "Get in there and help him shake it off... Purcell!" The silence at the other end told him he hit the target. "How are you doing? Did you kill any more of your own men today, *good buddy*? Did you murder any more honest cops to make room for your crooked lot? The new California Detachment of Hillbillies and Pricks."

"Matter of fact, it is me, Morgan." Purcell's screamed. "Now that I know you're close by, I'll come out and put you out of your misery once and for all, you hear me?"

Purcell ran to the entrance and motioned for his men to search.

They scurried out of their hiding places and spilled into the road.

"What happened to Carlston, Nate, and the others?" J.P. asked.

"They aided and abetted a criminal who conspired to weaken the national security of the United States," Purcell replied with disdain. "What do you think happened to them?"

J.P. covered the phone and asked Max to open the back gate. Max pushed the button, and the back door lifted in slow motion.

"Here is your rat, Purcell. See you around." He kicked Powell out, clicked off, and pushed the rear button, closing the liftgate. "Go, Max!"

Max peeled off in a hail of bullets, leaving the proper amount of rubber on the asphalt.

J.P.'s phone rang. "Missed me already?" J.P. tasked. "Or is it again? I wonder what Clancy has to say about this. May I have his number? He did not strike me as a person with a sense of humor. Maybe he will reward all of you the same way he did Officer Smythe."

Purcell shouted, "You don't stand a chance, Morgan. We have officers on every road leading in and out of here. Every law enforcement agency in California is after you. We'll get you, and when we do, you're dead. I'll see to it myself. I hope some Podunk cop doesn't shoot you. I want that pleasure for myself. Then I'll cut off your head and keep your skull on my desk as a reminder."

J.P. pulled the phone away from his ear, holding it as if it were a small dead animal. "Did you say something, Purcell? I got distracted, attempting to evade your invisible men covering all the roads. Until next time. Do not worry. You and I will meet soon enough, on my terms. Those were my friends, and you will answer to me for that." He dismantled the phone and removed the SIM card and the battery. He threw the pieces in a drawer.

CHAPTER 92

PURCELL PITCHED CARLSTON'S PHONE at the wall. He hit computer screens, broke a chair, a desk lamp, and two phones. His men walked in and waited patiently just inside the front door, weapons at the ready, with Powell still handcuffed between them.

Purcell retrieved Nate's weapon and shot Powell in the head without a single word. Purcell ordered his men to drag Powell's body to Creighton's cell and leave them both there. He wiped the gun, placed Nate's fingerprints on it again, and returned the weapon to its owner's holster. He picked up the radio receiver and the attached tape recorder and cradled them in his arms while he issued orders in a staccato tone. "Load the bodies in the chopper. I don't want anyone to find this mess too soon. When you're done, burn this place down. Take two Sheriff's cruisers and go after Morgan. Simpson will track him and patch the location to you. I want him now, more than ever. Dead or alive, I don't care. Whoever brings him to me gets to be my top deputy at CDoHP." Tiny balls of foaming spit formed at the corner of his mouth.

The men got to work and loaded all seven bodies. Purcell ordered the pilot to head toward the lake. The pilot cursed quietly, knowing he would have to scrub the helicopter again.

Two Sheriff's cruisers left in a hurry, lights flashing. The Sheriff's station erupted in a symphony of explosions, culminating with a giant fireball, visible for miles. Under the cover of darkness, Purcell heaved the bodies out of the helicopter in the middle of the lake and then ordered the pilot to return to Morgan's cabin. The pilot hovered two hundred feet above the structure. Purcell retrieved two incendiary grenades and dropped them on the roof. As soon as the pilot saw the grenades fall out, he took off in a hurry in pursuit of J.P.'s truck.

CHAPTER 93

I **N THE BACK OF** the Expedition, J.P. had been quiet for half an hour. They had seen the two fireballs light up the night sky and knew what that meant. He kept kneading his temples, as if he were trying to massage his brain into figuring it all out. He felt he was on the verge, yet one critical element still eluded him.

Max had pulled into a service tunnel and waited with the lights off until the three cruisers had passed by, and Purcell's helicopter had disappeared on a southern course. Then she drove down the mountain. "Where to?" asked Max as they reached the 210 Freeway.

"Dan and Chloe's. We need another vehicle they cannot link to us."

"What the hell is wrong with you?" Lisa laid into J.P. "You dropped the bomb, no pun intended, about the nukes, you drop-kicked Powell out of the car, and now you won't talk to us. That's crap, Morgan. What's going on? What else didn't you tell us?"

"Leave him be," Max said. "He's dealing with guilt, thinking things through. He'll let us know when he's ready." Max studied J.P. in the rearview mirror.

"What guilt?" Lisa showed concern.

"He blames himself for everyone at the Sheriff's station being murdered," Max answered in a whisper. "He'll torture himself for a short while, he'll come out of it, then he'll be useful again." Lisa nodded and respected the implied request. "However, I should throw his sorry ass out and let him roll down the mountain," Max blew some steam out of her ears. "Then catch up with him at the bottom and run him over a few times."

"Why?" Lisa queried, puzzled.

"The jerk planned to leave us behind at the cabin and go play hero by himself," Max answered, letting leftover vapors out through her ears

270

and nose. "The only reason we're with him is because Creighton and Powell showed up. He knows we're not safe there anymore."

"Is that true?" Lisa turned to J.P., incensed. Not getting an answer, she continued, "That's a terrible thing to do, J.P., really lousy. I thought we were in this together." She waited for a moment for a reply, turned forward, and smacked the dashboard. "Jerk."

They rode in silence until Max entered a residential neighborhood. "Lisa, trade places, please," J.P. said. Then he instructed Max, "Drive around a few times first. We want to make sure we do not bring these maniacs to Dan's front door. They have kids, for God's sake."

Max drove in a random pattern through the neighborhood. Satisfied that nobody had followed them, J.P. nodded to Max. She stopped at the end of a cul-de-sac and turned the SUV around, preparing it for a quick getaway. J.P. strolled to the last house of the cul-de-sac on the lakeside. The home backed to the water and had a large green area to its side.

Lisa opened the SUV door to follow. Max touched her hand. "Chloe Wilson."

At the mention of the name, Lisa shuddered, closed the door, and settled in the seat. She recalled Chloe from Morgan's trial. Chloe was a past love interest J.P. remained friends with after he married Alice Hunter. Against J.P.'s wishes, Anna called her as a character witness. Lisa had pushed Chloe to admit on the stand that she and J.P. kept the flame going despite both being married, and it could have been his motive for the murders. Chloe had jumped off the stand and started a fistfight with Lisa. Court Sheriff's deputies had to break up the scuffle, and Chloe cooled her heels in jail overnight for mouthing back to the judge.

A man opened the door, stretching and yawning. J.P. trailed him inside. The garage door sprung open and a shiny midnight blue Suburban exited with J.P. behind the wheel. Max followed J.P. to another residential neighborhood. They transferred everything from the Ford into the Chevy. J.P. removed the Ford's license plates.

J.P. took the 405 Freeway northbound and pulled off in the Disneyland area. He located a quiet motel close to the parks, with the VACANCY sign lit. He handed Max a wad of cash. "Check us in, will you? Two adjacent rooms, connected if possible."

PART THREE

July 3

CHAPTER 94

DISNEYLAND WAS OPEN AGAIN to the delight of millions of children, after the COVID-19 pandemic had forced it to close. Corelli and Timmons turned their backs on the brilliant park lights as they marched to the motel manager's office and rang the night bell.

Jack Martell sauntered out, sleepy, slippers dragging. "How may I help you, gents?"

Corelli shoved Martell back in the office. Both cops followed, closing the door behind. Alarmed, but not scared, Martell pointed to the register. "If you want the cash, you can have it. It's a measly $300. Everybody uses plastic nowadays." Jack's eyes popped open.

"The Big Man took care of you, Jacko. Time for you to return the favor." Corelli grabbed Martell by his shirt with a gloved hand and propelled him back in his chair.

Martell relaxed, realizing they would not hurt him. About a year before, Martell's younger brother, Sammie, got arrested with a sizeable amount of cocaine. Sammie faced a heavy prison sentence—or at least a hefty lawyer bill. A local cop had approached Jack on behalf of the Big Man and proposed a deal to get his little brother off the hook. The officer did not want money or anything like that. It was all very innocent, in fact. All he had asked for was access to the motel's security system and for Jack not to rent room 225 twice a week for a year. When the time came, Jack would have to return the favor without hesitation.

What was he going to say? No? Over the past year, now and then, the officer would return and lock himself up in the recording equipment room for a couple of hours, and that was that. It seemed such a small price to pay to keep Sammie out of prison.

"Oh, it's you guys." Martell lowered his voice.

Corelli let go of Martell's shirt and produced a stack of DVDs. "Let's look at your security system. Paw through these. Get your prints on all of them."

Martell grabbed keys and led them to the recording room. Corelli and Timmons stepped inside. They retrieved the stack of DVDs with Martell's fresh prints and started replacing selected ones in the archive. When they finished, they returned to the manager's office.

Timmons pushed Martell down in his chair. "At exactly 5:30 A.M., take out tonight's DVD, and replace it with a blank one, like you always do. Make sure you destroy that DVD and scatter the pieces where nobody can ever find them. Shortly after that, call 911 and report suspicious activity in room 225. When the cops get here, let them do their job. It would help if you were not forthcoming about anything. Let them ask questions on their own."

Corelli shoved two pictures under Jack's nose. "Inspect these pictures. Remember the faces. You will be very reluctant to betray your guests. Only after the cops ask several times, or threaten you, you tell them these two have been staying here now and then for about a year. The man always paid cash, always asked for the same room, 225. You rented it off the books and kept the cash, and you suspected nothing. You thought they were father and daughter staying here for the night. Is everything clear so far, Jacko?"

Martell nodded, eager to end the encounter. He reflected on how creepy Corelli sounded. If a snake could talk, it would sound just like that. "I replace tonight's DVD at 5:30 A.M. with a blank. Destroy the old one. Call 911 and cooperate reluctantly."

"What about them?" Corelli thrust the photos under his nose again.

"I thought they were father and daughter staying here after trips to Disneyland for about a year. Always paid cash off the books. Always room 225."

"Good. You play your part right, and not-so-tiny Sammie stays out of prison. You fuck this up, and he goes in forever. We'll find something to send you too, to keep him company. Now go back to bed. This next part does not concern you." Corelli lifted Martell by his robe and shoved him back toward his quarters.

Timmons and Corelli drove to the end of the motel where the staircase led up to room 225, the last room on that wing. They retrieved a long object wrapped in a tarp from the trunk. They carried it up the stairs with haste.

Martell opened the bottom drawer and picked up a bottle of tequila he kept for such emergencies, when he needed to calm his nerves. He took a long swig and then another, corked the bottle, and dropped it in the back drawer, then crossed himself several times. "Sammie, God only knows what you got us into."

CHAPTER 95

J **.P. OPENED HIS EYES** and studied the room clock. 7:05 A.M. He needed coffee. Gallons of it. He showered but decided against shaving and rushed out the door. He returned with baked goodies, fruit, and large coffees; knocked on the connecting door; and then pushed it open. "Rise and shine, my sleeping beauties. It is another gorgeous day in paradise."

Max launched a sham in J.P.'s general direction, without bothering to open her eyes. Chuckling, J.P. caught it with ease. Max stuck her head under the pillow, pulling the sides down with both hands, growling like a disturbed, sleepy lioness.

In the next bed, Lisa raised her head and looked at J.P. and then Max. "God, I hoped it was only a nightmare and when I woke up everything would be all right with the world again." She dropped her head on the bed, holding it between her palms.

"If you only knew how many times I woke up with that same feeling," quipped J.P. "I have coffee, bagels, fruit, and croissants. First come, first serve while supplies last."

He closed the door and switched the TV on for background noise. He settled on a local news broadcast station when he noticed his own face on the screen and raised the volume.

"Good morning, Southern California." The TV anchor's cheerful voice grated on J.P.'s sleep-deprived nerves. "We bring you breaking news. We have an update on John P. Morgan." Her face retreated to the bottom left corner of the screen, allowing a picture of J.P. from his Navy days to fill the screen. "Authorities want him for his involvement in the murders of several law enforcement agents. Morgan is armed, presumed mentally unstable, and extremely dangerous. Authorities believe he runs a major counterfeiting operation. When the multi-agency task force closed in on him, he engaged the agents, killing at least five of them. During his escape, he may have abducted or possibly killed this woman." Lisa's head shot replaced Morgan's picture. "Orange County Assistant District Attorney Lisa Jensen. Ms. Jensen prosecuted Morgan in the infamous multiple murder case that shocked Southern California a few years back. That trial earned him the nickname *The Butcher*—"

J.P. changed the channel to another news station. A few moments later, the courtyard of a nondescript motel appeared on the screen, and then a grainy picture replaced it. A handsome man, dressed in a sharp suit along with a tiny, teenage girl, climbed down the motel's outside staircase. A digital blur concealed the girl's face. J.P. fixated on the screen.

"... Local police officers found the body of the sixteen-year-old victim at a Disneyland area motel. Because of her age, authorities are withholding identity. The victim was last seen entering the room with this man, identified as Congressman Jack Hunter, Governor Hunter's son." A face shot materialized in the center screen.

J.P. had had no contact with Jack since Alice's death. However, Jack Hunter would never take a woman to a cheap motel, let alone a sixteen-year-old girl. He paused the broadcast and studied the frozen image. The lighting was odd, and the way Jack and the girl stood in relation to each other was unnatural. J.P. twitched his nose and pursed his lips. Another conundrum inside an already dangerous and complicated situation. He did not buy it.

"Congressman Hunter fled his residence this morning before the police arrived to question him," the voice droned on. "The Congressman's spokesperson claims she does not know where he is. She informed us the Congressman would make a statement later today, although she would not confirm details. The Governor's office has not yet issued a statement. Keep it right here, and we will keep you posted as the story unfolds."

J.P. fired up two laptops and connected them to the Internet via his mobile hotspot. Max and Lisa, still fighting sleep deficiency, ambled in, and sat at the table, reaching for coffee. They watched J.P. work, yawned, and shook their heads.

"Men. He wakes us up at the crack of dawn, and then he ignores us. I'm surprised he doesn't ask us to cook him breakfast, make more coffee, shine his boots and iron his shirt," Lisa wisecracked, attempting to get J.P.'s attention with a hand wave.

"Something is very wrong. We need to get going." J.P. looked up from the screen. "It seems things are about to get a lot worse."

Max and Lisa exchanged inquisitive glances and then walked to stand behind him. "Things can get worse? How?" scoffed Max. She studied the laptops over J.P.'s shoulders. "Jack Hunter. What about him?"

"I do not know, yet." J.P. brought up the story. "I just know that this story cannot be true. Jack is not that type of person, and he is not that stupid. Eat your breakfast. We need help. This is getting out of hand by the minute." J.P. continued to type, alternating his gaze between the two screens.

"Getting out of hand?" Lisa hissed. "As if we had a handle on it all along. Is that why we are running desperately for our lives? What work can you possibly have to do at this hour?" She sipped some coffee, frowned, and hunched her shoulders.

J.P. asked Max for a clean phone. He turned it on and dialed a number and then a series of access codes before his call connected to its destination.

CHAPTER 96

"**A** LIBABA'S PIZZA." THE DUTY sergeant answered, checking that the system activated the trace. "Pick-up or delivery?" He listened, placed the call on hold, read the info on the screen, then rejoined the call. "This request has old ingredients, sir. I'm afraid they are moldy and stink. Would you like to order something with fresher fixings, sir?"

The sergeant placed the call on hold again. He dialed another number, went through the encryption and identification routines, "Colonel, I have a man on the Alibaba line. He refused to identify himself. He called from an non-encrypted, yet untraceable phone using an ancient authentication protocol. It is still active, but it's a decade out of style. When I requested a newer one, he asked for you. I informed him there is no Ramos here. He ignored me and told me to find you right away and give you the following message: 'Für Elise'. Yes, sir, he meant Beethoven's thing. I asked. He said you'd know who he is." He listened to the other line. "Very well, sir. Here you go."

The sergeant repeated the phone number, ended the call.

CHAPTER 97

"WHO DO YOU THINK YOU ARE?" Eric Ramos started shouting as soon as his call with J.P. connected. "How dare you! You, murderous bastard! I should have killed you when I had the chance. I should have skinned you alive, then squashed you like a bug!"

J.P. set the phone down. There was no need to activate the speaker. When Ramos finished shouting, J.P. lifted the device. "Eric, are you done?" Another torrent of curses, invectives, and yelling followed. "Apparently not." J.P. flashed an innocent smile, twiddling his thumbs.

Max and Lisa observed with growing curiosity.

Eric's bellowing finally subsided.

"Eric, are you done now?" J.P. picked up the phone.

"Now I'm done. What do you want, asshole?" Ramos barked.

"I invoke the *Für Elise* clause. I need your help." J.P. held his breath.

"You lost the right to use it. How dare you!" Lieutenant Colonel Ramos, USMC, replied, letting each syllable drop like a hammer.

"Eric, we do not have time for a debate. All I am asking is to observe the clause and, in her memory, help me and Jack," J.P. whispered, closed his eyes and prayed in silence for his old friend to acknowledge the request.

"I'll listen, but I promise nothing. You're pond scum so far as I'm concerned. Lower than pond scum." Ramos expressed his feelings in a hissing voice.

"Fair enough. I need to find Jack right now."

"Did you have anything to do with that thing on the news? Did you frame him? It wasn't enough that you murdered his son and sister?" Ramos launched another verbal assault worthy of a squad of lunatics.

"You, too, think they set him up. That is terrific. We both know Jack would never do something like that. Even if he did, he would not be stupid enough to be caught on camera. There is something odd about the picture. It did not seem right somehow. I would need to look at the actual footage to know for sure, but I just got this feeling," J.P. reported in a hurry.

"What's your angle? How are you involved in this?" Eric asked.

"I have a hunch the same guys who are after me may have framed Jack."

"Who's after you? Wait, I don't want to know, and I don't care. I don't know why I want to believe you, but I will always help Jack. What do you want?"

"Jack needs our help. I must locate him, and you can get in touch with him."

"That's all you want? To contact him? What good is that going to do?"

"He has resources I can use," J.P. said. "He cannot because he has to hide for now. If they arrest him, he will suffer the same fate I did. Maybe he will be as lucky as I was and only lose everything and everyone he loves. Maybe he will end up in prison for life or worse. He may hate me, but I will not stand by and let these guys railroad him and ruin his life."

"We do this together. Take it or leave it." Eric's tone was flat and final.

"I do not want to get anyone else involved. These people are ruthless killers, not taking prisoners. They murdered their own men and some friends of mine. I do not want more deaths on my conscience," J.P. pleaded, knowing in his heart he was arguing in vain.

"Boy, am I glad to see you haven't lost your sense of humor. You know us, Marines. When our friends are in trouble, we scream and shake like little girls, and then run and hide under the bed. Did you think that would stop me? I'm not leaving Jack out in the wind because it might be dangerous for me. Where are you?"

J.P. sighed and then relayed the motel's address and room number.

"Thirty minutes, forty tops," announced Eric and ended the call.

CHAPTER 98

J.P. RETURNED HIS ATTENTION to the laptops. Max slammed the lids, missing his retreating fingers by a hair. "Who's Eric, and what's he got to do with Jack Hunter?"

J.P. knew there was no wiggling out of this one, not the way Lisa and Max watched him, both impersonating crouching tigresses, ready to pounce. "Jack, Alice, and I grew up together. Eric had a thing for Alice. He and I were from the wrong side of the tracks. He always followed her around, like a lovesick puppy. The three of us became thick as thieves. After high school, Jack and I went to Annapolis. He did it in part to piss off his old man, who had all these grandiose plans. Jack was going through his JFK phase, Navy, and then move on to his political career. Eric joined the Marines later. Jack, Eric, and I worked together for Naval Intelligence until Jack moved to DC. We were best friends until Alice died."

"Until you murdered her," Lisa interjected, earning herself a crusty look from Max.

"What about that clause? He was ready to rip your head off until you said 'Für Elise'. Then he became your best friend. Is it a hypnotic phrase used to control his mind? Does it work on other guys? Can you teach me, Papa Bear?" Max perked up.

J.P. smiled with the indulgence of a proud father. After all these years, it amazed him how Max could behave like a child. "Eric and I were both in love with Alice ever since we were kids. When we would fight, she used to get between us. One day, she tired of it and came up with this idea, a code word that Eric and I would have to observe and stop fighting—for Alice. She must have been thirteen. When Alice was born, baby boy Jack had trouble pronouncing 'Alice.' It came out like *'Aelis.'* *For Alice* became *For Aelis.* We thought it sounded cool. Being the consummate piano man, one day Jack played the first bars of Beethoven's *Für Elise* when Alice had invoked the clause. She dubbed it the *Für Elise clause.* It stuck. We were kids. When Alice would hum *Für Elise,* the clause would be in effect. Eric and I would have to set aside all our differences, or Alice would rain on both our parades."

"Hmm, she had you pussy-whipped any time she wanted. Not one, but two men. I should learn how to do that. Too bad she died," Max gibed in her childlike voice.

"You are something else, you know." Lisa reached over and covered Max's mouth.

Max blew raspberries and sat down, pouting.

"While we wait, let me check my voice mail. With all the phone changes, I might have missed the call from the California lottery. What is the jackpot up to?" J.P. accessed his account and whistled. "Fourteen messages since yesterday. I usually get less than that in a month."

"Something happened to B and C?" asked Max, worried.

"They are still at Martha's," replied Morgan. "I am positive they have been over spoiled out of their furry heads by now, but they are OK." Max's shoulders relaxed, and she let out a long breath. She closed her eyes and lifted her face upward, thanking God in a whisper.

"Who are B and C?" Lisa's curiosity overtook her. "What is it with you two and your codes? It's like you have your own private language."

"Bonnie and Clyde are our darling, misbehaving dogs. They are the reason J.P. may never go to any animal shelter by himself. An adult must accompany him at all times. That's me," Max answered in a solemn tone.

"You have two dogs and a cat?" Lisa asked as if it were the most preposterous thing she had ever heard.

Max nodded with a cheery grin.

The fourth message brought a surprise. "Mr. M, this is Carl at the towers. Something terrible happened. The old woman staying at your place, she apparently jumped off the balcony. The police want to talk to you. I know we're supposed to let you know first, but this is quite a dilemma. Please call me back ASAP," Carl droned on, excited, wheezing loud enough to mistake him for a leaf blower.

"What old woman? Does he mean Candy? J.P., talk to me. What happened to Candy?" Max jumped to her feet as if she had been sitting on hot coals.

"I know as much as you do, Max" J.P. answered in a paternal voice laden with worry.

Max moved to the bed, wrapped her arms around a pillow, and sobbed. The fifth message was from the Orange County Sheriff's Department requesting urgent contact about the fire at his house. The following four messages were pretty much of the same pleas from Carl. The tenth was from a police sergeant in Las Vegas informing J.P. that his guest was the victim of an apparent suicide, and that they needed to get a statement from the owner of the place. Then three more messages from Carl. The last message was from the Las Vegas PD.

"I know how much you loved Candy. God knows I loved her too. I am the one who got her killed. I should have never sent her to Vegas alone."

CHAPTER 99

J.P. SAT NEXT TO Max, caressing her hair.

"You are not my most favorite person, but it wasn't your fault." Lisa's face turned red. Her voice trembled. "It's ludicrous to assume Mrs. Richter killed herself. These people will kill anyone who interferes. We got in their way, and they murdered Mrs. Richter. They are all psychopaths. Cowards. Any way you want to look at it, you are not liable here."

"Thanks. That is probably the first gracious thing you ever said to me. However, it is my responsibility. I should have known they bugged her somehow. I was just too damn caught up in this bullshit and missed it." J.P.'s jaw ground on his upper teeth.

"What do you mean?" Lisa arched her eyebrows.

"I could not figure out how they pinpointed our location yesterday. I knew they had not tagged me. If they had found me, they would have done much worse. You were clean, since all you had on was the hospital gown. Unless they planted it subcutaneously or made you swallow one, you did not have a bug on you. Clancy ordered his men to kill you and burn the body. There was no reason to waste a tracker and leave potential evidence in the ashes."

"How can you be so sure?" Lisa continued. She bit her lower lip, thinking it had never occurred to her that anyone could have put a tracker on her while she was unconscious.

"If you had, they would have found it at the hospital when they examined you. An SAK exam means they looked over your entire body with a magnifying glass. That only leaves one possibility. They tagged

Candy. I made the error of thinking they had not cast a net that wide before I picked her up yesterday. That got her killed. My mistake."

"Don't be ridiculous. Following your line of reasoning, this thing could be my fault. If you hadn't followed the guys who kidnapped me the night before, you would never know about this and Mrs. Richter would be alive," Lisa said with renewed passion.

"You have a point there," replied J.P. "Let's stick with that version. I like it better."

Lisa hit him with a pillow. "I loved her, too. She's been like a mother to me, since I was in law school." She wiped a tear. "How did you figure it out?"

"The cabin. Very few people know the cabin exists. Only ten people know it is our place, and only eight of them know how to bypass the security traps." He looked at Max, who still had her arms wrapped around the pillow, hiding her tears in it. "Six of the people who knew the security measures died in the past three days, and two of them are in this room."

"Six of them died in the past three days?" Lisa asked.

"Anna, Candy, the two park rangers and two Sheriff's deputies I met with last night after we took Marie to Dr. Wilson's shop. Clancy's goons must have planted a tracking device on Candy before I picked her up yesterday. That is how they found us after the hospital incident and how they found her in Vegas."

"There is no other way?" Lisa's legal mind kept seeking other possibilities.

"Other than Max and me, there are only six people in the world who know that Max and I own that place in Vegas. Two of them are dead, Candy and Anna. Two of them do not live in the United States. The developer and Carl, his property manager, are out of the question. They have abundantly explicit instructions about that, and they both owe us too much to betray us under any circumstances. Everybody else there knows us only as Mr. M and Max."

"The employees there could have disclosed the information if they thought they were talking to cops." Lisa continued.

"Nope. They would not cross me. Say they would. How would the bad guys know about that place *before* Candy got there?" J.P. cocked his head, staring Lisa down. "That leaves Max and me. Max did not know where Candy was until she arrived at the cabin last night. I decided yesterday at the office, after you and I made our deal. They tracked Candy. They probably tortured her before they threw her off the balcony. She was an old woman, so she broke down and told them about the cabin and how to get around the perimeter sensors."

"These twisted psycho animals tormented an old woman and killed her. We need to eliminate them. Waste them like a colony of sick, infected rats." Max lifted her head off the bed, looking scarier than even J.P. had ever seen her.

"Easy there, tiger." J.P. stroked her hair. "Let's hold off on the mass murders. Killing is wrong, you know. I might have mentioned that few of times over the years."

"No," Lisa jumped in, her nails drawing blood from her own palms. "Max is right. These people are not cops, not even human beings. They are rabid animals. Nothing can justify killing innocent, helpless people. I'm with Max. Let's annihilate them."

"Way to go, Max," hooted J.P. "You converted Ms. Straight and Narrow over here from playing the law-and-order tune incessantly to reasoning like a human being, with actual emotions. Overnight. Bravo!" He clapped his hands.

"I am a human being with genuine feelings. When I'm an Assistant DA, I don't have the luxury of thinking and acting outside the law."

"Calm down," he chuckled. "I am messing with you. I am happy you had that reaction. I am glad to find out you are flesh and bone, like the rest of us."

"Jerk!" She followed with a fist to his shoulder. "Now I feel better."

A quick rap at the door sent them on high alert.

CHAPTER 100

PURCELL ANNOUNCED HIMSELF WITH a cough.

"There is a change of plans you need to know of." Clancy invited him in. "Golden Trident is implementing their contingency policy as of this morning. You saw the thing on the news about Jack Hunter. If any of our primary plans fail, the Big Man's assets will step in and correct the problem by any means necessary."

"May I ask what they will do and when?" Purcell fought to mask his annoyance.

"In case the people standing in our way avoid the surprises we set up for them, Golden Trident operatives will execute surgical strikes. Jack Hunter is the contingency plan for convincing George, since he is harder to eliminate through conventional means."

"How is that going to work? I mean, it's all bogus. What happens if someone figures it out and blows the whistle?"

"We only need the story to hold for the next twenty-four hours. After that, the devil may care. The world will have much bigger problems, and nobody will care about Jack. I feel sorry for him. He's a respectable man. However, we don't have the luxury of sparing anyone in this fight. He's a casualty of a war we should have fought and won long ago."

"I see. Do you need me to do anything to support this backup plan?" Purcell inquired.

"Not really. Corelli and Timmons replaced Sadowsky and Smythe. They are assisting Golden Trident with something related to the Big Man's plans. Give them some latitude. That part of the plan is being deployed as a security measure, should someone upset the apple cart this late in the game." Clancy shot Purcell a meaningful look.

"I don't think anyone can accomplish that, sir. We have every angle and every unforeseen event covered." Purcell sounded more convinced than he felt.

"I would have agreed with you until Morgan showed up," snapped Clancy. "Make sure he doesn't *'accomplish'* that. I don't want him interfering any longer. Check all possibilities again. Find new options. Figure out where he may show up. For God's sake, catch him. I need reassurances that you and your men are not the biggest mistake I made in planning this event."

CHAPTER **101**

J .P. MOTIONED FOR THEM to get on the floor. He picked up
a SIG and went into the adjacent room. He opened the door and
leaped out with the gun leveled.

Lt. Col. Eric Ramos, in USMC fatigues, holding a tray with two
large cups of coffee, about to knock again. He lowered his head, studying
J.P. with intelligent giant brown eyes over the rim of his mirrored aviator
glasses. "You called me here to shoot me in a public place? Here I am,
thinking of you and bringing coffee. You still breathe this stuff, right?"

"Good to see you, Eric. Thank you for joining us." J.P. lowered the
gun, guiding Eric into the room. "Ladies, Eric Ramos, jarhead. Enough
said. Eric, Max and Lisa."

"Wow! That's what you need help with. You're overwhelmed dealing
with these two gorgeous women. Why didn't you say so?" Ramos set
the coffees on the table. He deflected the two pillows that hit him
simultaneously with the ease of a trained warrior, grinning widely like
a caricature of a child. "Feisty ones, too. I like that. I sense trouble,
and you need my help. Enchanted, madam." He took Lisa's hand and
brought it to his lips.

"Apologize first, Jarhead." Max retreated as if Eric was a giant slimy,
venomous snake.

"Hmm, really spirited this one is. Her more I like." He laughed with
a good hoot, then abandoned the Yoda voice. "I must apologize to the
beautiful lady for my rude remarks. May I?" He took Max's hand and
brought it up to his lips, holding on for a second too long.

"Now that the comic relief has arrived, let's get to the action part,"
J.P. interceded, pulling a chair for Eric. "Good to see some things never

change. If the Marines had a clown division, Lieutenant Colonel Ramos would be its undisputed commander."

"Jarhead? Comic relief? Why, J.P., it's good to see you too." Ramos switched to an all-business tone. "I'm here to help Jack. If you hurt him, I will kill you. First, I'll torture you in unimaginable ways. I learned new things since we last saw each other." Eric stared at J.P. for a long minute, two statues sizing each other up.

"Sounds fair to me," J.P. replied, holding his gaze.

"I guess that'll have to do for now." Ramos rubbed his hands. He surveyed the room. "What's this big emergency you need Jack's help with?"

"Would you two give us a minute alone? Eric and I have a few things to clear up, and we have some catching up to do. This hungry-wolf look on his face could interfere with his concentration." J.P. pointed loosely toward the adjacent room. "Please get ready to go as soon as I am done bringing Eric up to speed."

Max and Lisa protested but eventually walked to the other room, slamming the door.

J.P. brought up the still pictures he had taken at the warehouse. Eric examined them once and then went back to the suitcases with Cyrillic markings. "Are these things real?" Eric scrutinized the interior of the first suitcase. "Please tell me this is one of your pranks, J.P."

"I wish it was, Eric. I want your professional assessment."

"The mythical Soviet-era suitcase nukes. Yield two, maybe three kilotons, if properly maintained. They are a nightmare, almost impossible to detect due to size, until they're ready to blow, and then, well, it's just too late. Are they three separate devices? Are you sure?"

"This is about as real as it gets. Look at the serial numbers."

"Let's go to the cops. We don't need Jack," Ramos said, standing up.

"There is a lot more to this story." J.P. flipped through the still photos to the pictures of the badges. "They all seem affiliated with law enforcement. I doubt they carry fake badges."

"You think rogue cops are playing with nuclear devices on US soil? That's beyond serious trouble. Let's say you're right. What does it have to do with Jack?"

A light knock at the door reminded them of the two women in exile.

"We are in this together. It's not fair to hide things from us. We're coming in." Lisa and Max stuck their heads in the room. They had both showered and changed.

J.P. nodded and closed the lid, inviting the women to rejoin them, and turned to Eric. "I do not know for sure. I know Jack, and you know Jack. I saw the news this morning. My first thought was 'there's no way Jack would ever do anything this stupid.' That is why I called you. You confirmed what my intuition told me. What if this is not about Jack?"

"How do you mean not about Jack?" Ramos thought for a moment, and then it hit him. "You mean it could be about his father?"

"Yes."

"Do you have any proof of this?"

"None, just a hunch."

"What does this have to do with George Hunter?" Lisa asked, struggling to keep up with J.P.'s line of reasoning.

"When I saw the news this morning, my intuition started screaming that this is not about Jack. It is about coercing his dad to do something that otherwise he would never consider doing. It would be the right point to apply pressure. Something Sadowsky said on Thursday prompted me to think back to the time they murdered Alice. I researched what George was working on back then, and I had a colossal surprise. He was prosecuting Hector Salazar, Don Alberto Salazar's son. Newport cops busted Hector with a boatload of coke, guns, and cash. Literally. Hector faced life in the slammer."

"How did you make the leap to this not being about Jack?" Ramos asked. "I'm still not convinced you had nothing to do with Alice's murder back then."

"Alice and Artie were killed, and George recused himself from the Salazar case to deal with their deaths," J.P. explained. "Phil Tomlinson stepped in for George. Two months later, Hector Salazar walked. Thursday, I learned the same mysterious Big Man who engineered that crisis killed Alice and Artie. He is financing, providing logistics and support to Clancy and his group of renegade cops for this *True Patriot Day* event."

"That's quite a stretch." Lisa moved closer to the two men.

"She shares your doubts. She was second chair for the prosecution at my trial." J.P. pointed at Lisa, causing Eric's eyebrows to arch all the way to the ceiling.

"I have no proof," J.P. laid it out. "Just parallels. Back then, Sadowsky and the Big Man strong-armed George. They are both involved in this. Back then, I woke up in a ditch with amnesia. Now Lisa is experiencing the same. I never had a reason to hurt Alice or Artie. I loved them both more than life itself. I kept quiet about everything because until last night I thought Alice's death was a message intended for me."

Lisa bit her lip, not wanting to add fuel to J.P.'s fire. She decided to share with the rest of them. "The DA's office had Hector Salazar dead to rights. After Phil took over, information started leaking. Then some evidence went missing. The chain of evidence got compromised." Her lip curled into a snarl. "Is Morgan correct? A thought crossed my mind. What if Phil knew who had killed J.P.'s wife and prosecuted him? That would explain some things he had had me handle at trial. He needed to insulate himself. That was why he needed me to second-chair with him. God, I feel so dirty and manipulated."

CHAPTER 102

"IT WAS PURE LUCK** Anna found that traffic tape showing I was fifty miles away when the murders occurred, and the fire started. Otherwise, I would be on death row in San Quentin right now or worse. However, I have no recollection of it. An entire week wiped out like a computer file irretrievably deleted," J.P. concluded.

The room fell silent, save for the air-conditioning unit working overtime.

"You mean I may never recall what happened the past week?" Lisa inquired, worried.

"We cannot retrieve chemically deleted memories. It's different from retrograde amnesia or events blocked by a traumatic experience," Max declared with authority. "Think of it as deleting files from a hard drive then overwriting the spot."

Stunned, Eric and Lisa turned toward Max.

"Max just handed in her PhD thesis in bioengineering." J.P. caressed Max's hair as he clarified. "This brings me to the real reason we need to end this today. I booked her and I on a two-week cruise, leaving next week. It is a graduation present for her, and I intend to enjoy every moment. This is my first vacation since Alice died."

"I can vouch for the fact J.P. adored Alice. Otherwise, I wouldn't have let him have her," Eric said. "What I don't get is what they could gain from this ruse with Jack and Governor Hunter. It is an election year, but this seems extreme."

"This is not about the elections. The *True Patriot Day* is the Fourth of July."

"That's tomorrow. We've got to do something." Ramos got to his feet. "Let's kick some ass."

"What do we do?" asked J.P. "We only have one shot at this. If we mention it to the wrong person, they take us out. Game over. There already is a trail of bodies a mile wide. They will kill four more people to protect their operation for another twenty-four hours."

"Let's go to the Feds." Ramos clasped his hands. "We can outsmart them for a day."

"Hell, they have been gunning for us full speed for the past two days. Only dumb luck allowed us to escape so many times. However, because we got away, other people paid with their lives," J.P. said. "We cannot take chances like that again. They could have moles."

"Then I agree with your assessment. We need Jack, the Governor, and the resources they have access to," conceded Eric. He took a step back. "Well, there is a slight problem."

"What is the problem?" J.P.'s voice turned hard as flint.

"I do not know where Jack is," said Ramos as he raised his hands in a defensive posture. "I never said I knew where he was. I only said I would help you. However, I have an idea."

"Do tell!" J.P. lent each word the impact of a sledgehammer pounding on concrete. "I should smack that silly grin off your clown face. Boy, how I fell for it."

"I called Mel. She was in DC and had no clue where Jack was, or she would have told me. She's flying in this afternoon, but I don't think she'll be much help right now. Jack would not want her involved in any of this. However, she gave me another idea. Mother Mary is at the estate. Opa's dying, and she's been staying there with him. She knows where Jack is. As you know, Mother Mary and I don't always see eye to eye. You—well, I don't think she has any lost love for you, either. We need to convince her we're on Jack's side, then she'll help."

"I will go see Mother Mary," J.P. said. "You guys watch the videos, look through the pictures, listen to the recording of our conversation with Powell last night. See what you can come up with, and we compare notes when I get back. Eric, you need to be up to speed, and three heads are better at figuring out what I missed."

"You know you have to speak to her in person?" Ramos asked. "I'm going with you."

"She knows I did not do it," stated Morgan.

"Who is Mother Mary?" Lisa asked, exasperated by the exchange.

"Mary Hunter, the first lady of California, Jack and Alice's mother," answered J.P. "To us, she was always Mother Mary."

"You want to meet with your dead wife's mother and try to get information on the whereabouts of her only son? The son who's in trouble, wanted by the police for a murder you claim they framed him for but have no proof to back it up?" Lisa shook her head.

"That just about sums it up," replied J.P. "Mother Mary knows or, at the very least, suspects, that I did not kill Alice and Artie."

"How do you know she knows you didn't do it?" Lisa kept gnawing at the same bone.

"I am still alive, am I not?" retorted J.P. with a disarming smile.

"If she knows, why hasn't she ever set foot in the courtroom during the trial?" Lisa asked, still attempting to piece it all together.

"Precisely. If she thought I had done it, she would have shot me herself, court or no court conviction. However, if she knows where Jack is, she will tell me."

"You're nuts. You don't know what this woman thinks. She could hand you over to the police herself," Lisa said, wondering why she cared. "She has a protection detail."

"She could. It is moving to see how much you care, Counselor. This is something I have to do. Unfortunately, given our time constraints, I must do it in person. I committed to keep you alive through all this. Just trust me a little longer, will you?"

"If something happens to you, all these people will have died in vain. The psychos will win tomorrow, and the world loses. Is this worth the risk?" Max broke her silence.

"I think J.P. has a chance," said Ramos. "He wouldn't be alive if Mother Mary believed he murdered Alice and Artie. If Mother Mary didn't kill him, her father would have. Wait until you meet Opa Schumann. He's an old WWII relic who fought on the German side."

"Settled then," J.P. said. "You get up to speed. I hope you will come up with new ideas because I am fresh out. I will be back, hopefully with Jack, in a couple of hours. Max, if something happens, you know the drill. Brief Lisa and Eric." He opened the door, turned, and then smiled at them. "This is the one and only time I will ever trust Colonel Ramos alone with two beautiful women. Exigent circumstances."

CHAPTER 103

THE OVERHEAD VENTS PROVIDED maximum flow cold, causing the papers on the table to flutter. The heat and humidity bordered unbearable in the congested room. Tempers proved harder to control than the room temperature. The Irvine PD Ad Hoc Task Force had unearthed an astonishing amount of information. None of it made sense, contributing to the swelling frustration of its members.

Lieutenant Baker finished rehashing the ballistics and DNA reports. The lab confirmed that the bullet Morgan admitted firing had shattered Ryder's femur.

"Most likely, that prompted his partner to kill him at the scene. That is one powerful commitment statement, people." Baker concluded his presentation.

"Yesterday, I spoke to my buddy at Florence PD about a call that got deleted from their logs. Remember that?" Old Man Sparks took the floor. "He spoke separately with the four officers dispatched there. They all said they didn't respond to any such call. Later, one of them approached my friend and insisted he should speak with Lisa Jensen. She was there that night. She made the call to 911 and met them upon arrival."

"Has anyone seen Ms. Jensen since yesterday?" Randy Sparks surveyed the room.

Everyone shook his or her head. Old Man Sparks nodded to his son, knowing his concern, and then resumed speaking. "The patrolman confirmed the address and disclosed that Ms. Jensen had two men tied up on the second floor. She claimed they had kidnapped and attempted to rape and kill her. Two other LEOs, cuffed and unconscious, were on the ground floor. The responding cop said he saw lots of equipment, trucks, Humvees, boxes, etc., in the warehouse. The patrolman claimed someone from the DOJ in Sacramento instructed them to forget the whole thing, invoking national security and whatnot."

"Where is Ms. Jensen? Why is she running, if she is a victim?" Lieutenant Baker focused everyone's attention on an overlooked issue.

"We took possession of her clothes, purse and phone. She couldn't be wearing anything but the hospital gown when she fled," Sergeant Pearce added. "That girl must be scared to death. I think she remembers things, and she's been playing us. She may be with Morgan."

"It makes no sense she'd run with Morgan," scoffed Lieutenant Simon. "Those two could never be near each other without a riot squad between them."

"You think she's running *with* Morgan." Stonehill pointed out the flaw in logic.

"We assume that, since she disappeared after he got here," Sparks added.

"The two killers may not have come alone, and someone kidnapped her again." Pearce changed his tune. "You know how I feel about Morgan. This shit's confusing. Had you asked me yesterday if I considered helping Morgan, you'd have lost some teeth. I did some checking up on our dead victims. Two of them are our own officers. Then we have James Smythe of the LAPD. He was a disgruntled cop with a history of reprimands and a penchant for violence in the line of duty. Nothing we haven't seen before."

"Not all police officers are angels," murmured one officer.

"According to his commanding officer," Sergeant Pearce ignored the comment. "Smythe's been detached to an outfit he never heard of. Last year, his lieutenant told everyone to forget about Smythe, keep quiet, and not rock the boat. Next victim is Patrick Allen of LBPD, similar behavior. The fifth body was not a cop. He's former state trooper Jon Sadowsky. His prints were on the bullets found in the gun Morgan fired at the hospital yesterday. He was one brutal cop, many charges of excessive force, bribery, assault, solicitation, etc. Nothing ever stuck, like he had a powerful guardian angel. Early last year, he quit. He told everyone he got a fabulous job with Golden Trident Security. Incidentally, Ryder, the man killed by his partner during the UCI incident, also quit his job with CHP and went to work for GTS. I called GTS. They had me chasing my tail for an hour. They wouldn't confirm these guys worked there. I don't like that place. I have a bad feeling about it."

"After Lieutenant Sparks informed us about the Florence warehouse, I requested CHP to trace the vehicles leaving the area yesterday morning." Lieutenant Baker took over. "I wanted to see if I could get their new location. Instead, I got a lot of lip service about camera malfunctions, incomplete recordings, and no data. I sent the request to Sacramento marked 'Urgent.' It came back 'backlogged due of lack of resources' and suggested I waited until after the holiday weekend. What kind of BS is this? We have a seven-dead-body count, four of them active cops, two ex-cops, and a lawyer. They give me the 'lack of resources' BS?"

"Let's summarize," Sparks took over. "Morgan stumbled across of a bunch of nasty people, maybe cops that went off the reservation. It's ironic. The only person who knows enough about them is a fellow everyone wants to shoot on sight. Given his history, they knew we'd gladly do it. What are they up to? Speculate, people."

They conjectured for another hour. They decided they did not have enough information, agreed to keep in touch, and hustled to start their day.

CHAPTER 104

"OFFICER SPARKS." MORGAN'S VOICE sounded jovial when Sparks answered his phone. "You are hard to find. You should be recuperating, living the good life."

"Morgan?" Sparks pushed his jaw up with his other hand. "You need to come in. We believe you. You're on to something, and it could be big. We need to know what you learned so we can stop them." Sparks gestured for his dad to track the call.

"So, they cleaned out of the warehouse already," J.P. hooted. "You will understand if I do not run straight to a cop shop. Please listen and do not interrupt. I know you are tracing this call. I need your help. I have information to trade. Can I trust you to do the right thing?"

"Goes without asking." Sparks sat up on the bed, ignoring the pain.

"Duly noted. I need two favors. This group's big event will occur on the Fourth of July. They call it *True Patriot Day*. It will take place all over California. For sure, they will hit Los Angeles, Bay Area, Sacramento, San Diego, and somewhere in Orange County. My source did not know where in OC. This group claims their self-assigned mission is about deporting illegal immigrants, America for Americans. The way they act, how little regard they have for human life, including their own brethren, it does not jibe. Check on Golden Trident Security. They provide logistics and support for this operation." J.P. allowed Sparks to ask questions.

"Come in with what you know. My dad and I will guarantee your safety."

"They also seem to be hell-bent on reinstating Trump as their choice President, although that does not ring entirely true to me," said J.P.

"OK, Morgan, I believe you stumbled onto something dangerous, Come in, please."

"On to the favors, then. First, they framed Jack Hunter. I do not know how, but they did. I am positive it relates to this *True Patriot Day* crap, probably to manipulate his dad. I do not have time to chase that lead down. Help me clear his name."

"Whooooooa." Sparks stuttered on the o" sound, dragging it out the way he would if he was pulling the reins on a runaway horse. "Do you know what you're asking? I'm a police officer. It's not my job to clear people of suspicion. That case is not even in our jurisdiction."

"Last time I checked, cops befriended cops. I promise you. You will not regret helping Jack, if we all live to see the sunset tomorrow, that is."

"What makes you sure Hunter didn't do it? They have him on tape with that girl several times in the past year. He was there with her last night, and he left alone. They found her dead shortly thereafter. Pretty slam dunk."

"If rogue cops framed him, it would be a solid job," J.P. pointed out.

"Maybe." Sparks realized J.P. had a valid point. So far, he had provided them only with reliable information and apprised them of facts they had not known.

"No 'maybe.' I have known Jack all my life. We served together in Naval Intel. He is the best, extremely smart, and has extensive counter-surveillance training and experience. Do you think he would be stupid enough to allow anyone to tape him going into a motel room with a child? He would not cheat on Mel. Jack abhors child molesters."

"You could be wrong. People change, maybe she lied about her age—"

"We can argue about this all day. You cannot convince me otherwise. If you rather not helped, tell me, and I will find someone else."

"OK," Sparks relented. "I'll do my best but give me something I can work with."

"Have them check the integrity of recordings and the motel. I bet that is where the fraud lies because that is the damning evidence. Again, my intuition says this connects somehow to that group of corrupt cops.

I do not know how yet. I have a hunch they targeted Jack to control or manipulate the Governor."

Old Man Sparks walked in and signaled his son to stretch out the conversation.

"If I do this, you surrender today. My dad will arrange it and take care of everything. You have my word," Sparks concluded, holding his breath and crossing his fingers.

"I will do it when I am ready. Help clear Jack of this crap, please."

"He should turn himself in and tell his side," said Sparks.

"I know you are doing your job. Remember, legal is not always right, and right is not always legal. Second favor. Anna Richter had a pendant on her, a heart-shaped locket, white gold with diamonds and sapphires, about an inch and a half across. I need it. I will trade all the evidence and information I have on these guys for that piece of jewelry."

"Ask her family to get it for you. Why involve me?"

"Her only living family was her mother. Cohorts of the men who executed Anna Richter threw Candy Richter off a balcony in Vegas last night."

"How do you know the locket isn't in the ruins of her home?"

"It is an electronic vault disguised as a piece of jewelry. I had it made specifically for her. Waterproof, so she never needed to take it off, even in the shower."

"What's so important that you're willing to trade everything for it?"

"Anna left this message for me the day before they murdered her. I know she backed up the information on that drive. I need the pendant to prove it." J.P. held a digital player to the phone and replayed Anna's last phone message.

CHAPTER 105

J.P. FIGURED SPARKS STILL attempted to stall him.

"The coroner and Irvine PD classified Richter's death as suicide," said Sparks. "Where did you get the murder or execution idea? If you're right, the pendant is evidence in that investigation. I can't just get it for you."

"Time is up, Sparks. There are a lot of lives at stake. Help me expose this, for truth's sake, if nothing else. You strike me as an honest man and a stand-up cop."

J.P. dismantled the phone and launched the parts out the window. "There goes another one. I wonder what the fine is for littering," he quipped.

He took a winding road leading into the back hills to an old iron gate with impressive ornaments. He punched the code to open the gate and returned to the SUV.

Seconds later, four men in dark suits surrounded him, pointing weapons at him. "On the ground. Lock your fingers, or we pump you full of lead," their leader yelled.

"This is all you get. I am unarmed." Morgan leaned against the hood.

Two dark-suited men holstered their guns and patted him down. "He's clean." They handcuffed him and then goaded him toward the main house.

"We got you now. And it feels so good," one of his captors whispered in his ear, his laugh sounding like a hyena on speed.

CHAPTER 106

ERIC STOOD AND STRETCHED his six-foot-one frame. They had just finished examining all the evidence collected by J.P. since Thursday night. "That's J.P. for you." Eric's voice was full of admiration and pride. "If there's any shit somewhere, he'll step in it and splatter it. What are they planning? Killing police officers and civilians like that means they believe they'll get away with it or they will escape prosecution."

"How can they escape punishment? Killing a cop is an automatic death penalty case." Lisa jumped in with both feet, baring her teeth.

"Not if they know the government will not charge them, or if they're sure that something bigger will occupy the minds of the people, government, and media."

"I'll do it myself, if I have to." Lisa's face turned red with fury. Max reached out to touch her arm. Lisa swatted her hand away. "I just watched something I never thought possible. To top it off, I owe Morgan for saving my life twice. Actually, three times. He got me out of Anna's home before the killing started. I can't believe I was there, but I saw it with my own eyes. Sadowsky's account of events related to the cases against J.P. and Hector Salazar is compelling. I'm not 100 percent convinced, but I feel it was the truth." She paused and lowered her voice. "Morgan could have masterminded it to clear his name. Why would he avoid the police? Then how did he pull the stunt at the Sheriff's station last night? All this is enough to drive me crazy. Why do they believe they would escape prosecution?" Lisa turned to Eric.

"We saw this time and again when we were with Naval Intel. Leaders of a new regime forgive all transgressions of those who helped in the transition—" Eric began.

"In third-world countries! This is America, for God's sake!" cried Lisa. "We have a constitution, laws, and a system of checks and balances that works."

"It all means nothing to the family staring at the business end of an assault rifle in the hands of a trained warrior or a psychopath who believes everything Trump is selling in his efforts to return to the Oval Office. I know it sounds impossible, but I bet J.P. concluded the same thing. He said nothing because he wanted to see what we figure out on our own."

"Why would he let us toil this way?"

"J.P. is fond of Einstein. 'I never teach my pupils. I merely provide the environment for them to learn.' He could not go to the authorities." Eric drew imaginary quotes around the word authorities. "One false move and all this died with him, with us, now. There is only one explanation. *True Patriot Day* will change California forever. If the people promoting this change execute cops on duty, their own troops, how good will it be for the rest of us?"

"What are we talking about here?" intervened Max.

"Factoring in the Jack Hunter development, I guess we're talking about having new state leadership tomorrow," Ramos said. "That's bold, but in today's political environment, if you have enough money and committed people, it can be done. Before the Trumpsurrection I would have laughed you out of the room if you suggested that. Now, I don't know."

"I know J.P. would never allow this to happen," Max declared. "Never."

"Do you know what it would take to accomplish that in California or anywhere in the United States? To remove an elected Governor and replace him and maybe the entire cabinet in one day? Because you couldn't just get rid of one. To be successful, all must go." Lisa worked herself up as if she prepared to argue an important case. Max and Eric shrugged.

"I'm sure we can find out right now." Eric pointed to the laptops.

"No need to. It was one question on the bar exam. I still recall it." Lisa tapped her foot. "The whole thing sounds alien, like a bad sci-fi movie script. God, what a world we live in."

"We can't let this happen. People who kill innocent women and children do not deserve to live, let alone be in command. I vote we find their nest and call the Marines to exterminate them," Max said in a calm, determined voice. "Nukes? On American soil. No, no, no."

"Normally, I would say we go to the Feds. Alert the media. However, we have no actual proof." Eric raised his hand like a traffic cop. "We have recordings and pictures of the materials. By now, I guarantee it, they abandoned that warehouse."

"That and our word should be enough." Lisa closed the laptop lids.

"Without the actual stuff," Eric continued, "the Feds will laugh at us. This is Fourth of July weekend. The APB labels J.P. a counterfeiter and cop killer. Nobody will take anything he says at face value. I get J.P.'s position. Jack can vouch for him to his dad, and the Governor can cut through the red tape and move mountains. We are about twenty-four hours from the conclusion of this operation. We can't afford mistakes. There are too many lives at stake."

"Did J.P. tell you he came to the same conclusions?" probed Lisa.

"He said nothing. We used to play this game—Jack, J.P., and I—at Naval Intel. J.P. beat the pants off us, but we got a few of them right. I'm one of the few people who knows how he thinks, mostly." Eric answered.

"What did he do for Naval Intelligence? I've been dying to know, ever since I got his service file during the trial." Lisa's curiosity took hold.

"What did he tell you?" snorted Eric.

"He said he was an analyst. The way he acts, he's no desk jockey."

"Technically, he was an analyst," replied Eric. "His nickname was *The Fantasist*. It's a treat to watch his mind work under duress. The consensus was that when the bombs fell, everyone would run for cover. J.P. would cook breakfast and plan for tomorrow."

"His file consisted of three, maybe four legible words per paragraph, usually his name and rank." Lisa leaned in a few more inches. "What did he actually do?"

"I think it's best to let J.P. answer that. It's his life." Eric sensed the conversation was sliding down a steep, slippery slope.

"Why did he quit and give up all his rights?" Lisa put her hands on her hips.

"What did he tell you?" Ramos repeated his question, aware he was now aboard a conversational runaway train, rushing downhill, with no brakes.

"Oh, spare me the bullshit, Colonel. What happened? He had a stellar career. One day, he resigns his commission in the Navy, gives up everything, and becomes a gumshoe. It was good stuff when I prosecuted him. Now it makes little sense."

"These are issues classified beyond Top Secret, stuff that will never see the light of day. Just leave it be." Eric attempted again to stop the imminent free fall.

"How can we trust you when you refuse to trust us?" Max joined Lisa's side.

CHAPTER 107

THE SUITS FORCED J.P. into a chair and assumed a daisy position around the room, keeping a safe distance, aiming their guns at his head. A stately blonde woman walked in and stopped three feet from Morgan. She crossed her arms on her chest, locked her ice-blue eyes on J.P., and studied him for a long time. Her face betrayed no emotions.

"Hello, Mother Mary," J.P. broke the awkward silence. "You still look as ravishing as ever. I am delighted to see you after all these years, circumstances notwithstanding."

"J.P. Morgan, as I live and breathe!" exclaimed Mary Hunter. She motioned for a chair and sat across from J.P. She cocked her head to one side and then the other. "The people on my detail, and the Governor's, would consider it an honor to shoot you."

"Are you going to let them?" J.P. lifted his arms out toward her. "Can you please ask them to remove the cuffs? If I wanted to get in unannounced, they would have never seen me."

"What makes you believe I will not ask them to do it as a favor to me? Shoot you, that is." Mother Mary leaned back in her chair.

"You know I am a lot of things. Cold-blooded murderer and child killer is not among them. We need to talk about Jack. Please." He exposed the handcuffs again.

"You could never lie to me, not successfully." She motioned to the head of her protection. "It's perfectly OK, Jim."

With great reluctance, Jim Honeywell ordered his men to remove J.P.'s cuffs. One of them detached the shackles and pocketed them. The rest of the detail kept their guns trained on J.P., fanning away from Mary Hunter to more advantageous lines of fire.

"Leave us alone, Jim. J.P. would never hurt me. He's like a son to me."

Honeywell objected with vehemence, but Mother Mary prevailed. "We'll be right outside, Mrs. Hunter. If we hear anything weird, we come in guns blazing," Jim barked.

"I know you may have doubts about my killing Alice and Artie," J.P. began. "Now I know I did not do it. I have a weeklong gap in memory surrounding Alice's death. Two nights ago, I stumbled onto info that points somewhere else. Soon I may prove who did it. I plan to have a heart-to-heart with him."

"Deep in my heart, I've always known you couldn't have killed them. If you tell me you didn't do it, I believe you. If you find him, do not waste the courts' time. This is between you and me, mother to son." She thrust her hand out.

"You have my word." J.P. reached out and shook her hand.

"Now what about Jack?" Mother Mary folded her arms in her lap.

"I know Jack did not do this crap." J.P. explained his line of reasoning. He touched on the events of the past few days and then concluded, "I need Jack. He has access to resources I do not. He has credibility with the Governor. Together, we can stop this madness."

"Why not go to the police or the FBI and let them sort it all out?"

"I do not know who to trust. From their point of view, this information comes from a cop killer, someone they think got away with murder before. Even if they do not shoot me on sight, I have no solid proof. That APB labels me a counterfeiter, which is enough to raise serious doubts and buy them time. Time we do not have. Unless we find their new lair soon, I have nothing but a video and some photos that anyone could claim I doctored. I would love to talk to the Governor directly, if possible." He handed her one of the flash drives he had prepared outside UCI Medical Center the day before.

"Oh, no. George will probably have you killed and buried out there. You stay away from him. Jack is a different story. You two grew up together. Let me deal with George when the time is right." She twirled the flash drive on her fingers.

"OK. How do I get in touch with Jack?"

Mother Mary sighed, hugged herself tight around the waist, stared J.P. straight in the eyes, and then spoke. "He's all I have left. I can't afford to lose him too. I told George he should be ready to step down if Jack had to leave the country. You understand, J.P.?"

Force him to step down as Governor. Hmm, could that be it?

"I give you my word. I will do everything in my power to clear Jack's name and keep George in the Governor's mansion."

Mother Mary wrung her hands, looking out the window at the exquisite garden. Her lower lip quivered, and then she caved under J.P.'s penetrating gaze.

"I'll hold you to it. You help him clear his name. I don't care about George's ambitions. He can retire, go fishing, and do whatever old politicians like him do after their careers end. Jack is still young. He has his entire life ahead of him. Get out of here and then call him. He's at the old cabin where you boys built that fort thirty years ago." She produced a small phone. "Go help my son. Your best friend needs you." Mother Mary stood and hugged J.P. tight.

"I heard Opa is dying. May I see him?" J.P. asked. "I may never get another chance."

CHAPTER 108

ERIC ROLLED HIS EYES at the manipulation attempt. "You realize if J.P. finds out I told you, he'd kill me? Not to mention if the word gets out, they will boot me from the corps and send me to Leavenworth for life. This information never left the Navy."

"Can it, Jarhead!" exclaimed Max. "That's the price for my trust."

"Kryptonite." Eric looked deep into her eyes. "I'll just have to have faith in you. You can never reveal that you know this. It may prove dangerous, and I don't mean J.P. I mean the people who want this kept under wraps at any cost."

Max and Lisa nodded in somber agreement, leaning forward shoulder to shoulder.

"Here goes nothing. J.P. plays by his own set of rules. You can always count on him to do the right thing, but his rule book aligns with the Ten Commandments and less with the prevailing laws. Anyway, J.P. can look at the same information we do and reach different conclusions. I don't know how he does it, but he's always right on the money. Well, almost every time, but even when he's wrong, it's not by much. After a while, we learned to let him have it." Eric paused and slapped his thigh. "Man, I can't believe I'm talking about it. You must understand. The Navy and the government kept a lid on this for a lot of years."

Lisa and Max drew closer to Eric.

"End of August 2001, J.P. was new at the Intelligence game, and didn't have a reputation for his abilities yet. J.P. pulls one of his usual tricks and comes up with five names of Arab nationals operating on US soil. J.P. was sure they planned something dreadful. He didn't know what. He only had one of his famous hunches. He wanted the law enforcement and intelligence people to know. He thought someone else might get additional evidence and figure out how to catch the Arabs. J.P. forwarded the info to the law enforcement and intelligence communities. A Naval Intel special liaison officer had to evaluate this kind of information prior to dissemination. Without the special liaison vetting, his info didn't leave Coronado." Eric took a sip of water.

"This was Thursday, August 30, 2001. The special liaison took off a day early to go down to Mexico for a weekend of fun. He had a place outside Ensenada, and he spent almost every weekend there. He liked the local underage girls, or so the story went. Nobody ever investigated it. His daddy made sure of it."

Ramos paused, staring at the wall, pondering if he should go for broke with the full story. This was treacherous territory, to say the least. "This was Labor Day weekend of 2001. The special liaison took one extra day after the official weekend. He returned to Coronado on September 5th. Whatever happened, we'll never know. He may have decided it was all bullshit and buried it. Fact is, the Special Liaison never officially endorsed the information for the Navy, and it didn't make it to the intelligence community or to any law enforcement agency that could have done something about it." Eric halted, playing with the water bottle.

Max snagged it with a scowling look, signaling for him to continue.

"September 11, 2001, three thousand people died. When the Feds released the names of the nineteen terrorists, all five names J.P. had exposed were among them. He lost it. He went to the liaison's office. Long story short, J.P. literally put him through a wall. The man was gargantuan, over 330 lbs. J.P. broke his jaw, nose, and a few ribs. The liaison was the son of a career US senator. They were out for J.P.'s blood. SECNAV settled it behind closed doors to avoid a gigantic scandal."

"Yep, that sound like Papa Bear I know," said Max. "For years, I tortured him in every imaginable way. He wouldn't talk about any of it. All he ever said was that he got disgusted with the way the Navy handled things and quit. I guess he was telling the truth, to a certain extent." Max broke the silence.

"That sounds like him. I know he can lie with the best of them, yet if you ask a direct question, he'll always tell the truth. Maybe not the whole truth, but if you learn to read between the lines and piece stuff together, you get everything. Unless he doesn't like you, and then he'll mess with your head, sending you down dark alleys until you can't figure out which side is up." Ramos flashed a sad smile. "Maybe I should have asked *him* about Alice."

Lisa turned away to conceal tears and the slew of emotions. She recalled J.P.'s poem the day before and his remark about the last lines. "He could have prevented 9/11. They should have given him a medal, not forced him to quit." The lawyer in Lisa jumped to attention.

"The senator had pull on the Hill. Anybody else involved in it, J.P. would have gotten the medal. God knows he got pretty much everything the Navy awards."

"Oh my God," Lisa added, frustrated. "I understand now why he said I had misunderstood him and misinterpreted the facts. At trial, I pointed out to the jury he quit the Navy during the war on terror, when the country needed him the most. I called him a coward who ran to safety to the civilian life rather than put his ass on the line."

"Anyhow," Eric continued. "Blink twice and J.P. makes Commander and by now he had built a reputation. *The Fantasist's* analysis and field experience were in high demand. The same Special Liaison botched up another operation, and a detachment of Navy Seals got ambushed and murdered. Every single one of them. That's the second tie J.P. lost it and went after the guy. He dragged him out of the office and tied him to the flag post. Not a good idea."

"Now I get it," Max whispered. "It happened five or six years ago on the anniversary of Alice's death. J.P. was feeling down that day. It was the only time I saw him feel sorry for himself, come to think of it. He said, 'I am responsible for the loss of over three thousand souls, but they only prosecuted me for three. It's a good ratio.' He wouldn't say anything else. I never understood what he meant. He thinks all those people died on 9/11 because he failed."

"Who's the Special Liaison?" asked Lisa, incensed. "Who is the son of a bitch? The Navy may have done nothing about it, but I will find a way to do it."

"Commander Theo Myerson. Eventually, he quit the Navy as well." Eric stretched his long arms. "The scandals were just too many and too big. After the Navy, he went into some unsavory business with people south of the border. He died in a confrontation with the Coast Guard. That man was a true sociopath, but Daddy had lofty plans, and J.P. scuttled them. That's the unofficial story. Can you trust me now?"

Lisa and Max nodded in agreement, and Max touched his shoulder, smiling at him.

"I screwed up big-time," Eric said. "I mean not giving J.P. the benefit of the doubt."

"You did," Max replied. "If it happens again, you'll answer to me."

"Does J.P. still keep those nine flags around?" Eric changed the subject. "Or are there more than nine by now?"

"Yeah," muttered Lisa. "What's that about?"

"Another thing I tortured him about." Max shook her head. "I don't know. He never told me, no matter how many times I asked."

"That I will let J.P. tell you about them," said Ramos. "I am not touching that with a ten-foot pole. I was just curious. I'm going to run out to get more coffee and snacks. I skipped breakfast today getting here. Would you ladies like anything?"

CHAPTER 109

J.P. FOLLOWED MOTHER MARY into a cluster of weapons aimed at them. She waved at the detail to put the guns away and headed upstairs. She tiptoed to an impressively large door, which she opened with unnatural ease. Mary Hunter asked the attending nurse to give them a minute alone with her father and then beckoned J.P. to come in.

J.P. advanced to the bed. The old man's eyes fluttered open, and he tried to sit up.

"Save your strength, Papa. J.P. is here to see you," Mother Mary whispered.

"Hey, Opa, how are you?" J.P. kneeled and enveloped the old man's hand in his own.

"It's been a long time, J.P. Where have you been?" The old man moaned, his voice a hint of what J.P. recalled.

"Here and there. Let's talk about you. Still wreaking havoc with the female help?"

"Same old J.P. All you can think about is women. Speaking of girls, that business with Alice?" He scrutinized J.P. with the intensity of a wild cat stalking its prey.

"I do not know for sure who did it. I am about to find out. I will come back and tell you about it. Deal?" J.P. squeezed Opa's hand, fighting back tears.

The old man nodded and then drifted away. J.P. lifted Opa's hand to his forehead and held it there for a moment. The fingers felt stiff and frail.

The old man's eyes flew open, and he grabbed J.P.'s wrist, pulling him down. "Don't go yet. I need to tell you a story."

"J.P. needs to take care of something. He'll come back. Then you can tell him all the stories you know," Mary intervened, avoiding eye contact with her father.

"No. I need to tell it now. Sit, J.P. It won't take long. I know Death is lurking outside." He gestured toward the immense door.

"Don't talk like that, Papa," Mother Mary pleaded, tears adorning her sky-blue eyes.

"You know, J.P., I was a boy of about fifteen in Berlin during the Olympics. We were on top of the world. The German people, I mean. Hitler and his cronies had all of us fooled, believing their crap. They spewed it all over the place—on the radio, in schools, in the newspapers, everywhere. Even I was fooled by them." He paused, catching his breath.

Mary Hunter leaned in again, imploring with her eyes.

"It will only take a moment." The old man's tone left no room for argument. "I was young and gullible, exposed to it day in and day out. There was this family of immigrants, Polish or maybe Czech. It was so long ago. They lived a few streets over. They had a daughter, Anya, a year younger than me. She was so beautiful that I couldn't help but fall in love with her the very first time I saw her." His voice trailed off, and he closed his eyes, reliving the teenager's love for Anya. His eyes opened slowly and regained their focus.

"I wanted to ask her to go out with me. In those days, things were simpler yet a lot more complicated at the same time. She was Polish or Czech. I was German. I never understood all that, but I never asked her out, either. We walked together to school a few times. One day, the Gestapo showed up, loaded her entire family in a truck, and hauled them away. Suspicion of being Jews or harboring anti-German feelings or some other crap like that. Who knows? Back then, they didn't really need a reason. They could always make one up. I never saw my beautiful Anya again." His wheezing sigh sounded like a small vacuum cleaner.

This was a rare occasion. Opa Schumann did not have a reputation for heart-to-heart talks. Mother Mary moved a little closer and listened, captivated.

"Later, I could never forgive myself for letting her go without even trying. What hurt the most was that the very people I believed in took her from me. They used the propaganda machine to spread the hatred and fear we breathed in. What harm could have Anya ever done to the German state? A sweet teenage girl?" He coughed several times and cleared his throat.

"I know you're wondering where this is going. I assure you, I haven't lost my mind yet." He chuckled, squeezing both Mary's and J.P.'s hands. "Anya was the most beautiful thing that happened to me as a boy." Opa beamed at his daughter. "Until I met your mother."

Mary straightened a strand of her father's hair and then kissed his forehead.

"Today," Opa resumed, "I see the same ingredients as in Germany in the thirties. I see the same limited thinking and justification of atrocities. The same hatred and fear bred into the mass consciousness. There are so many people willing to commit horrendous acts. They have no issues with shredding the Constitution, rationalizing everything in the name of the almighty national security and other such crap. J.P. don't let hatred and fear win again. This Trump character opened a door mankind should have welded shut and buried along with Hitler."

The old man coughed hard, and tears invaded his steel-gray eyes. "Someone, I don't remember the chap's name, once said this: 'The only thing necessary for the triumph of evil is that good men do nothing.' Don't stand by and let it happen again. I did when I was young. Look what Hitler did to the world. I thought I should tell you this while I still can. Whenever I mention it to George, he laughs at me and calls me a silly old fool. He's the one who's blind."

"Thank you, Opa. Be good. I will be back as soon as I can, and you can tell me more about Anya." J.P. stood. *How did he know what I ran into? Amazing.*

"Go on, J.P. Help Jack clear his name." Seeing his daughter's terrified look, Opa clarified, "You think you can keep that from me? I may not be the man I was, but I'm not a chump. J.P., the divine inspired me to tell you this story for a reason. I'm just the messenger."

"I love you, Opa. I will bring Jack and Eric. It will be like old days. You will teach us to pick up chicks, and we will get you real German beer, without Mother Mary knowing." He flashed a conspiratorial grin and winked.

Opa Schumann grinned and closed his eyes. J.P. and Mother Mary stepped out. She directed Jim Honeywell to escort J.P. off the estate. "Jim, you and your guys can never reveal his visit to anyone, especially the Governor. When the time is right, I'll tell George."

J.P. left the estate, followed by the furious looks of Mother Mary's protection detail lined up from the front steps to the gate, guns drawn.

CHAPTER 110

T HE IRVINE CHIEF OF Police was fuming, wiping heavy perspiration off his thick brow. He was a corpulent man, with a balding head. The heat added extra levels to his raging fury, making him sweat in places he did not know he could. He had spent the last twenty-four hours fending off the mayor, the media, and an assortment of politicians who needed to get their names in the paper. All of those hyenas "applying the right amount of pressure on the Irvine PD to solve the case, apprehend the murderers, and restore order," as one such A-hole put it. Nobody understood that, when they called and took up his time, fewer things happened. He had instructed his department to get Morgan any which way they could and cooperate fully with all law enforcement agencies operating in their territory, advance notice or no notice.

He hated the second part of that order, but the directive had come from Sacramento. On top of everything else, he had received a call from that arrogant DOJ a-hole, Clancy, who had scolded him in a milk-and-honey voice and had questioned his ability to command.

Clancy, the A-hole called again, interrupting the chief's Saturday morning golf routine. Clancy tore the Chief a new one. Then informed him that several officers under his command harassed other law enforcement agencies and respectable business establishments. The Irvine PD officers concocted accusations and asked impertinent questions.

Clancy then asked the Chief if his officers did not have enough to do, given the eight murders in their jurisdiction, blah, blah, blah. He then told the Chief that several of his lieutenants, sergeants, and officers were looking for ways to help Morgan. The Chief had summoned his department heads to his office for a spur-of-the-moment meeting.

"Help him? How in the world did this happen? Has the entire world gone mad? This department has enough to worry about handling the fallout from previous encounters with this maniac. What the hell is wrong with you people? I get calls from everyone under the sun asking when we plan to catch this freak, and you want to assist him. You want to give this department another black eye?" bellowed the Chief, issuing copious amounts of spit foam with each word.

"Sir, we have reason to believe—" Lieutenant Baker began.

"You have reason to believe nothing, Lieutenant," the Chief cut him off. "Yesterday I issued precise orders. You all disobeyed. I don't care about excuses and reasons. Do you understand? Here it is again: catch Morgan. Dead or alive, I don't give a damn. Just end this fiasco. That's your job. That's what I pay you for. You want to help Morgan, figure out a way to get him off the streets before he kills more cops. That's your job. Doing anything else is an insult to the memory of the officers he murdered."

Everybody knew the Chief got the job through sheer manipulation and political connections. His investigative skills had been the butt of jokes his entire career, but his political survival skills were top notch. The Chief paced the length of his office, alternating between clasping his hands and slapping them together. He stared at each man assembled in his office with a challenge in his eyes. He got more furious because of the cold treatment he received from his subordinates.

"Now get out of here, and tell everyone, if they want to have a job here, they need to follow all my orders. If anyone helps this a-hole Morgan, I will fire them on the spot. I don't care what the union has to say. This is still my department!" he yelled, slamming his small fists down on the top of his desk. His uncle's picture rattled. The uncle was the state senator who got him the job. His portrait grew larger with each promotion. What started out as a three by five now occupied an eight by ten in a golden frame. The betting pool had five-to-one odds that the next installment would be a portrait of his uncle on the wall, hanging where no one could forget the origin of the power behind the Napoleonic Chief.

The officers filed out of the office in silence. "Morgan's goose is cooked. We don't have enough to confront the chief, and he's wanted for killing cops." Baker summarized.

CHAPTER 111

ERIC BROUGHT BACK COFFEE, water, sandwiches, and fresh fruit. Max and Lisa had packed everything, except the laptops. Max gave Eric a quick update.

"J.P. mentioned something I thought strange. Anna's message ended with the words 'thank God for sunny days.' We listened to it a few times, and we think Anna may have said, 'thank God for Sonny Days.' Lisa recalled there was an Orange County Sheriff's deputy named Sonny Days. We looked him up. He died a month ago under strange circumstances. He was married almost forty years and had a daughter. Her name is Cher. I kid you not."

"I reward you with goodies. Tell me more." Ramos opened the boxes.

"What do you want to know?" Max chirped, grabbing a sandwich.

"I'd like to find out about you and J.P." Ramos handed Max coffee and a paper plate. "I know about Ms. Jensen. I followed the trial. I didn't make the connection until J.P. pointed it out. Truthfully, I never thought J.P. could stand to be near her."

"I would like to hear the end of the story, Max." Lisa jumped right in.

"I think J.P.'s right. That's our private story and no one else's business. I'll leave it at that. He's the closest thing I have for a parent, and I'm the closest thing he has for a family."

"No go, girlfriend." Lisa gripped Max's hand, pulling her back. "Not after what you shared last night. We need to know everything."

"No, you don't." Max glared at them. "J.P. is right. When this is over, chances are we'll never meet again. So, the less we get to know each other, the better."

"I now believe J.P. didn't kill Alice," Eric said. "I don't plan to leave my best friends hanging. I made that mistake once because I allowed rage and grief to blind me."

"We have work to do and no time for campfire stories." Max drummed under the plate.

"I need to know who I'm going into battle with. My dear ladies, do not kid yourselves. We are about to engage in mortal combat. How can we trust you if you refuse to tell us about you? Please satisfy an old soldier's curiosity."

Max measured Ramos up and down twice. "You're not that old. Try a fresh approach, before you crash and burn, Jarhead."

Max recounted the first part of the story in Reader's Digest fashion for Eric's benefit and then proceeded with the conclusion. "The first two weeks at the cabin, I tried to kill him a dozen times. He caught me every time. I half hoped he would finally put me out of my misery. He didn't. He just talked to me in his calm manner and assured me constantly that I would be OK. I recall little else from those days, except the pain, the burning sensation, and the need for a fix. Nothing else mattered much. Then Marie showed up."

"Who's Marie?" asked Eric.

"Marie was a few weeks old at the most. She followed us from one of our daily walks in the woods. J.P. didn't want her there at all."

"Who is Marie, again?" Ramos chimed in.

"Their five-hundred-pound pet bear, their cabin keeper when they're not up there," offered Lisa, urging Max to resume the story.

"Their what?" Eric's eyes bulged out. "This I got to hear."

"She is much more than our pet." Max's voice melted with affection. "She is like a sister to me. J.P. wouldn't hear of letting her stay. I cried, threw fits, things. She was so small and hungry. I couldn't conceive of Marie being on her own in the forest. I promised to stop trying to kill J.P. if he allowed her to stay. He thought Marie's mother would show up eventually and that the baby bear would go away with her."

"You have a pet bear?" Ramos asked, unable to hide his astonishment.

"Marie drank our entire milk supply in one sitting." Max placed her open palm on Eric's hand. "Several days and milk trips later, when the mother didn't show up to claim her, we took Marie to the vet. Dr. Wilson proclaimed her healthy and wanted to place her in a zoo. He said she was too young to survive on her own, and that we shouldn't encourage her to loiter near the cabin. I trashed his office. I grabbed Marie and ran out like a lunatic with the screaming bear cub in my arms." Max paused, laughing at the memory.

She played with her hair, and Eric's heart fluttered along with her tresses.

"I was irrational. J.P. calmed everyone down, and we took Marie back up to the cabin. Later that day, the two local park rangers showed up, trying to take her. I grabbed one of their guns and threatened to shoot them both if they didn't leave immediately. J.P. stood between us and got me out of that one by the skin of his teeth. The rangers didn't press charges. We eventually became close friends. They would come by now and then to check up on Marie. After a while, everyone accepted we were taking care of Marie until she was old enough. She's been with us ever since. Every time we go up there, we bring her food. She loves steak, sausages, hot dogs, and any kind of meat. Don't get me started about the bear claws. Last night, she saved our lives, didn't she?" Max looked for Lisa's support, who nodded in agreement.

"How? She refused to eat you?" Eric asked, mesmerized by Max and the story.

"No, you jerk. She got shot while she saved us. If she hadn't come in, we'd all be ashes by now, courtesy of the California Renegade Psycho Cop Club." Max withdrew her hand and recounted the story in as few words as she could manage. Then she stared at Eric. "If you ever make it to the cabin, I'll make sure she eats you. You might be tough to chew on, but she'll manage. She's got strong teeth." Max slugged Eric in the arm. He leaned closer to her.

"Marie saved my life," Max resumed. "After she showed up, I stopped trying to kill J.P., for a while anyway, until I hit sixteen. Then it was a completely new ball game. I don't know how I'll ever repay him. He saved me in every way there is. He taught me at home. I left high school at sixteen. I never thought I would even graduate before I met him. However, I went to college, and now I'll have my PhD before my twenty-fifth birthday. I never looked back on my former life. He's been behind me every step of the way, paid for everything. I don't know how he did it, where he found the strength not to wring my neck. He's far from perfect. I'll give you that. To me, he's the textbook parent, mentor, friend, and a lot more."

Lisa looked away.

Eric's mouth hung open in an approximation of a McDonald's clown's face. "J.P. did that? I feel so small for doubting him. My loss, I guess. That's what he'd say." The brawny Marine wiped a tear from the corner of his eye.

"Yes, he would. It is your loss because I think he's the most wonderful man in the universe. Knowing him the way I do, I understood there is no way he committed those murders. He doesn't have it in him." Max stood and stretched. Ramos took in her beauty, awestruck.

"That's what Anna and Candy used to say," Lisa mumbled. "Now they are both dead." She struggled with a slew of emotions ganging up on her. "This blows everything I thought I knew about Morgan out of the water. This unfamiliar man challenges my belief system. I feel like a cutter with a broken mast, in the middle of a hurricane."

CHAPTER 112

"YOU NEED A CIGARETTE BREAK."** Sergeant Pearce stuck his head in Baker's office. Old Man Sparks and Lieutenant Baker joined him outside. He held out the pack, knowing both had quit years ago.

"What gives?" Baker asked, pretending to draw on the cancer stick.

"I know what the chief said. Randy got a tip from Morgan," Pearce began.

Baker groaned at the mention of the name.

"Morgan told Randy that Jack Hunter didn't kill the girl found this morning." Pearce continued. "Despite the evidence, Morgan stood by Hunter. Jack is family to me. I called my nephew. He's with the forensics lab. I asked him to check the tapes. He called me back with a bomb. He doesn't know what to do. He's scared out of his gourd. He needs help."

"OK, I'll bite. What did he find?" Baker said with a resigned look. "Goodbye, pension. Bye-bye, happy retirement. Welcome, three-job weekends to pay for my kids' college."

"He explained the details, but they're lost on me." Pearce resumed. "He's 1,000 percent sure someone doctored the DVDs that show Jack Hunter with the victim. Not just the one this morning, all of them, going back a year. Someone altered the incriminating DVDs and planted them in the archive. The lab wouldn't have checked that without Morgan's tip."

The three seasoned cops exchanged worried looks. They were discussing a decorated former Navy officer, serving as US Congressman, the Governor's son, a man of impeccable conduct. If someone framed him for the sexually related murder of a child, he must have powerful enemies in all kinds of places. They understood why Pearce's nephew needed help. This had turned into a situation where the right move could make a brilliant career, and the wrong move could send one to an early grave. Possibly an unmarked grave.

"Randy went ballistic when he learned of the Chief's orders." Old Man Sparks broke the heavy silence. "He wants to discharge himself and march into the Chief's office. I had to promise him I would continue the investigation. Randy says Morgan will surrender with all the evidence if we clear Hunter. My gut says Morgan is on to something worth investigating. If we could get our hands on him and the evidence he has, we could go to the Chief or the Feds. Sticking our noses in some other PD's case will ruffle some feathers."

"I'm facing the same dilemma," Baker answered, tapping a foot against the wall. "My training and experience as a cop scream at me to trust Morgan. My life, my mortgage, my pension plan, my kids' college tuition, they all yell for me to follow the Chief's orders. Either way we look at it, it's going to end up bad. I wish we had more to take to the Chief."

"Do we sit on this and allow the events to take their course? Whatever these gents are planning cannot be good. They killed five cops. We will lose how many lives? I say we ignore the Chief, and we do what we know to be right." Old Man Sparks put out the cigarette.

"Why don't you go to the Governor with this?" Baker turned to Pearce.

"It would scream 'conflict of interests' all the way," Pearce answered. "I will not compromise Jack and the Governor. If I go to George, he'll have no choice but to act on the information. Jack will never be fully exonerated. His career would be over. I will call George and share this with him off the record."

"Let me make some calls." Baker made his internal decision. "The top Fed in LA owes me big time. I can steer him in the right direction and have their lab analyze the DVDs. He'll figure out jurisdiction. With a Congressman involved, that shouldn't be a problem."

CHAPTER **113**

"**T**ELL US ABOUT YOU** and J.P. How did you get together?"
Max pointed at Eric.

"The short version is I was nuts about Alice. She and Jack
went to a private academy. J.P. and I attended public schools a few
blocks away. I made it my mission to be around the private school in
the morning and after class to catch a glimpse of Alice. I was eleven."

"Some of them stalkers start very young." Max bumped Eric's
shoulder.

"One day, Jack and his buddies cornered me. They would have
beaten me to a pulp or worse. I was this scrawny Mexican kid aspiring to
their beauty queen. J.P. pulled me out and stood between them and me.
Even then, he was bigger than the rest of us, and he had street smarts.
He had this way about him. Nobody dared to take him on. His dad had
been in the service, died when J.P. was five or six, so he grew up mostly
on the streets. This one older boy stood up for me in front of four rich
white kids. I liked him instantly."

"Yeah, J.P. would do that," Max interrupted. "He's always like that,
protecting those in need with no regard for himself. It's what I love most
about him."

"Then he and Jack hit it off, and J.P. started hanging out with Jack
and Alice. J.P. had taken me under his wing, so we all became tight,
inseparable friends. The Three Musketeers, Alice being d'Artagnan.
We hung out at Mother Mary's house a lot. She practically adopted
us. One day, George said something to Mother Mary about taking in
all the strays and street urchins. She smacked him and yelled at him. I
don't think she knows I saw that. She loved us in her own special way,

and she accepted us in her home and her children's lives, even though we were from the wrong side of the tracks."

Ramos inhaled a sharp, deep breath, reminiscing, and then continued. "I think you should know this. You'll never learn it from J.P. A couple of months before he turned sixteen, J.P. disappeared for a few days. When he reappeared, there was something different about him. He had aged years. He didn't talk about it and canceled his sixteenth birthday party. Long story short, a year later, J.P. got detained trying to cash his dad's pension check. Cops called George. J.P.'s mother had died. For a year, he was alone taking care of his parents' home, paying the mortgage, and utilities. He acted like a grown-up. Mother Mary took him in, and he lived with them until he and Jack went to Annapolis."

"Makes sense why he adopted you." Lisa glanced at Max.

"We saw less of each other those years. Still, we got together every chance we had. I finished high school, and my family couldn't afford college. I knew I'd succeed if I could pay for it. I have a knack for cryptography, codes, all of that. Alice was going to Princeton when Jack and J.P. came up with the idea for me to enlist in the Marines, and I was hooked. A few years later, they worked in Naval Intel. I ended up being their counterpart for the Marine Corps at Camp Pendleton. We were inseparable again."

"You were all three Naval Intel at the same time?" Lisa asked, curiosity taking over.

"Yes. Those were the days." Eric grinned, ruminating. "Alice finished college, and life was peachy. All that time, we knew she would eventually marry J.P. That didn't keep me from hoping one day she would choose me over him."

"Nah, not a chance, Jarhead," quipped Max.

"Then came the Myerson incidents. J.P. was forced out of the Navy. Two years later, he and Alice eloped. Jack and Mel helped them. George went ape shit. I don't think he ever got over that. When Alice died, he was the first to blame J.P. It helped that he was the DA."

"Thank you for being a great friend to him." Max touched his arm.

"Some friend I was," Ramos scoffed. "When he faced certain death and needed a pal, I jumped on the wrong bandwagon. And it happened more than once. Look at J.P. today. When he heard about Jack, his first instinct was to help. He never doubted Jack's innocence or stopped to ponder his own safety. Now it makes sense why he didn't escape from jail while awaiting trial. I always wondered about that. He really didn't know whether or not he was guilty. Running, he might have never found out."

"I don't think that it would have been possible for him to escape," said Lisa.

"You don't know J.P. at all," retorted Eric. "If he wanted out, he would have waltzed out the front gate, arm in arm with half a dozen deputies, singing 'Kumbaya.'"

"I seriously doubt that. OC Sheriff's deputies are not that gullible." Lisa continued to defend her law enforcement brethren.

"It has nothing to do with the deputies. I know of several places he waltzed in and out of, a hundred times worse than the OC jail. J.P. is your worst nightmare or your best asset, depending on perspective. J.P. only got caught once. He is that good. Let me share the story. I haven't been able to wrap my head around it. It might give you an insight into the dark corner of the universe known as J.P.'s mind. This is another thing you can never talk about."

Both women made the zipper-drawn-across-their-lips gesture.

CHAPTER 114

"**J**.P. HAD A CONNECTION** to a scientist who wanted to defect but would not leave without his family. We are talking about wife, three kids, and his sick seventy-six-year-old mother. J.P. got approval to extract them, and he enrolled me and six other nut jobs into helping him." Eric laughed. "Half the medals Jack Hunter and I got were for supporting J.P. with his wild endeavors, inspired by his famous hunches. I digress. We contacted the scientist. On the way to the extraction point, the local military surrounded us. J.P. ordered us to get the family out, and he stayed behind to buy us time. There was no talking him out of it. We left him alone against more than thirty soldiers, armed to the teeth, with helicopter support."

"I get it," said Max. "With friends like you—"

"Max, stop it!" exclaimed Lisa. "Let him finish the story."

"Last we saw of J.P., the soldiers had him cuffed in an armored personnel carrier on the way to a military prison. We made it out, met with the sub that took us into international waters to the operational support ship. As we were preparing to fly back to the States, we got J.P.'s distress signal, requesting immediate extraction."

"Oh my God!" exclaimed Max. "You left him there, didn't you?"

"Yes, we did," sighed Ramos. "The captain asked me, and I said it must be a trap. J.P. might have been drugged into revealing the mission. We left him behind. *I* left him behind."

"I thought Marines never left a man behind," intervened Lisa.

"Not one of our proudest moments," parried Eric. "You have to understand. The political situation was very delicate. We couldn't take any chances to divulge the defection. We flew back to the States. Five

333

days later, a fishing vessel rescued J.P. He was knocking on death's door, floating in a dinghy in rough seas. Navy wanted to debrief him. Scuttlebutt has it that J.P. was so furious that he only gave the examiners his name, rank, and serial number for a week. He knew the risks but was mad at us for ignoring his extraction request."

"How did he escape?" Lisa's tone was almost shrill.

"Nobody knows," replied Ramos. "The Navy dispatched a two-star to intimidate J.P. He didn't get anywhere either. J.P. told him, on the record, that he craved a good burger, couldn't put up with prison food, so he went out looking for a burger joint. He said he couldn't find one over there, and he figured he would swim back to the US. The admiral blew a gasket. J.P. told the admiral that, if he didn't believe the story, he was welcome to refute it. Eventually, the Navy returned J.P. to active duty, against the two-star's recommendations."

"OK, that's all dandy," intervened Max. "But how did he escape from prison?"

"A few years later, we captured a spy. He told a story about a crazy American who incapacitated three guards, commandeered an armored vehicle, and drove it through the prison's administrative building onto the adjacent road. The prison warden sent everyone after the American. The legend, because I don't know how this can be true, has it they never lost sight of the armored vehicle, but when they finally stopped it, there was no one inside."

"Yeah, right," retorted Lisa. "He pulled a vanishing act in the middle of a chase?"

"I don't know how he did it, but he escaped." Eric smiled. "He can drive you nuts with stuff like this. Now I don't know this to be about J.P. I have no proof that's how he got out, but if the story is true, my nose tells me it was him."

A knock at the door brought them back to reality. J.P. walked in. "What is going on here? Never mind. I am not sure I want to know. Gather around, please. I have news. I would like to hear what you uncovered. Let's conceive an action plan and then end this thing." J.P. handed Eric Mother Mary's phone. "Jack is at the fort we built when we were kids. He is not picking up. Mother Mary thinks he has a handgun and a high-powered rifle. I doubt he would let me get close enough to hear what I have to say."

"What am I, the sacrificial lamb? Don't you think we should try the phone again?" Ramos challenged him in a mocking tone. He looked around for support.

"I thought that was why God created the Marines, to storm reinforced positions without fear of death, for the glory of God and good ole US of A," answered J.P. with a smirk. "Jack will not shoot you. He is a politician now. If he does, he will have no real friends left."

"Great speech. When this is over, you should become a motivational speaker," Ramos chided back. "Where do we meet up?"

"I guess back here. We need to bring you up to speed. Lisa and I uncovered something." Max bounced out of her seat.

"So, it is 'Lisa and I' now, huh?" J.P. tried a smart-ass comment.

Max stuck her tongue out at him. "Maybe nothing, but I have a strange feeling."

Max briefed him about the Sonny Days connection. J.P. absorbed the information.

"You are right," replied J.P. "It probably is nothing, but we have nothing else now. Let's go check it out while Eric retrieves Jack for us. Then we regroup and finish the action plan, with Jack's resources factored in."

J.P. asked Max and Lisa to put on body armor and do a weapons check. He slid inside his own body armor and covered it up with a short-sleeve shirt. Eric drove away while Max went to reserve the rooms for one extra night.

CHAPTER 115

"**W**HO IS THIS ELUSIVE Big Man," asked Lisa from the backseat.

"I have an idea. Nothing concrete yet, but I am sure that he was and still is in cahoots with your boss," J.P. answered.

"Let's go ask Phil. If you're right, and he was in bed with this Big Man, it means he's involved now." Lisa studied J.P.'s face in the rearview mirror, aware that his focus was away from the road. He had the same look on his face as he did before the high-speed chase started in Irvine. His eyes fixated across the street at the back of the restaurant's parking lot. She wondered what he saw that neither she nor Max could.

"Damn it! It is a trap. You called this one right, Max!" J.P. exclaimed.

"What trap?" Lisa leaned forward between the front seats.

"Hold on, and I will explain." J.P. pointed to the restaurant. He drove to the next strip mall parking lot and asked Lisa to hand him binoculars.

"Remove your body armor and T-shirt. Keep the shirt on," J.P. instructed Max.

"Going on a decade now, and I thought you'd never ask," Max teased him.

"I hardly think that's appropriate. I presume next you'll ask me to undress as well." Lisa pressed her lips into a thin line.

"Why would I? I need you to drive." J.P. shot her a puzzled look.

J.P. retrieved two SIGs from the bags in the back of the SUV, checked them, and handed them to Max, putting a small object in his pocket. He invited Lisa to the driver's seat and then climbed in the backseat and clarified his plan.

Lisa executed a U-turn and dropped J.P. off at a car wash. He disappeared behind the buildings. Lisa drove and pulled up to the entrance in the restaurant's parking lot.

Cornwall and Spencer observed the redheaded young woman stroll toward the restaurant entrance. The open shirt flapped in the light wind around her sleek, slender body, affording them a full view of the voluptuous curves bursting from the blood-red lace bra. The heart-stopping effect caused heads to turn all over. The driver of a Toyota Camry passing by ogled her. His wife smacked the back of his head, almost causing a crash.

"This angel almost makes up for staking out this dump!" said Spencer. Spellbound, he gawked at Max, who seemed oblivious to the furor she triggered in her wake.

J.P. tiptoed to the rear door of their cruiser. He removed the training flash bang from his pocket and armed it. He jerked the back door open, threw the mini grenade inside, slammed the door, dropped to the pavement, closed his eyes, and covered his ears.

Surprised, Cornwall and Spencer turned. Their eyes followed the object in landing on the backseat. The device disintegrated in a high intensity burst of light, smoke, and sound. All car windows shattered under the pressure, and the shock knocked the two cops into semi-consciousness. Sporting his *cat-that-ate-the-canary* smile, J.P. approached the driver's door as nonchalant as if he intended to ask for directions. He coldcocked Cornwall, walked around to the passenger side, and repeated the procedure. He kissed his fist for effect.

"Freeze, asshole! Police! Put your hands up and don't move!" The yell came from the restaurant's front door area, followed by the unmistakable sounds of yanked gun slides.

CHAPTER 116

J.P. RAISED HIS HANDS in slow motion. He heard another pair of automatics cocked for effect, followed by Max's milk-and-honey voice. "Drop those guns, boys. I thought they taught on the first day to check your blind spots."

The Sheriff's deputies raised their hands, weapons hanging from their trigger fingers. Max had stepped behind them, issuing instructions in an authoritative voice. "Throw down your weapons. You on the left, face down. Lock fingers behind your head. You on the right, cuff him. Any wrong move will be your last. Now handcuff yourself, hands behind your back. Lie face down. No heroics, Deputy. I don't want to shoot you." The man cuffed himself and kneeled. "Lie down next to him and behave." Max enjoyed giving directions.

J.P. busied himself with the cops in the cruiser. He retrieved their guns, twisted their arms through the steering wheel, and handcuffed them to each other. He motioned for Max to go inside the restaurant, and then he collected the weapons and backup pieces from the men on the ground. He picked up the deputies, piling them in the backseat of the damaged cruiser.

"Let Clancy and Purcell know I find this stuff boring. I do not mind kicking your asses, but carrying you around, that is quite a workout in this weather. I could get a heatstroke." He slammed the door and removed the memory card from the windshield-mounted GPS navigation system. "Thanks, guys. See you soon. Give Purcell and Clancy another message, will you? Tell them I said, 'No hard feelings. You did your best. They should be proud.'"

J.P. walked away, wiping his hands on his jeans. Max half-dragged a terrified woman from the restaurant. Cher tried to speak but could not put the words together.

"Cher, my name is J.P. Morgan. Your life is in imminent danger. If these people are here, it means they would have killed you as soon as they got us. I need you to focus. I have some questions for you. Do you have a car here?"

With trembling hands, Cher pulled a set of keys from her purse, fumbling with them. J.P. retrieved them from her fingers with gentle movements and pushed a button on the remote. A Toyota Highlander beeped and flashed its lights. "Max, you go with Lisa. Follow us."

They drove away, trailed by the puzzled looks of the crowd still gathering.

"Cher? May I ask you a few questions?" J.P. asked, taking the freeway. "First, are you married? Do you have children?"

"Divorced. You answer mine first," Cher shot back. "Who are you, people? You attacked those police officers and kidnapped me from my office."

"You probably know nothing about us, but I assure you, we saved your life. I am interested in one thing only. Afterward, I would like you to take your family to a safe place, where you can hide for a few days. Do you have such a place in mind?" Cher nodded.

"Your father, Sonny Days, did he leave something for me, or an attorney named Anna Richter?" J.P. resumed scanning the mirrors.

"Is this what—"

"We need to get you and your family out of danger. You need to go before they find you again. Since we made contact, you are no longer bait. You are now a loose end. So, the package Sonny left, what was it?"

"A digital tape in a sealed envelope addressed to Anna Richter, Esq."

"If it was sealed, how do you know what was inside?" J.P. pointed out.

"My mom found it in a secret safe my dad had in his home office. It had a Post-it note on it with instructions to be mailed in the event of his death under suspicious circumstances. The envelope looked old. I had my son check the address. It turned out that Ms. Richter's office was at a new address. I opened the envelope, addressed it correctly, and mailed it on Monday morning. What is this about?"

"Your son? Has he touched that tape?"

Cher nodded. Her hand flew to her mouth, and her eyes widened in terror. "Oh my God. He may have watched it. I had it in the house overnight. The following morning I thought it was moved. He's fifteen. He's into computer stuff. Is he in any danger?"

J.P. pulled over in the parking lot of a 7-Eleven and waited for Lisa and Max to join. He handed Max the keys to Cher's Toyota and gave Cher a wad of cash. "Use this. Only cash. No credit or debit cards, no checks. You will know when it is safe to return. You will also know if it is never safe to come back."

J.P. shared with Lisa and Max what he had learned from Cher and then instructed them to go with her. "Cher, this is Lisa Jensen. She is with the Orange County DA's office. This is Max. She is my daughter. I trust her with my life. You can too." He focused on Max. "If they were watching the restaurant, it means they know she mailed the tape. That means they are watching her mother's house. Create a diversion and then get Mrs. Days out of there safely. Send them out of town immediately. Meet back at the motel in an hour, ninety minutes tops."

He started walking to the Suburban and then turned back toward them. "One more thing. Her son may have watched the tape. See if he made a copy. Cher, please help us find it."

"Where are you going?" A worried look shadowed Max's face.

"Plausible deniability." J.P. hugged her and kissed her temple.

CHAPTER **117**

PURCELL'S PHONE CHIRPED, WAKING him from the much-needed catnap. "What now, Cornwall?" He listened and then clicked off without a single word and launched his phone straight into the wall. "Message received, Morgan," he mumbled. "That was not a brilliant idea. I have to reprogram all those numbers into a new one. But it felt terrific."

He decided against informing Clancy of this new failure. He was not ready for another tongue-lashing from that bureaucrat. He wanted to kill the men who failed. Four supposedly seasoned officers ambushed like a bunch of Boy Scouts, first time in the berry bushes.

Purcell called Simpson. "Dispatch two teams Sonny's widow's house for backup. Morgan may show up there. Tell them to stay the hell out of view and not fail. No more mistakes, you hear? Simpson, bring me a new secure phone ASAP. I dropped the old one."

He walked into Clancy's office. "I recommend we deploy everything today," said Purcell. "Not just the materials for San Francisco. If someone takes Morgan seriously, at least we'll have all principal assets in place for *True Patriot Day*. We owe it to our fallen comrades to ensure the complete success of this part of the mission."

"We need to close the book on Morgan." Clancy paced in an intricate pattern. "Maybe then we can focus exclusively on the job at hand. You're right. Deploy to the farms for final preparations and have everything in place tonight. Call everyone in. We'll have a final meeting tonight. Get dinner for everyone. Get the suitcases and the money in position this afternoon before the troops get here. I need my helicopter for the afternoon. I have to fly to Sacramento for a little while. I'll be back here around seven thirty, eight o'clock at the latest."

CHAPTER **118**

CHER DID NOT WAIT for the Highlander to come to a complete stop. She made a beeline for her son's bedroom and dragged him away without bothering to explain. Mark broke off, grabbed his favorite backpack, and stuffed his laptop, tablet, game console and assorted electronics in it. Cher pushed him in the car and took over driving. "We have to get my mom."

Max asked, "Is there a way to bring your mom out through a back door?"

"Yes," Cher answered. "There is an alley running behind the house."

Max pulled out a phone and asked Cher for Mrs. Days's number. "Ask your mom to call the police and talk to someone she can trust. Request that person to show up at her house with a couple of uniforms to provide an escort. Afterward, have her wait five minutes, then dial 911, and report smelling gas or smoke. We will try to get her out through the back door."

Cher glared at her as if Max had five eyes and seventeen arms.

"We're here to help. It's a lot to take in, but you need to trust us to get you and your family out alive," Lisa offered from the backseat.

"You think my grandma's house is under surveillance? Cool. Is this like an adventure?" Mark asked, absentmindedly squirming in his seat.

"No, Mark, not cool. We have to leave without as much as a clean shirt. Totally not cool." Cher jumped all over him. Her face was flustered, and her nostrils flared. "I'm sorry, honey. I'm scared too. This is so unexpected."

"Mark, last weekend, your mom had a digital videotape in the house," Lisa segued, "the one your grandma gave her to mail."

"Yeah, I know which one you're talking about. There was a something like a snuff film on it. I think it was a bad, lousy-quality homemade movie. Why?"

"You watched that tape?" Cher asked, twisting to look at her son.

"I skipped through it, mostly. At first, I had thought it might be something cool, soft-core porn or a police operation." Mark kept his nose buried in the video game screen.

"Soft-core porn?" Cher almost lost control of the car.

"Mom, I left kindergarten ten years ago. I'm a teenager. I'm supposed to be disgusting," Mark replied with a straight face, and a quick smirk crossed his face.

"You watched that tape?" Max stepped in, tugging at Mark's game console. "This is serious. It could spell mortal danger for you and your mom."

"I told you. I fast-forwarded through most of it, looking for the interesting parts. It was a lousy-scripted homemade flick. Some masked dudes threatened and beat up a pregnant woman. Brutal stuff, though. They killed her and her little tyke. Lots of blood and gore but borrrrinnnngggg. I watched a few minutes and lost interest. They set the house on fire at the end. That was attention grabbing, but it wasn't enough to make up for the rest."

"Did you make a copy by any chance?" Lisa's pulse quickened. Mark may have misinterpreted the tape, but his description matched the facts of the case and Sadowsky's account of Alice Morgan and little Artie Hunter's deaths.

Max leaned over the seat, near nose to nose with Mark, waiting for his answer.

"I don't know." Mark cleared his throat, shifting his gaze out the window.

"Mark, you are not in trouble. This is very important," Cher cut in.

"I did, sort of." Mark hesitated. "I don't know if it's still there."

"What do you mean?" Max straightened up, and her head hit the roof.

"I converted it to a digital file, but I deleted it yesterday to make room for new stuff. I never had the time to download. I was going to do it tonight."

"Where is the drive?" Max bounced in her seat like a beach ball. Mark pointed to his backpack. "Thank you, Mark. Thank you!" Max leaned over and kissed him on the cheek.

He pulled the hard drive and handed it to Max, without asking questions.

Cher turned onto her mother's street and stopped two blocks away. They watched as an unmarked police cruiser and a black and white pulled in her mother's driveway. A plainclothes detective and two uniformed cops walked into the house. A fire engine turned the corner, siren blaring, and stopped in front of Mrs. Days's home.

"Go," Max urged Cher, who shifted into Drive and pulled away from the curb. "Turn here and park. Go through the rear entrance and bring her to the alley."

Max slid into the driver's seat and pulled up to the intersection with the alley that ran behind the Days's home. An unmarked police sedan barreled down the alley, pursuing Cher. Max gunned the Highlander and rammed it with the Toyota's brush guard. The impact propelled the Chrysler into the concrete base of a light pole. Max jumped out with her gun leveled in front. The two occupants of the cruiser battled the deployed air bags.

Max yelled, "Don't even think about it. Cuff your hands through the steering wheel."

Max holstered her gun, then pivoted on her left foot, and executed a full pirouette. Her right foot hit the man behind her in the head. The blow tossed him into the middle of the road, where he landed with a loud thump. Two bullets slammed into Max's torso, tossing her onto the pavement, face up, arms apart, hair radiating around her like a fallen angel. Her eyes closed in slow motion, and her head dropped to the side.

Cher and her mother scrambled into the alley.

"Hello, ladies. We've been waiting for you." Corelli smirked behind them.

The two women sauntered hand in hand toward the depressing tableau at the corner. Max lay motionless on the ground. Corelli leaned over her and took the hard drive from her jeans pocket, grabbed the gun, and then checked her pulse. A sinister grin flashed on his lips.

TRUE PATRIOT DAY

The man Max had kicked in the head struggled to his feet, rubbing his temple, while his partner kept a gun trained on Lisa and Mark. Timmons passed escorting duties and strode to the damaged Chrysler. He removed the cuffs, binding his colleagues to the steering wheel. They joined the others, forming a tight shooting group around the three women and Mark.

Satisfied, Corelli turned to face the prisoners. "Where is Morgan, so we can end this charade?" He treaded to Lisa, patted her down, and disarmed her, handing the guns to Timmons. He checked Cher, her mother, and her son for weapons. He grabbed Lisa's arm, squeezing hard. "Where is he, sweetheart? Or you'll end up worse than your girlfriend there."

Lisa shoved him away. Corelli backhanded her across the face.

"I am Assistant DA Jensen." Lisa stepped up to him.

A gun barrel pushed her chin up from behind, and her eyes radiated hatred.

"You wanna see how far you can take that comedy act?" Corelli frowned. "Before you say you don't know, let me add that the first one to try that approach earns a bullet on the spot."

Cher stepped between Corelli and Mark, attempting to shield him with her own body. "We don't know where—" A silenced round tore through her thigh. She let out a piercing scream and tumbled to the ground, pressing on the wound. Mark lunged at Corelli. Mrs. Days locked her arms around him and whispered, "Bide your time. It might save your mother's life."

Timmons ambled to the trunk of the damaged cruiser and returned with a small blanket, which he threw at Cher. "Here, wrap that wound. I don't want you to bleed to death yet."

CHAPTER 119

MAX, WHOSE BODY ARMOR had stopped the bullets, regained consciousness during the ride over. From the second story deck, Purcell watched with satisfaction as his men unloaded the human cargo from the two cruisers and Cher's Highlander.

Max glanced at Purcell, her eyes oozing contempt. Lisa was still furious with herself for letting her guard down. Magnetized by watching Max deal with the cruiser and the cop attacking her, Lisa did not notice their backup creep up from behind the Toyota.

Clancy walked onto the catwalk at Purcell's side. He turned to Purcell, unable to hide his short-lived pleasure. "The only one missing is that Goddamned Morgan." Clancy slapped the rail. "If the Big Man is correct, now that we have the women, he'll come to us."

Purcell walked down, inspected Cher's leg wound, and called for a medic. "Take the others to the briefing room and watch them at all times. When the medic is done, have her join them," Purcell ordered his men before he walked back upstairs to Clancy's office to gloat.

Purcell and Clancy stepped into the briefing room and stood by the door, surveying the captives. They wanted to appear at ease and in control. However, they knew the battle was far from over with Morgan still out there.

"This is a one-time offer," started Purcell. "Whoever tells me where Morgan is, walks out of here alive. If you don't know or refuse to talk, you are of no use to me."

"What happened to you? You were an Army Colonel. You took oaths to protect those who couldn't do it themselves." Lisa shot back.

"Save it. I want Morgan so bad I can taste it." Purcell squared his shoulders.

"Let everyone else go," Max intervened, staring Purcell down. "J.P. doesn't care about them. Unfortunately, no matter how much I wish it, J.P. will not stay away. He'll come for me, and when he does, I'll help him rip your heart out and feed it to you in pieces. Payback for Anna and Candy. You have my word."

"My, my, what a valiant little lady," Purcell teased her, breaking eye contact. "I have an army of God's best trained warriors, itching to get their hands on Morgan."

Max scoffed. "Two or three armies… maybe you'd have a shot at levelling the field. You have no idea the wrath you unleashed when you killed our friends. Let the others go."

"How selfless, offering yourself to save the others. Not interested. I want Morgan, and until I get him, I'll hold all of you here. If he doesn't show up, when I tire of your whining, I'll shoot you one by one." He pointed to Cher, who sobbed, holding on to Mark.

"I didn't know he existed until he showed up at my work today. My son and my mother never met him. We're not a part of this," Cher pleaded in a meek voice.

"Are you sure you don't know where Morgan is? What if I shot your son?" Purcell aimed his hand with his index finger extended at Mark's right thigh. Cher's her heart leaped into her throat, and she began panting. She drew her body over her son's.

"Start with his leg. Will that jog your memory? How high on his body will I get?" Purcell stepped forward. "You think I'll reach anything vital before your recall improves?"

Cher's heart threatened to break through her breastbone. Her eyes darted between Mark and Purcell, alternating between love for her child and disdain for her son's assailant. "You know my dad was a cop," Cher said. "He'd be rolling in his grave if he knew about this."

"Poor, sentimental old fool, Sonny. Now tell me where I can find Morgan, and we can all go home," Purcell cut her off.

"You knew my father?" Cher struggled with the inference in the statement. She stole a glance at her mother and then returned her attention to Purcell. "You are a disgrace."

"We arranged his accident. He grew a conscience at the worst possible time," Purcell exulted to impress his power upon her. He glanced at his wristwatch. "The offer expires in five minutes, starting now. The first one to give up Morgan gets out of here unharmed. The rest of you, well, I'm sure I don't have to explain. Tick, tock."

Clancy and Purcell walked out, leaving two guards with the hostages.

"Here I am again, captured by the same lunatics with badges, tied up like a ham. All this running, trying to get away from them was for nothing." Lisa let out a self-deprecating short laugh. "How does a girl get rid of the likes of you?"

One guard smirked, checking his watch. "No worries. Morgan will join you any minute now, and then you can stroll into hell hand in hand. This time, neither of you gets away."

Max got out of the chair and settled on the floor with her back against the wall, stretching her long legs across. "You should do the same. We'll be here a while. We might as well get comfortable."

The first guard advanced toward her, sporting a threatening look.

"Leave them be. It doesn't matter. We'll be able to keep a better eye on them if they attempt to move," the second guard called out.

The first man shot the hostages a dirty look and then returned to the table.

Max set her head on Lisa's shoulder, burying her face in her hair. "Push my locket against my breastbone. It activates the Bat Light."

"No talking. No touching. Sit separately, or I will shoot you." The first guard jumped out of his seat as if he sat on live electrical wires.

CHAPTER 120

J.P. PROCESSED THE GPS memory card he had taken from Cornwall's cruiser. He examined the chip for crumbs, frequently visited places, while monitoring Phil's home. A series of short tones beckoned his attention. He read the text message: the code RIBT, *Redhead in Big Trouble*, followed by a set of GPS coordinates. He matched the location to coordinates retrieved from the SD card. Max and Lisa were now hostages. That changed everything. He took his frustration out on the computer keys and then drove away.

No time for you, Phil. You caught a big break. I will be back, though.

J.P. peeled off and headed for UCI Medical Center. It was time to share information, get reinforcements and resources. He could not investigate and handle the situation by himself.

Sparks dropped the TV remote control. His mouth opened, wide as a cave entrance. "Morgan, you have one hell of a way to surprise me."

"How are you feeling? Is there any long-term damage?" J.P. stepped up to the bed.

"None. A few more days here, a month or two on crutches, and I'll be good as new. I owe you for pulling me out of the line of fire," Sparks replied. His phone was in the drawer, and the nurse alert button behind him. No way to raise an alarm without spooking J.P.

"I am not talking to you as a police officer. This is man to man." J.P. said. "I need you to listen carefully. I want to finish what I need to say. You want that as well."

"It would be fruitless anyway to try and catch, or corner you. If you didn't have your exit strategy planned out, I guess you would have never come in," said Sparks with a resigned look. He settled in a more comfortable position and motioned for J.P. to talk.

"You owe me nothing. You served. You know we never leave people in harm's way."

Sparks nodded, fighting back a myriad of conflicting emotions.

"Thank you for helping Jack." J.P. continued. "I heard on the news on the way here. The Feds took over the investigation. They are reviewing the evidence at their labs."

Sparks kept his gaze trained on J.P. without a word.

"Second. The pendant?"

"There was no pendant or jewelry. Her car key was in the ignition. She had no other keys on her or in the car when she jumped."

"When they pushed her," J.P. corrected him. "I have a riddle for you. Who is it you never notice on the side of the road?"

Sparks shrugged, though a curious expression altered his mien.

"The cops. You notice their cruiser and the car they stopped. You thank your lucky star they do not have time for you, and you keep driving."

Sparks nodded again. It made sense.

"Maybe personal effects got switched?" J.P. asked. He felt his heart sinking.

The phone in J.P.'s pocket chirped. He lifted a finger toward Sparks, answered it, and listened for a few seconds. "Yes, I know. I do not have time for that." J.P. clicked the phone off. He flashed a smile and mouthed to Sparks, "He will call back."

CHAPTER 121

HIS PHONE CHIMED AGAIN, and J.P. answered it in an apathetic voice. "You do not get the hint. I am busy. I know... I am booking a seat on the next flight to Australia. I do not plan to be here for your *True Patriot Day*... If you had the guts to do it, you would not call me for permission... I will call you when I have time for you." He clicked off again.

"You didn't care much for him," Sparks said. He scanned the room again for a way to send a message unnoticed and then settled in bed, disappointed.

"Purcell, the tactical commander of this rogue outfit, he wants me to know he has my friends, and he will let them go if I turn myself in, or he will kill them if I do not, blah, blah. The usual psychobabble. We both know he is lying, just going through the motions."

"What if he hurts them?" Sparks sat up in bed too fast and let out an agonizing groan.

"Let him sweat. He wants me. He intends to kill everyone, anyway. We know too much, and these bozos do not want witnesses. This way, I keep him off-balance until I am ready to deal with this band of knuckleheads. So long as he has my friends, he knows I would go in. If they are dead, all bets are off."

"You're not going in by yourself, are you? What are you going to do?"

"I will go in. He is a conniving bastard, and he thinks he outsmarted me. It is a trap. He expects me to go back to the vacant warehouse in Florence. I know they relocated to another warehouse, nowhere near Florence. He does not know I have their new location, which suits me just fine." Noticing Sparks's inquisitive look, J.P. added, "I got the GPS coordinates from the emergency burst transmitter my daughter carries, and I did some recon on Google Earth."

"I see. If you know where they are, let's go get them. I'll call my dad. He'll get the FBI involved, DHS, anyone who will listen." Sparks pulled the blanket off his legs and tried to get out of bed. He groaned in pain and grabbed the rail on the bed to steady himself.

J.P. pushed him back in bed with a gentle hand, surprising for his size. "Easy, cowboy. You need to sit this one out. You did your job, and I thank you for that. Now listen to me because I have a date with these jerks."

Sparks bit his lip to mask the pain. He knew J.P. was right. The only thing he could do was to lie down and wait for the stories. He smacked the bed.

"This is everything—video, audio recordings, photos, location of their new lair." J.P. handed Sparks a flash drive and then placed a firm hand on his chest, pinning him down.

Sparks's puzzled expression mimicked that of a cat sprayed by a water hose.

"They have three, I say again, three suitcase-type, Soviet-era nuclear devices. Confirmation photos and video are on the flash drive. My best guess is they intend to detonate the nukes tomorrow to create an unmanageable crisis and statewide panic."

Sparks struggled to sit up, but J.P.'s powerful arm held him down. "Easy there, tiger. You could rupture those stitches, and then your entire department will have a reason to come after me for injuring a cop." He winked.

Sparks blew out a loud, exasperated sigh and relaxed, slapping the mattress again.

"You kept your promises. I have to break my word about surrendering. If I live past tonight, I am all yours. I have to go help my baby girl and, ironically, the woman who tried to have me put to death. I will leave the original recordings with Lt. Col. Eric Ramos, USMC, or with Jack Hunter, for authentication. Good luck, and speedy recovery, Sparks."

"You're going in alone? Are you insane?" Sparks skirmished, trying to sit up.

"Do not worry about me. I have a plan." He tapped his temple. "I also made a promise to your partner yesterday. This is for him too."

"You talked to Coop?" Sparks's eyebrows rivaled the McDonald's logo.

"Manner of speaking," J.P. said. "He did not answer me, nor did he blink any of his three eyes. He died protecting Anna's mom. I owe him. Someone among those crooked cops knows who killed Alice and Artie." Then J.P. added in a soft voice, "You understand, right?"

"Morgan, don't do anything stupid," Sparks pleaded, halfhearted. "If you find the guy, bring him in, and let us deal with him. Don't let him ruin your life again."

"Is that what you would do if you were in my shoes?"

Sparks recognized the debt-of-honor, and he could not fault Morgan. "I have a question for you, Morgan. Why are you doing this? I mean, you had every reason to let me die yesterday. You had no duty to help with this mess." Sparks held his gaze on J.P.

"When I was young," J.P. chided, "there was a gunny at Camp Pendleton. He trained Jack Hunter, Colonel Ramos, and I to shoot. The gunny was incredible with any firearm. He shared philosophical tidbits. One of them was, 'If you do not stand for something, you will fall for anything.' It stuck with me. I try to do the right thing, not necessarily the popular one."

"You are a rare breed. I wish I had a chance to know you better." Sparks stuck out his hand. "Maybe when this is over, we can revisit our relationship."

"You are a good man. I am sorry for what happened to you and your partner. Thank you." J.P. accepted the handshake and lowered his head in a salute to Sparks.

The two men stared into each other's eyes, acknowledging a bond neither of them would have thought possible two days earlier.

CHAPTER 122

P URCELL STUDIED MAX'S PHONE with disbelief. He could not accept that Morgan dismissed him like that. Twice. He turned off the device, even though he knew it was impossible to trace. He tried tracking Morgan's phone first. After twenty minutes, Simpson filled the air with technobabble and said the phone was untraceable in real time. He could only get a general area. The proverbial needle in a ten-square-mile haystack.

"We can't locate Morgan, unless he wants us to," Simpson said. In Purcell's mind, Simpson's gadget collection did not replace a single trained soldier. An army of one. Hooray!

"How would you like to get another shot at Morgan?" Purcell walked into the warehouse and summoned Cornwall.

"There is nothing else I would like more, sir," Cornwall answered, smacking his lips and licking a few drops of saliva.

"He'll be at Site C shortly. He's bound to pull some stealth crap, maybe bring back up. He thinks he's got me fooled with his bravado, but he'll be there. Take a few men, set up a welcoming party, and get his ass to me pronto. Feel free to rough him up, but I want him alive. Check him for tracking devices. This jerk is a regular jack-in-the-box full of nasty tricks. Do not engage him if he's not alone, or you believe he has support nearby. Snipe him and then get back here. We have urgent things to take care of."

"Yes, sir." Cornwall disappeared to collect his friends, all of them eager to make up for the fiasco at Cher's restaurant.

CHAPTER 123

INSPIRATION HIT AS J.P. drove out of the UCI lot. He rummaged through the equipment bags and retrieved an old Nokia phone. "This is J.P. You know I do not call in favors, but you can wipe the slate clean. The most powerful gang operating in South Central LA. I need their leader's number, and background info. Ten minutes. Thank you."

The Nokia beeped. J.P. scanned the text message. Shortly after, it rang. "You're late. Are you getting old or something?" J.P. asked in a friendly, mocking tone. "Great job on this. Yes. Squared away. You owe me nothing."

J.P. clicked off and perused the files attached to the text message. He connected the phone to the laptop, transferred the new files, wiped its memory, and then copied several files onto it. Satisfied there were no traces of the calls to his source, he dialed the gang's leader number on the same Nokia phone.

"Who da fuck dis?" came the angry answer.

"Who I am is unimportant. I have important business to discuss with your boss. Put him on," J.P. replied.

"I da boss, mo'fucke'." The voice sounded irritated. J.P. waited. When he did not answer, the voice continued. "You got som'ing t'say, talk to me. Or git lost, dipshit."

"The message I have is for your boss only. If he is not on the phone in the next ten seconds, I will take my business elsewhere. You can explain to him later why his bunch will no longer be the most powerful gang in South LA. Maybe your posse will still be in the top ten." J.P. drummed his fingers as the man bellowed over the blaring background rap music.

Trumpet came on the line. His voice was stylish, velvety, better educated. The music ceased. "This better be good, my man. You have any idea who you're messing with?"

"Name of your cousin who is doing two dimes in San Quentin for a murder committed by his baby brother. Three seconds, go."

"You are something," Trumpet replied, scornful. "Why would I tell you that? Convince me you are not a cop or some idiot trying to set me and my crew up to get killed."

"The clock is ticking. If you do not want to play, I take my business somewhere else."

"Darnell Stanton. Now, how do I know you're for real?"

"Your actual name is Cornelius Aurelius Stanton. You have two elder sisters, Amanda and Babette. Your nickname is Trumpet, coined when you were ten years old, and you mooned your school principal in his office. Then you let out a fart so loud it sounded like a trumpet. You joined the Black Angels of LA as a drug runner when you were eleven. At fifteen, you ended up in juvie for an assortment of charges, and you enjoyed their hospitality until you turned twenty-one. When you got out, you killed the leader of the gang and took over—"

"So, you read my unwritten autobiography. Or you're a sick pig. Maybe I should be respectful and say a *policeman*? That whole litany stinks of Big Brother shit to me."

"I am not a cop, but I have been bumping into them all over this place where they keep the dough. The pigs have lots and lots of money. It is their off the books retirement plan. I am calling you as a fellow businessman. You have the firepower and live bodies we need to mount an operation and get our hands on the money. There is more than enough to split with your crew, and we can all live happy long lives. Deal?" J.P. crossed his fingers.

"I'm listening."

"I will send you some information. Look through it, and if you are interested, call me back. If I do not hear from you in five, I will go to the next name on my list." J.P. ended the call and then forwarded the files transferred to the Nokia earlier.

Less than a minute later, Trumpet called back, excited and ready for action.

J.P. laid out his plan. Trumpet listened without interjecting, acknowledging every so often with a whistle.

"Deal," said Trumpet. "We'll be there. This better be for real."

CHAPTER **124**

J.P. KNOCKED, AND THEN let himself into the motel room. Eric had finished briefing Hunter. Jack retreated from the table, the clouds over his head getting darker.

"Thank you for helping me. I heard that man's account. Until we have solid proof or independent, third-party confirmation, this changes nothing between us." Jack rattled through his speech as fast as he could.

"I can live with that. Set your feelings aside. We have bigger issues. I only have a few minutes. They have Lisa and Max at these coordinates." J.P. handed the GPS tracker to Ramos.

"They've got Max? You're so damn calm about it. We have to get her out of there. Let's go." Eric jolted as if seared. "And Lisa, of course."

"That changes things," intervened Jack. "We should call the Feds."

"Do you think we can take on a fortified position, defended by former military, armed to the teeth?" J.P.'s eyebrows arched. "Without massive casualties? I will go in by myself, assess the situation, and render assistance from inside. I will make sure they keep all of us alive for a while. I will buy you three, four hours tops. After that, you can probably write us off. Jack, you have access to resources none of us can reach or use. By any means necessary, get the FBI, DHS, CBI—what the hell, get the whole alphabet soup there. ASAP."

"I'm still wanted by the Feds and the police," Jack Hunter replied, clenching his jaw.

"In a short while, you will be in the clear, maybe not entirely, but they will listen to your side of the story without throwing you in jail right away."

"You never asked if I did it." Jack's tone was skeptical.

"I know you did not do it." J.P.'s gaze remained riveted on his friend's eyes.

Jack looked away without a word.

"Your dad is not wanted," J.P. said. "I am sure you can get a message to him. If we do nothing, come tomorrow, there will be a new Governor in Sacramento and a layer of dead people blanketing the entire state. The more I thought about it, the more I am sure they framed you to force your dad to step down and clear the way for their people to take over."

"Lisa said it would be impossible to replace the government overnight," Eric intruded. "There are contingency plans in effect, stipulating who takes over what position in the event of death or incapacitation. But, do you recall the destabilization games we kicked around years ago? What's the fastest way to create an instant need for new leadership?"

"An unmanageable disaster or crisis paired with incapacitated or ineffective leadership. Any team ready to step in and take charge becomes the logical choice. The firefighter-arsonist-and-rescuer scenario." Jack's brain shifted into overdrive. "I think it could be the case here. They strike major populated areas, and we have statewide mayhem. They install a provisional government, pretending they can 'manage the crisis.' Four months left to elections, and then we have brand-new 'legitimately' elected leaders in California."

"It would be next to impossible. There are many safeguards in place for that exact reason. You would need an army and a boatload of money. However, yes, I guess theoretically, it's possible," Eric concluded.

"What if they had years to plan it, and enough money to prepare? What if they had access to all levels of the government to control the flow of information by using disgruntled law enforcement types? All former Special Forces, military trained personnel who believe they would be the power elite of tomorrow?"

"I guess it can be done," admitted Jack. "How do you think they plan to control the entire state? They need to issue orders, share information, coordinate efforts in real time."

"The infrastructure is in place," J.P. pointed out. "Law enforcement and emergency personnel trained to manage a crisis. The new leaders need to provide direction and issue marching orders, hence the CDoHP. After the disasters, they deploy and implement a swift plan of action. People will eat it up."

"I see. You could call the Feds. They are not local cops," Jack insisted.

"Would you leave that to chance? I would have assets to monitor inquiries, quash requests, or delay long enough for the plans to take effect." Ramos sounded convinced. "J.P. may have some of it wrong, but every minute we sit here arguing, they get closer to their goal."

"All this to get Trump back? The worst President in US history," scoffed Eric.

"There is something else going on here. Trump is the window dressing," replied J.P.

CHAPTER 125

"**H**OW DO YOU MEAN?**"** asked Jack. "We all heard that Powell guy."

"I still do not buy it," said J.P. "He was nothing but a pawn in someone else's game. A misguided kid. I have been racking my brain, and it finally hit me."

"What?" Eric and Jack asked simultaneously.

"You have seen everything I saw. What do you think?"

Jack and Eric exchanged inquisitive glances, then they both shrugged.

"OK, slowpokes," quipped J.P. "We do not have the time to play. What is missing?"

Eric answered after a while, "There is no Trump paraphernalia anywhere. Son of a bitch. What do you think this is really about?"

J.P. clapped his hands. "Give the man his dues. OK. Let's say you wanted to take over California or the entire country. That would take armies of followers, years of coordinating in secret and billions of dollars."

"Hmm," answered Jack. "You're right. It seems these guys have everything they need."

"Yeah, but things still do not line up for me," continued J.P. "The timeframe and other thins do not fit. How about a wraparound false flag operation?"

Eric summed it up. "You mean like a false flag inside a false flag? That's interesting."

J.P. placed his hands on his friends' shoulders. "The armies are there. Festering, disillusioned, ready to explode. All you would need is a spark to light their fuse and you would have an army of followers ten or fifteen times the size of the entire US military, all carrying weapons, and dedicated to the cause."

"Damn it," exclaimed Jack, pounding on the table. "J.P., you may have something there. All those Trump supporters who think the election was stolen and they railroaded Trump. The perfect storm waiting to be unleashed. I have to call my dad."

"I agree," Eric said. "This is too big for the three of us."

"I will go in alone. You and Jack talk with George and bring the cavalry. Hell, bring the national guard, the Army and the Marines while you are at it." J.P. slapped Eric's shoulder. "If we do not do this, I fear tomorrow California will be knee-deep in rivers of blood."

"I guess you're right. What do you mean you're going in alone? Are you suicidal? I can't let you do that." Eric reached for J.P.'s arm.

"If we barge in there with an army, there will be a heated fire exchange. I cannot take that risk. Max is in there. I think I can still get my hands on the proof Anna found. I also hope to get confirmation of the Big Man's identity."

"Confirmation? You figured it out!" Eric exclaimed. "Tell us. Jack may play tough, but he believes you. He's just being Jack the Stubborn."

"Sadowsky said that I knew the Big Man, but everyone thought he was dead. It got me thinking. He loves money, talks incessantly about having his billions, and runs Golden Trident Security. Who does that remind you of?"

"Could be a former SEAL. US Navy SEALs has a logo that includes a golden trident. What are you thinking?" Jack answered with his own query.

"Bingo," replied J.P. "Who do we know who bragged he could have been a SEAL who loved money more than anything, and was a sadistic psychopath?"

"When you put it like that, Theo Myerson. But he's been dead for years," Eric replied. "Not a moment too soon, if you ask me."

"Is he? What do we know about his death? I mean factual information, hard facts, not hearsay." J.P. drummed his fingers on the table.

"He was aboard a yacht that smuggled money and drugs for the Salazar cartel. Acting on a tip, the Coast Guard intercepted. The boat blew up. The Coast Guard searched for two days. They found nothing, except pieces of the hull and fake money, hundreds and twenties. Everything sank in shark-infested waters too deep to explore," Jack reported.

"It's circumstantial. You're right more than you're wrong, J.P., but I'm not convinced. I watched the Coast Guard video." Eric defended Jack's position.

CHAPTER 126

J.P. STARED AT ERIC then at Jack. "Here is another bit of circumstantial evidence. Do you recall the SEAL detachment that located three Soviet-era suitcase nuclear weapons while taking down a Russian arms dealer in Uzbekistan? The incident that pissed me off so much I tied Myerson to the base flagpole with the 'Imbecile or Traitor' sign around his neck?"

"Yeah, I remember that," replied Eric.

"We got definitive confirmation the nukes were real. Before the SEAL team could extract the weapons, our boys who executed the takedown mission were massacred. The bombs disappeared, never seen again," J.P. concluded.

"We never figured out who did it. What's that got to do with this?" asked Eric.

"The Intel lead on that operation was Myerson. The team leader dispatched to retrieve the weapons cache was our classmate at Annapolis," answered Jack.

"Now these lunatics are playing with three suitcase nukes. I do not believe in that many coincidences. I am ready to bet the serial numbers on file are the same as the ones in my pics." J.P. challenged them. "Think like Naval Intel people and tell me how you would make everyone think you died in that explosion."

"There was an unconfirmed report that the boat was smuggling cash back into Mexico for Don Alberto Salazar. Supposedly, it was $180 million. They never recovered the real money. Don Alberto foamed at the mouth, blamed Uncle Sam for stealing the money and using the boat explosion as a cover-up. That was a contributing factor to those ugly drug wars in Mexico. Goddamn Theo Myerson." Eric's voice escalated.

"I would have scuba gear towed under the boat, including an underwater sled for a quick getaway, and place the charges on the hull to create a diversion. Damn it. He didn't die in that explosion." Jack inhaled sharply. "The more I think about it, the more it makes sense. He's psychopathic enough to conceive and justify the *True Patriot Day* crap. Where would he get the capital to finance it? Oh my God, the cash on that ship was counterfeit. He switched it before they sailed, blew up the boat with all the witnesses, and kept Salazar's money."

"I guess we agree it could be Theo," J.P. summarized. He changed in a long-sleeved shirt and handed his body armor to Jack. "You will need this. I will get corroboration and Theo's location. I believe he used Alice's death to force George off the Hector Salazar case. The way Alice and Artie died stinks of his raging fury." J.P.'s voice turned to a hissed whisper. "Sadowsky never said it explicitly, but I am sure he did it."

"We'll find another way to bring him to justice. No sense in you taking the risk of getting killed before we get there with the reinforcements," Jack pleaded.

"Why can't I go?" asked Ramos. "Jack can organize everything by himself."

"You and Jack need to coordinate this. Jack still has to stay out of sight for now." Morgan pointed to the device left on the table. "This is an encrypted phone. I know George has a similar one. I will do my best to stall them long enough for you to bring the cavalry."

"What is a realistic time frame?" inquired Jack, standing tall and square-shouldered.

"It is 4:38 p.m. Call it 5:30 p.m. by the time I get there. You be in position by 8:30 p.m. I will secure Lisa and Max and then make my move from inside a few minutes before 8:45 p.m. Be ready to storm the castle and take control of the situation at 8:45 p.m. sharp. Let's hope we live through this. If not, it has been a real pleasure working with you again."

The men bumped fists in a triangle and synchronized their watches.

"You're going in unarmed?" Jack's expression resembled a pug's face.

"I got my weapon up here." J.P. tapped his head. "You know me. I dislike killing people if I can help it. Mosquitoes are a different story."

They all cringed at the implied reference to a night the three of them had spent in a parasite-infested African swamp, trapped behind enemy lines. At one point, they had considered surrendering just to get away from clouds of mosquitoes the size of hummingbirds.

"You want to take down a bastion of crazy people, you send in a madman. When was the last time it made a difference whether J.P. went in armed or unarmed? Remember Operation Black Catapult? Too bad, it's classified." Eric burst into laughter. Jack and J.P. joined in.

"Guns and ammo are in the Chevy. The original recordings are in the office safe for authentication. Mother Mary and Officer Randy Sparks of the Irvine PD have copies," J.P. concluded. He wrote the office address, alarm code, and safe combination and handed the slip of paper and keys to Jack. "Thank you, and good luck. Come and get us."

"One thing I have to know, just in case we never meet again," said Ramos.

"What is that?" asked J.P.

"How did you get out of that prison when you got caught buying us time to escape?"

"Is that what got your panties in a bunch?" J.P. hooted.

"Yeah, a little." Eric backpedaled. "We figured you were toast."

"OK, here it goes." J.P. smirked. "I would not want you to mess things up tonight. Once the drugs wore off, getting out of the cuffs was the hardest part. I took out the guards and went for the armored vehicle. I drove through the administrative building, put it in gear, dropped a toolbox on the gas, pointed it to the road, and jumped out while it was breaking through the outer walls. I hid in a bathroom until everybody gave chase. Then I strolled to the beach."

"Son of a bitch." Ramos slapped J.P.'s shoulder. "Only you could come up with something like that. OK, J.P., now I'm sure our odds have improved substantially. We'll see you at eight forty-five on the dot, with the federal cavalry in tow. Good luck, buddy."

"I forgive you," J.P. said, gently smacking Eric's shoulder.

"What for?" Eric queried.

"I know you made the final assessment that they had compromised me."

"You knew? All this time, and you said nothing?" Eric swallowed hard.

"Of course, I knew," quipped J.P. "No worries, I would have done the same thing."

"The hell you would," retorted Jack and Eric at the same time.

CHAPTER 127

"**P**URCELL, YOU'RE NOT GOING to believe this!" an excited guard screamed into his radio. Purcell's foul mood had worsened since he had not heard from Morgan, and he was ready to reprimand his man. He heard commotion downstairs and rushed out of Clancy's office. His eyes bulged out of their sockets.

Morgan strolled in, thumbs hooked in his jeans pockets. He filled the warehouse with an off-key parody of Inner Circle's *Bad Boys*.

"Bad cops, bad cops,

whatcha gonna do,

whatcha gonna do,

when they come for you?"

"Shut the hell up and hit the floor!" Purcell bellowed, leaning over the rail.

J.P. carried on the mockery, unfazed. He stood in the middle of a circle of a dozen men, who kept their weapons trained on him.

"Nobody naw give you no break.

Feds naw give you no break.

Soldier naw give you no break.

Good cops naw give you no break."

J.P. ended with an extravagant bow, straightened up, stared at Purcell, and then lowered his gaze to the men surrounding him. "I am here to deal with the big boss, no caca." He smirked. "That one up there," he continued, pointing to Purcell, "is just big caca, no boss."

Purcell crushed the railing with white knuckles in a futile attempt at maintaining composure. Nobody had dared to speak to him like that in a long time, if ever.

"Stop kidding yourself, Purcell." J.P. beamed, taking inventory of his surroundings. "You are a big, fat nothing. Get the real boss out here. I am talking about the anal-retentive reedy pain in the ass who executed Jamie Smythe. Clancy is the *real jefe*, is he not? I have recordings and information to trade with him for my friends' lives."

"Check him for weapons and bugs and then bring him to me!" Purcell yelled.

"Whoever has too many teeth, please approach. I am here to deal with Clancy, not the clown up there, who could not lead a bunch of hungry hyenas to the chicken coop." J.P. made a dismissive gesture. He glowered at the ring of armed men, sure of himself.

"Coldwell, you check him," ordered Purcell.

J.P. heard movement behind. Someone had holstered a weapon and took a step toward him. He leaned forward; his right leg shot backward and caught Coldwell square in the chest. The blow sent Coldwell flying. He landed with a loud thump, the back of his head bouncing off the concrete floor. J.P. brought his foot down slowly amid a dozen guns being cocked.

"Good puppies. You need direct orders from the actual boss, remember?" He spun in slow motion and glared at each one of the men surrounding him. "Let's end this charade. As they say in the movies," he lowered his voice, distorted his face into a horror mask, and faked an alien accent, "'Take me to your leader.'"

Purcell's face turned ashen. Controlling his temper became impossible. He wondered what Morgan may have concocted. Shooting him could prove more dangerous to the operation. Walking in here with such confidence, he must have something up his sleeve. "Search him and put him with the others." Purcell issued orders and then slammed Clancy's office door.

"It would be easier if you allowed us to search you." Timmons stepped forward, holstering his weapon.

"Ask nicely," retorted J.P.

"What?" Timmons asked.

"Be polite. Where are your manners, boys?"

"OK, Morgan. You heard the man. May we please frisk you?" Timmons looked as if he thought J.P. must be out of his mind.

J.P. extended his arms at shoulder level, palms down. Two men sprung forward and searched him from head to toe. They found the Nokia phone and a flash drive on a lanyard around his neck. They handcuffed him and then marched him to join the hostages.

CHAPTER 128

MAX AND LISA SAT shoulder to shoulder on the floor with their backs against the wall. Next to them, Sonny Days's terrified family huddled together.

"You had to be the macho man and waltz in here. You couldn't stay away or bring the Army or the Marines with you. Are you that stupid, J.P.?" Max asked with contempt.

"You let them catch you? You know they'll kill us all and go on with their plans. While you were out there, we had hope. How are you going to honor your word and keep me alive now?" Lisa slumped, looking away, fighting tears and feelings of disaster.

"Thrilled to see you, my ladies. What a warm welcome." J.P. took a quick bow. "I did not want to live in their new world, anyway." He looked at Max, who had a tear streaking down her cheek. He kissed her cheek and then he settled between her and Lisa. "If we die, I would rather die with Max by my side. I am here, baby girl. I promised I would never leave you."

Parker barged into the room, followed by Coldwell, still rubbing his chest. "We'll take over here. We both have unfinished business with this bag of shit." Coldwell walked up to J.P., grabbed him by the front of his shirt, threw him down across from the hostages, and kicked him hard in the back. "Get on your knees, shithead!" Coldwell yelled, spit flying from his lips. "I guess you're not such a hotshot now, are you?"

J.P. complied, stole a quick glance at his shirt's left cuff, and then looked away fast and guilty. Parker patted him down, coming up with a handcuff key concealed in the shirt's cuff. He waved it in front of J.P.'s face with a scowl.

Lisa let out another groan as if hit with a baseball bat.

"You cannot blame a guy for trying." J.P. winked at Max and Lisa.

"Check him again. He is a jack-in-the-fucking-box full of cheap tricks, one unpleasant surprise after another," hissed Parker between clenched teeth.

Coldwell frisked J.P. again. He found nothing this time. Then he pushed J.P. on the floor next to the other hostages, mumbling something about revenge under his breath.

"How are my favorite girls? What did I miss?" J.P. asked in an amused tone.

"I thought you were this fearless guy who would swing on a vine and rescue us. Instead, you surrendered. Then you gave away our only chance." Lisa kicked him in frustration.

"You are exceedingly cute when you are mad, Ms. Jensen. Remind me to piss you off more often," J.P. said in a soothing voice. "The vine thing is overrated. I did that two nights ago, and then you went back in. I pried you out of their hands at Anna's place. Yet here you are again. I will not count the hospital incident because they never actually got their hands on you." J.P. stole a sideways glance at Parker. "They say third time is a charm. Maybe you can find it in your heart to trust me just a little longer. We will be out of here in no time."

Lisa scoffed and rolled her eyes.

"You do not really believe these semi-trained monkeys can keep us here?" J.P. tilted his head in Parker and Coldwell's direction, who watched the exchange with confident grins.

"They have guns. We have handcuffs on our wrists," snarled Lisa.

"Oh, ye of so little faith," replied J.P., settling on the floor as if he intended to nap.

"I like you, Morgan. You're one cool customer. I respect that. I will ask the boss for the privilege of shooting you dead before the night is out," Parker said, sitting down.

"Dream on, and get in line," J.P. retorted. "You are the bozo who executed four cops two nights ago because I got inside your *impenetrable fortress*. Talk about anger and self-control issues. You took your best shot at the hospital and failed again. You shot two more of Irvine's finest, and you forgot your partner there, if I am not mistaken. Wake me up when the truly competent people get here."

"Who do you mean?" Parker jumped to his feet, his face covered in crimson patches.

"You know, the ones who can make sound decisions and carry them out," delivered J.P. in a flat tone, and then he closed his eyes and pretended to sleep.

Parker rushed to J.P., kicked him with the tip of his boot, and then punched him several times. He sauntered back to his chair and plopped into it, letting out a satisfied sigh.

Lisa moaned in exasperation, feeling J.P.'s pain. Max closed her eyes, leaning back against the wall. Throughout the entire exchange, Cher, her mother, and her son sat still, their faces contorted in terror. Their last chance of getting out of this alive had marched in voluntarily and joined them. To add insult to injury, he was antagonizing the armed captors.

CHAPTER 129

PURCELL MARCHED IN, SPORTING a triumphant sneer. Simpson followed him, carrying a laptop. Purcell strode over to J.P. and kicked him. "Wake up, smart ass. The boss will be here in about an hour. He asked us to provide entertainment until then, courtesy of the Big Man. He wants you to die knowing. The Big Man wanted me to relay this message: 'Alice being your wife was an unexpected bonus'."

Simpson finished setting up the equipment and turned on the TV.

"Sadowsky and Jamie got this off your lawyer before they gave her private flying lessons. She turned out to be a lousy student. Enjoy the movie," Purcell added.

J.P.'s expression reflected a deliberate lack of interest, annoying Purcell even further.

Alice appeared on the giant plasma screen. *Pregnant as a blimp*, J.P. recalled her pun with adoration. She looked worried. She sat at the kitchen table in their Irvine home.

On cue, J.P. sat up right. He knew what it was—the proof Anna died for, the recording of Alice's murder, the thing he had been seeking since Thursday, the reason he had spent the last decade in hell while his body remained on Earth.

Two masked men wearing surgical gloves sat across the table from Alice. The shaky video suggested a third person behind the camera. Alice looked terrified as she helped Artie climb on her lap. She wrapped her arms tight around him, pushing his head full of unruly hair against her chest. J.P. recognized the first masked man at the table to be Sadowsky—same body and voice, ten years younger. The second assailant looked familiar too.

Hello, Theo. Still an asshole. You cannot help who you are.

For a while, there was nothing but alternating threats from Myerson and Sadowsky. Myerson handed Alice a sheet of paper and instructed her to read it into the camera. Alice swatted it away and then demanded they leave her house. They haggled for a while, and then Myerson reached over the table and slapped Alice across the face. He ordered her to read the prepared statement facing the camera. Alice refused, her hand rubbing her cheek.

Myerson staggered around the table, grabbed Alice's hair, and pulled her out of the chair. Alice screamed in pain and let go of Artie, reaching up to free herself from Myerson's iron grip. Little Artie leaped to his feet on the chair and placed a precise kick to Myerson's groin, sending him to his knees, doubled in agony.

Mark, Lisa, and Max let out a glorious yell. Years too late, but it warmed J.P.'s heart.

Alice fell back in the chair, hugging Artie's tiny body, anticipating the retaliation. Sadowsky pointed a silenced gun at her. Alice took no chances with Artie's life. She picked up the paper. "I'll read it. Leave the boy alone." Her gloomy voice turned J.P.'s soul inside out, and he felt his heart pierced by thousands of razor-sharp knives.

Myerson yanked Artie out of Alice's arms. She fought with all her might, earning a shove that sent her skidding across the tiled floor. Myerson propelled Artie into the wall. The boy slammed his head and slid down like a broken puppet, sobbing. Alice bolted off the floor and picked up Artie, checking the back of the kid's head. Myerson jostled her from the boy. She slapped his hand away, and Myerson smacked her again, knocking her down.

Blood started flowing freely from Alice's broken nose and lip. Artie opened his eyes, saw his aunt bleeding, braced himself with his back against the wall, and thumped Myerson in the shin with the heel of his boot. Myerson hopped around on his other foot and then retaliated, kicking Artie in the chest.

At Morgan's trial, the Orange County Medical Examiner described that blow as "*the most severe blow I have ever seen administered to a child. It crushed the boy's sternum, sending bone shards into his heart and lungs. His lungs filled with blood, drowning him and rendered him unable to even cry out in pain. The child died slowly in indescribable agony.*"

A chorus of painful groans arose from the hostages. J.P. focused on the screen in complete silence, keeping a face devoid of emotion. Inside, he felt his blood approaching the boiling point, and he bit his tongue, until he felt blood draining down his throat.

Just you wait, Theo. I will find you, and I will repay you. With interest.

On the screen, Myerson steadied himself by placing his right hand on the kitchen counter near the sink. Alice struggled to her feet, protecting her belly with her arm; rushed up to the counter; and seized a two-pronged fork with sharp metal tips used for checking meat temperature. Mustering all her fury, Alice brought it down on Myerson's hand. The fork went through his hand and shattered against the granite countertop. Myerson howled in agony.

Alice dived to check on Artie, who spurted blood through his mouth and nose. He could not breathe. The child's petrified eyes reflected his awareness of imminent death.

CHAPTER 130

S TILL WAILING, MYERSON PULLED out the remains of the fork, dropped them in the sink, and attempted to clean the splinters. He gave up and grabbed a butcher's knife from the block on the counter. He hurled himself at Alice with no restraint.

The coroner had described the attack at trial as "*twenty-six savage stabs, twenty of them fatal blows on their own. The victim had forty-one defensive cuts on her hands, arms, and upper body. My conclusion is she fought her attacker bravely yet uselessly before receiving the first of the twenty fatal blows.*" The coroner had continued to describe the attack as "*one of the most, if not the most vicious attacks I have witnessed in my career. This assault was perpetrated by what could only be categorized as an enraged animal with no semblance of self-control. This was without a doubt a crime of passion.*"

The four women and Mark cried bighearted. A single tear streaked from the corner of J.P.'s eye down his stony face. He knew he had entered the "zero-feelings zone" as he called it, a state of complete calm and control where his mind functioned in perfect harmony and generated fascinating, often deadly, solutions. Here, all obstacles ceased to exist or matter.

On the screen, the third masked man had set the camera on one side and rushed to stop Myerson. His efforts earned him a stab wound on his left arm. Cher and Mrs. Days gasped.

Seconds later, it was over. Alice and Artie lay dead on the floor, drenched in blood. Myerson walked into the service bathroom and returned with two towels. He wrapped his hand in one and gave the other to Sonny. Myerson ordered them to set fire to the upper level while he turned on all the faucets on the ground floor.

The tape ran until the assailants drove away in Alice's SUV. It now made sense to J.P. why the seventy-eight-year-old neighbor, Mrs. Constantine, testified at J.P.'s trial that she saw him leave the home, when the fire started. She had spotted the killers drive Alice's SUV, but she did not get a close look inside it. In those days, as a symbolic gesture, Alice and J.P. drove *The Twins*, two Infiniti QX80 SUVs, both black on black, indistinguishable from each other.

Simpson reappeared and packed the gear. He left without a sound.

"Oh, J.P., I'm so sorry. You should have never seen that. It was so horrible." Max crawled over and sobbed on his chest, her body shuddering with every hiccup.

"This is hard for me to admit. I was wrong about everything. If we get out of here, I will make sure they set the record straight," Lisa declared in a compassionate voice.

Lisa edged closer but did not dare to disturb J.P. and Max's embrace. She sobbed, unable to wipe the tears. She felt as if she had watched the murder of her own family.

"I now understand what Candy meant. The people who really count, they know the truth. The rest, well, it does not matter," J.P. replied, staring at Max and then Lisa. "Make sure nobody ever sees that video, especially Alice's family. Do you understand what I am asking?"

Lisa looked at him, puzzled, and Max nodded between uncontrollable sobs. Even though she now admired J.P.'s effectiveness, Lisa could not fathom a way out of their current predicament.

"Don't you worry about that. We'll bury it with you to keep you warm. Not a soul will ever see it again—or you." Parker spat the words.

J.P. dropped his chin on Max's head. Lisa touched her shoulder to his.

Cher, her mom, and Mark mourned their own loss all over again. "There is no reason to deny it. The man filming was my husband. I— we owe you a heartfelt apology, and I pray you can forgive him and us. He wasn't an evil man," Mrs. Days said, her voice shaking. She blinked, attempting to clear up heavy tears.

"I appreciate it. He tried to stop the madness. He probably was a good man in a hard spot," replied J.P. in a dismissive, ice-cold but a cordial tone.

Purcell reentered the briefing room and pointed to Morgan. "The boss is here. He's graciously allowing you five minutes."

Showtime. Drum roll, please.

CHAPTER 131

SEATED AT HIS DESK, Clancy was twirling J.P.'s flash drive by the lanyard. Contempt radiated from his narrow, rigid face. Clancy measured J.P. up and down with condescension. "John Paul Morgan. Finally, a face to go with the name that's been a thorn in our side. I'd say it's a pleasure to meet you, but it's not." Clancy waved Purcell out.

Reluctantly, Purcell stepped outside and closed the door behind him.

Clancy continued to twirl the little computer drive. "Let me guess. Copies of this will go to the Feds, the media, the Governor's mansion, the White House, and other people who, you believe, can stop us. Unless we let you and your women go."

J.P. did not respond, and Clancy resumed. "Maybe I am presumptuous. Would you like to outline your own terms?"

"Such limited imagination. It will cost you more than that. To compensate, I will throw in a big bonus for you, something you should not refuse."

"What could you have that I'd be interested in?" asked Clancy, anxious.

"Let all others go. No exceptions, no arguments, no haggling. I will stay here, until after the *True Patriot Day*, as insurance that they will not talk. You leave Sonny Days's family alone and allow Ms. Jensen to return to her former life, as if this never happened. Maxine and I will leave the country for good as soon as I deliver my bonus. Until then, every four hours I will need access to a computer to delay the release of the evidence on that stick. Upon setting me free, I will give you the information to retrieve and destroy all copies and you may enjoy your Attis fetish and reign in peace."

"What's this 'Attis fetish?' Are you trying to piss me off?"

"You get a pass. It is a rather obscure reference. Attis was the God of rebirth."

"I see. What do you offer, and why are you so sure I'd desire it?" Clancy rubbed his chin, emphasizing the last words with a drawl.

"I want Theo Myerson's location, the bastard who financed your operation. Myerson is not negotiable. I will make sure he never creates another problem for anyone. Let's face it. We are here because of this temper. It must eat you alive that you have to rely on him. When it is over, I promise I will forget everything I know about you and your plans. If you did your homework, you know that my word is stronger than any written agreement."

"You live up to your reputation, Morgan. You figured out Theo's identity. I'm not sure even his dad knows he's alive. Tempting offer. I'd love nothing more than to be free of him."

"Yet you choose to keep him around. As unpredictable as he is?"

"Theo said you were good. As enticing as it sounds, I'll pass." Clancy's eyes betrayed a slight shadow of fear. "You tell me how to retrieve this information and disable your Internet bomb. I promise you all die a quick and painless death. Best I can offer. Take it now because tomorrow morning it will no longer matter."

J.P. stood, strode to the door, and knocked on it with his head.

"No counteroffer? You're walking away from the table like that?"

J.P. turned and stared into Clancy's face with cold, unforgiving eyes. "I do not bargain. I made you a magnificent offer. If you refuse my proposition, I will take care of things my way. You now have my terms. If I were you, I would agree."

"You are a different breed. I expected you to barter with something, beg, threaten, whatever. Instead, you just up and leave. I don't get it," Clancy muttered.

"Yeah, you do not get it. You never stopped to consider that your scheme has no chance of success. All you will accomplish is kill and hurt a lot of innocent folks. Then the American people will see you for what you are and put you down like a rabid dog. Best-case scenario, you will go down in history as a footnote on the page dedicated to deranged mass murderers."

"Careful there, Morgan," Clancy barked. "I'm not someone you should toy with."

"All I care about is Theo." J.P. continued, unfazed. "He hurt my family and framed me for it. I think I earned the right to thank him in person." J.P. faced the door again.

"Get back here and sit down!" Clancy yelled, jumping to his feet. "What do you mean our operation will fail? You do not understand what we have planned or for how long. We covered every contingency. We even allowed for wild cards like you."

J.P. took his time getting comfortable in the chair and then yawned. "Delusion of grandeur is one of the deadliest mistakes a man can make. Hey, it is your funeral. I will tell you what I know, and then we talk about why your plan cannot succeed. If I get it wrong, please correct me. Though I fear someone promised you something that you cannot achieve."

"By all means, dazzle me." Clancy made an elaborate, inviting gesture, leaning back in his chair. "I read your file, and I've got to admit. I'm curious."

"I figured it out. So will others. You have eyes on the Governor's mansion, but decided to bypass the old-fashioned, democratic way. Why bother with elections when you can make sure you slip into the job? You create a statewide disaster and then force George to step down. Maybe you will try to use this thing with Jack. Then you step in with *unparalleled leadership skills* and guide California out of the crisis. When the dust settles, you assume the part of provisional Governor until the elections, when you, a genuine American hero, are a shoo-in as Governor, and then it all looks legit. Who would dream of running against you? If someone finds the courage, I am sure the loyal psychos of the new CDoHP would dispose of the inconvenience."

J.P. asked for water. Clancy trudged to his private refrigerator and retrieved two bottles. J.P. motioned to his handcuffs. Clancy ordered Purcell to switch J.P.'s handcuffs to the front, and then waved him out.

J.P. took a long swig. "Tomorrow you intend to detonate the three nuclear bombs. Simultaneously, you launch a Biochemical attack with tainted money, fake money, but who cares? It will spread the agent and cause havoc among the unsuspecting population."

"So far, you live up to your reputation." Clancy's blood drained from his gaunt face.

"You coerce or assassinate all legitimate successors to the Governor's office, leaving the path wide open for you. I have not figured out how you fit in, or how you will get them all in one place, or how you will blackmail or threaten them all into resigning. Maybe getting three or four of them in one place at the same time is possible. All eight or nine levels, I do not know. However, I am sure you planned this whole thing to the last detail. You have been at it for years. I stumbled onto your scheme two days ago. I have to hand it to you, though."

"How do you mean?" Clancy asked, startled.

"*True Patriot Day* sounds much classier than *Night of the Long Knives*." J.P. shook his head. "In over eight decades, humanity has learned nothing from it."

"What else?" Clancy labored hard to hide his genuine feelings and ignore the bait.

"The CDoHP, your private army of lunatics, is a delicate touch. I admire your idea to use the disheartened, delusional Trump supporters who think you work to bring him back. Imagine their surprise when they figure out you never intended that, you just used them."

"The CDoHP members are not lunatics. They are all true patriots."

CHAPTER 132

"***TOMATO, POTAHTO,***" **RETORTED J.P.**, offering nothing else.

"What!?" Clancy barked.

"Something my nephew used to say. He heard us say *potato, potahto, tomato, tomahto*. One day, he combined them. *Tomato, potahto*. It became the family inside joke."

"I'm starting to like you, Morgan." Clancy smirked. "Too bad we're on opposite sides. Would you work for us? There is an influential position for you in our organization."

"Not in a million years on principle alone," said J.P. "I miss Artie. He was six years old, and he kicked Theo in the nuts for picking on his aunt. Brave little man, just like his dad."

"I watched the tape, too. I'm truly sorry about your family. You're right. Theo is a psychopath, but he has his uses." Clancy pursed his lips. "No dice, Morgan. I may not like him, but he's not the person I would cross. Let's finish our story. What else you got?"

"Where was I? Oh, yeah, the CDoHP. They think they are doing a great, patriotic thing, protecting California and all that. What you have in mind is for them to be your private legionnaires, carrying out your agenda, the occasional murder of the opposition to your regime. Again, nothing original. Countless despots tried it since before man learned to stand upright. Hitler and Stalin only introduced the concept to the modern world."

Clancy leaned back in his chair, full of himself. "I think it's a stroke of genius and accurate test of leadership, being able to foresee problems and provide an immediate solution."

J.P. ignored the bait and continued. "The CDoHP deploys in the middle of the crisis. They become hubs with direct lines of communication to you and your cronies. They coordinate the hordes of unsuspecting Trump supporters who still have not figured out how democracy works, or maybe they just do not care. They will take arms, fight and kill innocents for *their President*."

"What's wrong with that?" asked Clancy. "Someone has to channel that anger and resentment into something that will change this country. We will cause the rebirth of this nation, free of bloodsucking illegals, criminals and all those blacks, browns and inferior races who think they measure up to true Americans. Trump's loyalists are perfect. After all, they bought the stolen election myth for months, some for years. If you frame it right, they'll believe anything."

"Yeah. I am sure you have patsies stashed somewhere, with compelling evidence around their necks, of planning and executing the nuclear and Biochemical strikes. I bet they will prove to be card-carrying members of some international terrorist group. Whatever will justify sending our soldiers in harm's way again and hurting immigrants and further oppress minorities. War is always good for big business."

"Don't be so negative," Clancy cut him off. "It is in man's nature to relish war. The financial consequences are there for those who provide stewardship."

"Tell that to the veterans missing body parts or to the families of those who never came back. All that so you and your bunch of self-entitled assholes can make another buck, buy another Ferrari or a bigger yacht." J.P. grimaced. "You are a disgrace to the entire human race."

"You seem to be so sure that you're the one on the moral high ground," Clancy scoffed. "People like you do not understand what it takes to make history happen, to change the course of a country, to get it back on track. Don't lecture me about—"

"Whatever you need to tell yourself." J.P. dismissed him. "I will not engage in a debate with you. Obviously, you believe that whoever has more money and power, is automatically right. Let's get back to the patsies you plan to use. I bet none of them have a record of entering the United States legally, or they are all known as Trump opposers.

All this built on psychosis, mass killing of Americans, oppression, discrimination and the intent to propel us into war."

"I'm impressed. You nailed it, pretty much. I would say over 90 percent. There is one major aspect you got wrong." Clancy paused for effect, waiting for J.P. to ask. Disappointed, he resumed. "The succession line. As of two hours ago, I am the Attorney General of California. As the AG, I can summon all of them for an emergency meeting, where they would be vulnerable."

His creepy smile was too much. J.P. fought hard to stop himself from killing Clancy on the spot. Max, Lisa, and the other hostages would pay with their lives if he lost his temper. J.P. understood why everyone had deferred to him for the past few days.

"The old AG died last week," gloated Clancy, answering the unasked question. "He suffered a massive heart attack, courtesy of our Doc Death Jones. He expired in the ambulance. Did you ever meet the doc? He's a genius at killing a man or a million." Clancy let out a sinister chuckle he had learned from Myerson.

"Your family maintains controlling interest in several pharmaceutical companies, both here and overseas, right?" J.P. cocked his head to one side.

"As a matter of fact, we do. What's it to you?"

"I bet all those companies had the foresight to stockpile medication that tomorrow will be indispensable to California. They will offer their entire supply to Californians. At a significant profit, of course. Probably more money than you made with the COVID vaccines."

"There is nothing wrong with making money. That's what capitalism is all about." Clancy flashed a wide grin. "That's probably the one thing Trump got right."

"Easy on the fake hero worship," scoffed J.P. "You may end up believing in him yourself."

"Careful, Morgan," Clancy spit his words. "Trump lacked vision and the discipline to implement the plans to make America great again. I will return America to the true Americans. Make it the greatest country on God's green earth and make certain it stays that way."

"Hmm. I wonder who is going to cook for you and clean your mansions then."

Clancy blew an exasperated sigh. "Let me tell you why I will succeed where Trump failed. Trump is a megalomaniac, or I should say a MAGAlomaniac. He just had to trumpet all his ideas, thoughts, and actions before he did anything. Do you know why the January 6th insurrection failed? Because Trump wanted to give the final orders and lead the insurrection personally and be present when his followers executed those who opposed him. There was a second wave of true patriots, armed to the teeth, staged and waiting to attack the Capitol on Trump's personal orders. However, Trump wanted to announce his intentions to the world, to appear this great leader who guided his followers into the final battle to change America. The cowards and traitors around him cut him off, shut down all communications and isolated him in the White House. That gave the biggest coward and traitor of them all, Mike Pence, time to send in the National Guard. Without direct orders from Trump, most parties didn't attack."

"I see. You are going to let them know after you took over, when it will be too late. In the meantime, why not make a few more billions hurting the people?"

"Well, I could use additional funds for my next political campaign," gloated Clancy.

"If you expect me to congratulate you, dream on. You are not the first psychopath in history to use mass murder to land a job he is not qualified for." J.P. yawned.

"Now, now. That's not polite. You know nothing about my qualifications."

"What is next for you? Governor of California is not enough?"

"All my life, they have bred me for the Governor's seat and one day for the President's office. I come from a long line of blue-blooded American patriots." Clancy issued a politician's smile, looking down his patrician nose.

"President of what?" J.P. kept a straight face. *Gotcha!*

CHAPTER 133

"**O**F THE UNITED STATES!** What other presidency matters?"
Clancy bellowed, leaping to his feet. His face turned into an
upside-down eggplant.

"Oh," said J.P. "I thought you were thinking about the Psychos R
Us Club. I heard their president retired, Alzheimer's or something."

Clancy circled the desk and hit Morgan in the face. The blow sent
J.P. tumbling backward with the chair. J.P.'s nose started bleeding.

"Enough with the psycho crap. We're not psychopaths. We're
genuine American heroes, true patriots who did something about the
plague overtaking our society, while the rest of you are busy watching
TV. Tell me how to disable the Internet bomb and recover all copies,
or I will start with that pretty redhead of yours. We'll slice her up and
force-feed the pieces to you. Let my men have a little fun before the
operation begins, to release some pent-up tension. I'll make sure Purcell
glues your eyelids open for the show."

"I will let you think about it. You should consider my offer seriously
before you continue with the empty threats." J.P. got off the floor and
then strode to the door. "I wonder what Trump and his zealots would
do if they found out about your plans. Now, I am half tempted to escape
just to lead them here to ask you that question in front of them."

"We'll reinstate Trump for a short while. Someone has to keep my
seat warm in the Oval Office." Clancy gloated.

"I am not sure I am down with that, Governor. One Trump term
was enough. You, in the White House? No way, no how!"

"What can you do about it? I hold all the chips." Clancy shoved his
chin forward. "We got all of you!"

"I am glad to hear you think that. I know they are ice chips, and it is summer outside. It will come to you. Right now, you are not rational. I would blame it on the pressure around here. It is an unsuitable environment for clear thinking. Have it your way."

"Let me tell you why our operation will work like a charm. You'll appreciate the elaborate planning and everything we're doing to save this great country from disaster."

Morgan sauntered back. He lifted the chair with his foot and settled in it. "OK. Amaze me, although I doubt it will impress me. I do not sympathize with petty dictators."

"Here it goes." Clancy appeared to be at his wit's end.

J.P. had pegged Clancy as the tyrannical, self-important type. He knew Clancy would take great pride in his discourse. *The longer, the better.*

"We tired of seeing our beloved country's resources depleted by the illegal immigrants, criminals, lazy blacks and spics, and terrorists from all inferior races. Do you know how much money we'll save when we stop spending it on illegals? Do you know that crime would drop by over 60 percent if we got rid of them? Our education system's in trouble, yet we send illegals to college, and they take our jobs. Add another 20 percent if we rein in all those blacks and browns who rob everything from the true Americans and bleed this country dry."

J.P. yawned and took another sip of water.

"Our prisons are full," Clancy continued through clenched teeth. "Because they prefer to live in our prisons instead of going home to starve. Damn leeches. Those poor people on the border are sick and tired of dealing with the invasion of bloodsuckers. Let's not mention what it costs this country to process and deport their asses or hold all those criminals in prisons." Clancy argued his case. "It is our sacred duty to rid California and eventually the United States of the parasites who bleed this great country dry. We'll make sure America grows back into the number one world superpower. Everyone will listen and quiver when America speaks."

"What about constitutional lawyers, ACLU, and organizations that champion human rights? You think they are just going to lie down?" J.P. asked.

The question caused Clancy's face to turn white splashed with red blotches. "We got that covered. We change the laws that protect illegals in California. The lawyers, ACLU, and the entire lot can take it to the Supreme Court. While the Supreme Court fiddles with the case, we process and deport all the illegal immigrants we can find. Even if the Court ruled against us, we'll file lawsuits, appeals, and injunctions on California's behalf. CDOHP will kick the rest of them out of the country. It will be California and then America for Americans only."

"Trump tried and failed. The KKK tried and failed. Plenty of other wannabe despots."

"I already explained why I will succeed where Trump failed," Clancy groaned. "He wanted to do too much at once and drain the swamp at the same time. Did you see how terrified the swamp creatures were? They pounced on him and deprived him of all his rights to a fair impeachment trial. The Democrats held on to Articles of Impeachment longer than it took them to reach a decision to impeach him. Why? Because they were scared out of their minds when they saw the number of patriots willing to fight for Trump. Then they threatened and forced Trump's legal team to quit a week before the trial. Without giving him a minute longer to prepare for the most important trial of his life, they pushed the trial in the Senate. Even petty thieves are entitled to a continuance to prepare a proper defense with a new legal team."

"I do not recall Trump asking for more time to prepare."

"They withheld everything from the public. The abysmal performance of his legal team did not matter in the end, because everyone's mind was already made, before the trial started. When I'm President, the hordes of Trump loyalists will get a much stronger and dedicated leader, who will get things done rather than brag about them and give the other side time to interfere. Whether or not the Grand Ostrich Party will support me."

"Just out of curiosity," yawned J.P. "Did you start the CODIV-19 pandemic?"

"No," replied Clancy. "But I wish I had. It would have been a brilliant move to weaken the whorish political system and make tons of money. It proved to be the perfect storm to facilitate implementing our plans."

J.P. stole a glance at the clock on Clancy's desk—7:42 p.m.

"You have time. This is the end of the line for you and your friends." Clancy wallowed.

"I am hungry. I am sure the growing teenager is starving, and the ladies are too."

"We're having pizzas delivered here shortly. We'll share with you."

"Pizza." J.P. twitched his nose. "I guarantee Lisa and Max will argue against it. Can you get healthier stuff? Even death row inmates have their choice of a last meal."

"Beggars can't be choosers. You get the pizza or nothing."

"Pizza it is. I hope it comes with salads. When will it be here?"

"In ten or fifteen minutes. We'll have dinner, and then we need to get out of here and get in position. Big day tomorrow, you know."

"One thing bothers me. How did you convince them all to go along with this madness? Trump's followers think they are getting Trump back and see nothing else. But the rest?"

"We recruited only men 100 percent convinced it is imperative to rid this great country of the plague brought by illegals." Clancy trumpeted his reply.

"How did you convince them to go along with the nuclear and the Biochemical attacks? Murdering and hurting millions of Americans. Even psychopaths and Trump's devotees know their own families and friends will get hurt along with Trump opposers."

"I said enough with the psychopathic stuff. You are the true mental case, thinking you can derail progress." Clancy spat his words like flaming arrows.

"One last question. What did you promise Tomlinson for prosecuting me ten years ago? What did you promise him now for his support in this mess? I lied. It was a two-part question." J.P. stood again and turned toward the door.

"Phil is Theo's buddy. Whatever happened back then, that's between the two of them. I never met Phil until we started planning this operation. He'll get a new job. I won't tell you which one." Clancy played coy, waving his finger. "OK, he'll get my current job."

"What did you promise Theo as a reward? Money? It is the only thing he cares about. Please tell me he will not be your new treasurer. You, fool. Poor Californians."

"You are something else entirely. You never give up. I can't tell you."

J.P. kicked the door. Purcell opened it, grabbed J.P. by the neck, and shoved him back. He switched Morgan's handcuffs to the back. "Sir, dinner is here. You can address the troops as they eat, and then we can deploy all personnel." He stood at attention.

"Mm, dinner." J.P. smacked his lips. "I thought you handled important matters."

Purcell elbowed him. J.P. gasped for air, "Did you demote him to steward? You finally figured out that he lied on his résumé? Do not blame him. The last few years have been tough."

"Enough with the obnoxious act!" Clancy roared and instructed Purcell, "Take him back, and get the troops ready. I'll address them in fifteen minutes, then we're out of here."

"One more thing, Governor, sir." J.P. pushed the last button with a southern drawl.

"What now?" bellowed Clancy, leaning on his fists planted on the desk.

"Oops, I forgot to mention that I took extra insurance before I came here tonight."

"What insurance? Morgan, I need no more problems." Clancy jutted his chin.

"You have not checked my phone? Purcell, are you asleep at the wheel again?" J.P. switched his gaze back to Clancy. "I forgot you demoted him to handling pizza deliveries."

A blow to the solar plexus, directed with evil pleasure by Purcell, cut off his speech.

"Enough, Morgan. What did you do? Called the Feds?" Clancy yelled, attempting his best poker face while he bit the inside of his cheek.

CHAPTER 134

"I MAY HAVE SENT pictures of the pallets with money and your location to the local gangs," J.P. answered. "It slipped my mind to mention the money was counterfeit. I may have told them to surround this place and make sure nobody left. If they do not get a call from me, they will storm the place to get the money. This just came to me because it is about time for me to contact them and delay the assault."

"Are you insane, Morgan? What in God's name possessed you to do that?" Clancy screamed after Purcell had closed the door.

J.P. shrugged. "It seemed like a good idea at the time. I had a short time to choose between notifying Trump zealots and inviting the local gangs to rob you. Gangs are easier to motivate with money. Sorry if interferes with your plans to take over the world."

"This is a complication I didn't foresee. LEOs or Feds we could deal with. Gangs that think we have hundreds of millions of dollars? That's a different story. Those animals would do whatever it takes to break down the doors and storm the warehouse. I must hand it to you, Morgan. You are one hell of a destructive force." Clancy's body tensed. "We should have recruited you first. It would have saved me the ulcers."

"We moved everything out in position for tomorrow." Purcell issued a meek laugh, calling J.P.'s bluff. "Bet you didn't know that."

"It will make no difference. I bet they will barge in to see for themselves." quipped J.P.

"You idiot. How do I know you're not pretending?" Clancy grabbed J.P. by the throat and shoved him into the wall.

"I walked in with a phone on me. Have your techsverify. Unlock code is 666333. 666 is for you, 333 for Purcell. I think he is only half the monster you are."

Clancy shot Purcell a murderous look and punched J.P. in the solar plexus.

Purcell barked into his radio. "Simpson, check Morgan's phone. Who did he call?"

"Yes, sir," acknowledged Simpson in a worried voice.

Morgan motioned with his chin to the chair he had sat on before. Without waiting for permission, he strode to the couch instead and sat down. "Mind if I catch my breath waiting for Simpson's report? Tell him to hurry. I should make that call soon, and I am starving."

Clancy and Purcell exchanged worried looks, both calculating the odds of overcoming the additional problem Morgan had just dumped in their lap.

"Back to my question. How did you sell this to the people following you? They have to realize you are a band of domestic terrorists," J.P. asked as if commenting about the weather.

"We are not terrorists," Clancy snapped. "We are freedom fighters. True Patriots. We took the initiative, and did something before the country sinks under the weight of this debt, most of it caused by illegal immigrants, blacks Mexicans, criminals, and their progeny. We will not allow California or the United States to collapse under cost of dealing with those fuckers."

"Never mind that," J.P. scoffed. "I heard the argument from Hitler, Mussolini, Saddam, Milosevic, and the list goes on. Butchers pointing fingers at innocent people, trying to justify their own homicidal tendencies. Phew!"

"We talked enough. Sit there and shut up!" yelled Purcell.

A shy knock interrupted the silence. Purcell threw the door open, startling Simpson, who dragged his feet, eyeballs glued to his shoes.

"I'm afraid I have some bad news, sirs."

"Out with it." Clancy massaged the dancing earthworms at the sides of his head.

"I checked Morgan's phone, and we have a problem. He wiped the phone clean—"

"Skip the technobabble, if you want to live," hissed Purcell.

"Yes, sir. He called a mobile number and spoke for four minutes. Then he sent these pictures." Simpson handed Purcell two sheets of paper with close-up pictures of the money and the pallets, four to a page. "The recipient called him back in less than one minute. They talked for another eight minutes. He didn't make or receive any other calls from this phone."

Purcell studied the pictures and then passed them to Clancy, who took one look at them and started shouting at Morgan. "Why the fuck did you do that?" He marched to the couch and unleashed a torrent of punches. J.P. protected his face as he allowed Clancy to unload.

J.P. wiped the blood from his reopened nosebleed on the nearest throw pillow. He glared at Clancy and spoke in a calm, determined manner. "I am tired of being confused with a training dummy or a piñata. Do that again, and I will forget the abort codes. Let them storm this place and kill you like the rabid animals you are. You got that, Mr. Wannabe Governor?"

Purcell stomped to Morgan. J.P. shifted his unforgiving hard gaze to Purcell.

"Leave him be for now." Clancy waved Purcell away. "We have a tremendous problem. Who did he call?" he asked Simpson, his eyeballs protruding from their sockets.

Simpson had left the data out on purpose, hoping he would not become the lightning rod for both Purcell's and Clancy's fury. "The guy's nickname is Trumpet, sir."

Morgan laughed long and hard, catching the fear in Simpson's eyes.

"What's so funny, dickhead?" Purcell screamed.

"Your own men are terrified of you. There is no chance they will stand by you when this little charade goes south. Which will be soon, I promise."

"Shut the hell up, Morgan. Who is this Trumpet? Simpson, spit it out already." Purcell's neck arteries resembled cartoon pipes under pressure.

"Rumor has it…" Simpson started evasively.

"Rumor has it? Or he *is*?" J.P. helped stir the pot.

"OK. He is the leader of a gang called the Black Angels of LA." Simpson frowned in J.P.'s direction, wiping sweaty palms on his pant legs one at a time.

Purcell pulled his gun and aimed it at Morgan's nose. He placed one hand on J.P.'s shoulder and leaned into J.P. with his entire weight. "If those bastards attack, there will be a bloodbath. You and your women will die for some counterfeit money that isn't even here. You have been the biggest pain in my ass, but I will have my revenge tonight."

"Revenge is poison for the soul. I lived with it for years. Once you figure out how forgiveness works, you may find peace." J.P.'s line stunned Purcell into holstering his pistol.

"We need him to keep those idiots out of here," Clancy said through pursed lips. He looked at Simpson. "Call this Trumpet and let Morgan give them the signal to stay out. Tell him we moved the money already." He switched his menacing gaze to J.P. "You try anything funny, and you'll have raw pieces of your redhead girlfriend on your pizza for dinner. Clear?"

"Crystal, Governor."

"Stop screwing with me, Morgan. I only have so much patience. Now call that gangbanger." Clancy turned to Purcell. "Send someone to check around and report any signs of them. Make sure our men stay out of sight. Have them report only to us."

CHAPTER 135

SIMPSON DIALED AND ACTIVATED the speakerphone, holding it up for J.P.

"'Bout fuckin' time, man." Trumpet's man answered on the first ring. "Boss man bin waitin'. Here da boss man." Trumpet's man covered the microphone, yet excited voices in the background breached through. J.P. cleared his throat and locked eyes with Clancy.

"You're late. I hope you're not trying to back out of our deal because I don't like being jerked around." Trumpet's voice sounded annoyed.

"We do not have time to argue. I only have a few seconds. I called to let you know the place is still crawling with dirty cops. Stay out of sight. I will call you when it is time. It looks as if they are getting ready to leave soon."

"Hurry the fuck up. My men are antsy to shoot the mother-fucking pigs and take their money. I don't know how long I can hold them." Trumpet's pitch increased with every word.

"It is not as if I can kick all of them out of here. They will go when they are ready. You just play it cool and remember what I told you. Do you recall?"

"I know, I know. Stay out of sight, keep the warehouse surrounded, under surveillance from afar, catch all the pigs who try to split, and keep them on ice until we get the dough. Hurry the fuck up. We have important things to do." Trumpet ended the call.

Clancy kicked the couch, screaming in frustration. He turned to Purcell. "Get me information about these animals. Let your men know we may have a threat, but don't tell them anything else. Just be vigilant.

Let them have dinner while we assess the situation and then decide how to move out without engaging those blasted gangbangers."

"Should I call everybody else in, to deal with them?" asked Purcell.

"Not yet. Maybe we can get out of here without a battle." Clancy kicked J.P.'s feet. "I was going to have you shot, Morgan, so you'd die a soldier's death. For this, I'll make sure all of you suffer. I'll make you watch your friends die first, knowing they agonized because of you. Why couldn't you mind your own fucking business?"

Purcell coughed to get Clancy's attention. He gestured toward Morgan.

With the speed of a glacier, J.P. got to his feet and ambled toward the door. "You will not forget to bring us dinner, will you, Governor?" J.P. asked.

Clancy slammed his fists on his desk, sending papers flying everywhere. He picked them up and stuffed them into a large briefcase he kept by the foot of his desk. "Simpson, destroy all records. Erase all archives. We're not taking any chances tonight. Any records we need to keep put everything in my file case. Purcell, assemble the men and feed them. As soon as the scouting party comes back, we'll start the deployment. Morgan, I'll deal with you later. You have sealed your own fate."

Purcell shoved J.P. into the briefing room. He ordered Coldwell and Parker to keep an eye on him until the meeting with the troops was over. Coldwell resumed cleaning his gun. Parker shot J.P. a vicious look, salivating with anticipation.

Morgan ambled to the space between Lisa and Max and then dropped to the floor.

Seeing the fresh blood and bruises, Lisa asked in a soothing voice. "Why do you keep antagonizing them? You have a death wish?"

"Why do magicians use gorgeous, half-naked aides?" retorted J.P. with nonchalance.

She examined his demolished face, shaking her head, wondering if he had lost it. Seeing his family butchered had been trying for sure, and a human being could only take so much.

"Keep your eyes open," he whispered.

"OK, I'll bite. Why do you do it?" Lisa asked, nibbling on her lower lip.

"You sure? It could get ugly, and you may end up hating me even more."

"I don't hate you, J.P., not anymore. Yes, I want to know. Are you out of your mind or just downright stupid? I mean, you look worse than the old punching bag at my gym, yet you come in here smiling as if you just won the lottery. What's your angle?"

"Remember, you asked for it, Lisa." J.P. shrugged, flashing a mischievous smile. "What is your worst fear as a single woman? I mean, we all have our insecurities. What are you always afraid a man may not like about you?"

"That's a very personal question. I will not dignify it with an answer."

"OK." J.P. settled back between her and Max and closed his eyes.

"What's the trick? I don't get it," Lisa said, her lips trembling.

"You refused to take part, remember? If you want to play, you must answer truthfully," J.P. retorted without opening his eyes.

"OK. I'll tell you. If you ever repeat this to anyone, I will torture you in unimaginable ways and then kill you myself." She leaned into Morgan and whispered in his ear, "I'm afraid men will think my ass is too big or too fat. Tread carefully, Morgan."

"No need to worry about getting any bruises from sitting on this hard floor. There is plenty of cushioning on your bottom." J.P. delivered the line with the precision of a metronome, keeping his eyes closed and a naughty smile on his lips.

"You dolt. How dare you use that against me? You are such a moron, J.P. Morgan, just when I was beginning to like you." Lisa kicked him with both legs while ping-pong sized spitballs flew out of the corners of her mouth.

"Serves you right, Counselor. You should never tell that to any man," Parker said, tilting his head back. They continued to hoot while Lisa adopted a pouting posture.

J.P. inquired, "What has been on your mind for the past two minutes?"

"I'm not speaking to you... obnoxious jerk. Get away from me."

"Stop being such a baby." J.P. scooted closer and whispered, "I think your ass is small, shapely, and attractive." He smacked his lips playfully. "What has been on your mind for the past minutes?" pressed J.P.

Lisa's frown resembled the aftermath of an avalanche. "Several ways I could make you pay dearly for that," she scoffed. "I warned you to be discreet and use it wisely. Jackass!"

"I mean, besides that. What else did you think about?"

"I had no time for anything else." She glowered. "I had enough on my mind trying to figure out appropriate punishments for you."

"Precisely."

Her eyes lit up, and she tossed her head back. She giggled with her entire body, resembling a little girl trembling with delight. "You are something else, J.P. Morgan."

"Enough with your stupid games and banter!" Coldwell shouted. "Sit there quietly until the boss gets back. Risky business, but I guess it works for you, Morgan. I would kill you if you did something like that to me."

Lisa settled closer to J.P. and opened her mouth to ask something.

"I said be quiet there!" Coldwell said in a menacing voice, rising to his feet.

CHAPTER 136

TWO STERN-FACED MEN entered the briefing room, and the aroma of hot pizza permeated from the boxes they carried. Coldwell and Parker ate while the additional guards watched. When the hostages finished eating, the men collected the empty pizza boxes, leaving Parker and Coldwell alone with the captives once again.

J.P. checked the time on Max's wristwatch—8:35 p.m.

Intermission is over. Time for the second act. Jack, Eric, I am counting on you to be out there. Otherwise, this will be a very short second act.

J.P. wriggled, seeking a comfortable position. "Any other entertainment scheduled? I am a little sleepy after all that grease. I don't want to fall asleep and some wonderful spectacle."

"You keep quiet, you hear? I'm itching to shoot you, asshole. Don't give me a reason." Parker jumped to his feet. Silence fell over the room.

"I will need a diversion soon," J.P. mouthed silently to Lisa and Max.

Lisa and Max acknowledged with one blink each. Their faces remained locked with mystified expressions. What diversion did he think they could create, handcuffed and guarded?

J.P. winked again and then pretended to go back to his nap.

"Hey, Parker." J.P. yawned, displaying his best bored-to-death expression. "Or is it Porker? I do not have my glasses on me. How many more people do you have to kill before you qualify as a mass murderer?"

"What did you say?" Parker sprung to his feet as if he had been sitting on a lava bed, his nostrils flaring. He leaned across the table, his eyes darkening with every passing second.

"You heard me. I guess right now you are just a lowly serial killer. I bet your mom is proud enough, but not you. Not yet." J.P. glanced at Parker.

401

Coldwell had just finished reassembling his gun. He slammed the magazine in and then placed the weapon on the table. He crossed his arms on his chest and leaned back in his chair.

"You want to say that again, asshat?" Parker leaped and grabbed J.P. by his shirt, lifting him to his feet, away from the hostages.

"For god's sake, J.P., would it kill you to keep your mouth shut?" Lisa blurted out.

"You qualified for the mass murderer status already? Is that what you find insulting?" J.P. continued, unfazed, keeping his gaze trained on Parker's face.

"Shut the hell up. I'm not in the mood for your crap. My best friend is dead because of you." Parker shoved J.P. away from him and pulled out his silenced Berretta. He smacked Morgan in the face with the gun, sending him backward, across from the other hostages.

"I thought you executed him for getting injured, by me no less." J.P. licked the blood off his lips and glared at Parker with that defiance that teenagers adopt when confronting their parents. "They sent two clowns to kill an unarmed woman with amnesia. You idiots shot the wrong people and then each other. What a lousy comedy act." J.P. hooted.

Parker yanked the slide on his weapon, chambered a round, and bent over J.P., thrusting the silencer in his cheek. "Shut up, shithead. I swear I'll shoot you, no matter what the boss says." He lifted J.P.'s chin with the barrel of the gun, his finger trembling on the trigger. Parker's face turned fiery red, heavy perspiration rolling down his face.

J.P. kept his eyes riveted on Parker's face. Parker lowered the gun and stepped away, trying to get his emotions under control.

"Diversion," J.P. mouthed to Lisa and Max.

"You bitch." Max kicked Lisa in the knee. "Look what happened because of you."

She tried to hit Lisa again, but Lisa retreated out of reach.

"You, slut! He came here for you," Lisa joined in, spitting her words like bullets.

"I'm the slut? Every time you look at J.P., you drool like a bitch in heat, and I'm the slut? Huh. You have some nerve, lady."

"You, little tramp," Lisa hissed venomously and then added in a mocking tone, batting her eyelashes, "'Oh, my J.P. this, my J.P. that. He's my world. He raised me, and he did nothing to me.' Like anyone's going to fall for that."

"Cool. Chick fight." Coldwell leaned forward on his elbows, smirking in anticipation.

Parker holstered his gun and seized both Lisa and Max by their hair. "Cut it out. All of you shut the fuck up. Not another sound." Parker shoved Lisa and Max away from each other.

J.P. pounced in one fluid move and grabbed Parker by the neck with his left hand, pushing him down. Simultaneously, J.P. collected the silenced Beretta out of Parker's holster with his right hand. In midair, his left knee took over, pinning Parker to the floor. Parker went down hard, trying to break his fall with both his hands. J.P.'s knee remained planted squarely on Parker's spine. His left hand clutched the back of Parker's neck, burying his face in the carpet. J.P. aimed the Beretta at Coldwell's forehead.

Coldwell grabbed his own gun and pointed it back at Morgan. In the warehouse, the troops cheered and applauded Clancy, and then they yelled, "America for Americans!"

"Put the gun down, Morgan. You're outnumbered. You don't stand a chance. Where can you go?" Coldwell asked in a shaky voice.

"That is what they keep telling me, but I am hardheaded." J.P.'s voice turned to ice. "It may appear we are pointing guns at each other, but it only seems so."

Parker struggled under J.P.'s knee, unable to make a sound. "Calm down, Parker, or your spine will suffer irreversible damage." J.P. redirected his attention to Coldwell. "You. Pay close attention. I have a silenced weapon with a round in the chamber aimed at your forehead. I assure you I can put a third eye in it for you before you know what happened. You have a loaded gun, but no round in the pipe. You get better results if you throw it at me."

"Are you willing to risk it?" Coldwell glanced at his gun and then at the door.

"I watched you all night. You followed your safety training. Every time you took the gun apart, you released the slide before you inserted the magazine. The chamber is empty. I am pissed and itching to shoot some assholes tonight. Do you want to be the first one?"

"You know there are over a hundred of us down there. You'll never get out of here alive, none of you." Coldwell made a last-ditch effort, attempting to conceal shaking hands.

"All the more reason you do not have to die playing the hero tonight. Just to be clear. I do not count to three or any of that nonsense. When I get bored, I shoot. Silenced slug with the ruckus your friends are making down there, I doubt they will figure it out anytime soon."

"You win." Coldwell set the gun down, raising his hands. "For now."

CHAPTER 137

J.P. INVITED COLDWELL TO lie on the floor, face down. Behind him, J.P. heard five loud exhales, each rivaling a small hurricane. Coldwell settled on the carpet with his fingers interlaced behind his head. J.P. reached behind his back with his left hand, ignoring the handcuffs dangling from it. He pulled the handcuff key and tossed it to Max.

Max and Lisa turned back-to-back and removed each other's cuffs. Max sprinted to the table, picked up the gun, chambered a round, and pointed it at Coldwell's head. "See? No round in the barrel, jackass. Excellent choice."

Lisa uncuffed Cher and then secured Parker and Coldwell with their hands behind their backs. She removed their backup weapons and J.P.'s manacles dangling from his left wrist. Then she rummaged through the supply cabinets and returned with a roll of packing tape. "You should stock up on duct tape. This is going to hurt." She wrapped their legs and mouths in about a dozen layers. "All done. What's next?"

Max flew into J.P.'s arms, kissing him on the cheeks and forehead. "You are certifiably, irreversibly nuts. That was beyond crazy. What is wrong with you?" She let go, slugged him in the shoulder, and then hugged him again.

"I love you too. I said 'diversion,' not start World War III."

"No harm, no foul," Lisa offered. "I figured it out, and I went along for the ride. Speaking of that, where did you get the key? They took it away when they brought you in."

"They found the key I wanted them to find. You two make excellent assistants. Maybe we should take this act on the road, make some money with it." He turned to the Days family. "Are you guys OK? Anyone else hurt?" Cher was hugging Mark so tight his breathing had slowed down, and his face gained a light purple tint.

"What if they used flex-cuffs or rope?" Lisa smacked J.P. gently on the forehead.

"I had a different trick planned." J.P. winked and turned to Mrs. Days.

"Thank you," Mrs. Days said, rubbing her wrists. "That was a neat trick, but they could have killed you, Mr. Morgan. We're OK, except for my daughter's leg, but it's just a flesh wound. She'll be OK as soon as we get her to a doctor. How do we get out of here?"

J.P. measured the wall separating Clancy's private office. He traced an imaginary shape on it with the tip of the silencer. "There is nothing on the other side of the wall. In the opposite corner is a trapdoor to the roof. We can climb the fire escape down the side. They will be busy downstairs for a while." He checked his watch. "The cavalry should be here by now, ready to storm the fortress. What do you say we get out of their way?"

He stepped back, calculated the position of the studs, and shot the entire clip, creating the approximate shape of a door. He reloaded with a clip he had retrieved from Parker. "We proceed by hand." J.P. hit the wall with his shoulder, and the drywall shattered. He kicked the other side with his foot, and then they all worked on breaking down the drywall. All hostages joined in, breaking away the wall pieces.

Coldwell made a noise, attempting to attract attention. Max walked up to him and clubbed him with the butt of his own gun. She moved to Parker and administered him a similar blow. Lisa joined her, took the pistol from Max's hand, and hit Parker twice in the face. "That's for Arlene. She was my best friend and a wonderful woman." Lisa walked over to Coldwell and pistol-whipped him too. "Just because I'm pissed," she hissed, seeing Max's look.

"It's about damn time you got mad, sister," retorted Max.

They filed through the hole between two metallic studs. J.P. went last and headed for the trapdoor. As expected, he found it locked. He lifted a neck pillow from Clancy's chair and then shot the lock through it. The ambient noise drowned the report of the gun. He pushed the trapdoor open and then slid down. He knew he had triggered a silent alarm. He activated the speakerphone on the desk and dialed.

Cher urged her mother up the stairs and then Mark, and she followed them.

"Nine-one-one. State your emergency." The crisp voice drew J.P.'s attention.

"Patch this line to the local police, FBI, State Police and DHS. Be quiet, and keep the line open, no matter what you hear," J.P. whispered, leaning over the phone.

When the Days family was out of sight, J.P. shoved Lisa toward the stairs.

"What about you?" Lisa grabbed J.P.'s arm.

"Do not worry about me. I am not done yet. You two get out. Eric and Jack are outside."

"If you're not leaving, I'm staying with you," Max stated with conviction.

"Me too," Lisa joined in, adopting a defiant stance.

"Leave now, before I shoot you myself. This is not what I came here for." J.P. gripped them both by the arm and propelled them toward the stairs.

"No way, you big bully. We're staying." Lisa squirmed to free herself from his grasp.

The kick tore the door off its hinges. Clancy walked in behind four armed men.

"Throw your guns down!" yelled the SWAT-clad men. J.P., Max, and Lisa let their weapons drop to the floor.

"You are resourceful. I'll give you that, Morgan. Again, too bad you're not working with us." Clancy ordered his men to take positions at his sides. He lifted his radio and ordered Purcell to chase down and apprehend Sonny Days's family.

"Heil Clancy." J.P. stood at attention and clicked his heels. His right arm shot up then his fist bounced back over his heart. "I do not know that I could. Not my style."

"I should have killed you the first time I laid eyes on you. However, that is one mistake I will easily correct now." Clancy reached for an MP5 from his men and pointed it at Morgan.

"If you kill me, all that stuff goes to the people and the media. *True Patriot Day* will be nothing but the biggest mass murder in US history. You will be just like Hitler when the Allies reached Berlin. Please keep in mind your new best friends, the local gangbangers. I should probably call them again soon." J.P. smiled and checked his watch with a deliberate motion.

"Maybe I cannot shoot *you* yet. However, you'll tell me what I need to know." Clancy aimed the gun at Max's gut. "Or she dies first, slowly and painfully, while you watch." He shifted the sights of the gun to Lisa. "Then her, equally slow and painful. Oh, nothing personal, Ms. Jensen. Your boss wanted me to deliver a message. He appreciates all your services over the years, and he meant *all of them*. However, with his new job coming up, he won't need you anymore. You might say you could be a hindrance."

Lisa's look required no clarification.

In the warehouse, all hell broke loose. Warning shouts erupted, followed by minor explosions, gunfire and screams.

"You two. Check it out." Two men peeled off.

"A contingent of unknown people invaded the warehouse and started shooting," one of the SWAT team members reported from the catwalk.

CHAPTER 138

"**C**EASE FIRE! CEASE FIRE!**"** The unmistakable baritone voice of Lieutenant Colonel Ramos boomed. "We ask that you surrender, and we will spare your lives."

"Go out there and help. Those are gangbangers trying to rob us," Clancy ordered.

Three of them started down the walkway toward the stairs. Clancy handed the MP5 back to his last man. "Keep an eye on them until I return. Nobody comes in here."

"Is anyone there? Was that gunfire?" the 911 operator screamed.

Clancy sprinted to his desk and read the LCD display. He hung up without a word.

"Nine-one-one. I can handle this. Keep them here until I get back." He grabbed the portable file case and then climbed on the fire escape as the firefight resumed in the warehouse.

Morgan grabbed the heavy paperweight from the desk and hurled it at the last standing SWAT member, closing the distance to him in its wake. The fake rock connected with the man's nose and sent him flying backward. J.P. body-slammed him, ripped the MP5 out of his hands, and hit him under the helmet, in the back of the head, before handcuffing him.

Max flung herself at the fire escape and grabbed Clancy's ankle, just as he was about to disappear onto the roof. She yanked hard, bringing him down. He crashed with a loud thud. The portable case file landed on the floor and broke open, sending a flurry of papers through the room. Max pounced on Clancy. She turned him over and placed her knee on his spine. "You don't get off that easy. You killed my friends and tortured an old woman to death."

J.P. retrieved the backup piece and extra magazines from the downed SWAT cop. Lisa collected the guns they had taken from Coldwell and Parker and then joined J.P. by the couch.

In the warehouse, the firefight seemed more subdued. Eventually, it slowed down to the occasional brief burst or single shot. Eric's voice roared once again. "This is Lieutenant Colonel Ramos, United States Marine Corps. We offer you one last chance to surrender peacefully, and we will spare your lives. We surrounded the building with a battalion of recon Marines. Put down your weapons. Come out with your hands above your heads."

"We fight to the last man and the last round. There is no surrender!" Purcell's voice roared in reply. Several *Hoorays* rumbled in support.

The noise got the departing SWAT men's attention, and they rushed back in. The first one caught a three-round burst from the MP5 in J.P.'s hands. He fell on his back, unconscious. The other two opened fire. J.P. and Lisa scrambled for cover behind the couch. Max leaped a fraction of a second before three rounds passed through the space where her head had been.

"Kill them all!" bellowed Clancy. He bounced to his feet and climbed the fire escape under the cover of gunfire from his SWAT detail. Max watched helplessly as he vanished out of sight. She smacked the floor and screamed in frustration, hiding behind the bureau.

J.P. switched the MP5 to fully automatic and handed it to Lisa. "Spray and pray," he said, pointing to the door.

She placed the weapon above the back of the couch and squeezed the trigger. The two SWAT officers plunged for cover on the walkway. J.P. stood from behind the couch to the side with a sidearm in each hand and shot all four knees out. Lisa ran out of ammo and pulled the MP5 down to reload. J.P. sprinted to the two SWAT officers wriggling on the floor and snatched their weapons. Lisa handcuffed them back-to-back. J.P. dragged the other unconscious SWAT cops and shackled all four of them like a human pyramid.

Max dashed toward the fire escape, pursuing Clancy.

"Damn it, Max!" J.P. yelled after her. "Max, get back here!"

"Have you ever killed anyone?" Lisa surveyed the room with scowling eyes.

J.P. gave his best impression of Arnie. "Yeah, but they were all bad guys."

The two conscious SWAT officers moaned in pain. Lisa walked through the hole in the wall and returned with the roll of packing tape, shaking it playfully. "Time to be quiet, girls."

"Son of a bitch got away, but the good guys are here. There is a sea of cop cars all around us," Max reported, sliding down the ladder submarine-sailor-style. She pointed at the tied-up SWAT. "What have you two been up to while I was chasing the bad guy?"

J.P. stretched his neck and took in the picture. Cops, Navy SEALs, and Marines, scattered throughout, hiding behind trucks and boxes, waited each other out. Jack, clad in J.P.'s bulletproof vest, squatted next to Eric, clad in US Marines' combat uniform. Multiple dead and injured bodies strewn around completed the horrific tableau.

"We get to keep that BBQ date with Marie," quipped J.P.

They ventured on the bridge and crouched, as gunfire erupted.

"What was that about gangbangers?" Lisa inquired, looking worried.

"I took an extra insurance policy, in case Clancy intended to shorten our life span."

Lisa's face reflected pure confusion. "What kind of insurance do gangbangers offer?"

"No need to worry about them. They are only interested in the money. Clancy and Purcell already moved it into position for tomorrow's strike."

Lisa resumed her interrogation. "How did they find out about the money?"

"It is a long story."

"Give me the headlines."

"I may have sent them pictures of it."

"Only you could come up with that. Let me guess. You didn't tell them it was counterfeit, did you?" Lisa asked, delight lighting up her face.

411

"It was a brief conversation. I was in a hurry to get here. Some details may have escaped me." J.P. displayed a sheepish grin.

"It figures." Lisa slapped her thigh and let out a short laugh. "I don't think it's such a good idea to have them barge in here in the middle of this firefight. It will only lead to unnecessary deaths. Morgan, stop them before anyone else gets hurt."

"I would not worry about it," replied J.P., making a dismissive gesture with his hand. He continued to scan the entire warehouse floor.

"Those gangs are armed, drugged and dangerous. If they think there's money here, they will come in. There could be bloodshed, more useless deaths. Stop this, J.P."

"I said not to worry." He flashed his *cat-that-ate-the-canary* smile. "I only had GPS coordinates for this place, so I gave them the address of the other warehouse in Florence."

CHAPTER 139

LISA LOOKED THUNDERSTRUCK AND struggled to find her words. Max rolled her eyes in mock disbelief. They imagined with pleasure the gangs assaulting the empty building. It felt fantastic to have a chance of ending the madness and return to their lives.

"You better pray they never find out who sent them on the wild-goose chase," said Lisa, barely able to contain her delight. She turned to Max. "Is he always like this?"

"You get used to it after a while. Otherwise, it's enough to drive you up the walls."

Gunfire subsided again. J.P. stole a look and located Purcell hiding behind a Humvee. He sprinted to the wall end of the catwalk and vaulted over the railing, ignoring Lisa and Max's shouts. He landed on top of the truck twenty feet away; tumbled on the canvas, discounting the pain caused by the metal beams; and rolled on the van beside it. He leaped on the Humvee, using it as a launch pad to propel himself onto Purcell. J.P. and Purcell hit the floor hard, and their guns clattered away. They sprung to their feet and faced each other.

"Your time has come, asswipe. Make your peace with whatever God you believe in." Purcell pulled an army KA-BAR knife and hurled himself at J.P., who sidestepped with ease.

Lisa lifted her head above the rail, taking in the situation. Then she stood and shouted, "I cannot believe all of you signed on to use nuclear and Biochemical weapons on the American people! These mad men tricked you into following their irrational agenda!"

"Are you crazy?" J.P. turned his head, motioning for her to get down.

Purcell nicked J.P.'s shoulder. J.P. stepped out of the way and smacked the back of Purcell's head, sending him headfirst into a Humvee. Purcell retaliated with a stab, missing J.P.'s throat by an inch. J.P. snaked his arm around Purcell's, stepped under it, and nearly tore Purcell's limb out of the socket. Purcell howled in pain as his bones and joints let out a sickening, crunching sound. Purcell recovered the knife with his left hand and retreated.

"Your boss chose to save himself." Lisa continued to preach. "If you stop fighting, we can end the insanity together and save countless lives."

"What proof do you have? I didn't sign up to use nukes or Bio-weapons! I have family." one officer yelled back. Two more voices supported him.

"Don't listen to her. She wants to trick you into surrendering to the gangs they called in to rob the place. We fight to the last man and the last round for our way of life, for a free country!" Purcell screamed, cradling his injured arm.

"Think about it. What is the biohazard gear for?" Lisa carried on.

"You have a death wish or something? Stay down until this is over," Max said.

A three-round burst from an MP5 narrowly missed Lisa's head as Max pulled her down. Lisa nodded, jolted by the narrow miss.

Purcell and J.P. resumed their death dance in a larger opening between vehicles. Purcell assailed in a constant madman-style. His disabled arm hung at an unnatural angle, giving him the look of a wrathful gorilla. Purcell's men came out, pointing their weapons at J.P. Marines and SEALs stepped out, aiming their rifles at Purcell's troops, who lowered theirs but stood their ground. They formed a circle between trucks, watching the fight.

"Purcell, I do not want to kill you. Your boss ran out of here like a rabbit. He chose to save his neck. All I want is Theo's location." J.P. shifted his weight, staring Purcell down.

"You know," Purcell stopped with a stunned look, "you're too late, Morgan. I will kill you tonight. Nobody ever caused me this much embarrassment in my entire life."

"Have it your way. All I want is Theo," repeated J.P. pointing toward the entrance. "There are more Feds out there than I knew existed. Your *True Patriot Day* is a bust."

Purcell responded by lunging at J.P., who stepped aside and hit Purcell in the temple, propelling him headfirst into the Humvee again.

"Give me Theo's location, and let's end this."

"Not in a million years. I will suck your eyes out of that fucking skull!" shouted Purcell, attempting to headbutt J.P., who avoided it without effort.

Soldiers and cops advanced into a tighter ring around them. Lisa and Max joined Eric and Jack's side. A dozen injured officers wriggled, moaning on the floor. One of the Marines bled from a nick on his left shoulder. Medics started tending to the wounded.

"No more useless death. Your leaders intend to use nuclear devices on our friends and families. We are talking about American lives, on American soil!" Lisa cried as loud as her lungs allowed her. Her face reddened with the effort. She wriggled free of Max's grasp.

Tactical lights created slices of darkness and brightness from the top windows. A bullhorn blasted, "This is Special Agent in Charge Paulson of the FBI. The building is surrounded. Drop your weapons and come out single file with your hands on your heads."

"Please, listen to us," Lisa pleaded. "I know it in my heart that you were not part of the plan to massacre Americans throughout the state."

"Shut up, bitch! You're ruining everything!" bellowed Purcell. He turned on her.

J.P. seized him by the throat and twisted his knife hand. J.P. slammed Purcell face down on the ground and kneeled on his spine. "Stay down."

"I'll kill all of you, motherfuckers. You don't understand. You can't prevent history from taking its due course." Purcell wriggled under J.P.'s knee, frothing at the mouth.

Jack took a pair of handcuffs from a cop, collected the knife out of Purcell's hand, and cuffed him. He lifted Purcell to his knees. "Knock it off. It's over."

"Brainless, fucking traitors. You won nothing. This is not even a setback." Purcell doubled backward with a sinister snigger. "We will still prevail. Tomorrow, America will experience its rebirth and take its rightful place in the world again."

"What is wrong with you? Do you want to die?" J.P. grabbed Lisa's shoulders.

Jack escorted Purcell away from the group and passed him off to two Marines. "We need to end this before the FBI barges in here." Jack addressed the men. "We want no more violence and death. I will step outside to negotiate with the Feds."

Purcell broke loose from the Marines. Using his dislocated arm, he grabbed an MP5 from one of his men and aimed at Lisa behind his back. "You, Goddamn bitch. It's all your fault." The MP5 barked a three-round burst, its report louder than a series of explosions.

J.P. leaped over and shoved Lisa out of the way. The first bullet went through, nicked the top of his right lung, and then lodged under Lisa's left shoulder blade. The second one pierced his right trapezius muscle. The third one bounced off his right temple. J.P. crashed backward into the truck and slid down into a heap. The bullet passing through J.P.'s chest spun Lisa towards the truck's hood. She rebounded and fell in slow motion on top of J.P., wailing in pain.

CHAPTER 140

MAX AND ERIC FIRED simultaneously. Purcell's head burst like a watermelon at the shooting range, spraying blood, brains and bone shards on the people standing around him.

Max let the gun fall and hurled herself on top of Lisa and J.P. "No, no, no... noooooo."

"Enough!" yelled Jack, stepping out in the open. "Everybody, weapons down."

"You heard the man. Let's have a cease-fire and tend to the injured. Whoever is in command, acknowledge," said Ramos, stepping in the middle of the human circle.

"Since Purcell is dead and Mr. Clancy left, we no longer have a commander. We accept the truce." Simpson spoke up, drawing approving nods from his men.

Max pushed Lisa off J.P., dragged his body flat on the cement slab, and then checked his pulse. She listened for his heartbeat. She heard nothing. "We need doctors and ambulances. Now!" Max glared at Jack and Eric, who sprinted toward the warehouse exit.

Timmons reached inside the nearest truck and brought two blankets and a First-Aid kit. Max tore a blanket out of his hands and threw it over J.P. Timmons stopped Lisa's bleeding. Two cops assisted Max in performing CPR on J.P. She shoved them out of her way.

"This getting-shot thing hurts like hell." Lisa sat up, cursing.

Max examined her shoulder, probing for the lodged round. "The bullet didn't have enough energy to go through your shoulder blade. That is good news. There is no shattered bone. You'll be OK. Keep your arm still." Max glared at Timmons. "Keep an eye on her."

"It's not that bad." She squinted at Timmons with grateful, agony-filled eyes. Timmons draped Lisa's shoulder with the second blanket, removed his belt, and secured it in place.

Max sat on the floor cradling J.P.'s head in her arms, sobbing and rocking him with the gentleness of a mother holding her child. "He's not breathing, Lisa. I think he's dead."

The circle tightened around them. Lisa crawled over to J.P., feeling for a pulse. She leaned over J.P.'s body, ignoring the free-flowing tears streaking her cheeks, and cupped his hand in hers. "You need to wake up, J.P.," she pleaded between hiccups. "You must give me a chance to redeem myself." She looked at the circle of hard-faced men and women surrounding them. "Two days ago, I would have sent him to death without shedding one tear. I would have celebrated with the best steak and champagne money can buy. Two days ago, I wanted him dead, and he couldn't stand me. Yet he came to help at incredible risk to himself."

Max started pummeling J.P.'s chest. "Don't. You. Dare. Die. On. Me. You promised you'd never leave me. You always keep your word. Wake up, J.P. Waaaaaakke uuuupppp."

"He's gone. I'm so sorry," uttered Lisa, placing J.P.'s hand on the ground. "I get it now. That's all he lived for all these years, to learn for sure he didn't murder his family."

"He still has *me*." Max shot Lisa a sideways glance filled with contempt, and Lisa's words died in her throat. Max continued to thump J.P.'s breastbone with animalistic fury. "Wake up and finish this. Don't you dare leave me with this mess on my hands."

Max shoved Lisa and Timmons out of her way and resumed CPR. She gave J.P. mouth-to-mouth and resumed hammering on his chest. Blood had left her lovely face, and she looked twenty years older, pale as a ghost. Devoid of energy, Lisa kneeled at their side, weeping.

J.P.'s chest wound spurted blood, and Max let out a triumphant yelp and then lowered her ear to his chest. She heard weak, erratic heartbeats. She kissed his forehead several times and then leaped to her feet. She seized a TAC radio and yelled into the mike. "Eric, Jack, J.P. is alive! Barely! He needs to go to the hospital right now!"

CHAPTER 141

OTSIDE THE WAREHOUSE LAY a surrealistic scene. Nearly one hundred federal agents pointed their weapons at twice as many local cops. The police officers had encircled the Feds. A sea of emergency vehicle flashing their lights surrounded them. Three SWAT vans and a mobile command center loomed at the edges. The tactical lights illuminated the entire area like a billboard. All weapons turned on Jack and Eric as they emerged.

"My name is Jack Hunter. Who is the scene commander?"

Commotion ensued, and then SAC Paulson, wearing an FBI bulletproof vest, strode through the ranks and stopped face to face with Jack. A few steps behind him jogged a heavyset man in his late fifties, wearing body armor marked *POLICE*. He introduced himself as Captain Jenkins. They both claimed to be the scene commander.

"Two scene commanders. It figures," scoffed Jack. "EMTs can go in. Hold off on anyone armed. We need to come up with a plan to make sure the bloodshed doesn't resume."

Agent Paulson lifted his radio and issued orders while Captain Jenkins continued to argue jurisdiction and procedure. Jenkins wanted to send his men in first to secure the scene under his authority. He also wanted to arrest Jack. Paulson informed him that Jack Hunter had already surrendered to the FBI, and Jack was technically in his custody.

Ramos's earbud tinkled with Max's excited voice, sharing news about J.P. being alive.

"Acknowledged. Stay put, Max. EMTs are coming in now. J.P. will be first one out." Eric pumped his fist in the air and motioned emergency personnel to hurry into the warehouse.

Around them, the paramedics rushed in, their gurneys and equipment rattling.

"We need to negotiate the rogue outfit's surrender. We must show some tact. If you storm in there, you may set off a nuke or release the plague in LA," stated Jack.

"What do you propose?" Audible grudge marked Jenkins's voice. "We sit on our hands while the gangs rob the place and get away clean?"

"Is there a place where we can talk in private?" asked Eric.

Jenkins pointed to his mobile command center. Paulson ordered the technicians to turn the recorders off and step outside. Ramos brought them up-to-date. With every word he spoke, the faces of those present became longer, and dread filled the cramped command center.

"Where would cops get nuclear and biological weapons?" Jenkins interrupted.

"Captain, Congressman Hunter and Colonel Ramos called us. Governor's orders are to minimize exposure to the site. That's why we didn't want local support until we assessed the situation," Paulson replied, drumming his fingers on the monitor next to him.

"You're in cahoots with a child murderer and a renegade Marine!" yelled Jenkins.

"Why am I a renegade, again?" Ramos's jaw danced under his cheek.

"We got a call for help. A band of turncoat Marines attacked LEOs on US soil. Even if you're acting in good faith, this is my town and my jurisdiction, Lieutenant Colonel."

"Agent Paulson, please remove this idiotic bureaucrat before I do something all of us will regret." Ramos inhaled sharply, the tension in his muscles threatening to rip his fatigues.

"You can't talk to me like that. This is my turf. You hear me, Lieutenant Colonel? Soon I'll have you busted down to private and thrown in jail for this." Jenkins worked himself into a good semblance of a squat body armor topped by a ripe tomato.

Jack struggled to contain his amusement. He knew the only reason Eric had not reacted was to make Jack's situation easier. Ramos did not put up with Jenkins's kind.

"Stand down, Captain." Paulson's voice was firm and glacial. "There could be nuclear or Biochemical weapons in that warehouse. The last thing we need is a turf dispute that would cause this area becoming uninhabitable for centuries."

"Fellow LEOs are under attack by gangs and need help. That's how we play it. If you don't like it, call my chief. Only he can order me to stand down." Jenkins stood defiantly.

"Normally, I wouldn't do this." Jack pulled his phone. "Don't worry, Dad. I'm with the FBI now. The cat's out of the bag. The situation is deteriorating, courtesy of the stubborn local police. We cannot locate and neutralize the special items, so long as the locals mark their territory. I'll let you talk to Captain Jenkins." Jack handed the phone to Jenkins with a disgusted look. "Governor Hunter would like a word with you."

Jenkins took the phone with apprehension.

"Here you go. Agent Paulson is in charge until *Daddy* gets here. Don't try to run, you hear? I'll be watching you." Jenkins returned the phone to Jack, posturing.

"Let's see if we can talk everybody down and locate those weapons." Jack motioned for Paulson and Ramos to follow. Jenkins fell in step. Eric glanced at Paulson.

"Captain Jenkins, you coordinate out here." Paulson stopped Jenkins. "Secure a perimeter five blocks around. Make sure your men pay attention to anyone, especially media, who might try to break through. Hold everybody trying to leave until this is over."

"I'm not letting him out of my sight." Jenkins pointed at Jack.

"I am in command, and I decide where resources get allocated. You stay out here and manage your personnel. There will be twenty federal agents arriving shortly from San Diego. When they get here, they will relieve my men who will join us while we interrogate everyone." Paulson clarified his position. Jenkins protested, spitballs flying with every breath.

"Captain, please follow my instructions, or I'll have you relieved. File all the complaints you want. Now, I only want to hear two words. Otherwise, I'll have you arrested for obstruction and interfering with a federal investigation." Paulson stood his ground.

"Yes... sir?" Jenkins replied in a throaty voice.

"You got it. Contact me only through my people. Otherwise, I trust you are capable to sort it all out here." He turned to follow Jack and Eric in, stopped, and pivoted back to Jenkins. "Do I need to remind you that everything discussed so far is confidential?"

Eric returned to the mobile command center. Jack walked inside the warehouse with Agent Paulson. Jack approached Captain Eisenhower, Eric's second in command. Around him, Marines, SEALs, and cops talked to one another in a friendly manner. When they saw Paulson, some weapons came up. Jack raised his hands and stepped between them.

"This is Special Agent Paulson of the FBI. He is the scene commander for now. You will address your grievances to me. He is not in a position to grant any favors." Jack held his palms up, quashing the chorus of complaints. "We have to work together. This is the time to set aside our differences and manage this crisis to a safe resolution."

"What will happen to us now?" Cornwall asked in a worried voice.

"It will be up to the Governor and the US Attorney, but we'll note your individual cooperation," Paulson replied in a professional voice.

Scoffs and unpleasant comments followed. Eventually, the crowd broke up, and they started searching the warehouse.

CHAPTER 142

"**Y**OU NEED TO ACTIVATE the contingency plans, all of them," Clancy launched into a tirade as soon as Myerson answered. "The Feds and local police showed up at Site B. After all that preparation, that pain in the ass, Morgan, screwed up our designs."

"Fucking Morgan. Where are the bombs and the money?" Myerson inquired.

"I had them moved into position this afternoon. Nobody will find them in time, but we still need the contingency plans to ensure that the mission succeeds. See to it."

"I will. You take care of your end of the deal, and I'll take care of mine. Keep in touch." Myerson's voice trembled with anxiety and anger. "Make sure nobody spills the beans about our true plans. We can always call for Trump's followers to help us finish this."

"Wait!" Clancy yelled. "We may need the sand coons and the spics alive as insurance for tomorrow. Make sure the warden keeps them alive."

"The warden will keep them alive until the nukes go off and not a minute longer. Those are the warden's orders. He will follow them to the letter," boasted the Big Man.

CHAPTER 143

GOVERNIOR HUNTER ARRIVED IN his chopper, as the search dwindled down. A battalion of Marine Expeditionary Force and two companies of National Guard arrived minutes later. A contingent of Irvine PD led by Lieutenant Sparks and Sergeant Pearce showed up to support Jack and Eric's team. Governor Hunter OK'd everyone's presence and help.

Agent Paulson briefed George Hunter and Colonel Smith, the Marines' commanding officer. Lieutenant Sparks, Sergeant Pearce, Jack and Eric joined the small group. "We searched the warehouse and found no traces of nukes, money, biological or chemical agents. We interrogated everyone and learned that early afternoon two trucks, three Humvees, and a mixing chamber vehicle left for destinations unknown. Three metallic crates matching those suspected of containing the nuclear devices were in the Humvees. Nobody knows what was in the big trucks, but they left fully loaded." The Governor absorbed the news with distress.

"The general conclusion is that only the top leaders and the teams that left with the materials had knowledge of that phase of the operation. Without further info, we are searching for a few needles in a haystack the size of California. Despite statewide BOLOs on the vehicles, none of them have been located yet," concluded Paulson.

"Are we doing anything proactive to locate and neutralize the threat?" the Governor asked, his voice trembling. Hunter's face became spotted with tiny red dots.

"We are speculating where the most likely strike points are. There is not enough time to evacuate every major city. There is serious resistance to going public with the story." Paulson resumed. "Panic will clog every road in the state by futile attempts to flee."

Colonel Smith decided to use the briefing room as the temporary command center and the old security office as a communication center. Governor Hunter assumed command.

Jack, Eric, Agent Paulson, Colonel Smith, Lieutenant Sparks, and Sam Miller, the leader of the NEST team, stood by to assist the Governor.

Jack briefed his dad on Sadowsky's statement and the existence of the recording of Artie and Alice's murder. The Governor listened, biting the inside of his cheek.

PART FOUR

July 4

"**C**HP PULLED OVER THE mixing chamber truck on Highway 62, at the 10 Freeway. They arrested the driver. He demanded to talk to Purcell, Clancy or a lawyer from a big Sacramento firm. A HazMat team is examining the truck." Lieutenant Sparks summarized.

"I'm going to get some shut-eye, or I may end up setting the bombs off myself," Miller announced, walking through the wall into Clancy's old office. "I had the weekend off."

Eric had been pacing the room. He scribbled "WWJPD" on the lower right corner of the board, took a step back, and scanned the California wall map again.

"What does that mean, Ramos?" asked Colonel Smith.

"It's an old thing from the time we worked together at Coronado. It stands for 'What Would J.P. Dream?'" replied Eric, tossing and catching the marker.

"Who or what in the hell is 'J.P.'?" Smith inquired.

"J.P. Morgan," Jack answered. "He discovered this scheme. All the intel we have results from his efforts. Otherwise, we would have found out about it on the news."

"Oh, that J.P. Why isn't he here?" Colonel Smith stood and lifted his radio.

"Purcell, the second in command of this outfit, shot J.P. earlier. He is fresh out of surgery, not awake yet, last time I checked." Jack surmised, joining Eric at the map.

"We must think like him," stated a raspy voice from the doorway.

"Good luck with that," Ramos chuckled. He turned toward the door and studied Sparks, who leaned on crutches, flanked by two uniformed Irvine PD officers.

"Who are you? How did you get in?" Paulson jumped out of his seat.

"Randy? You should be in the hospital." Old Man Sparks faced the group. "This is my son, Officer Randy Sparks. They shot him during the fiasco at UCI on Friday."

"Sir." Sparks faced the Governor. "Morgan stopped by to see me before coming here. I saw the evidence on the flash drive he gave me. This is the worst crisis California ever faced."

"It doesn't answer the question. Why are you here?" inquired George.

"To assist and pay my debt to Morgan." Sparks glanced at his cast. "May I sit down?"

"By all means, Officer, let's hear what you have to say." The Governor pointed at the seat next to him. "A fresh pair of eyes might be just what we need at this point."

Sparks gave a quick rundown of both encounters with Morgan.

The Governor's phone chirped. He scanned the screen and then stood, rubbing his eyes. "My wake-up call. I have a conference at ten o'clock this morning. I should cancel it."

"A conference scheduled on the Fourth of July?" Jack asked, stifling a yawn.

"The top members of the cabinet are meeting to discuss an emergency," George answered. "The new AG called for it last night—"

"What happened to Jim Simmons?" asked Lisa from the doorway. Her voice was coarse, and her left arm hung in a sling. She had borrowed a sweatshirt three sizes too large to cover up her bloody clothes. Beside her stood J.P., pale as a ghost, right arm wrapped tight against his chest, his shirt stained with blood around the bullet holes. A large bandage covered his shaved right temple. Behind them, Max's scowling expression required no interpretation.

Jack and Eric rushed to support J.P. to one bed. Lieutenant Sparks and Max guided Lisa, helping her sit down next to Sparks and Hunter.

"You look like the living dead." Jack addressed J.P. "What the hell are you doing out of the hospital? You got shot only hours ago."

"That seems to happen a lot these days," J.P. replied, hinting with his head to Sparks.

"Were any of you discharged?" Eric's gaze shifted from Lisa to J.P. and then to Sparks.

"What do you think?" thundered Max. "They bolted out of there like bats out of hell against medical advice. I could barely keep up with them."

"It's good to see you up and about, Ms. Jensen," offered George Hunter. He ignored J.P. and walked away from the beds.

"No big deal, just a scratch." Lisa winced. "Though without painkillers, I'd be Spider Woman right now. Back to my question, sir."

George Hunter acknowledged J.P.'s presence with a reluctant nod and resumed his talk with Lisa. "Jim died last week of a massive heart attack. Richard Clancy is the new AG."

"Clancy called the cabinet meeting for today?" Lisa asked. "Doesn't that worry you?"

"I didn't think of it until now. He called as soon as I signed the executive order, making him AG. He said he had information to share with the leadership, and it couldn't wait until after the weekend. He asked for a meeting today, and I set it for ten o'clock at Mary's dad's home." George Hunter rubbed his chin. "Sounds like the perfect setup to take all of us out."

"I can vouch for that. Earlier tonight, he admitted to me that was part of his plan." J.P.'s voice was weak and throaty. "He had the old AG murdered. Who else is attending?"

"He wanted everyone there, the entire cabinet and a few others. He insisted that the Lieutenant Governor, the President of the Senate, and the Speaker of the Assembly be there. He also asked for the Treasurer, said there was a need to allocate a special budget to correct this problem. They scheduled the Lieutenant Governor to attend that thing at the Rose Bowl. He hasn't confirmed either way yet. Everyone else is a definite attendant," replied Hunter.

"That's the entire succession line down to the AG." Lisa bit her lower lip.

CHAPTER 145

"**H**OW DID EVERYONE PLAN** to arrive for the meeting?" Smith chimed in.

"Most of them will drive or fly into John Wayne and then drive in. Clancy's been riding around in that damn helicopter since Jim died, as if he's the most influential man in California's history. He asked for permission to land at the estate for the meeting."

"Oh my God," Sparks interjected, leaping to his good foot and joining in. "He will not be in the helicopter. Morgan, you said one of the intended targets of the attack was 'somewhere in Orange County.'"

"Clancy dispatched the helicopter with one nuke to ensure none of you survived, and then he would step in as the new Governor," added J.P.

"It makes sense. To achieve the maximum effect, a nuclear weapon must detonate at a certain altitude," Ramos uttered in a pensive voice.

"That is one diabolical yet bold plan," offered Paulson. "Where does that leave us?"

"They moved the nukes and the money out of here before our raid," muttered Jack.

"Get a list of every aircraft cleared to fly over California today. Cross-reference the list with this group and the AG's office. Notify the FAA that all non-commercial flights over California are grounded or rerouted until further notice," Paulson commanded into his radio.

"I don't think we have the authority to do that." The reply sounded hesitant.

"The Governor is behind this." Paulson glanced at George, who nodded. "Screw the noisemakers. This is about saving lives. Blame it all on me."

"He would not be on that helicopter," said J.P. "Hmm..."

"What does that mean?" Jack questioned J.P.

"We've been looking for these things somewhere, right?" cried Sparks.

"Yes. That's how it usually works," George said, his eyes darting around the room.

"But we are searching at random." J.P. felt his heartbeat quickening, and he beamed at Sparks. "Great catch. Let's find out if they were told to stay away from certain areas."

"Geniuses." Paulson whipped out the radio. "Wake everyone up, the ones we arrested here tonight, and the wounded. Interview them again." Paulson pointed to Lisa and J.P. and then to Sparks. "Even if getting shot makes me smarter, I don't want to try it."

"Sir." Smith stood at the Governor's side. "I would like permission to deploy armed aircraft and personnel at strategic locations to intercept and neutralize the threats."

"Approved. But, Colonel, please hold off on starting a war."

"I'm afraid this war has already started, Governor. All I can promise you is that we will do our best not to allow them to cripple us with their first strike."

CHAPTER **146**

CLANCY PACED IN FRONT** of the pilots, hands clasped behind his back, head held high. In the background, the three helicopters, rotors hanging, resembled giant sleeping birds. "You'll soon depart to fulfill your missions. Today is the most momentous day of your lives. At the end of this task, you'll earn your place in history, your families' freedom, and their right to live in this great country. America will be the greatest country again. Questions?"

"No, sir," the pilots answered in unison.

"Get to preflight preparations. Dismissed." Clancy walked to the barn, avoiding a small pool of jet fuel that had leaked from the refueling truck.

Clancy examined the work of technicians who had been laboring over the final details of arming the nuclear weapons. "Are you done here?"

"Yes, sir. If we could address payment for emergency handling and extra travel time, we'll be out of here in a flash," answered their leader, wiping his hands.

"I'll handle it as soon as the banks open on Monday," Clancy cut him off.

"This job was super-rush and cash on completion," the man insisted.

"Where am I going to get that kind of cash at this hour, on the Fourth of July? I'll handle it tomorrow. I'll add a 10 percent bonus for handling this so quickly and professionally. Is that acceptable?" Clancy's attitude showed he encouraged no further discussion.

"I guess so. Thank you, sir." The man took a quick step back.

Clancy strode to the main house. He motioned for his newly promoted chief of staff to follow him into the private study. "Take a team and intercept them as soon as they leave."

CHAPTER 147

"**W**E HAVE TWO AWACS,** four drones, NEST, Disaster Assistance Response Teams, and Army Radiological Advisory Medical Teams ready. Smith updated the Governor.

"Should we request FEMA assistance and federal government support for any negative outcome?" Smith asked the Governor in a whisper.

"We can't fail, Colonel," intervened Paulson. He got on his radio and threatened to send everyone to Alaska. He clicked off and reported, "So far, nothing mind-blowing. We believe the other two nuclear attacks will be in the Bay Area and LA, but there is no consensus on locations. If we add the Governor's wife estate, it accounts for the three nukes."

"The 49ers new stadium and the Rose Bowl," said Ramos. Curious eyes scrutinized him. "Both Northern and Southern California are hosting festivities, games, and all-day parties. They invited me to attend the Rose Bowl celebration, before I got involved in this. The Rose Bowl makes sense from two perspectives. The Lieutenant Governor may be there."

"Find the closest airfields and look for helicopters authorized to take off this morning!" exclaimed Jack. "Good catch, Eric. I didn't think of that."

Hunter called the President to request permission to engage in preventing the impeding disasters. The President replied, "George, don't kill civilians. I don't want to justify it on TV."

Jack, J.P., and Sparks argued on the couch. The Governor finished his briefing call to the President and addressed them. "Care to let us in on your disagreement?"

"It's not a disagreement," Jack replied. "We have a difference of opinion over the most effective delivery method for the tainted currency. We are convinced they'll use aircraft to deliver the contaminant to ensure the maximum dispersal pattern. However, I'm thinking helicopters. Randy and J.P. believe they will use small planes."

"Elaborate, please." Colonel Smith stepped closer.

"They did not plan on getting caught," J.P. said, wheezing. "They would use helicopters for the nukes, because the explosions would obliterate the aircraft, and after the fact, they could spin the story." He stopped, fighting visible pain.

"If they use helicopters for the money, there will be witnesses." Sparks picked up. "Drop a bunch of money from a chopper, it gets noticed. Planes fly higher. By the time the money hits the ground, the aircraft is long gone, and it ensures a larger dispersal area."

"They planned to get away with it and blame it on patsies. It makes sense. I think they are right," Lisa said, patting J.P. and Sparks on the shoulders, causing both to wince.

"Where was the mixing truck coming from?" Eric stopped in front of the map.

"What truck?" Lisa attempted to connect the dots.

"CHP intercepted the mixing chamber truck J.P. photographed. We think they used it to contaminate the bills with a Biochemical agent." said Jack.

"If that assumption is correct, that truck would return from an airport. A hangar would provide enough privacy for that entire job," put in J.P., his voice growing weaker.

"J.P., we appreciate you are here and everything you did. I think you should go back to the hospital right now." Jack voiced everyone's opinion.

"I am OK," J.P. said with a light chuckle. "It only hurts when I breathe."

"Go on." Colonel Smith pointed to Ramos, his ears perking up. "I understand Mr. Morgan's reluctance to leave. Wild horses couldn't drag me away right now."

"Any airports along Highway 62?" Jack completed his friend's thought.

Eric's finger was already tapping the Twentynine Palms Airport icon.

"Get the base commander on the phone," George ordered Colonel Smith.

"Sir," Smith shook his head. "If they scheduled their aircraft to fly from there, General Rollins is in on it. Nothing goes on at that base he doesn't know about."

"Handle it the best way you see fit, Colonel," George Hunter commanded.

"General, send all nearby available troops, hazmat teams, NEST and DARTs unannounced," Colonel Smith relayed orders to the air support operational commander.

"Dispatch local LEOs to the airport. Check with FAA for flight plans out of Twentynine Palms," Lieutenant Sparks relayed the order to police and FBI assets.

"I hope we reasoned correctly. We know we are guessing with no solid basis." Lisa summed it up, closing her eyes in prayer.

"The FAA reports no out-of-the-ordinary or new flight plans filed out of the Twentynine Palms Airport," Agent Paulson communicated in a matter-of-fact voice.

"No flights left Twentynine Palms this morning. A check of all hangars and structures yielded no results. The team reports General Rollins is threatening to order his men to open fire, unless someone explains to him what's going on," Colonel Smith informed Hunter.

Max and J.P. studied the map. Sparks joined them, fighting to maintain his balance on crutches. He looked over their shoulders, sensing the frustration build-up. "What do you see?"

"That's just it," replied Max, tapping her foot. "Nothing but desert, miles and miles of empty space and sand. That truck had to be returning from somewhere out there."

"There is nothing out that way but the new prisons south of Cadiz," Governor Hunter joined them. "This private outfit built them. I remember signing the bill a few months ago."

"Say that again!" cried Sparks and Lisa simultaneously.

CHAPTER 148

"**E**VERYTHING IS IN PLACE** on my end. The money's been processed and loaded. Backup teams are in position, ready to carry out the contingency plans. You make sure your helicopters deliver their payloads on time, and we are home clear, no matter what George's people are doing," said Myerson, sipping from the expensive crystal tumbler.

"Pilots are ready to go and eager to complete their missions. They bought the whole thing," replied Clancy. His tone was once again upbeat.

"Why wouldn't they? It was official." Myerson let out his signature evil chuckle.

"Are you prepared for your part in the aftermath? Do all our men have credentials and proper instructions?" Clancy asked, though he knew the answer.

"Of course. Relax, Governor. We took care of everything. By noon, you'll take your place at the helm. Then we start preparations for the White House."

"I trust you will take care of all the details on your end from here on. Let's talk again at 9:00 A.M. to confirm," replied Clancy in a buoyant voice. "Then I'll be on my way to Sacramento."

"My people will start spinning up the Trump cells everywhere. Have Purcell issue the order for all CDoHP personnel to move into position and take control of all troops. This is it, Governor. See you Sacramento."

CHAPTER 149

"**O**UT BY BRISTOL DRY LAKE**, this private outfit, Golden something, built five maximum-security prisons." George Hunter sensed his statement carried strange importance.

"Golden Trident Security, by any chance?" J.P. said, visibly animated. His energy had shifted, and pain no longer seemed to bother him.

"Yeah, that's it. We dispatched a team from Justice and Corrections on Friday for the final inspection." George looked puzzled.

Sparks dropped his crutches as he yelled, "Yeah!" then collapsed to the floor, missing the chair by an inch. "They have their own airstrip or airfield. Their spokesperson gave a presentation at a law enforcement seminar. He hammered it to death."

"That's it," added Lisa. "Phil's been talking about this new place for months."

Smith and Paulson both started shouting orders on their radios. Governor Hunter issued instructions of his own. Ramos called his troops to help coordinate.

"This time, I know we got it right." Jack's voice sounded confident.

Sparks winced in pain. Lisa handed him a couple of her own pain pills. "Max wouldn't allow us to leave the hospital without them. We owe her."

Paulson's private phone rang. He answered it with a perplexed look. "Franks, what the hell?" Paulson's face reddened and dark thunder clouds gathered above his head. "We need him alive, but you have my blessing to soften him up." Paulson punched a hole in the drywall.

"Agent Paulson, your hand is bleeding." Jack broke the silence afterward. The entire evening, Paulson was the calmest of them all. His reaction had everyone on the edge.

"They have a mole in the bureau. Son of a bitch disappeared in the confusion. My people cross-referenced this outfit and stumbled on calls to a private phone they tracked to our own ASAC, James Harrelson. His cousin is one of the people hurt during Colonel Ramos's incursion." Paulson kicked the desk with all his might. "This is my fault."

"That's bad news," Ramos said. "But it's not your mistake. Can we find him?"

"I'm sure he went into hiding, and he'll wait for the storm to pass. He knows that if we get him, he will be in a world of hurt," Paulson replied with obvious pain. "The matter is that he knows all our plans. He has an FBI issue radio, and I bet he's been listening in."

"Why are you blaming yourself?" asked the Governor.

"Harrelson did not inform me of the Bristol Dry Lake facilities, even though the men we arrested talked about it. Last night, I instructed local LEOs to contact me only through my men. As second in command, he chocked the flow of information. Franks just figured it out." Paulson faced George Hunter. "You may relieve me now or when you decide it's appropriate."

"Not your fault, Agent. No sense in crying over spilled milk. Let's find the WMDs," Jack intervened. "From here on, we use military communications only."

"My men switched to mobile phones, but they are sure Harrelson overheard the orders about Bristol Dry Lake," Paulson said, avoiding Jack's eyes.

Lisa retrieved a First-Aid Kit, waking up Sam Miller. She tended to Paulson's hand.

"What's new? Have we found anything yet?" asked Miller.

Before anyone could answer, Paulson's phone chirped. "I'll put you on with Congressman Hunter. Deal with this please," Paulson handed Jack his phone.

"Update from the FAA. DOJ requested clearance for two helicopters to fly from SFO and Van Nuys Airport to test surveillance gear and provide support to local law enforcement. According to their respective departure times, they should be on the ground at their assigned airports, yet neither of them is where it should be," Jack concluded.

"The AWACS have radiation detection gear. They fly too high to detect weak sources. If they store the bombs in lead-lined boxes, it's damn near impossible. They would have to be on top of the source. Can we ask them to come down to twelve thousand feet?" Miller asked.

"That would cut effective area to one-fifth. We don't have another detection aircraft in range," Colonel Smith answered, glancing at the map. "We do not equip the domestic drones with radiation detecting gear, and the sources are too weak to be picked up by satellites."

"We need to concentrate on the Bay Area and Greater LA, right?" asked J.P., glancing at Eric. "Stadiums as targets reduce the radius to only a few miles."

"I'll re-task them. Can you give me something definite to make the move effective?" Colonel Smith turned to Miller, hope permeating from his voice.

"For now, move them closer to Southern Bay Area and Northern LA. I'll have new parameters for you by the time they are in position. Ask them to drop to fifteen thousand feet and report anything that shows up on their scopes, even if it only seems to be a ghost."

"Will do. Anything else we need to know or do in the meantime?" Smith inquired.

"NEST choppers are in San Fran and LA. The Navy has a few of them at Lemoore, but they have a limited range, although the moment they get a scent it would be the real thing. As soon as the AWACS sniff something, vector in the NEST helicopters, and call me. I'll start running numbers." Miller returned to the adjacent room with his bag and briefcase.

"I'll lend him a hand," Max said, following Miller into Clancy's old office.

CHAPTER 150

THE FLEET OF MARINE vehicles approached at breakneck speed.

The plane crews scrambled to take off, abandoning vehicles and gear on the runway.

"Strauss, that aircraft could carry WMDs. They do not get off the ground under any circumstances. Exercise caution," Colonel Alexander ordered his second in command.

Six Humvees broke off and cut across the field toward the runway. It was agonizingly clear they would never catch up to the planes. Major Strauss attempted to raise the plane crews on the radio. He gave up and switched frequencies. "Montreal, you must prevent the planes from taking off without blowing them up." Strauss turned his eyes skyward.

"How in God's name do I do that?" Lieutenant Montreal looked at the radio, puzzled.

"May I, sir? I always wanted to try this." Gunnery Sergeant Addison asked.

Montreal made a by-your-leave gesture. Addison ordered two Humvees to stop and then leaped out, accompanied by three soldiers. They fanned out and raised antitank weapons, aiming at the speeding aircraft. Addison explained to his men what he wanted to accomplish.

"For God's sake!" yelled Montreal. "They could have nukes on board."

Addison turned and winked. "Look on the bright side, LT. If we screw up, we'll be soaring with angels before we realize what happened." Ignoring Montreal's scowl, he returned his attention to the runaway and ordered, "Fire."

Four streaks of rocket fuel exhaust marked the trails of the speeding RPGs. On impact, the combined explosions rocked the valley surrounding the airstrip. Two charges detonated about one hundred feet in front of each aircraft, creating small craters. The planes' wheels dipped into the smoldering holes and broke off. The giant birds slid on their noses and bellies, churning up dirt and tarmac pieces until they came to a full stop.

The troops cheered victorious, observing the occupants of both planes sprint across the runway to the hills on the opposite side. "Outstanding job, *Master* Gunnery Sergeant Addison." Montreal patted Addison on the back, beaming with pride. "Now, catch me some rabbits."

"With pleasure, sir." Addison motioned for the vehicles behind them to pursue. A Texas-sized grin flashed on his sunburned face.

CHAPTER **151**

"PRESERVE SAMPLES, THEN BURN** it all. Squeeze the crews for info," Colonel Smith ordered. He turned, facing the Governor. "We found an amount of money consistent with four pallets. Our troops detained the aircraft, pilots and crews tasked with spreading it."

"Thank God," uttered Hunter, gesturing with urgency for Smith to continue.

"The pilots received new orders only minutes ago. Someone told them to take off, because they were about to get robbed. They had directions to fly toward San Diego and Sacramento and drop the money along the way, in the most heavily populated areas. They refused to acknowledge instructions to wait on the ground for FAA approval. They know the bills are counterfeit and claim it was all part of a test tracing program approved by DOJ." Smith remained at attention.

"Unbelievable. They wanted to infect the entire state with this plague. This could affect millions of people, children. Who can conceive a plan like this? Who can carry it out without question?" George Hunter sat down and dropped his head in his hands.

"I don't think the pilots and crewmen knew what they were in for. They were not using protective gear. Either they received inoculations, or, more likely, they're not supposed to survive. Interesting fact, pilots and crews asked for Purcell or Clancy by name and insisted they'd speak only to them or a Sacramento lawyer, just like the truck driver." Smith concluded.

"Biochem threat contained. Question the pilots and their crews. We need to find those damn nukes," Jack Hunter reminded them.

"Any other ideas, people? Anything, no matter how crazy it sounds. I'd like to find them before we see mushroom clouds." He slipped an arm around his dad, something he had not done for years, and his father patted his knee.

"A ground crew member at Van Nuys Airport recalls the pilot of the chopper missing was pissed last night. He was ranting about an unscheduled trip to get some new equipment installed. The pilot left without a flight plan," Lieutenant Sparks said in a somber tone.

"Did you ask the tower where he went?" Paulson jumped in.

"Tower tracked him due north. Ground control does not know where he went past the mountains. We're checking with SFO," Lieutenant Sparks reported.

"No one thought to mention it earlier?" Paulson turned to face a group whose hearts were pounding with eager anticipation.

"The pilot of the chopper scheduled to fly from SFO received a similar call last night. He flew south for retrofitting. He told the ground crew he needed to test something and then fly to get the new equipment installed," Lieutenant Sparks relayed the news.

Colonel Smith ordered both AWACS to merge and concentrate on the area between San Francisco Bay Area and Los Angeles, hoping for a break.

"Let's recap. The Biochem stuff was at the new prisons, which they controlled. We know the helicopters are somewhere north of LA and south of San Fran." Jack said.

"That's a mighty big area," Colonel Smith scoffed, pacing in front of the map. "Without something more specific, it'll take weeks to check it."

"Airports have radiation detectors and too many prying eyes. I think they are using helicopters to deliver of the nukes to avoid that. Choppers can land pretty much anywhere, but their range is more limited than a plane," J.P. said.

A knock at the door interrupted him. A female Marine Corporal ambled in, carrying a portable, secure radio. She scanned the room, unsure of what to do. She snapped at attention.

"Sirs, I am not sure about protocol here."

"Don't worry about protocol, Corporal," said George Hunter.

"Sir, yes, sir." She faced Colonel Smith. "Sir, I have a Major Strauss on the comm, who will only speak with you. He asked that this channel be private, sir." She handed the radio to Smith, then she continued to stand at attention.

"This is Colonel Smith. What do you have for us, Major?"

"Colonel, this is rather strange, sir. I think it relates to our problem. We sent patrols to check the prison buildings. One patrol met resistance and gunfire."

"Cut to the chase, Major."

"Yes, sir. We found seven women and fifteen children, sir. Three women and six children are Arabs. The rest are Latinos. They all have bizarre stories to tell. They arrived here on private planes to be with their fathers, husbands, whatever. The two Latina women are sisters-in-law. They've been held captive for five days now. Two days ago, the guards moved them off premises and allowed them to speak with their husbands briefly by phone. They returned to the confinement area just a few hours ago."

"What is it about, Major?" George Hunter asked over Smith's shoulder.

"Who is that?" Strauss exclaimed as if the radio had burned his ear.

"That was Governor Hunter," Colonel Smith clarified. "Continue."

"Two of the women had photographs of their husbands. You will not believe this, sir. The two pilots we detained are their husbands. We got similar stories from all of them. Four are relatives of the pilots or crewmen of the planes with tainted money," Strauss reported.

"We need the names of the helicopter pilots." Jack jumped in.

"Identify yourself," snapped Major Strauss.

"That was Congressman Hunter. His orders come from the Governor and the President. The pilots' names, Major?" Colonel Smith cut in, leaning into the radio.

"Abu Said Harami and Jose Chaquerres," answered Strauss without hesitation. "I'm sending pictures and bios to your location, sir."

"Major, Jack Hunter again. Take the families outside. Let them see their loved ones are safe, then interrogate everyone again. We need to find out everything they know."

"Yes, sir. Out," replied Strauss.

"Clancy and his lot thought this through, and they almost got away with genocide. They waged war against all Californians. We must find and hang them, like war criminals, every single one of them," Ramos pitched in and resumed pacing.

"That's quite a speech, Eric. I wish it were possible," George Hunter said and then exhaled. "I have to update the President."

"They coerced innocent pilots into carrying out acts of terrorism, acts of war. They used their families against them. That's unconscionable." Lisa shook her head in disgust.

"We still need to find those nukes." J.P. grounded everyone in a quiet, calm voice.

"The FAA and military radars tracked the helicopters part of the way. A combined report showed their last known headings to intersect in the Peachtree Valley. I vectored in the AWACS from Northern California to investigate," reported Colonel Smith.

"Agent Paulson, cross-reference land ownership in the area with information we have." J.P.'s voice dissipated with each word. "Clancy's family might own land there. Or Myerson's."

CHAPTER 152

"C OLONEL SMITH, SIR," Major Strauss's voice boomed from the secure radio.

"Go ahead, Major."

"The moment the pilots and crewmen saw their families, they started talking. Their accounts are the same. They wanted to bring their families to America and experienced unusual bureaucratic delays. A few weeks ago, someone from the DOJ promised to straighten all the paperwork and bring them in. In exchange, they had to help the government crackdown on terrorist cells and drug dealers. They've been told the chemically treated they would use money to track patterns of the drug trade supporting terrorist activities. The warden threatened, if they broke silence, their families would be sent back and never be allowed to return to the US."

"Any information about the helicopters, the pilots, location of the bombs?" Jack grabbed the mike out of Smith's hand.

"None, sir," replied Strauss in a pained voice. "All we got are the names and various bits of useless info from the families. Nobody here knows where they are right now."

"Sirs, we have contact with a potential source of radiation," reported the AWACS plane on course to the Peachtree Valley.

"Drop to ten thousand feet and put the pedal to the metal. Vector in on that source at maximum speed and keep this channel open at all times." Colonel Smith took charge. Smith ordered the standby units to take off from San Francisco, Los Angeles, and Lemoore Naval Air Station. He instructed them to converge and dispatched back up on the ground.

A few minutes later, the AWACS reported the faint source had vanished. "What do you mean, you lost the source? How can it disappear?" Colonel Smith berated the officer.

"I only report the facts, sir. I don't make them up," the AWACS technician answered. "One moment, it was there. The next, it faded, and then it was gone, just like that."

The second AWACS, flying in from the south, reported seeing a faint source of radiation, approximately thirty miles due south of the coordinates given by the first AWACS.

J.P. jumped in. "They took off toward their intended targets. Colonel Smith, redeploy assets from the south to intercept the source on the southern course. Keep all other units going on their present course. Seize and bring them down any which way you can, Colonel." J.P. glanced at the Governor, asking for silent approval.

Smith issued the orders in his darkest voice, with quivering lips.

"They took off, sirs. The remaining source split up," the technician aboard the northern AWACS barged in. "We are now tracking three faint sources. One headed north to the Bay Area, the other two south to LA. The sources headed south are about thirty miles apart, sirs."

"God help us now!" exclaimed Hunter, and he picked up the phone to call the President.

Ramos took charge of the aircraft task force. "Establish contact with the pilots and force them to land by any means necessary."

Colonel Smith issued orders at a furious pace, scrambling every available unit to intercept. Lisa touched his tense arm and startled him. "Ms. Jensen? What do you need?"

"The helicopter pilots don't know their families are safe. They believe the penalty for breaking radio silence is losing their loved ones. You may never get them to answer," she said.

"Thank you, Counselor." Smith grabbed the radio mike and commanded Major Strauss to bring the families of the two helicopter pilots to his side.

"Three choppers, two pilots identified. Who is the third?" wondered J.P. out loud.

"I've been asking myself the same question," Colonel Smith joined in. "I cannot wrap my head around it. He must be someone they keep the family at a different location."

"Or someone fanatically loyal to the cause and determined to see it through, even if it costs him his life," Ramos added. "Someone with nothing to lose."

"The most dangerous enemy there is." Paulson frowned. "God, please help us stop this madness."

CHAPTER 153

"**H**OW THE HELL DID** they find the planes? The leak must be on your end." screamed Myerson, spittle forming spider-egg-sized white balls at the corner of his mouth.

"I don't know. There was nothing at Site C to link the prisons to any of our activities, so Morgan couldn't figure it out from that," Clancy replied, taken aback by Myerson's reaction. "Maybe someone arrested at Site B talked. I don't know."

"Did you mention anything to that asshole, Morgan? I told you he could pull crap out of thin air. You should have killed him first chance you had. That was a huge mistake."

Clancy considered relating J.P.'s stunt involving the Internet bomb and gangbangers. He decided against it. He did not wish to hear any more belittling comments from Myerson. "We never broached the subject. He somehow deduced we intended to use the money as a delivery agent for the genetically altered Y. pestis, although he didn't know what it was. He never asked, and I didn't tell him anything." Clancy closed his defensive speech.

"At least tell me that the choppers are on their way!" yelled Myerson.

"They took off a few minutes ago. I'm sure this place is still a secret." Clancy tried to sound reassuring, though his voice faltered.

"We can still do this. It will not be as spectacular, but it will be effective enough." Myerson decided. "Make sure your men carry out their assignments without fail. We cannot afford to screw up now, for god's sake."

"I never liked the idea to use the bubonic plague your Doc Jones cooked up on the American people." Clancy backpedaled. "Maybe it's better—"

"Grow a pair, Governor. If you want history to remember you as a great savior, you must create a little havoc. Omelet, eggs."

"Whatever. I had to eliminate the technicians you sent to my ranch. They demanded immediate payment, and I didn't like their attitude. They were dangerous loose ends."

"Did they finish the work?"

"Yes."

"They served their purpose. Let's regroup and carry on. This is too important. One or two million casualties is a small price to pay. Totally acceptable."

CHAPTER 154

MAJOR STRAUSS REPORTED HE had the families standing by. Smith ordered them patched through to the pilots. A scared woman's voice, speaking Arabic, called out her husband's name several times then broke down, sobbing and pleading.

No response.

After an awkward silence, another woman, speaking Spanish, equally hesitant, implored her husband to answer. She let him know they were all safe, including his sister and nephew. Her voice broke up, and a second woman took over and spoke in a sweet, low tone, calling to her brother in both English and Spanish.

"It's not working. You may have to shoot them down," Strauss interceded.

"Isabella, es de verdad? ¿Eres tú, mi hermanita?" A man's voice came through the waves. ("Isabella, is it true? It's you, little sis?")

The first Spanish-speaking woman interceded and launched into a torrent of words, half-talking, half-yelling. She pleaded with him to follow the task force's instructions.

"This is Jose Chaquerres. I am prepared to surrender, Colonel Smith." The man's voice switched to heavily accented English. Smith directed him to switch frequencies and follow the commands of the aircraft shadowing him. Chaquerres acknowledged his new orders.

Harami asked to speak with his family. Shortly after they established contact, the wife launched into her own tirade. She pleaded with desperation drowned by heavy tears. Harami then acknowledged the directive to turn around and follow Chaquerres to Lemoore Naval Air Station.

"The third helicopter pilot is Adrian Hunsacker, Mr. Clancy's pilot. He's headed for Orange County with papers for today's meeting," Harami answered the unasked question.

"Pull all the information you can find on Hunsacker. Now," Paulson instructed his team. "Send local police to get the next of kin and have them on the horn ASAP."

"Cock-sucking, camel-fucking, filthy piece of shit, you couldn't keep your cowardly mouth shut. There's no room for pieces of crap like you and that spic in this country. I wish I had the time to kill you and your families myself. To make sure no spineless dimwits like you ever walk on this sacred ground." Hunsacker's enraged voice burst. Then the radio fell silent.

The AWACS tracked Hunsacker on a southern course, parallel to the 5 Freeway, two hundred miles north of Los Angeles. Three helicopters from Camp Pendleton's Third Marine Aircraft Wing intercepted him and flew half a mile behind. Two MH-60R Seahawks from Lemoore joined the convoy. The group made its way south at a steady 120 miles per hour. Behind them lined up an ever-growing fleet of military and emergency response aircraft, carrying personnel and equipment to address the nuclear threat.

"Hunsacker has terminal colon cancer and a few weeks left. His sister reports he's been talking about doing his patriotic duty and going out like a true warrior. It's my assessment that he's aware of his cargo. He intends to detonate that bomb," Paulson informed the Governor.

"Oh, my dear God. How do we stop him?" Lisa's hand covered her lips.

"Short of shooting him down, there is little we can do. If we do it, we need to take him down over the Angeles National Forest before he reaches populated areas," said Smith.

"Will the nuke go off if we shoot him down?" asked George Hunter.

"I don't know, Governor." Sam Miller chose his words with care. "These are old weapons. I'd say there is an even chance the nuke goes off if the helo crashes or explodes."

"What's the predicted damage? Safe minimum distance? The affected zone?" George asked in a crescendo voice. "How many casualties can we expect if it detonates?"

"I estimate safe distance to be two to four miles. We don't know the nominal yield, if they were properly stored and maintained. Altitude and topography are determining factors. Number of casualties depends on terrain, population density, wind direction..."

"Good enough," George cut him off. He turned to Smith. "Scramble the fighter planes from Edwards. Prepare to shoot it down."

Smith acknowledged and issued the orders.

"Can we push him out to sea and shoot him down?" asked Hunter. "It's got to have a smaller impact if the detonation is over the water or, even better, under water."

"I don't think it's a viable option, Governor," Max answered. "The closest his present course will take him to the shore is east of Santa Barbara. Even if we get him over the water, it will be an equal, if not worse, ecological disaster in the Santa Barbara Basin and an even greater loss of life, human and non-human, but still life."

The Governor scanned the room for additional input. He encountered only sad eyes, supportive of Max's assessment.

"We understand the gravity of the choice that rests solely with you, the most difficult decision of your career." Jack stood next to his father "We are with you, Dad."

George nodded at Jack and then addressed Colonel Smith.

"Patch me through to Hunsacker. I'll attempt to reason with him before we proceed with the violent alternative." Hunter sighed and sat down on the bed next to Sparks, who placed his hand on Hunter's shoulder and squeezed.

"I don't envy you, sir. No matter how glamorous it sounds to be Governor and all, I don't know that I could make this decision without hurling my guts out."

"Get me a bucket, Officer," replied George. He buried his head in his palms and rocked it. "This will be my legacy? Nuclear holocaust?"

"Colonel Smith, sir. You have an urgent call from Lemoore Naval Air Station, sir."

"Put it through," answered Smith. "Maybe some good news for a change."

"Colonel, Admiral Armstrong at Lemoore. I'm afraid we have grimmer news."

A collective groan erupted, and the group flocked around Smith.

"Our techs examined the bombs in the two helicopters. They welded the casings to the frame of the aircraft and the shells booby-trapped. They're rigged to go off on impact. They retrofitted the bombs with receivers. The bad guys can remote-detonate."

"This is Col. Marcus A. Smith, USMC. I acknowledge receipt of the message, Admiral. Thank you," Smith replied in a voice reminiscent of a hollow cemetery bell.

"We jammed the frequencies here to protect the bombs on the ground. My men are working to find a solution to fry the circuitry and safely render the weapons non-operational. It should work, given the advanced age and lack of sophistication of Russian electronics. Unfortunately, it will take some time. We have no solution for the airborne one. The best jamming transmitter we have must be within a quarter mile to be effective. Preferably less. I already dispatched it south."

CHAPTER 155

"**T**HIS SUCKS. IT BLOWS** any which way you look at it. It's a no-win situation," Sam Miller ranted loud enough to get everyone's attention. "I have a crazy idea. I think you'll have a hard time finding volunteers to carry it out, but it could work."

"Spit it out, Miller. Time is of the essence," barked Paulson.

"If we can force the chopper below two hundred feet and disable it, the bomb may not go off on impact. It'd be better over a dense forest to soften the impact. We position the frequency jammer on top of it until the ground teams arrive." He laid out his plan.

"You are a genius. I could kiss you right now." J.P. sprung to his feet.

"Don't let the earring fool you," Miller imitated Joe Pesci.

"What do you have in mind, J.P.?" asked Ramos.

"I need a secure channel to the pilots in pursuit." J.P. said.

Colonel Smith picked up the radio mike and keyed it on.

"All units in pursuit of helicopter Hector Lima one-niner-six," Smith instructed. "Follow Mr. Morgan's directions to the letter."

J.P. took the mike and explained his plan and completed his speech. "We will present new ideas as they come to us, based on how this situation unfolds."

"This is Commander Hawkes, leader of the task group pursuing Hector Lima one-niner-six. Are you sure, sir?"

"Yes, I am," replied J.P., crossing his fingers.

"I hope it works, sir. This sounds more like mass suicide, though," scoffed Hawkes.

Jack yanked the mike from J.P.'s hand. "Admiral Armstrong, I know you're monitoring, sir. The Governor asked you to send your best pilots for this mission. Can you send them to relieve...'?

"I am the best helicopter pilot in this man's Navy, sir." Hawkes cut in. "Who is this?"

The angry answer brought wide grins to Jack's and Eric's faces.

"This is Congressman Jack Hunter. Then act like it, Commander."

"Aye, aye, sir," Hawkes retorted in an annoyed tone. A moment later, he added, "With all due respect, screw you. Sir."

"That's the spirit, Commander." Jack smiled, handing the mike to Eric.

"Many lives are at stake. You make this happen. If there is no way, you find a way, Commander. Understood? This is the only chance to avoid a nuclear event." Ramos said.

"Aye, aye, sir. I promised my kids we'd watch fireworks together tonight."

"You keep that promise, Commander. Any way that does not end in a nuclear event will do. Good luck and happy hunting." Ramos keyed off and then turned to Jack, "That was such a J.P. thing to do. It's rubbing off on you already."

"Speaking of the devil. Where is J.P.?" Jack asked, scanning the room.

"He was here a minute ago," Lisa said. "He can't be too far."

"Someone should find him before he gets in trouble," chided Eric. "At times like this, he's worse than a three-year-old after eating three pounds of candy."

"Sir, AG Clancy contacted your office to confirm the 10:00 A.M. meeting," Paulson reported to George Hunter. "When he learned you canceled it, he demanded to speak with you. Unfortunately, someone disclosed your location. We tracked his phone near Dos Amigos. CHP units, a chopper, and a drone have been tasked to locate him. He'll be in custody shortly."

Jack and Eric overheard the report and approached.

"You must leave immediately." Paulson held Hunter's elbow. "We intercepted another call from Clancy to Hunsacker. They are using encrypted phones. NSA is working on it, but we may not know in time. We must assume the target package has changed, and Hunsacker is heading this way, sir."

"Dad, you must go now. We'll do everything in our power to stop that lunatic. It's possible Clancy has contingency plans that ensure he becomes Governor."

"You must let all other state officials know their lives may be in peril," Max said.

Governor Hunter decided that fighting them would be counterproductive. He thanked everyone for their dedication, loyalty, and patriotism. He then left the room, escorted by the members of his security detail.

"This way, sir. We must hurry. We have to evacuate you by car, sir." The protection detail leader guided George toward the catwalk.

"Why?" asked Paulson and Hunter simultaneously.

"Morgan commandeered the Governor's helicopter," Smith replied, approaching them.

CHAPTER 156

"THAT ANSWERS THAT QUESTION," stated Jack. "Where is he going?"

"Damn you, J.P.!" Max's voice sounded like a screeching hawk. "I would bet my bottom dollar he is on a collision course with Hunsacker."

"Get a hold of his pilot, and have him return here ASAP," Paulson instructed Smith.

"Good luck with it," scoffed Eric. "I guarantee he'll throw the pilot out and fly the damn thing himself. Again. He's done it in—never mind. Leave him be. He didn't earn the nickname *Chop Nuts* for nothing. It's not as if he can cause any harm being on the scene."

"Eric is right. J.P. usually keeps going long after the body parts start falling off." Jack picked up Eric's explanation. "Then someone must follow him around and pick them up, so we can glue him back together after he gets the job done. I'm worried by the fact he's hurt. He's in no condition to fly, not that it would ever stop him."

"Say that again, Colonel." Smith advanced toward Eric with a puzzled expression.

"He can't cause any harm on the scene—"

"No," Colonel Smith interrupted. "What was that about *Chop Nuts*?"

"Oh, that." Ramos backpedaled. "It's just a nickname J.P. picked up along the way."

"In 2000?" asked Smith.

"That's right," replied Eric, a light bulb going off on his face. "You were the deputy commander on the scene where it happened."

"Are you saying Morgan is *Chop Nuts?*" Smith asked. "Man, I've been looking for this *Chop Chop Nuts Nuts* since that day to shake his hand."

"Yes, sir," Eric answered. "That's the *Chop-Chop Nut-Nuts* you probably remember. We shortened it later to *Chop Nuts.*"

"My God!" Smith exclaimed. "I have a commendation and a medal in my drawer for him. I always thought he was CIA and wondered when the Company became so modest. I sent them the medal, and they returned it with a note that said, 'Not necessary.'"

"What are you talking about?" intervened Lisa.

"Sorry, Lisa," Eric replied. "That incident is classified."

"You boys and the 'classified' crap," scoffed Lisa.

"Normally, I'd agree with Ramos," Smith interceded in a conciliatory tone. "But I will tell you. We were fighting a large rebel faction in... a nameless country. One of our choppers was shot down, and nine of my Marines got trapped below a ridge on the riverbank. The rebels, about fifty of them, advanced toward our boys under the cover of another fifty or so, armed with heavy machine guns, light artillery. We had no options to rescue our men. *Chop Nuts*—I mean, Morgan was returning from a classified mission aboard another helicopter. He commandeered the aircraft, threw his pilot into the river and proceeded to the scene."

By this time, everyone in the room had gathered around Smith, listening intently. "Morgan positioned his helicopter over the river directly in front of the rebels and emptied the guns and rails, launching everything at the bad guys. While taking heavy fire from all directions, he forced the rebels to keep their heads down long enough for the two rescue choppers to swing in at water level and extract our Marines. I never knew who had saved our bacon that day," Smith concluded with a broad smile.

"What happened to J.P.?" asked Max. "Obviously, he made it out, but how? Is this another one of those magic tricks?"

"When he ran out of ammo, he pointed the aircraft at the rebels and jumped into the river." Smith broke into a full body laugh. "He saved our nine Marines and killed more than twenty rebels that day. He floated down the river for a couple of miles before we pulled him out of the drink. Then he disappeared without a trace, hence the thought he was CIA."

"You mean he intentionally destroyed a helicopter?" asked Paulson incredulously.

"That's not what the incident report says." Smith smiled. "Hell, I was ecstatic to write that report instead of nine letters to my men's families. I'd do it all over again."

"Let's hope he doesn't do *that* again," said Paulson. "Throwing the Governor's pilot out of the chopper over land might be counterproductive."

"No worries," intervened Jack. "J.P. can fly choppers, but I doubt he can land them. He hasn't landed one yet, but he crashed two that I know of."

"Two?" Lisa's curiosity turned her voice shrill.

"Different story for another day," said Jack. "I'll make sure my dad's pilot complies with J.P.'s crazy ideas. J.P. has always been nuts, but not suicidal."

CHAPTER 157

A **FLIGHT OF TWO** USAF F-22A Raptors joined the pursuit. Despite continuous hailing and pleas, Hunsacker never broke radio silence after berating Chaquerres and Harami. He called Clancy instead. When he learned of the two pilots' surrender, Clancy had pitched a fit and then ordered Hunsacker to reach his objective at any cost.

Hunsacker noticed two Hueys, and a Seahawk boxed him in. "What are you up to?"

The third Huey gained altitude and then, without warning, plunged on top of his bird. Hunsacker noticed it late and panic-dived to avoid a collision. He dropped 150 feet. He considered they intended to disable his rotor by slamming their skids into it and forcing him to land. "Not gonna work, boys. I forgot more about flying than all of you learned so far."

Hunsacker sped up and attempted to regain altitude, but the more powerful UH-1N Hueys mimicked his movement. The Seahawk crowded him from the rear, forcing him to stay in the box. Hunsacker plummeted another hundred feet and sped up, only to find his maneuver mirrored again. He glanced up and saw the colorful Viper painted on the underbelly of the third Huey. "You think you're a hotshot, huh? Let's see what you know," he yelled to no one.

While scenarios of evading his pursuers twirled in his head, Hunsacker scanned the surroundings for a way out, any solution to his crowding problem. Ahead, like an ominous barrier, stood the mountains that separated Los Angeles from California's Inland Valley.

"You bastards. You wanna push me down so I won't be able to fly over the ridge. No worries, I intend to use the freeway. I need to think my way out of the proverbial box," Hunsacker muttered to himself, his eyes darting across the landscape.

He was off course, headed for the mountainside rather than the valley to his left, where the freeway snaked through the peaks. Hunsacker banked hard right and pushed down the nose of his helicopter, hoping his followers would follow suit. He reversed his turn, attempting to shake free. To his dismay, the three Hueys and the Seahawk emulated his actions with uncanny precision. He found himself an additional two hundred feet lower, still boxed in.

"Cocksuckers! Back off right now, or I'll blow you out of the sky!" Hunsacker yelled into his throat mike. His body broke into a sweat storm, his heart pounded, and he felt his chest tightening as though a heavy metallic band twisted around it.

"No can do, Hunsacker. Your instructions are to land the aircraft immediately, or we have orders to shoot you down. You served. You know how it is. This is your only courtesy call," Hawkes replied.

Hawkes switched frequencies and ordered all choppers to move in. All four helicopters crowded around Hunsacker. The formation flew with a mere fifty feet clearance between rotors. Hunsacker tried another maneuver, only to find his followers echoing it, almost as if they read his mind. The Huey on his port side got nearer, forcing him to make a slight course correction to avoid a midair collision. The new course took him further away from the freeway. He was unable to cross the mountains into Southern California at his current altitude.

The Huey above him surged ahead and nose-dived, almost touching his chopper's rotor. Unnerved, Hunsacker lost another hundred feet of altitude. An intricate ballet followed as he pulled every trick he had learned during his army pilot career, which had started during the last years in Vietnam. He slowed down several times, forcing the Seahawk to apply its own brakes to avoid slamming into the tail rotor. Still, he could not break loose from his pursuers.

Hunsacker called Clancy to report his new predicament.

CHAPTER 158

"**Y**OU HAVE A NEW TARGET.** Detonate over Site B. Use any means to complete your mission. We will hail you as a patriot and a martyr," Clancy assured him. "Call me when you're in position. The fate of California, and possibly the world, rests with you now."

Clancy ended the call, then dialed Myerson's number and updated him.

"Unbelievable," screamed Myerson. "How the hell did this happen?"

"The fucking cowards, the sand coon and the spic surrendered. You must ensure your teams deliver on the contingency plan, or we're finished." Clancy was furious, and his voice broke up. "Kill their damn families."

"I say we cut our losses and head for my place down the peninsula, just in case. We can always turn around if we succeed. If not, we just hunker down for a while and wait for our next chance." Myerson's voice betrayed unadulterated fury.

"I'm not ready to bail out. I invested so much in this, and you assured me there was no chance of failure!" yelled Clancy, foaming at the mouth.

"This is not the time for pointing fingers. I'm offering you safe haven. However, if you'd rather take chances with the death penalty, be my guest. Someone will cut a deal and rat you out for shooting Smythe and ordering the other killings."

"Hunsacker will succeed. We shouldn't give up." Clancy grasped at straws.

"He may, but the odds have changed. I know when to hang up the gloves. Take my advice and meet me there. If it works out, you can assume your throne as if this hiccup never happened." Myerson laughed like a hyena.

"I guess you're right. I'm heading back south. I'll be on my way down as soon as I can safely get through," Clancy conceded with a deep sigh. "Send in the special teams to take all of them out. Maybe we can still turn this thing around from afar. Let Trump's name keep the momentum going. We'll wait at your place for the dust to settle, and then we'll return to take our rightful place."

CHAPTER 159

H UNSACKER THOUGHT OF A maneuver he had perfected after his return from Vietnam. He was flying below the height of the ridges looming ahead. The Angeles National Forest Mountains was a volcanic formation with steep canyons running between tall crests. With an eye on the 3-D terrain scope, he plotted a fresh course. He slowed his aircraft and wiggled left to right to make room. As his escorts adjusted, he sped up and headed toward a narrow valley.

The helicopter convoy flew in the deep canyon, the rotors of the outer birds only a few yards from trees and ravine walls. The gulley forked and Hunsacker made his move. He sped up, feinting toward the rift on the right. His escorts, as expected, emulated his actions.

Sporting a sinister grin, Hunsacker banked hard left, slowed down, and dropped to a few feet above the gulley. His smaller craft gave him an advantage in the narrow confines.

The Seahawk behind him could not drop fast and low enough to cut him off. The big copter weaved, trying to avoid the trees that grew angled on the canyon walls.

An eight of a mile behind, Hawkes sped up his Seahawk and fired a warning salvo, cutting Hunsacker's path toward the pass. The other helicopters scrambled back in position around him while Hunsacker gloated. "That's how it's done, cocksuckers. Anytime you need lessons, I'll be happy to oblige. If you crowd me again, I'll blow you to kingdom come."

The Hueys and the Seahawk caught up to Hunsacker above the western end of a small town, a mere six miles from the freeway. The three Hueys took station around him. Hawkes positioned his Seahawk on top. As soon as they had him sealed in properly, Hawkes renewed his attempts to make radio contact. He reiterated his orders to land.

Hunsacker filled the air with curses and invectives. With his last maneuver, he gained enough altitude to clear the first ridge lying just beyond the towns of *Lake of the Woods* and Frazier Park. He continued south toward the massif ahead, standing over seven thousand feet tall, several hundred feet higher than Hunsacker's altitude. He attempted a host of tricks, but he had no luck in luring his escorts into a trap.

The convoy approached within a mile of the northern slopes of the massif. Hunsacker felt the warm sweat as it ran down the inside of his flight suit; he smelled his own body odor as the perspiration overwhelmed the soap from his early morning shower.

Hunsacker selected another canyon on the side of the ridge and prepared to evade his followers. The group tightened around him. Hunsacker simulated a left turn. He banked hard right and then left and slowed to a hover. He yanked the joystick, forcing the helicopter to gain altitude, ending slightly higher than the Huey on his port side. Hunsacker dropped his craft like a rock, damaging the rotor of the Huey with his skids. He banked hard left and headed toward the freeway. The damaged Huey hit the side of the gulley and disintegrated into an orange ball.

"Sirs, Captain Thomas's aircraft is down. I believe there are no survivors," Commander Hawkes, reported, biting into his lower lip until he felt a coppery taste.

A collective feeling of sorrow reinforced the commitment to stop Hunsacker. The escort caught up with him, and they boxed him in tighter. The second Seahawk shadowing the convoy sped up to maximum speed to replace the downed Huey.

"Want more lessons? I'll take you down one by one until I get tired, and then I'll set the bomb off. Sayonara, cocksuckers." Hunsacker straightened his aircraft above the freeway.

"Sirs, I don't know if this idea will work. Hunsacker's aircraft is smaller, lighter, and more maneuverable," Hawkes offered in a strained voice.

J.P.'s voice reflected his passion and resolve. "Commander, we have to make it work. We will shoot him down, if there is no other way. However, do you want to be the man who allowed a nuclear weapon to detonate in the United States? I do not."

"That's not fair," Hawkes replied. "We're doing everything we can."

"I know, Commander. You know the stakes. Get it done. Or your son may witness different fireworks today." J.P. outlined the final steps of his plan.

As the freeway curved eastward, the military choppers squeezed Hunsacker. They forced him west toward the uninhabited areas. Hunsacker fought hard, his eyes scanning the canyons separating him from the Pico Canyon Oilfield.

Much like a synchronized flock of giant geese, the convoy flew over the town of Val Verde towards Pico Canyon.

"Oh, you boys want more lessons. Who's next? A damn Seahawk or another Viper? Makes no difference to me." Hunsacker's overconfident tone grated on everyone's nerves.

The ridge in font of him was the last obstacle that prevented Hunsacker from reaching the populated areas of Southern California.

Instead of crowding him, the surrounding aircraft moved away.

"You pussies have no guts." Hunsacker laughed. Their silence was unnerving. He increased speed and climbed, desperate to clear the ridge. Hunsacker's face turned into a mask of horror. His eyes bulged out, almost touching the inside of his visor.

Beyond the ridge, four AH-64 Apaches rose as one to block his path, angry birds of prey ready to sink their talons into his helicopter. The Governor's chopper soared a hundred feet above them. Despite the distance, Hunsacker sensed J.P.'s intense scrutiny. His spine tingled. The trickle of sweat turned ice-cold down his spine. Hunsacker slowed down his aircraft and hovered one hundred yards above the forest. He knew he was stuck. He howled in excruciating pain and frustration; the sounds swallowed by the noise of the machinery.

CHAPTER 160

THE TWO RAPTORS BEGAN circling a couple of thousand feet above, like two eagles twirling in the warm air, waiting for their prey.

"End of the line," Hawkes stated, hovering above Hunsacker's bird. "Hunsacker, set your aircraft down and walk away. Comply, or we open fire in fifteen seconds."

"You, cowards. Mother-fucking traitors. I will never surrender. I will take all of you with me." Hunsacker sprayed droplets of foam on his microphone.

Hawkes keyed his mike once. The Huey behind Hunsacker fired a quick burst into the side of the massif.

"That was your shot across the bow. Land and walk away, now." Hawkes continued, unfazed by Hunsacker's insults. Hunsacker howled in frustration.

Hawkes changed frequencies. "Prepare to disengage at max speed." Hawkes turned and nodded to his crew chief, Petty Officer Wagner. The chief replied with a thumb-up. "On my mark. Three... two... one. Break, break, break."

All other helicopters, except Hawkes's Seahawk, flew away at maximum thrust. The choppers groaned from the stress of the maneuver. Wagner dropped a large gray object out of the Seahawk. Hawkes began ascending as fast as his aircraft could manage. The Seahawk grumbled and creaked from every joint as the crew held its collective breath, along with thousands of people locked in common prayer for the success of the crazy maneuver.

"Oops!" Hawkes exclaimed over the radio. His voice strained with effort, as if he had been lifting the Seahawk by himself.

The tool case hit Hunsacker's rotor. The blades bent and shattered. The aircraft lost altitude and tilted toward the woods below. Hunsacker battled for control, but the propeller had become a useless mess of twisted metal shards. He half-landed, half-crashed nose first into the tall trees. The leftover rotor sliced through treetops and crumbled. The bird leaned nose down, tail in the air, rear blades still spinning, like a seagull hunting for fish under the surface of the water.

"You, and whoever came up with this plan, owe me a new toolbox, Commander." Wagner slid the helicopter door closed. "You have no idea how much paperwork they require."

"Sirs, target is down and incapacitated! I say again, target is down! We have no detonation!" Hawkes roared, his voice vibrating.

Everyone in the command center jumped up as one. Sparks hopped on his good leg and then fell backward on the bed. He ignored the pain, rejoicing along with the rest of them. Max and Lisa hugged each other and then Eric and Jack.

"Sirs, the pilot is alive. He climbed in the cargo area with a sidearm in his hand," Lieutenant Commander Hawkes reported. "He's holding it like a hammer."

"Marines, shoot him!" yelled J.P., signaling his pilot to return to the downed chopper.

"Sir?" sounded the baffled reply.

"He's trying to detonate it. Marine snipers, take him out!" J.P. shouted and then removed his headset and reached the sniper rifle.

"Roger that" came the calm response from Lieutenant Martin. He patted the back of his sharpshooter. "Sergeant."

Marine Sergeant Lopez lay flat, his legs spread wide, on the floor in the cargo area of the Viper Hueys five hundred yards away. The sniper aimed at the downed craft and rushed the shot. The round bounced off the bomb casing, four inches in front of Hunsacker's nose. In reply, Hunsacker hammered at the housing surrounding the nuclear weapon like a madman.

J.P. broke the side window with the butt of the high-powered rifle and then stuck the barrel out. He slowed down his breathing and heart rate and then cleared his mind. He targeted Hunsacker's ear, the butt of the rifle firm against his injured shoulder. He squeezed the trigger. The recoil of the powerful rifle sent waves of pain through J.P.'s body. He observed Hunsacker's head explode in a cloudburst of blood, brains, and bone shards.

Then everything went black.

"Target is down permanently," Hawkes exclaimed, losing the battle to conceal his satisfaction. "No detonation. We call this one a win for the good guys, sirs. Seahawks have the scene secured. Send in the mop up crews!"

Hawkes waited for the cheers to calm down and then resumed. "Exceptional flying and shooting, Marines. Happy Independence Day, everyone." He flashed a grin wider than the Mississippi. "Whoever came up with this idea, I owe him a case of beer."

"Oh, damn. He passed out." The Governor's pilot barged in.

"Who passed out? Hunsacker?" Smith broke away from the celebration.

"No." The pilot sounded annoyed. "Mr. Morgan. He dropped the rifle out the window. I'm sending coordinates for the ground crews to recover it. I'll take him to UCLA Trauma Center. I'm twenty minutes out."

CHAPTER 161

"**A**CKNOWLEDGED. BREAK EVERY SPEED** record and get him there alive!" Jack yelled. He turned toward Paulson and invited him to make the arrangements.

Eric pulled Jack aside. "You go be with Mel. I'll deal with this."

"I have to call the President. Mel is with your mother." Hunter patted Jack's shoulder.

"Why are you here?" Jack queried. "You should be as far away as possible."

"Being Governor has its perks." George's condescending tone did not surprise Jack. "I have a state to run, and only four months left before the elections."

"Before you go," Jack pulled his father aside, "I saw that recording J.P. made two nights ago. The person talking was there when Artie and Alice were murdered. I'm sure J.P. had nothing to do with it. Most likely, Theo Myerson murdered them."

"They are dead because of him, whether or not he killed them." The Governor made a dismissive gesture. "Nothing will convince me otherwise."

"Sadowsky suggested they killed them as a message to you," insisted Jack. "Alberto Salazar hired Myerson to free his son."

"I had no beef with Myerson." George shot his jaw forward. "J.P. did."

"Dad, wait until we see all the evidence. There is a recording of the actual murders."

"She should have never been with him. If she had married someone appropriate, she would still be alive." The Governor walked away, his lips pursed.

"Dad!" exclaimed Jack. "That's not fair. He's one of my best friends. He saved my life more times than I care to remember."

The Governor stopped on a dime and pivoted on his heel to face his son. "Best friend? Since when? He is also responsible for your son's death. My only grandson."

"He is not," declared Jack in a forceful tone. "Yesterday he risked his life to help me. He got the FBI involved and helped clear my name."

"That's what he wanted you to believe. It probably served his purposes somehow. He has been nothing but trouble for our family." George walked away. "I should have let him go to juvie, not bring him into my home. He's been a curse ever since."

Randy Sparks stepped forward. "I can confirm that, sir. Morgan came to see me in the hospital and convinced me to help your son. He asked for nothing in return."

George Hunter studied Jack, Sparks, and Lieutenant Sparks for what appeared to be an eternity. "It doesn't matter. My daughter made a huge mistake marrying him, and she paid with her life. I must call the President. Happy Fourth of July, gentlemen." He strode out of the room.

CHAPTER 162

"**C**ONGRATULATIONS, GEORGE." PRESIDENT **CORNELL'S** exuberant voice pleased Hunter. "Your leadership in this time of crisis was unparalleled."

"Thank you, Mr. President." George basked for a moment. "I did everything in my power to avoid this disaster. My men also intercepted the assassination squads dispatched to eliminate the successors to the Governor's seat."

"Can we keep the entire incident under wraps? We cannot afford to have this pop up in newspapers or worse, on TV or the Internet. Last thing I need is to fan the flames over this new Trump fiasco."

"No need to remind me, sir. I'm up for reelection in November. However, I just learned this may have had nothing to do with Trump. The bad guys here in California fooled everyone into thinking they were fighting to return Trump to the White House. They just took advantage of the situation and national divide to further their own agenda."

"Jesus," sighed the President. "When will we get rid of this Trump character and his Machiavellian delusions? He's done more to tear this country apart and divide the American people than all our enemies combined."

"I agree, sir," Hunter commiserated. "At least Hitler was very charismatic. About these events, we can order everyone to keep quiet. The US attorney can offer incentives to the people arrested and those who will be detained shortly." The Governor paused for a long moment, searching for his next words.

"What is it, George?" The President felt the tension in George's voice.

"There are two civilians involved." George's voice reflected discomfort.

"John Paul Morgan!" the President exclaimed. "They briefed me. He and a girl are the only civilians. How do we convince them to keep this secret?"

"The girl's name is Maxine. I don't know her last name. She's his... I don't know what she is. She's too young to be his lover. My wife and I raised J.P. after his mother died—"

"Immaterial, George. I get it. They have some relationship. What can we offer the two of them to make sure they will keep quiet about this?"

"Clancy's cohorts burned down his home and his cabin. We could offer him full reimbursement and other enticements under a sealed agreement."

"From what I learned about him, money will not do it. He is a man to whom honor, duty, and the welfare of others are paramount. Something along those lines will work better."

"He had a brilliant career until the second incident with Senator Myerson's son. What a shame." George allowed his voice to dwindle at the end of the sentence.

"Do you think he'd be interested in coming back? I'm sure we can arrange it. That would solve the secrecy problem." The President replied.

"I agree, Mr. President. If he were active duty Navy, his clearances would ensure his cooperation. He'd make sure this Maxine girl kept her mouth shut."

"Do you think, if we offer it, he might accept?" The President's voice bubbled.

"He serves at your pleasure, sir. If you order him back, he must comply."

"Splendid idea, George. As always, you're the most unscrupulous and manipulative politician I know." The President laughed.

"Thank you, Mr. President. I only have the country's best interests at heart. We cannot afford a scandal of these proportions or another division so close to elections this year."

"I'll speak with the Secretary of the Navy and find a way." The President's demeanor remained upbeat. "I like it. You're still the same-old fox, George."

"I aim to please, sir." George Hunter's voice betrayed a hint of satisfaction.

"I'd like to meet this man. Why don't you bring him with you next time you are in DC, and I'll fit you on my schedule for a private meeting?"

The President ended the call before George protested.

EPILOGUE

CHAPTER **163**

J.P. TOOK IN THE LUSH Irish green grass that felt like a silk carpet, extending as far as the eye could see. Millions of rainbow-colored flowers in shapes he had never seen enhanced the splendor of the tableau. Brightness permeated from everywhere at once, although no source was visible in the picture-perfect cloudless sky. A young girl steered her translucent pony toward him. The little angel floated above the miniature horse in a cloud of butterflies and hummingbirds. She laughed with her entire being as only children can, filling the air with vibrant giggles. She blew kisses to her audience with both hands.

J.P. turned his head and discovered Alice, wrapped in a blanket of golden white light. She radiated pure love, smiled, and waved her delicate hand. Serenity covered her beautiful face, and her bright eyes blended in with the cerulean sky. J.P. knew she was the girl's mother. Next to Alice stood a young boy clad in a cowboy's outfit, a large hat low on his brow.

The girl brought the pony to a stop in front of J.P. and sang in a sparkling, innocent voice. "You did it, Daddy. Bravo." She clapped her tiny palms in delight.

J.P. tried to move closer to hug her. Not one muscle obeyed him, and he found himself forced to observe, unable to interfere. The little girl took off, standing on her pony once again.

Alice glided over, beaming, happy, and content. She reached out to J.P. Her hand felt warm and soft, like an angel's touch—so light, so affectionate, so full of love.

"It's not your time, babe," she proclaimed in a melodic voice. "We'll be right here, waiting for you when the time comes." She blew him a kiss and floated away after the little cherub, her image dissipating in the light.

"Remember, my love. Mexico," she whispered and then vanished.

"Bye-bye, Daddy." The angel sent him smackers with both hands. "We love you."

J.P. struggled to catch and smooch her and tell her how much he loved her and Alice, how he would never leave them. The opening bars of Beethoven's The Destiny Symphony echoed in his head, and the scene dissolved. His mind screamed in vain. *Not yet! Wait! I need more time with you! I want to be with you! I am ready!*

The boy stepped forward and then pushed his hat higher on his forehead. Artie.

J.P. ached to grab his nephew and race to catch the girl and roll with them on the lavish grass, but he felt pinned under a tremendous weight.

"Howdy, par'ner," said Artie in a burst of childish, peaceful laughter. He pointed at J.P. and continued. "You don't b'long 'ere, Mis'er." He chuckled and switched to a serious voice. "I need you to go back and help look after my sister." He waved his hands.

Artie's face faded into the light, and then the picture turned pitch-black. J.P. felt the burden lift to render him weightless. However, it was too late. They were all gone.

J.P. opened one eye and focused it on Max's face. Her giant emeralds glimmered with joyful tears, a smile brighter than the sun at noon radiating from her lips.

"It's about time, you, big bucket of lug nuts." She hugged him, kissed him, climbed into bed, and wrapped herself around him as best she could, nearly cutting off his air supply. Max babbled like an excited child.

J.P. ignored the sharp pain he felt all over his body. "Who... are you?" J.P. displayed the most puzzled look in his repertoire.

CHAPTER **164**

MAX FROZE AND LIFTED her head to study him. The doctors said that the round to his right temple, and the subsequent shocks, may have caused a concussion.

J.P. flashed a childish grin and reached out to touch her cheek.

She mock-pounded his chest and then settled back down, connecting her entire body to his. "Never scare me like that again. If you dare to die on me, I'll revive you just to have the satisfaction of killing you myself." She kissed his temple.

"How long was I out? What did I miss?" J.P. returned the caresses.

"Two weeks. It's all over. Tomlinson killed himself. Clancy vanished without a trace. Nobody knows where Myerson is hiding. Feds are all over it but, so far, nothing."

"What are you talking about?" J.P. stopped the torrent. "I was only half-kidding about the memory loss. I have a hard time connecting all the dots."

"What's the last thing you remember?" Max raised her head.

J.P. cocked his head to one side and then answered in a tentative voice, "I sort of recall a knife fight with Purcell... then nothing."

"Oh, boy." She filled him in, telegraphing the events, from Purcell shooting him and Lisa to Hunsacker's desperate race to assassinate the Governor.

J.P. gave her his undivided attention. At some point, he slapped his forehead and signaled for Max to be quiet.

"Remember, my love. Mexico." What the hell? Alice and I had no fond memories of Mexico. Almost every time we went south of the border, she got sick. Aha!

"Give me your laptop and a clean phone." J.P. did his best to sit up and failed. The machine behind him produced menacing tones. Max protested, pushing him down.

"Just get them for me. Please, Max," J.P. cut her off.

She handed him her computer and searched for a phone. Max craned her neck to see what J.P. was doing with a quizzical expression.

J.P. concluded the phone call. "You get triple your fee if I get the pictures today and a $5,000 bonus for that phone number. Get to it."

Max finished bringing him up-to-date. She did it all with the delight of a child, jumping from one subject to the next, and concluded, "Bonnie, Clyde, and Banker are still in the hog heaven known as Martha's Orchard. You have a lot of explaining to do with the insurance folks. Both the house and the cabin burned down the same day, along with my favorite bikes."

"No good deed ever goes unpunished." He sighed in pretend surrender. "Now I am homeless, too. Did they burn down the towers?"

"No, but we are both homeless in California. My lease ended. I gave up my apartment at UCLA." Max pouted. "I wanted to come back home after the cruise. But there is no home."

Two nurses entered, carrying a food tray, an IV bag, and medication. J.P. lifted the lids off the food plates, twitched his nose, and then pushed the tray away. "If I have to wrestle bunnies for their lunch, they should be Playboy bunnies."

"Stay right there. I'll get the biggest steak you ever ate. Not the best thing for someone coming out of coma, but you can handle it." Max ran out the door.

The head nurse entered, sporting a scowling look. "Boy, am I glad to see you awake. Hurry up, get well, and get out of my hospital. Since you got here, it's been a nightmare."

"What did I do?" asked J.P., shocked, as if he had walked into a surprise party.

"Plenty, Mister. That one called the Governor to make sure we allowed her to spend every day and night in your room." The nurse pointed at the door and kept going, getting more incensed with every word. "Can you believe that? Not the Governor. Worse, actually. She called his wife. That girl barely left your side since they transferred you here. We should have never accepted you. Don't get me started on the Marines, the Navy boys, the Feds, and the Police fighting to cover your door. The entire wing is out of this world. My nurses have heart palpitations all day long. They are worse off than the patients."

"Heart palpitations?"

"All these good-looking, hard-bodied, armed young men in uniform trolling through here at all hours of the day. What do you think? Well, now that you're awake, I want my hospital back to normal." The head nurse stomped her feet, walking around the bed.

"Yes, madam," replied J.P.

"Then there's the other one. She came by every morning and every evening, like clockwork. I'm surprised the two of them didn't get into a fight, both being so bossy and possessive. Phew. You sure know how to pick them, boy. Good luck with them."

"What other one?" asked J.P., confused. *Anna and Candy are dead. Who is left?*

"The blonde one from the DA's office. She shoved that badge in our faces so many times. Lisa something or another," she scoffed, studying J.P.'s vital signs on the monitor.

"Lisa Jensen?" His mind attempted to make sense of the news flash.

"That's the one. What a piece of work. She had her arm in a sling and wouldn't stay put for one minute. She's as crazy as you are. I heard you stepped in front of a bullet. Then you left the hospital AMA, after surgery, did something stupid and nearly drowned in your own blood. You two deserve each other." The nurse finished her checkup and left, mumbling.

CHAPTER 165

A **CLOUD OF BALOONS** erupted through the door with Lisa attached to the strings. Max followed, and the room filled with the distinctive aroma of grilled steak and onions. J.P. salivated as his eyes bobbled back and forth from Lisa to the container in Max's hand.

"Thank you for saving my life. I don't know how I'll repay you. I'll do my absolute best, if it takes the rest of my life." Lisa planted a kiss straight on J.P.'s lips and held him tight.

He enjoyed her perfume and her embrace, while his mind worked feverishly to put the pieces together. She smelled of spring flowers and fresh soap.

I woke up on a different planet. Forget the planet. What universe is this?

"It is not as if I had a choice. I gave my word to keep you alive. It would have been a real shame to lose you at the very end," J.P. chided, searching for a handle on the situation.

The three of them sat in silence, holding hands for quite some time.

Jack Hunter walked in, shadowed by Eric Ramos, clad in uniform, sporting his new full colonel eagles. Jack, Eric, and J.P. did a three-way fist bump.

George Hunter escorted Mother Mary and Melissa Hunter into the room.

Mel's skin glowed, and her entire being radiated pure bliss.

Ah, that sister.

The Governor allowed his wife and Mel to approach the bed while he kept his distance. He shook hands with Jack and then, with great reluctance, with Eric. "Good to see you again, Ms. Jensen. I'm glad you're OK," he said to Lisa.

Hunter ignored Max, who returned the favor, pretending to look out the window.

Mother Mary sat at J.P.'s side, took his hand, and kissed his forehead. "George and I are in your debt. I don't think we'll be able to make proper reparations. We owe you the most heartfelt apologies for doubting you. We watched the tape of Alice's and Artie's murders—"

"Damn it, Lisa," J.P. cut Mother Mary off. He sat up, ignoring the new wave of excruciating pain shooting through his body, and the blaring alarms originating from the hospital equipment. "I specifically asked you not to allow Alice's family to watch it."

"The court asked to see it to clear your record of any charges." Lisa lowered her gaze.

"I never asked you to do any of that. I was OK with the way things were that night. I wanted to know for sure that *I* did not do it. Why put their family through that?"

Lisa continued to study her shoes with enormous interest. A tear rolled down her cheek, streaking her light makeup. She ignored it.

Mother Mary pushed J.P. down on the bed with a gentle hand. "It's not her fault, J.P. I demanded to see it. Do you recall what you swore to me at Papa's home?"

"What did you pledge to her?" George stepped closer, wearing a troubled expression.

"That is between Mother Mary and me. If she thinks you need to know, she will tell you herself." J.P. squeezed Mother Mary's hand.

George turned toward his wife. She stared at him, defiant. "Oh, for the love of God, Mary. Not some vigilante crap. We cannot afford the appearance of condoning something like that. I hope you talked about it in private, at least."

"I can't be involved with that either," muttered Lisa.

J.P. stole a sideways glance at her. Everyone else focused on the Governor.

Realizing he would get nothing else out of them, George Hunter stepped into the hallway and returned holding a thick envelope with the seal of the Secretary of the Navy on it. He flashed his most brilliant, rehearsed politician's grin and then opened the packet with grandiose gestures. He held the papers at arm's length, squinting to read the elegant print.

"I will not read the whole thing... 'At the request of the President, the Secretary of the Navy used her discretion and retroactively rejected Commander John Paul Morgan's letter of resignation, effective to the date he submitted said letter of resignation. Commander John Paul Morgan retains his commission as a US Navy officer, effective the same date. All rights, privileges, and clearances are fully restored and augmented, as applicable.'"

Hunter lifted his eyes from the paper, and he surveyed the room, beaming his best prepared grin. "You should stand for this, but we understand. 'Furthermore, Commander John Paul Morgan, US Navy, is hereby promoted to the rank of Captain, retroactive five years from today's date.' That was issued on July 8. Congratulations, Captain Morgan."

CHAPTER **166**

"**H**IP, HIP, HOORAY!"** Jack and Eric shouted in unison, clapping a storm.

The entire room erupted with congratulations, applause, and cheers.

Eric adopted a pose reminiscent of the famous rum label. "Permission to come aboard, Captain Morgan, sir?" He lowered his voice to a conspiratorial whisper. "You will serve your famous liquor on your fine ship, right? We have a lot to celebrate."

"Who suggested this scheme to the President?" J.P. asked in a hoarse, barely audible voice, stunning everyone into silence.

George issued a bright full-face smile and looked with apprehension at Lisa and Max.

"They know everything," stated Eric.

"Everyone knows they shouldn't have forced you out of the Navy." Hunter said.

"It sounds like a payoff and shackles," replied J.P. dryly, shifting his gaze to Jack.

Noticing J.P.'s annoyed look, Jack stepped forward and stood by the bed, placing a hand on his friend's shoulder. "Did you ask for this, Dad?"

The pressure built in the room akin to being trapped inside a boiler.

Max asked the question on everyone's mind. "J.P., what got into you?"

"Help me out here, Jack." J.P. settled back on the pillow.

"I got your back, buddy." Jack squeezed J.P.'s good shoulder. "The *True Patriot Day* incident has to remain secret for obvious reasons. All parties involved are law enforcement or military. That means clearances, accountability, or, in some cases, lighter sentences. The two wild cards are J.P. and Max. I guess Dad asked the President to reinstate J.P., give him back his clearances, and promote him retroactively. That made J.P. a Naval officer at the time of the incident. Did I get everything right, Dad? Why would you do that?"

Uncomfortable stillness covered the room like a thick, heavy blanket. All eyes focused on the Governor, whose face displayed small pink dots.

"George, would you care to comment?" Mother Mary turned to face her husband. "You never mentioned the other stuff when we talked about this."

"You make it sound evil. We corrected a wrong decision made by a weak Secretary of the Navy under political pressure." The Governor studied his reflection on his polished shoes.

"Cut the speech, George." Mother Mary's face reddened. "You couldn't trust him? Even now, after you watched that tape with your own eyes?"

"The real reason we did it was to help J.P. and thank him for his invaluable service. This episode must remain secret. Can you imagine what would happen if the word got out? The entire state would be in disarray. It could lead to anarchy."

"And it could cause you not to be reelected in November, right, *Governor*?" Mother Mary was not in the mood for pulling punches.

"J.P., you cannot be that ungrateful—" began Max, fighting her emotions.

"No more fighting on my account. I appreciate the intention, but I am not accepting this." J.P. picked up the paperwork and shoved it toward the Governor.

"It's not up to you. You're back in the Navy. You got a couple of medals, too." George lifted the envelope, attempting damage control. "The President wanted the highest honors awarded to you for going far beyond the call of duty. He didn't know how to get it through Congress. It raised too many questions we didn't want to answer. This nation owes you a debt of gratitude it can never repay. You are a genuine American hero, son."

Sarcasm drenched J.P.'s words. "The draft ended about the time you went to college."

"There is no need to be disrespectful, J.P. The President ordered it. You serve at his pleasure. He insisted you accompany me to the White House as soon as you're able to travel. You may not refuse. Presidential privilege," George snapped back.

"You covered all your bases, didn't you? OK, fine, I will think of another way out of this." J.P. shook his head in disbelief. "As to the medals, they should award them to Anna and Candy Richter, and all the people who paid with their lives to stop this *True Patriot Day.*"

Max and Lisa both gleamed with pride and anticipation, alternating glances between J.P. and the Governor. After a few moments of awkward silence, the Governor and Mother Mary left the room. For a while, the only movement in the hospital room was that of the balloons bouncing against the ceiling and each other.

CHAPTER 167

MAX'S LAPTOP BEEPED, SIGNALING new email messages. J.P.'s signature *cat-that-ate-the-canary* smile grew on his face. He studied Lisa, calculating, and then he closed his eyes and breathed out a loud sigh.

I feel like crap for doing this, Lisa, but it is for your protection.

"I would like Anna's locket back, please. I want to keep it as a memento."

Lisa pondered, her hands mimicking a can of earthworms. "How did you know?"

"I could not imagine what you were doing at Anna's that night. I thought you went there to *get* something. You were at Anna's covering for Tomlinson, to drop off the pendant Theo's goons got from Anna when they killed her. Sadowsky and Smythe interrupted you before you could plant it. You knew that if it disappeared, Candy and I would raise hell and forever question the suicide ruling."

"You know I don't recall any of this." Lisa fought back enormous tears. "I found it when I got my purse from Irvine PD. They took all my stuff from UCI. I have been trying all this time to figure out how I got it. Someone wiped the drive clean."

"I figured as much," J.P. surmised.

"I don't recall seeing that recording before the night of the 3rd. Please, believe me," she implored. Her nails left deep incisions in her palms, and her body trembled like a leaf.

"The fact remains, you knew who killed Alice and Artie. You covered it up. Anna confided in you because she intended to exonerate me. You ran to Tomlinson, who called Myerson. That put Anna in their crosshairs, and Myerson had her murdered."

"I never meant for that to happen. I don't recall any of it. Please accept this as the truth. The woman who did those things ceased to exist that night at the warehouse... when I saw the recording." She grabbed her purse and darted out of the room. Giant tears were free falling from her eyes, and hiccups made it almost impossible to breathe.

"J.P., you can be such an ass. You barely woke up, and you alienated the Governor and a woman who cares deeply about you," Max said, frowning.

"I will figure out a way to apologize to her later," J.P. replied in a flat voice. "We have some decisions to make. She may find them objectionable, being an Assistant DA and all."

"You're a jackass. You could have asked her nicely." Max kept at it, pouting.

"I know where Clancy and Myerson are." J.P. turned to Eric and Jack. He swiveled the laptop, so everyone could see the screen. "Do you remember Theo's little love shack on the beach in Ensenada? He used to spend his weekends there, screwing local teenage girls."

J.P. played still pictures of Clancy and a fat man drinking scotch and smoking cigars on the deck of a home overlooking the ocean. "I had my PI buddy in Ensenada snoop a little, and that is what he found at Theo's place." J.P. pointed at the display.

"He had plastic surgery, but there is no doubt. That's Myerson," Eric stated, confident.

"I'll call the FBI and my dad." Jack lifted his phone. J.P. stared at him with a quizzical expression. "What do you have in mind?" Jack asked, canceling the call.

"I am not about to give them a chance to skate on this because of fear of political embarrassment." J.P.'s voice was hard enough to cut steel. "Last thing we need is to drag the Trump connection back into the limelight."

"You want us to take them out ourselves?" Eric's eyebrows arched all the way to the ceiling. "Don't get me wrong, you can count me in. But that's not the J.P. I know."

"Eric and I can't go incognito to Mexico. You're in no condition to do it either, now that you're back in the Navy," Jack added in a quiet voice. "Let the Feds handle it. They will black-bag extradite them, need be."

"Let's first vote on it, Jack—you, Mel, and me. Do we go to the authorities and take the risk they get away or make things worse by further dividing the country?" J.P. sat up, sending the alarms into a renewed flurry.

"No questions asked. No clemency. That animal butchered my baby boy, Alice, and your baby girl. All of it to spring a drug dealer out of jail. No fricking mercy. That's my vote," Mel hissed, packing every word with a ton of venom as she fought back heavy tears.

"What you're suggesting is not realistic. We'll find another way. We'll bring them to justice," Jack pleaded, alternating his gaze from Mel to J.P.

"What the hell is wrong with you, Congressman? This numbskull murdered your son and your only sister. *Pregnant* sister. They framed you as a child molester and killer. They just about killed or injured millions of people. Do you think anyone wants to let them fight it in open court and expose the *True Patriot Day* fiasco? Knowing Theo, he would love the chance."

"Fuck you, J.P.," Jack retorted, shooting Morgan a murderous look.

"That is the Jack Hunter I remember," countered J.P. with a smirk.

"After all these years, you still know how to push my buttons. It's the two of you anyway, so my vote doesn't count. How's that coming from a US Congressman?" He chuckled.

CHAPTER **168**

"**L**ET'S CALL IT DIVINE justice." J.P. dialed the number from the email.

"Quien eres? Que quieres?" an angry man answered, his breathing labored as if it had interrupted him from a strenuous activity. *("Who are you? What do you want?")*

"Don Alberto, we both know you speak perfect English, so spare me the theatrics. Your years at Stanford were not that wasted," J.P. said in calm, measured English.

Jack and Eric exchanged appreciative looks, while Max and Mel quizzed each other.

"Who are you? How did you get this number?" Salazar got madder.

"Call me *El Gringo Loco*, the Crazy Yankee. I have early birthday and Christmas presents for you."

"What will this cost me, Gringo Loco?" The drug lord exhibited a mild curiosity.

"Today? Absolutely nothing. With your permission, I reserve the right to call on this favor at some future time, though."

"What makes you believe you have anything I want?" Don Alberto Salazar regained his courage after the initial surprise wore off.

"Let's not waste time arguing."

"What do you have to offer?" Salazar asked in a voice filled with distrust.

"Don Alberto, are you still missing that $180 million?" J.P.'s delivery was impeccable.

Even through the phone, they could feel Don Alberto Salazar soaring to his feet as if electrocuted and heard his breath grow in intensity.

J.P. smiled with renewed confidence. His theory had just been confirmed.

"Are you offering some assistance with collecting on that particular debt?" There was even less conviction in Salazar's voice now, but it had piqued his interest.

"Not sure, but I can put you in touch with the debtor." J.P. played coy.

"The *hijo de puta* is dead. You need to come up with a better story, *Gringo Loco*." Don Alberto's reply was dismissive, his breathing still sounding like a small tornado.

"Are you sure?" J.P. toyed with him. J.P. read him the address of the villa in the pictures. "You will find him there, along with the guy who helped him spend your money. I am sending their pictures now. Run the fat bastard's prints before you let him talk you out of it. He will have a two-pronged scar on the back of his right hand."

"Why the prints?" Don Alberto sounded surprised.

"He had cosmetic surgery. Only for his face, not for his soul," replied J.P.

"Let me have that address again. If you're right about this, you can choose your reward. Whatever you want, no questions asked," conceded Don Alberto.

"I have one suggestion," J.P. hissed.

"Oh yeah? What's that, *Gringo Loco*?" Apprehension laced Salazar's tone again.

"Take your sweet time." J.P. clicked off and then looked up at Jack and Mel.

"Je... sus! Remind me never to piss you off!" exclaimed Jack, on the verge of tears. He looked at Mel, "Are you OK with this, babe?"

"It's the next best thing to squeezing the twit's neck between my own two hands." Mel smiled between oversized tears and hugged Jack, clenching her fists behind his back.

"How did you know where to look for them?" Jack asked.

"Alice whispered it to me when she kicked my ass back from the other side," J.P. answered, his eyes misting up with the faintest trace of tears.

They watched him for a long minute, their curiosity growing by the second. J.P. remained silent, and his gaze ventured out the window. "On to you, Colonel Ramos." J.P. switched his penetrating gaze from Eric to Max. "You finally got my girl. We are even."

Eric blushed. Max punched his arm and snuggled up to him. She bit her lower lip, almost drawing blood and locked pleading eyes on J.P.'s face.

"I told you, he'd figure it out, Jarhead. I still don't know how he does it."

Mel and Jack joined the giggling party, embracing Eric and Max. They all clustered around J.P.'s bed, congratulating and encouraging him.

"I need to get out of here. Today," J.P. said in a firm tone.

"Out of the question. You can barely sit up, and you want to leave the hospital? No way, no how. Remember what happened last time?" Max looked at Jack and Eric for support. "The doctors could barely drain the blood from your lung before you drowned."

"What is so pressing?" Worried, Jack scrutinized J.P.'s serene face. "Take your time, buddy. Relax. Enjoy the nurses waiting on you twenty-four hours a day. We can arrange some sponge baths for you." He winked.

"Among the things I have to do is... I would like to go somewhere to celebrate the arrival of your new family member." He pointed at Mel's midsection and hooted.

Jack lifted Mel in his arms, whirling around the room. He kissed her, and the world around them ceased to exist. It was only the two of them, wrapped in a blanket of adoration for each other. Max and Eric gave them a few seconds and then joined in the group hug celebration.

"If you tell me the sex of the baby before she does, I will kill you! I will figure out a way to make it look like an accident!" Jack mock-threatened J.P.

"What is it about politicians and cheap promises?" J.P. goaded him.

"How did you figure that out?" Jack burst into laughter. "We only found out this morning. You're full of surprises today, more than usual."

"Artie," replied J.P. offering nothing else. "We should ask Ms. Jensen to join us. Maybe she will forgive my outburst of rudeness," J.P. stated with a sheepish grin.

"Good luck with that." Max tapped his healthy shoulder. "If I were Lisa, I wouldn't give in that easy. I'd make you grovel for months."

"I also want to take flowers to Alice's grave. And Artie's," answered J.P., ignoring Max's remarks. "I think they are ready to forgive me for taking this long to find their killers."

In silence, they all examined J.P. with perplexed looks, except Max who looked away.

"My God, you've never been to their graves." Mel's hand flew to her mouth. "Jack, Eric, get him out of here. Now!"

Jack and Eric scrambled to arrange J.P.'s discharge.

"Oh, J.P.," whispered Max. "I think I should share with you the other glorious news. Dr. Wilson called me to let me know Marie was OK, and he released her. She is pregnant with twins." She burst into her childish giggle. "We'll have two new cubs to play with."